THE HUMAN RESOURCES REVOLUTION:

WHY PUTTING PEOPLE FIRST MATTERS

THE HUMAN RESOURCES REVOLUTION:
WHY PUTTING PEOPLE FIRST MATTERS

RONALD J. BURKE

Professor of Organizational Behavior
Schulich School of Business
York University, Canada

CARY L. COOPER, CBE

Pro Vice Chancellor (External Relations)
Professor of Organizational Psychology and Health
Lancaster University, UK

ELSEVIER

Amsterdam • Boston • Heidelberg • London • New York • Oxford
Paris • San Diego • San Francisco • Singapore • Sydney • Tokyo

658.3
H 91892

Elsevier
The Boulevard, Langford Lane, Kidlington, Oxford OX5 1GB, UK
Radarweg 29, PO Box 211, 1000 AE Amsterdam, The Netherlands

First edition 2006

Notice
No responsibility is assumed by the publisher for any injury and/or damage to persons
or property as a matter of products liability, negligence or otherwise, or from any use
or operation of any methods, products, instructions or ideas contained in the material
herein, Because of rapid advances in the medical sciences, in particular, independent
verification of diagnoses and drug dosages should be made

British Library Cataloguing in Publication Data
A catalogue record for this book is available from the British Library

Library of Congress Cataloging-in-Publication Data
A catalog record for this book is available from the Library of Congress

ISBN-10: 0-08-044713-9
ISBN-13: 978-0-08-044713-1

For information on all Elsevier publications
visit our website at books.elsevier.com

Printed and bound in the Netherlands

06 07 08 09 10 10 9 8 7 6 5 4 3 2 1

Working together to grow
libraries in developing countries

www.elsevier.com | www.bookaid.org | www.sabre.org

ELSEVIER   BOOK AID
            International   Sabre Foundation

Contents

Contributors

Chris Brewster
Henley Management College, UK

Ronald J. Burke
Schulich School of Business, York University, Canada

Saba Colakoglu
Department of Human Resources Management, School of Management and Labor Relations, Rutgers, The State University of New Jersey, USA

Cary L. Cooper
Lancaster University Management School, Lancaster University, UK

Maxine Dalton
Center for Creative Leadership, USA

John E. Delery
Department of Management, Sam M. Walton College of Business, University of Arkansas, USA

Evangelia Demerouti
Department of Social and Organizational Psychology, University of Utrecht, The Netherlands

Niclas L. Erhardt
Department of Human Resources Management, School of Management and Labor Relations, Rutgers, The State University of New Jersey, USA

Brenda E. Ghitulescu
Katz Graduate School of Business, University of Pittsburgh, USA

Terry R. Halfhill
Division of Business and Economics, Pennsylvania State University — The Eberly Campus, USA

Jeffrey Herman
Department of Psychology, George Mason University, USA

Sven Kepes
Department of Management, Sam M. Walton College of Business, University of Arkansas,
USA

Carrie R. Leana
Katz Graduate School of Business, University of Pittsburgh, USA

David P. Lepak
Department of Human Resources Management, School of Management and Labor
Relations, Rutgers, The State University of New Jersey, USA

Michael P. Leiter
Centre for Organizational Research and Development, Acadia University, Canada

Lynn Markiewicz
Aston Organization Development, Aston University, UK

Mary Beth Mongillo
Dell Inc., Round Rock, USA

Tjai M. Nielsen
School of Business, George Washington University, USA

Robert A. Roe
Department of Organization and Strategy, University of Maastricht, The Netherlands

Helen Shipton
Aston Business School, Aston University, UK

Paul Sparrow
Manchester Business School, Manchester, UK

Riki Takeuchi
Department of Management of Organizations, School of Business and Management,
Hong Kong University of Science and Technology, Hong Kong

Bas van Diepen
Department of Organization and Strategy, University of Maastricht,
The Netherlands

Ad van Iterson
Department of Organization and Strategy, University of Maastricht,
The Netherlands

Michael A. West
Aston Business School, Aston University, UK

Jack W. Wiley
Gantz Wiley Research, USA

Gabrielle Wood
Department of Psychology, George Mason University, USA

Stephen J. Zaccaro
Department of Psychology, George Mason University, USA

Acknowledgments

The roots of this collection go back to my graduate school days at the University of Michigan. The faculty in the Organizational Psychology Program emphasized research that had potential applications for improving organizational effectiveness. Floyd Mann, Jack French, Stan Seashore, Dick Hoffman, Norm Maier and Basil Georgopolous, among others, were pioneers in this regard. I thank them for planting the seeds. Since then, teaching in MBA programs has convinced me that a new and different take on human resources management was necessary if we were to satisfy both human and organizational needs. I hope that this collection moves us in the right direction. I thank our international contributors for their efforts. Preparation of this collection was supported in part by the Schulich School of Business at York University.

This is my first undertaking with Elsevier; their staff has been helpful and professional at all times.

Finally, I dedicate this volume to my children — Sharon, Rachel and Jeff — who continue to fill my life with joy.

Ronald J. Burke

I would like to dedicate this book to the people who taught me most about human resource management, my children — Scott, Beth, Laura and Sarah.

Cary L. Cooper

PART I

Human Resources as a Competitive Advantage

CHAPTER 1

The Human Resources Revolution[1]

Ronald J. Burke

The world of work and organization has become increasingly demanding and turbulent (Burke & Cooper, 2004). Ulrich (1997) lists eight major challenges currently facing organizations. These are: globalization, responsiveness to customers, increasing revenue and decreasing costs, building organizational capability, change and transformation, implementing technology, attracting and developing human capital, and ensuring fundamental and long-lasting change. Thus, levels of competition among organizations have increased. Most organizations today can copy technology, manufacturing processes, products, and strategy. However human resource management (HRM) practices and organization are difficult to copy, thereby representing a unique competitive advantage (Pfeffer, 1994, 1998). To be successful in the future, organizations will have to build organizational capability (Beatty, Huselid, & Schneir, 2003; Pfeffer, 1996). Human Resource (HR) professionals and HRM practices will be required to create value by increasing organizational competitiveness (Applebaum & Batt, 1999; Applebaum, Bairley, Berg, & Kalleberg, 2000; Ferris, Hochwarter, Buckley, Harrell-Cook, & Frink, 1999).

Traditional views on competitive advantage have emphasized such barriers to entry as economies of scale, patent protection, access to capital, and regulated competition. More recent views have highlighted a different source of competitive advantage, a firm's HRs, and human capital (Huselid, Jackson, & Schuler, 1997). New demands facing organizations as a result of heightened competition, globalization, and technological advances have put a premium on creativity and innovation, speed and flexibility, as well as efficiency (Kaplan & Norton, 1996). The critical firm assets do not appear on a balance sheet but reside instead in people and management systems (Ichniowski, Kochan, Olson, & Straus, 1996). The role of firm strategy, HRs and HRM in firm performance is being rethought (Burke & Cooper, 2005). Rather than seeing the HR function as a cost, a HRM system that supports a firm's strategy should be seen instead as an investment, a strategic lever for the organization in creating value (Becker, Huselid, & Beatty, 2004).

[1]Preparation of this Introduction was supported in part by the Schulich School of Business, York University. Sherry Kang assisted in the literature review.

The 1990s witnessed a growth in research interest in examining the link between HRM strategies and practices and a firm's financial performance (Becker & Gerhart, 1996; Koch & McGrath, 1996; Kalleberg & Moody, 1994; MacDuffie, 1995). Studies have shown a strong positive relationship between the two, and this relationship has been observed in studies of one firm, one industry, and multiple industries (Becker & Huselid, 1998). Becker and Huselid have shown in three separate national surveys (over 2400 firms) an economically significant impact of human resource management practices on several measures of firm performance. They observed a link between changes in the sophistication of a firm's HR architecture and dollar change in market value per employee suggesting three stages of HRM practices on firm performance.

How do we create organizations that add value to investors, customers, and employees? Organizational capability is the key and both HR professionals and line managers need to work together to achieve this. Pfeffer (1998) articulates the reasons why a people-based strategy pays dividends. High-performance management practices (selective hiring, extensive training, sharing of information, etc.) lead to performance results (innovation, productivity) while being hard to copy; in the long run profitability is maintained.

HRM practices influences employee skills through the acquisition and development of human capital (Stewart, 1997; Wright, McMahan, & McWilliams, 1994). Effective recruiting and selection practices can provide the firm with highly qualified applicants. Training and development opportunities contribute to increasing human capital (Bartel, 1994). HRM practices can also influence levels of motivation through the use of performance appraisals, pay-for-performance incentives and internal promotions systems based on merit (Brown, Sturman, & Simmering, 2003). HRM practices can also influence the design of work so that highly motivated and skilled employees can use what they know in performing their jobs (Wright & Boswell, 2002).

The past decade has produced research evidence supporting the critical role HRM plays in the success of an organization. This evidence has been generated in a variety of different types of organizations including manufacturing, professional services, and health care (see Becker, Huselid, & Ulrich, 2001; and Liker, 2003).

Why Don't we use HRM Best Practices?

Considerable research has shown that organizations do not use current or innovative HR best practices (Johns, 1993; Rynes, Bartunek, & Daft, 2001)). In fact, very few HR practitioners even read the research literature (Terpstra & Rozell, 1997, 1998). HR research has become increasingly technical, making it more difficult to keep up with the literature (Hitt, 1995). It may also be that HR practitioners do not see the HR research as being relevant useful in meeting their needs (Adams, 2003; Buckley, Ferris, Bernardin, & Harvey, 1998; Ford, Duncan, Bedeian, Ginter, Rousculp, & Adams, 2003).

Rynes, Brown, and Colbart (2002) surveyed HR managers to determine their beliefs if HR best practices were consistent with the latest research findings. It was assumed that HR professionals were the ones responsible for spreading information about effective HRM to their organizations and help line managers develop HRM strategies to achieve business objectives. They concluded that HR practitioners lacked knowledge about best practices supported by research evidence.

Rynes, Trank, Lausson, and Ilies (2003) conducted a study of business recruiters' espoused preferences for students with both technical and behavioral skills. Students tend to believe that recruiters favor technical skill. Although recruiters indicated a preference for students who combined both, they gave the same employability rating to students who only took functional/technical course work. There is considerable evidence that business students are skeptical about the value of courses in HRM and OB (Rynes & Quinn, 1999).

Yancey, Wagner, Baxa, Alkhourui, and Haugen (2003) believe that HR practitioners and HR researchers move in different circles (i.e., belong to different professional associations, read different publications, attend different conferences). They surveyed 45 industrial-organizational psychologists examining where they published, what conferences they attend, and what they knew about the HR practitioner community. Their findings indicated that industrial-organizational psychologists shared their research ideas with each other rather than with HR practitioners.

What can be done about this state of affairs? Rynes et al. (2003) believe the first step is to see this crisis in HRM/OB legitimacy as a systemic problem, not a local one. Other suggestions include: more clearly defining the HRM/OB knowledge base, forming alliances with other teaching disciplines having greater legitimacy, doing better research on the teaching of HRM/OB, being more critical of negative practices and proposing even more positive organizational futures (see Cameron, Dutton, & Quinn, 2003, for examples). Ferris, Barnum, Rosen, Holleran, and Dulebohn (1995) advocate the development of business-university partnerships to minimize the chasm between science and practice. Organizational executives identify the questions and problems in their organizations on which they would like to see research conducted.

The HR function has, for a number of reasons, been typically viewed by executives as peripheral to the successful performance of their organizations (Ulrich, 1997). HRM, as a course in most MBA programs, is often not seen as useful as offerings in finance, marketing, or information technology. Yet, managers with full-time work experience report that their major challenges involve people. It is vital that the HR function embrace a role that more directly impacts on organizational effectiveness (Beatty & Schneir, 1996; Ulrich & Beatty, 2001).

Case Studies of HRM Practices

Becker and Huselid (1999) synthesize findings from five case studies of firms known to be leaders in strategic HRM (Herman Miller, Lucent, Praxair, Quantum, Sears). The case studies are reported in Barber, Huselid, and Becker (1999), Harris, Huselid and Becker (1999), McCowan, Bowen, Huselid, and Becker (1999), Artis, Becker and Huselid (1999), and Kirn, Rucci, Huselid and Becker (1999). They draw three broad conclusions (p. 287):

1. the foundation of a value-added HR function is a business strategy that relies on people as a source of competitive advantage and a management culture that embraces that belief;
2. a value-added HR function will be characterized by operational excellence, a focus on client service for individual employees and managers, and delivery of these services at the lowest possible cost; and

3. a value-added HR function requires HR managers who understand the human capital implications of business problems and can access or modify the HR system to solve those problems.

Why Don't Organizations Emphasize HRM?

What is surprising, however, is the slow rate of diffusion of the use of HRM practices across organizations (Osterman, 1994). A survey of US businesses showed that only 16% had at least one innovative practice in each of the four major HRM policy areas (flexible job design, worker training, pay-for-performance compensation, and employment security). A study of 3300 US workplaces concluded that the use of high-performance work systems was relatively rare. About one third had tried a formal TQM program, and about one quarter used benchmarking programs to compare their practices and performance with other organizations. The fact that it is difficult to specify the particular HRM practice that contributed to enhanced firm performance may be one more reason for the lack of diffusion.

Although the use of best HRM practices has increased, only a minority of firms use them. And, somewhat surprisingly, successful HRM practices are not necessarily the ones adopted; instead firms often opt for those easiest to adopt (Strang & Macy, 2001). Practices adopted sometimes fail and more often are discontinued. Implementing such programs is difficult. Implementation needs to be monitored and approached in a planned and comprehensive way (Pil & MacDuffie, 1996).

Pfeffer (1994, 1998) identifies several internal and external barriers to the use of effective HRM practices. Four internal barriers are noted. First, CEOs touted as heroes are often those who succeed in the short term by destroying the human system rather than achieving long-term competitive advantage through people. Second, unproductive theories of human behavior in the workplace are endorsed. Employment relationships are couched in economic transaction terms rather than in human and social terms. Third, organizations use language that diminishes trust, cooperation, and self-management. Fourth, managers are resistant to and cynical about the implementation of new HRM practices because of the past history of management practices in their companies (deskilling, fighting unions, and management control). Among external factors, Pfeffer believes that labor laws, at least in North America, mitigate against organizational change. The legal system applicable to the employment relationship makes it harder to use people to competitive advantage.

There are also other internal sources of resistance to implementing HRM practices. These include: the loss of jobs, status, and pay through the removal of hierarchy; the costs, benefits and uncertainty of change; inadequate measures of the benefits of change, and hiring managers from outside who do not understand ways to obtain competitive advantage through people in their new companies.

Pfeffer (1998, p. 132) finds the following sources of resistance to utilizing HRM best practices. Organizations desire to do what everyone else is doing and to follow the crowd — the problem is that the conventional wisdom is incorrect. There are managerial career pressures, derived from the need to "make the numbers" and to have a track record that makes one "mobile", pressures that create an emphasis on short-term financial results.

There is a persuasive belief in leadership and a tendency to overvalue things we have helped produce, making delegation difficult. There exist demands for accountability and reproducibility in results and decisions that destroy the benefit of expertise, which is inevitably dependent on tacit knowledge. Career trajectories — who gets promoted — all too often reward financial results rather than HR or people management. There is an excessive focus on measuring short-term costs and neglecting to assess the returns of those costs and investments. The business press and management education touts "mean" or "tough" management. There exists a management education and training focus on finance and accounting rather than on HRs or organizational behavior. There is a greater normative and economic value placed on being a skilled analyst, on knowing, compared to the value placed on being able to manage people, on doing (Pfeffer & Sutton, 2000). Finally, the capital market primacy over other stakeholders and demands for short-term performance make long-term investments in people more difficult.

Implications

We may be on the threshold of a renaissance in the application of HRM knowledge and best practices. Organizations may have no choice given the critical importance of dealing with the increased level of global competition and pace of change (Risher & Fay, 1995; Horibe, 1999; Bamberger & Meshoulam, 2000; Goldsmith, Gandossy, & Efron, 2003). In addition, a lot of threads are coming together (TQM, re-engineering, learning, core competences) to give higher priority to HRM. Consider the following conclusions, which we believe to be valid:

1. Human capital has become the key to competitive advantage.
2. The traditional relationship between people and organizations has been shattered; a new relationship is needed.
3. We now know a lot about individual competence and development and organizational effectiveness.
4. We now know a lot more about changing organizations to deliver "best practices".
5. There is an urgent need to create peak performing organizations and we know how to do that.

To the extent that organizations can unleash the hidden value in their people, they will increase their chances of success, particularly as knowledge and intellectual capital become more important. Some companies have achieved high levels of performance over a long period of time. Why are these companies successful? The accumulating research evidence has identified powerful reasons that are applicable to almost all organizations (O'Reilly & Pfeffer, 2000). Employee commitment and motivation come from involvement and the ways that people are treated. Organizations have found that giving people a stake and say in what they do is important in building high levels of commitment. It is possible to use the ideas, thoughts, and wisdom of the people who do the work everyday to help the organization become more productive and efficient. This requires leaders of organizations to have the courage to put people first if they are to successfully meet these challenges.

This Collection

This collection reviews the most current thinking and evidence on HRM practices associated with high levels of current organizational performance and likely to be responsive to the new challenges facing organizations over the next two decades. HRM has become critical to organizational success and more firms have come to realize this. Hence the title — The Human Resources Revolution. HRs will need to be mobilized in new ways to meet the demand of this period of time. These HRM practices are shown to be a key part of the managerial jobs not merely the domain of the HR department (Burke & Cooper, 2005). Building on a comprehensive framework incorporating HRM practices, strategies, and organizational needs, traditional HRM functions are addressed in a new way.

It specifically addresses the following key questions, among others. What HRMpractices characterize effective organizations? What emerging HR challenges face organizations in their search for managerial talent? How do peak performing organizations develop and nurture talent? Why are HRM practices becoming more critical for success in the new world of work (Cooper & Burke, 2002)?

Readers of this collection will gain a better appreciation not only of why reinventing HR is vital to continued organizational success, but how this has been done in a variety of organizations in Europe and North America. The rhetoric that "people are our most important asset" has in fact been realized in organizations that have made HRM a central aspect of managerial accountability.

Much of the current HRM writing is aimed at the HR professional. Our approach, while still relevant for this audience, positions HRM activities as a central feature of the managerial job having demonstrated value to organizational success. Our approach is therefore similar or compatible with Pfeffer's (1994, 1998) work.

This volume also directly addresses the concern that HRM has not received its due. What can be done about this and why it is critical to continued organizational performance and innovation? It also provides concrete research evidence as well as company best practice showing the tangible benefits from reinventing HRs-the strategic positioning of people, as the key element in sustaining peak performance.

References

Adams, A. M. (2003). Mitigating risks, visible hands, inevitable disasters, and soft variables: Management research that matters to managers. *Academy of Management Executive, 17*, 46–61.

Applebaum, E., Bairley, T., Berg, P., & Kalleberg, A. L. (2000). *Manufacturing advantage: Why high performance work systems pay off*. Ithaca, NY: Cornell University Press.

Applebaum, E., & Batt, R. (1999). *The new American workplace: Transforming work systems in the United States*. Ithaca, NY: Cornell University Press.

Artis, C. R., Becker, B. E., & Huselid, M. A. (1999). Strategic human resource management at Quantum. *Human Resource Management, 38*, 309–313.

Bamberger, P., & Meshoulam, I. (2000). *Human resource strategy: formulation, implementation and impact*. Thousand Oaks, CA: Sage.

Barber, D., Huselid, M. A., & Becker, B. E. (1999). Strategic human resource management at Quantum. *Human Resource Management, 38*, 321–328.

Bartel, A. P. (1994). Productivity gains from the implementation of employee training programs. *Industrial Relations, 33,* 411–425.

Beatty, R. W., Huselid, M. A., & Schneier, C. E. (2003). New HR metrics: Scoring on the business scorecard. *Organizational Dynamics, 32,* 17–121.

Beatty, R. W., & Schneier, C. E. (1996). New HR roles to impact organizational performance: From partners to players. *Human Resource Management, 25,* 19–27.

Becker, B. E., & Gerhart, B. (1996). The impact of human resource management on organizational performance: Progress and prospects. *Academy of Management Journal, 39,* 779–801.

Becker, B. E., & Huselid, M. A. (1998). High performance work systems and firm performance: A synthesis of research and managerial practice. *Research in Personnel and Human Resource Management. 16,* 53–101.

Becker, B. E., & Huselid, M. A. (1999). Strategic human resource management in five leading firms. *Human Resource Management, 38,* 287–301.

Becker, B. E., Huselid, M. A., & Beatty, R. W. (2004). *Workforce success metrics: Creating a human capital scorecard for the CEO.* Boston: Harvard Business School Press.

Becker, B. E., Huselid, M. A., & Ulrich, D. (2001). *The HR Scorecard: Linking people, strategy and performance.* Boston, MA: Harvard Business School Press.

Brown, M. P., Sturman, M. C., & Simmering, M. J. (2003). Compensation policy and organizational performance: The efficiency, operational and financial implications of pay levels and pay structure. *Academy of Management Journal, 46,* 752–762.

Buckley, M. R., Ferris, G. R., Bernardin, H. J., & Harvey, M. G. (1998). The "disconnect" between the science and practice of management. *Business Horizons, 41,* 31–38.

Burke, R. J., & Cooper, C. L. (2004). *Leading in turbulent times.* Oxford: Blackwell Publishers Inc.

Burke, R. J., & Cooper, C. L. (2005). *Reinventing human resource management: Challenges and new directions.* Oxon: Routledge.

Cameron, K., Dutton, J., & Quinn, R. P. (2003). *Positive organizational scholarship.* San Francisco: Berrett Koehler.

Cooper, C. L., & Burke, R. J. (2002). *The new world of work.* Oxon: Routledge.

Ferris, G. R., Barnum, T., Rosen, S. D., Holleran, L. P., & DuLebohn, J. H. (1995). Toward business-university partnerships in human resource management: Integration of science and practice. In: G. R. Ferris, S. D. Rosen & D. T. Barnum (Eds), *Handbook of human resource management* (pp. 1–13). Oxford: Blackwell Publishers..

Ferris, G. R., Hochwarter, W. A., Buckley, M. R., Harrell-Cook, G., & Frink, D. S. (1999). Human resources management: Some new directions. *Journal of Management, 25,* 385–415.

Ford, E. W., Duncan, W. J., Bedeian, A. G., Ginter, P. M., Rousculp, M. D., & Adams, A. M. (2003). Mitigating risks, visible hands, inevitable disasters, and soft variables: Management research that matters to managers. *Academy of Management Executive, 17,* 46–61.

Goldsmith, M., Gandossy, R. P., & Efron, M. S. (2003). *HRM in the 21st century.* New York: Wiley.

Harris, B. F., Huselid, M. A., & Becker, B. E. (1999). Strategic human resource management at Prazair. *Human Resource Management, 38,* 315–320.

Hitt, M. A. (1995). Academic research in management/organizations: Is it dead or alive? *Journal of Management Inquiry, 4,* 52–56.

Horibe, F. (1999). *Managing knowledge workers: New skills and attitudes to unlock the intellectual capital in your organization.* Toronto: Wiley.

Huselid, M. A., Jackson, S. E., & Schuler, R. (1997). Technical and strategic human resource effectiveness as determinants of firm performance. *Academy of Management Journal, 40,* 171–88.

Ichniowski, C., Kochan, T. S., Olson, C., & Strauss, G. (1996). What works at work: overview and assessment. *Industrial Relations, 35,* 299-333.

Johns, G. (1993). Constraints on the adoption of psychology-based personnel practices: Lessons from organizational innovation. *Personnel Psychology, 46*, 569–592.

Kalleberg, A. L., & Moody, J. W. (1994). Human resource management and organizational performance. *American Behavioral Scientist, 37*, 948–962.

Kaplan, R. S., & Norton, D. P. (1996). *The balanced scorecard: Translating strategy into action.* Boston: Harvard Business School Press.

Kirn, S. P., Rucci, A. J., Huselid, M. A., & Becker, B. E. (1999). Strategic human resource management at Sears. *Human Resource Management, 38*, 329–335.

Koch, M. J., & McGrath, R. G. (1996). Improving labor productivity: Human resource management policies do matter. *Strategic Management Journal, 17*, 345–354.

Liker, J. K. (2003). *The Toyota way.* New York: McGraw-Hill.

MacDuffie, J. P. (1995). Human resource bundles and manufacturing performance: Organizational logic and flexible production systems in the world auto industry. *Industrial and Labor Relations Review, 48*, 197–221.

McCowan, R. A., Bowen, U., Huselid, M. A., & Becker, B. E. (1999). Strategic human resource management at Herman Miller. *Human Resource Management, 38*, 303–308.

O'Reilly, C. A. III, & Pfeffer, J. (2000). *Hidden Value: How great companies achieve extraordinary results with ordinary people.* Boston, MA: Harvard Business School Press.

Osterman, P. (1994). How common is workplace transformation and who adopts it? *Industrial and Labor Relations Review, 47*, 173–188.

Pfeffer, J. (1994). *Competitive advantage through people.* Boston: Harvard Business School Press.

Pfeffer, J., & Sutton, R. I. (2000). *The knowing-doing gap: How smart companies turn knowledge into action.* Boston: Harvard Business School Press.

Pfeffer, J. (1996). *Competitive advantage through people: Unleashing the power of the workforce.* Boston: Harvard Business School Press.

Pfeffer, J. (1998). *The human equation: Building profits by putting people first.* Boston: Harvard Business School Press.

Pil, F. K., & MacDuffie, J. P. (1996). The adoption of high-involvement work practices. *Industrial Relations, 35*, 423–455.

Risher, H., & Fay, C. (1995). *The performance imperative: Strategies for enhancing effectiveness.* San Francisco: Jossey-Bass.

Rynes, S. L., Bartunek, J. M., & Daft, R. L. (2001). Across the great divide: Knowledge creation and transfer between practitioners and academics. *Academy of Management Journal, 44*, 340–356.

Rynes, S. L., Brown, K. G., & Colbart, A. E. (2002). Seven common misconceptions about human resource practices: Research findings versus practitioner beliefs. *Academy of Management Executive, 16*, 92–102.

Rynes, S. L., & Quinn, T. C. (1999). Behavioral science in the business school curriculum: Teaching in a changing institutional environment. *Academy of Management Review, 24*, 808–825.

Rynes, S. L., Trank, C. Q., Lauson, A. M., & Ilies, R. (2003). Behavioural course work in business education: Growing evidence of a legitimacy crisis. *Academy of Management Learning and Education, 2*, 269–283.

Stewart, T. (1997). *Intellectual capital.* New York. Doubleday-Currency.

Strang, D., & Macy, M. W. (2001). In search of excellence? Fads, success stories and adaptive emulation. *American Journal of Sociology, 107*, 147–182.

Terpstra, D. E., & Rozell, E. J. (1997). Why some potentially effective staffing practices are seldom used. *Public Personnel Management. 26*, 483–495.

Terpstra, D. E., & Rozell, E. J. (1998). Human resource executives' perceptions of academic research. *Journal of Business and Psychology, 13*, 19–29.

Ulrich, D. (1997). *Human resource champions.* Boston: Harvard Business School.

Ulrich, D., & Beatty, R. W. (2001). From partners to players: Extending the HR playing field. *Human Resource Management, 40,* 293–307.

Wright, P., McMahan, G. C., & McWilliams, A. (1994). Human resources and sustained competitive advantage: A resource-based perspective. *International Journal of Human Resource Management, 5,* 301–327.

Wright, P. M., & Boswell, W. R. (2002). Desegregating HRM: A review and synthesis of micro and macro human resource management research. *Journal of Management, 28,* 247–276.

Yancey, G., Wagner, S., Baxa, J., Alkouri, K., & Haugen, E. (2003). Is the dissemination of knowledge about industrial-organizational psychology too insulated? *Psychological Reports, 92,* 723–730.

CHAPTER 2

Why Putting People First Matters[1]

Ronald J. Burke

Organizations today are facing challenges on several fronts in their efforts to remain competitive (Ulrich, 1997; Wright, Dyer, & Takla, 1999). These include the need to increase productivity, the prospects of expanding into global markets, new technological developments, responding to changes in the marketplace, containing costs, developing a skilled and flexible workforce, and bringing about significant organizational change. These challenges are emerging in the context of changing needs of the workforce, changing attitudes in the broader society, and heightened legal requirements (Cappelli, 1999; Goldsmith, Gandossy, & Efron, 2003). These demands are making it both more important and more difficult for organizations to be successful. There is a greater emphasis on organizational results (Risher & Fay, 1995). Not surprisingly, more organizations are looking for ways to improve their performances (Ashkenas, Ulrich, Jick, & Kerr, 1995; Galbraith, Lawler, & Associates, 1993; Heskett, Sasser, & Schlesinger, 1997; Lawler, 1992; Lawler, Mohrman, & Ledford, 1995; Nadler, Shaw, Walton, & Associates, 1995; Pfeffer & Sutton, 2000; Tushman & O'Reilly, 1997).

Wright et al. (1999) report results of interviews and surveys of 232 human resource (HR) and line executives. They found the following to be pressing organizational challenges: greater competitiveness globally, rapid technological advances, some labor shortages, changes in the psychological contract, dealing with organizational change, need for more effective management of people, the need to increase their talent pool, and the creation of high commitment work systems were impacting their ability to be successful.

McKinsey and Company (1998), based on interviews with over 5000 managers and executives, found that 65% of executives thought they had insufficient talent among their top 300 leaders and only 12% strongly believed that they retained most of their top performers.

Pfeffer (1998) notes a downward performance spiral as organizations address real performance problems such as low profits, high costs, poor customer service, and low stock prices. Typical organizational responses include staff layoffs, greater use of part-time and contract staff, a restriction of hiring and promotions, freezes or cutbacks, and reduced

---

[1] Preparation of this chapter was supported in part by the Schulich School of Business, York University.

investment in training and employee development. Employees respond, in turn, by reducing their job involvement, exhibiting lower job satisfaction, decreasing their effort, increased accidents and greater turnover. These individual behaviors have the effect of increasing the performance problems that led to the organizational responses in the first place. Thus, the downward spiral continues.

Some organizations do see increased profits in the short run through cost-cutting efforts. In addition, cost cutting can be done in ways that minimize their impact on the long-term success of the organization (Cascio, 2002). But these somewhat successful initiatives fall short of achieving peak performance.

There is considerable empirical evidence that the use of effective human resource management (HRM) practices increases firm performance (see Burke & Cooper, 2005). Why should this be the case? Performance increases because employees work *both harder and smarter*. Employees work harder because of greater job involvement, greater peer pressure for results, and the economic gains based on high performance. Employees work smarter because they can use their knowledge and skill acquired through training and development in the jobs themselves in getting the work done (Lawler, 2003; Osterman, 2005).

In addition, effective HRM practices are likely to reduce the direct and indirect costs of employee grievances (Applebaum & Batt, 1994). Finally, performance benefits are likely to be seen in the elimination of jobs whose main responsibility is to monitor people whose main job is to monitor other people. Such administration overhead is costly, both in the salaries paid to those who hold such positions and in the diminished contributions from those being monitored. Trained, motivated, self-managed, and broadly skilled staff can dramatically reduce administrative overhead costs (Pfeffer, 1994).

The traditional views on competitive advantage have emphasized such barriers to entry as economies of scale, patent production, access to capital, and regulated competition. More recent views have highlighted a different source of competitive advantage, a firm's human resources and human capital (Bamberger & Meshoulam, 2000; Druckman, Singer, & VanCott, 1997). New demand-facing organizations as a result of heightened competition, globalization, and technological advances have put a premium on creativity and innovation, speed and flexibility, as well as efficiency. The critical firm assets do not appear on a balance sheet but reside instead in people and management systems (Becker, Huselid, & Ulrich, 2001; Becker, Huselid, & Beatty, 2004). The role of firm strategy, human resources, and the role of HRM in the firm performance is being rethought (McWilliams, Van Fleet, & Wright, 2001). Rather than seeing the HR function as a cost the HRM system that supports a firm's strategy should be seen instead as an investment, a strategic lever for the organization in creating value (Wright & McMahan, 1992).

Wright, Dunford, and Snell (2001) note two competing views on the potential for HR practices to serve as a competitive advantage. Wright, McMahan, and McWilliams (1994), distinguishing between a firm's human resources and HR practices, suggested that HR practices could be copied by other organizations. Thus, human resources (skill and motivations of people) were the source of competitive advantage. Lado and Wilson (1994) propose that a firm's HR practices, as a system, can be unique and a source of competitive advantage.

The past decade has produced research evidence supporting the critical role that the HRM plays in the success of an organization (Koch & McGrath, 1996; Koys, 2001; Gelade & Ivery, 2003; Huselid, Jackson, & Schuler, 1997; MacDuffie, 1995; Ichniowski, Shaw, &

Prennushi, 1997; Wright, Gardner, & Moynihan, 2003). This evidence has been generated in a variety of different types of organizations including manufacturing, professional services, and health care (Becker, Huselid, & Ulrich, 2001; Cooke, 1994; Liker, 2003; Wright, McCormick, Sherman, & McMahan, 1999).

The 1990s witnessed a growth in research interest in examining the link between HRM strategies and practices and a firm's financial performance (Becker, Huselid, Pickes, & Sprott, 1996). Studies have shown a strong positive relationship, and have been observed in studies of one firm, one industry and multiple industries (Becker & Huselid, 1998). Becker and Huselid have shown in three separate national surveys (over 2400 firms) an economically and significant impact on several measures of firm performance. They observed a link between changes in the sophistication of a firm's HR architecture and dollar change in market value per employee suggesting three stages in influence of HRM practices on firm performance. The first stage represents the development of a professional HR capability. The second stage involves the development of HR excellence by the HR function but with a modest influence on firm performance. In the third stage, the HRM system achieves a dramatic impact on financial performance. The HRM system at this stage has achieved both operational excellence and is supportive to (consistent with) the firms strategic goals.

HRM practices influence employee skills through the acquisition and development of human capital (Stewart, 1997). Effective recruiting and selection practices can provide the firm with highly qualified applicants. Training and development opportunities contribute to the increasing human capital (Bartel, 1994). HRM practices can also influence levels of motivation through the use of performance appraisals, pay-for-performance incentives, and internal promotions systems based on merit. HRM practices can also influence the design of work so that the highly motivated and skilled employees can use what they know in performing their jobs (Bailey, 1993). In summary, the contributions of employees can have an impact on firm performance and HRM practices can influence employee contributions through their effect on motivation, skill, and participation in decision-making.

Pfeffer (1998) writes, "The returns from managing people in ways that build high commitment, involvement, and learning and organizational competence are typically on the order of 30 to 50 percent, substantial by any measure" (p. xvi). He later adds, "substantial gains, on the order of 40 percent or so in most of the studies reviewed, can be obtained by implementing high performance management practices." (p. 32). HRM matters.

The sources of competitive advantage today are different from what they were 20 years ago. Today how firms manage their workforces is the major competitive advantage — the organization, its employees, and how they work. Pfeffer (1994) argues that HRM practices likely to be successful are not faddish, it is not hard to understand them, or why they work, and they are not contingent on a firm's particular organizational strategy.

Although we are beginning to understand more about effective HRM practices, significant challenges remain in the application of this knowledge. First, it takes significant time to achieve a competitive advantage through the workforce. Organizations doing well may feel no need to change; organizations doing poorly may face immediate pressures making it also unlikely to change; organizational doing poorly may face immediate pressures, making them, too, unlikely to change. There also may not be enough communication of best-practice knowledge. In addition, managers may know something that researchers do not. Finally, some HRM practices may be risky and often fail.

HRM Practices and Firm Performance

There is considerable evidence that a range of HRM practices have been shown to reduce staff turnover (Arthur, 1994). In addition, HRM practices have been found to be associated with organizational productivity (Wright et al., 2003). Finally, some work has explored the links between individual HRM practices and corporate financial performance (Becker & Gerhart, 1996).

Ferris et al. (1998) offer a social context framework to explain the relationship between HRM systems and organizational effectiveness. In this framework, organizational culture affects HRM systems employed, which in turn influences organizational climate, which in turn influences employee attitudes, that then shape employee behaviors resulting in organizational effectiveness. Flexibility and organizational reputation are both affected by some of the above concepts and in turn influence organizational effectiveness directly. These authors then offer examples of specific variables within each of these components and indicate how these variables relate to other components in the framework.

Three reviews of the HRM and firm performance research literature have been reported. Kling (1991) reviewed 17 studies using quantitative measures of productivity, quality, and financial performance comparable across firms. He focused on three specific practices-training, compensation linked to firm or worker performance, and employee involvement in decision-making that were implemented together. He concluded that use of these practices was associated with greater productivity and that the gains from interrelated HRM practices were greater than when each practice was implemented alone.

Ichniowski, Kochan, Levine, Olson, and Strauss (1996), based on a review of research evidence on HRM practices, conclude that these innovative workplace practices can improve organizational performance. They suggest that three practices were particularly important in this regard: increasing worker participation, making work procedures less rigid, and decentralizing managerial tasks.

Dyer and Reeves (1995) address some issues within the SHRM field in their state-of-the-art review. First, they believe that bundling, HRM practices that are mutually reinforcing and synergistic, was likely to lead to heightened productivity. Second, they conclude that there was evidence that HRM practices do in fact influence productivity. And third, there seems to be relatively little support for the contingency perspective, the notion that effective HRM practices depend on the situation of the firm.

Huselid (1995) examined the links between systems of HRM practices and firm performance in a sample of almost 1000 US firms. He used 13 HRM practices that factor analysis reduced to two factors: Employee skills and organizational structures and Employee motivation. His results showed that the use of these HRM practices had an economically and statistically significant effect on both intermediate employee outcomes (turnover, productivity) and short and long-term measures of corporate financial performance. Little support emerged for a contingency perspective.

Arthur (1994) compared two HRM strategies in a study of 30 US steel mini-mills. One strategy emphasized control and attempted to reduce labor costs or improve efficiency by enforcing employee compliance with specific rules and procedures. The other strategy emphasized commitment and focussed on developing highly motivated and committed employees through employee involvement in decision-making and training in group-problem solving. He found that the commitment approach resulted in greater labor efficiency and lower scrap rates. Turnover was higher in the control-oriented mills, but their hiring and training costs were low. Turnover in the commitment-oriented mills, while lower, had a more negative effect on labor efficiency and scrap rates.

Banker, Field, Schroeder, and Sinha (1996a) undertook a longitudinal field study examining the impact of work teams on manufacturing performance. Both quality and labor productivity improved over time with the use of work teams.

Welbourne and Andrews (1996) examined the impact of HRM in enhancing the performance of initial public offering (IPO) companies. Two HRM variables, human resource value and organizations-based rewards predicted initial investor reactions and long-term company survival. Rewards had a negative relationship with initial performance and a positive relationship with long-term survival.

Banker, Lee, Potter, and Srinivasan (1996b), using a contingency framework, investigated the effects of an outcome-based incentive plan on sales, customer satisfaction, and profit. Contingency factors included competitive intensity, customer profile, and behavior-based control (supervisory monitoring). The outcome-based incentive scheme had positive relationships with the performance measures (intensity of competition, proportion of upscale customers) and negative relationship with level of supervisory monitoring.

Delaney and Huselid (1996), in 590 for profit and non-profit firms, found positive relationships between HRM practices (e.g. training, staffing selectivity) and perceptions of firm performance.

Davidson, Worrell, and Fox (1996) found that the presence of an early retirement program, a strategic HRM response, was associated with favorable views of investors.

Schneider, Hanges, Smith, and Salvaggio (2003) reported the results of a study of the relationship between employee attitudes and organizational performance with both sets of variables measured at the organizational level of analysis. Employee attitude data from 35 companies over eight years were analyzed at the organizational level against financial returns (return on assets, ROA) and market performance (earnings per share, EPS) using cross-lagged analyses. Statistical significant relationships across various time lags were observed for three of the seven employee attitude measures. Overall job satisfaction and satisfaction with security were predicted by ROA and EPS more strongly than the reverse, through some of the reverse relationships were also significant. Satisfaction with pay had a reciprocal relationship with ROA and EPS.

Schneider and his colleagues integrate the literature on high-performance work practices (HRM) with their findings as follows. HRM increases production efficiencies which, in turn, increases organizational financial and market performance which, in turn, increases pay and security to employees and a more positive company reputation, resulting in higher levels of employee positive outcomes (Cameron, Dutton, & Quinn, 2003).

Batt (2002), in a nationally representative sample of call centers, examined the relationship of HRM practices, employee quit rates and organizational performance. She found that quit rates were lower and sales growth higher in call centers that stressed high skills, employee participation in decision-making and in work teams, and HR incentives such as high pay and job security. Quit rates partially mediated the relationship between HRM practices and sales growth; call centers with lower quit rates indicated greater sales growth.

Carpenter, Sanders, and Gregersen (2001) propose that CEOs with international experience create value for their organizations and themselves through their possession of a valuable source and unique resource. They found that US multinationals performed better with CEOs with international assignment experience, particularly when this human capital was bundled with other organizational resources and capabilities.

Perry-Smith and Blum (2000), based on a national sample of 527 US firms, reported that organizations with more extensive work--family policies have higher perceived firm-level performance. In addition, there was partial support for the hypothesis that the relationship between work--family bundles and firm performance was stronger in older firms and firms employing a larger proportion of women.

Konrad and Mangel (2000) examined the adoption of work--life programs and the impact of work--life programs on productivity. In a national sample of 658 US organizations, they found that the percentage of professionals and the percentage of women employed were positively related to the development of more extensive work--life programs. In a sub-sample of 195 public, for profit firms for which productivity data were available, they observed that work--life programs had a stronger positive impact on productivity when the percentage of women, and professionals, was greater. Such programs can have an impact on employee retention, reduction of absenteeism, and supporting or increasing employee autonomy resulting in more favorable employee attitudes, which in turn enhance productivity.

Guthrie (2001) reported a positive association between the use of high-involvement work practices and employee retention and firm productivity. Interestingly, high turnover was associated with lower productivity when use of high-involvement practices was high and with increased productivity when use of high-involvement work practices was low.

Delery and Doty (1996), using three modes of theorizing in SHRM (universalistic, contingency, and configurational), showed that each perspective offers theoretical arguments that explain significant levels of variation in financial performance. Seven SHRM practices were considered.

Konrad and Linnehan (1995) considered the question of whether formalized human resources management structures promoted goals of employment opportunity and affirm active action. They examined antecedents and outcomes of formalized HRM structures in over 100 organizations, measuring the presence of "identity conscious" and "identity blind" HRM structures. They report that identity-conscious structures were associated with some positive indicators of the employment status of women and people of color.

Terpstra and Rozell (1993) found that organizations using the employee selection processes recommended by industrial–organizational psychologists (validation studies, structured interviews, cognitive ability tests, validation of application form questions, and investigation of the usefulness of different recruiting sources) enjoy superior performance (higher profit margins, higher annual growth in profit, and higher annual sales growth). But few organizations use these processes.

Wright et al. (2003) studied the effects of HR practices, organizational commitment, and the operating performance and profitability of 50 autonomous business units within the same organization. Performance measures were based on company records obtained after the assessment of HR practices and organizational commitment. They hypothesized a causal chain with HR practices leading to organizational commitment, which in turn led to operational performance (e.g. quality, productivity), which in turn led to expenses, which in turn produced profits. Their data provided support for the hypothesized relationships.

Huselid et al. (1997), using data from senior HR executives and line managers from 293 US firms, examined the effects of HRM staff competencies and both strategic and technical effectiveness on three financial indicators of firm performance. HRM effectiveness was found to be significantly associated with HRM staff competencies. HRM effectiveness was also related to firm productivity, cash flow, and market value.

Skaggs and Youndt (2004), using data from 234 service organizations in 96 different industries, report strong relationships between firm's strategic positioning toward customers, and their emphasis on human capital (more time and money spent on training, selecting staff with higher education and greater experience). In addition, using measures of both return on equity and return on investment as measures of firm performance, certain combinations of strategic positioning, and human capital practices (e.g. selection and training) produced higher performance levels.

Fulmer, Gerhart, and Scott (2003) used data from publicly traded firms in the "100 Best Companies to work for in America" listing and comparing them to both companies in the broader market and a group of matched firms on a number of firm-level performance measures. They found that companies on the 100 Best list had stable and positive workforce attitudes and generally performed better than companies in the broader market and, in some cases, performed better than the matched sample of companies.

Zacharatos, Barling, and Iverson (2005), in two studies, examined the relationship between use of high-performance work systems (HPWSs) and occupational safety. In the first study, data were collected from 138 HR and Safety Directors. Respondents indicated the prevalence of 10 high-performance management practices (e.g. employment security, training, teams, information sharing) and provided the number of lost time injuries and days lost due to eight specific types of injuries over a one-year period (2000). They found a significant relationship between HPWS and occupational safety. In the second study, data were collected from 189 male employees of two companies. Respondents rated the prevalence of HPWS practices, and described the safety climate in their firm, their personal-safety orientation, and numbers of safety incidents. They tested and found support for a model in which HPWS practices had direct effects on trust in management and safety climate, both of which in turn had direct effects on personal safety orientation and safety incidents.

Besides providing support for the association of HPWS practices and occupational safety, Zacharato and her colleagues confirmed three other aspects of HRM previously reported. First, their HRM practices overlapped considerably with those identified by others (Pfeffer, 1994, 1998; Becker & Huselid, 1998; Ramsay, Scholarios, & Harley, 2000; Way, 2001). Second, their measures of these HRM practices were found to be desirable psychometric measurement properties. Third, these HRM practices formed a single underlying construct — a HPWS.

Cutcher-Gershenfeld (1991) has shown in 25 work areas of a large unionized manufacturing firm that those areas characterized by transformational relations had lower costs, less scrap, greater productivity, and greater return to direct labor hours than areas with traditional (adversarial) labor–management relations.

Way (2001) studied HRM practices in a sample of small business firms having fewer than 100 employees. Seven HRM practices were considered with date being typically collected from plant managers. Two dependent variables were included: workforce turnover and labor productivity. Use of HRM practices were found to be associated with lower employee turnover and with perceived productivity but not with labor productivity.

Whitener (2001), based on a sample of 1689 employees from 180 credit unions, reported that use of HRM practices affected the relationship between perceived organizational support and organizational commitment.

Watson Wyatt (1999), in a survey of over 7500 US workers, concluded that companies with highly committed employees experienced greater three-year total returns to shareholders than companies with low commitment. They found that HRM practices and trust in management had the strongest relationships with building employee commitment.

MacDuffie (1995), based on a 1989–1990 survey of 62 international automotive assembly plants, found support for two hypotheses: (1) that innovative HRM practices affect performance when they are elements in an internally consistent bundle and not individually and (2) HRM bundles contribute most to performance when they are integrated with manufacturing policies within a flexible production system.

Tsui, Pearce, Porter, and Tripoli (1997) found that employee attitudes and performance were superior under high involvement employment relationships in which employers invested in employees compared to three other types of employee–organization relationships.

Linking HRM Practices to Firm Performance

The HRM system is an important element in making an organization effective. But how does HRM contribute to firm performance and effectiveness? What mechanisms link HRM practices to firm performance? Bowen and Ostroff (2004) introduce the notion of "strength of the HRM system", individuals sharing a view of expected and rewarded behaviors, to explain how individuals are motivated to adopt particular attitudes and behaviors that affect organizational performance.

They consider two common approaches to the HRM-firm performance relationship:

1. *The systems approach*: A bundle of HRM practices affect firm performance directly.
2. *The strategic approach*: The fit between HRM practices and a firm's strategy — the horizontal fit of HRM practices and the firm's business strategy affects firm performance. HRM practices produce knowledge, skills, and behaviors so employees behave in ways that support the firm's business strategy. Both the systems view and the strategic fit view take a macro approach in that both link HRM practices to employee characterstics which in turn enhanced performance.

Bowen and Ostroff suggest that climate serves as one such mediating variable. They focus on HRM process instead of HRM content. HRM process refers to how the HRM system is designed and managed. A strong climate signals to employees what is important, what is expected, and what is rewarded.

Different business strategies are linked to different HRM practices. Thus an innovation strategy leads to HRM practices supporting innovation, while a customer service strategy leads to HRM practices supporting service. In their thinking, HRM practices define roles that first influence individual behavior and then organizational performance. HRM leads to organizational culture that then leads to firm performance. Thus, HRM content and process must be integrated effectively for strategic HRM to be linked to firm performance. It is critical that HRM send clear messages to employees resulting in a shared understanding of what is important (a strong culture). HRM practices are communicated (can be seen as communication) from employer to employee.

They identify three key features of a strong HRM system:

1. *Distinctiveness*. The HRM system must be attention grabbing, visible, understandable, relevant and legitimate.
2. *Consistency*. The HRM system must be consistent internally, consistent over time (stable), and consistent with the values of senior management.
3. *Based on consensus*. The top management must be in agreement.

A strong HRM system in their view — serves as a link between HRM practices and firm performance.

Effective HRM Practices

Effective HRM practices are long established and well known, easy to understand what they are and why they work, and are not contingent on an organization's strategy. Pfeffer (1994) lists 16 interrelated HRM practices, for example. No organization does all 16 or all 16 well. And an organization can do all 16 and fail because people are only one factor in the success of an organization. These are not easy to implement. Their implementation requires involvement, effort, and responsibility of all employees. Some employees will resist, some may leave, and some are used to and feel comfortable with low commitment and not using their minds.

Pfeffer's original list of HRM practices include the following:

* Employment security conveys a long-standing commitment of the organization to its people. Employees respond in kind.
* Selectivity in recruiting means you hire better people in terms of performance, signaling to all that high-performance expectations exist, and the organization is an excellent one.
* High wages attract more and better applicants who stay. Firms can be more selective in hiring and high wages signal that the organization values its people.
* Incentive pay shows that the organization values performance and shares performance gains with all its people.
* Employee ownership aligns the goals of people with managers and shareholders.
* Information sharing makes more people knowledgeable and powerful.
* Participation and empowerment pushes decision-making to lower organizational levels where hands-on experience resides.
* Use of teams and job redesign increases communication, coordination, disciplined effort, data collection and monitoring, and peer supervision.
* Training and skill development increases problem-solving skills and ability to use knowledge.
* Cross-utilization and cross-training increase motivation and employment security.

- Symbolic egalitarianism increases communication, reduces "us" versus "them" attitudes and focuses people toward a common goal.
- Wage compression reduces competition, increases cooperation, and signals that all people matter.
- Promotion from within encourages training and development, increases the likelihood that managers understand the business, increases trust between management and employees, and serves as a reward for good performance.
- Long-term perspective supports the necessary long-term commitment to implement effective HRM practices.
- Measurement of the practices suggests that HRM is important and provides information on how well these practices are being implemented.
- An overarching philosophy connects the individual HRM practices into a coherent system, offers a rationale explaining what the organization is doing and why, and supports experimentation to achieve effective HRM practices. A philosophy, a system of values or beliefs about what the organization holds about the basis of its success and its approach to HRM, ties all the individual practices together.

These 16 HRM practices are not fads but reflect long-standing ideas about how to manage people.

Pfeffer (1998) later listed 7 broader HRM practices, not 16. He combined some and eliminated others that dealt with implementation. These seven were: employment security, selective hiring, self-managed teams and decentralization, high compensation contingent on performance, training, reduction of status differences, and the sharing of information.

O'Reilly and Pfeffer (2000) identified six HRM levers in common across eight outstanding organizations. These were: alignment of values, culture and strategy, hiring people for fit with the values and culture, investing in the training and development of all staff, widespread sharing of information, the use of team-based systems and tying rewards and recognition to desired behaviors and results.

Alignment of HRM Practices

In their discussion of strategic HRM practices, several writers focus on alignment — the alignment of HRM practices with each other (internal consistency or alignment) and the alignment of HRM practices with an organization's strategy (external consistency or alignment).

Pfeffer (1998) suggests that the alignment process start by examining the organization's particular strategy. The next step involves identifying a small number of critical competencies or behaviors that are needed to implement the strategy. A consideration of the various HRM practices that will support the demonstration of these competencies and behavior is undertaken. The final step is a check to make sure these HRM practices are internally and externally consistent. Pfeffer provides an illustrative example of how a firm can assess external congruence and internal consistency.

Can the HRM practices observed in high-performing firms be labeled as "best practices" or are they so specific to a particular firm that generalization across firms become meaningless — you will recall that Pfeffer (1998) proposed seven "best practices". These seven elements all emphasize the performance — enhancing aspects of the HRM system and each is part of an integrated high-performance HRM system.

Best Practices versus Contingency

The internal fit perspective suggests that the use of an internally consistent system of HRM practices would be seen in better firm performance in all cases. This would lead to the identification of specific HRM practices leading to important firm outcomes. The contingency perspective, on the other hand, raises the question of whether any HRM practice can only be seen as "best" in the context of a particular firm's strategy, industrial sector or environment.

The universal approach is the "best practices" perspective and implies a direct relationship between particular HR practices and performance. The universal approach documents the benefits of HRM across all contexts. The contingency approach suggests that an organization's strategy adds to (or detracts from) the impact of HR practices and performance. The main effects versus the interaction (or moderation) effects. These can be complimentary not competing views. They are not mutually exclusive. In both cases HRM policies and practices matter.

It is likely that bundles of HR practices have more impact on performance than individual practices, suggesting that internal consistency or fit among HR practices matters (Becker & Huselid, 1999).

It is also possible for evidence to support *both* a best practices and a contingency perspective. That is, some HRM practices and good internal fit may lead to high performance across all firms. But firms that tailor their HRM practices to their specific strategy sector or environment may achieve additional performance gains.

Youndt, Snell, Dean, and Lepak (1996) considered universal and contingency models of the HRM — performance relationship in manufacturing settings. Data were collected from 97 plants and generally supported a contingency approach to HRM. Human capital HR systems, linked with a quality manufacturing strategy were associated with multiple dimensions of operational performance (employee productivity, machine efficiency, customer alignment).

Datta, Guthrie, and Wright (2005) provide support for both a universal approach and a contingency approach for the effects of HRM practices and firm effectiveness in a sample of 132 publicly traded firms in manufacturing. Firms using more HRM practices were more productive in terms of labor productivity. Three industry characteristics were found to moderate this relationship: capital intensity, growth, and differentiation. Greater use of HRM practices was associated with higher labor productivity in industries having lower capital intensity, higher growth, and higher product differentiation.

HR's Role in Monitoring HRM

Beatty, Huselid, and Schneier (2003) observe that as the workforce becomes more valuable to organizational success in the knowledge economy, HR's role becomes increasingly important. HR needs to become a player instead of a partner that can be eliminated or outsourced

(Beatty & Schneier, 1997; Ulrich & Beatty, 2001). A historic problem for HR was the absence of workforce measures. They offer an HR scorecard based on Kaplan and Norton's (1996) business scorecard. Workforce success has three elements: mindset, competencies, and behaviors. Four HR system components are then developed: HR competencies, HR practices used to produce key HR tools, and the integration of the HR system with the firm's business strategy.

Benchmarking and HRM Adoption

Sanchez, Kraus, White, and Williams (1999) emphasize the role of benchmarking in the adoption of high-involvement HRM practices. Imitation may be more common when the practice is ambiguous and intangible (i.e., HRM practices). Others argue that the imitation of HRM practices needs to fit the environment of a particular firm, suggesting that the imitation of HRM practices may not be effective if they do not fit. Benchmarking is the continuous measurement and examination of practices against organizations thought to be practice leaders. Benchmarking is likely to speed up the imitation process. They collected data from 107 HR directors using questionnaires. Respondents indicated the extent to which their firms had each of 12 HRM practices, used benchmarking, and had resources to support growth. They found that the effects of resources on the use of high-involvement HRM practices were mediated by the use of benchmarking. Organizations having more resources for growth and also using benchmarking had more high-involvement HRM practices. Benchmarking, when coupled with organizational resources, proved to be a fertile ground for the adoption of HRM best practices through imitation.

The Gap between Research and Practice

Case studies and research projects conducted over the past two decades have shed considerable light on the characteristics of successful and satisfying work places. We know what needs to be done to satisfy both human and business needs (Katzenbach, 2000). If you accept these statements to be true, why are so few organizations implementing best practices?

Some of the reasons for the gap between research and practice lie within the researchers themselves (Mohrman, Gibson, & Mohrman, 2001; Dossahoy & Berger, 2002). They spend most of their time communicating with other researchers and little time conversing with practitioners (Blanton, 2000; Boehm, 1980). Much of the scholarship of the research community is not read by most practitioners or even most academic researchers.

One must also look at the teaching programs of most MBA courses. Many of the professor in schools of business are, themselves, researchers, or the consumers of research findings. Few business schools teach OB or HRM in ways that illustrate the usefulness of this knowledge to increase organizational health and performance (Pfeffer, 1998). Traditional OB texts review countless motivation theories and leadership theories which, if entertainingly presented, can be interesting to students, but the link between these concepts and bringing about peak performance is thin at best (Ferraro, Pfeffer, & Sutton,

2005a,b). Few business schools address the implementation of concepts, models and research findings.

One might expect that line managers would not be aware of the current thinking on unleashing potential of staff but that HR managers read and used the academic literature that had higher financial performance than those that did not.

Implementing Effective HRM Practices

It has been estimated that about three-quarters of all organizational change efforts fail. Ulrich (1997, p. 157) offers 10 reasons why change efforts do not produce results:

1. Not tied to strategy
2. Seen as a fad or quick fix
3. Short-term perspective
4. Political realities undermine change
5. Grandiose expectations versus simple successes
6. Inflexible change designs
7. Lack of leadership about change
8. Lack of measurable, tangible results
9. Afraid of the unknown
10. Unable to mobilize commitment to sustain change.

Pfeffer (1998) offers some thoughts on bringing about change to achieve competitive HR advantage. Management must take responsibility for fixing those problems found to exist. Then strategic choice must be exercised. To what extent are the HRM practices and policies externally consistent; that is, produce the skills and behaviors necessary to compete given the firm's strategy and the competitive environment it faces? People must feel a need for change, a need to do things differently. This can be assisted by data showing that current practices are not working, identifying ways in which evolving company strategy impacts on HRM, and seeking external stimulation through plant visits, other companies, seminars.

Ulrich (1997, pp. 158–159) summarized seven critical success factors for change. These are fairly widely known, yet most change efforts fail. Organizations and change agents have done a poor job of translating this knowledge into action.

- *Leading change*: Having a sponsor of change who owns and leads the change initiative.
- *Creating a shared need*: Ensuring that individuals know why they should change and that the need for change is greater than the resistance to change.
- *Shaping a vision*: Articulating the desired outcome from change.
- *Mobilizing commitment*: Identifying, involving, and pledging the key stakeholders who must be involved to accomplish the change.
- *Changing systems and structures*: Using HR and management tools (staffing, development, appraisal, rewards, organization design, communication, systems, and so on) to ensure that the change is built into the organization's infrastructure.

- *Monitoring progress*: Defining benchmarks, milestones, and experiments with which to measure and demonstrate progress.
- *Making change last*: Ensuring that change happens through implementation plans, follow-through, and on-going commitments.

How does one start? First, senior management must establish a philosophy, goal, or vision. This means publicly and repeatedly stating the importance to the organization's success. Language that respects people, used as leaders, acting on these beliefs, being available and approachable. Senior management has a key role in developing an overarching philosophy or vision for their HRM initiatives (Gratton & Truss, 2003). Second, it is critical to make some changes with immediate impact (immediate visible results generate support and widespread commitment to make going back almost impossible); to take action of some sort. Try experimenting. Finally, companies seriously committed to effective HRM practices use measurement of their efforts as a central feature of their efforts (Becker et al., 2004). Measurement serves several purposes. It puts attention on these practices. It provides feedback on the implementation of their HRM practices.

To the extent that organizations can unleash the hidden value within their people, they will increase their chances of success, particularly as knowledge and intellectual capital become more important (Horibe, 1999; Stewart, 1997). There is a sense that organizations today need new ways of functioning to be successful (Tushman & O'Reilly, 1997). Many organizations have apparently got this message. Although still involving only a minority of the workforce, there has been a steady increase in the number of large organizations taking such changes (Applebaum & Batt, 1994; Pil & MacDuffie, 1996).

References

Applebaum, E., & Batt, R. (1994). *The new American workplace: Transforming work systems in the United States.* Ithaca, NY: Cornell University Press.

Arthur, J. (1994). Effects of human resource systems on manufacturing performance and turnover. *Academy of Management Journal, 37*, 670–687.

Ashkenas, R., Ulrich, D., Jick, T., & Kerr, S. (1995). *The boundaryless organization: Crossing the barrier to outstanding performance.* San Francisco: Jossey-Bass.

Bailey, T. (1993). Organizational innovation in the apparel industry. *Industrial Relations, 32*, 34–49.

Bamberger, P., & Meshoulam, I. (2000). *Human resource strategy: Formulation, implementation and impact.* Thousand Oaks, CA: Sage.

Banker, R. D., Field, J. M., Schroeder, R. G., & Sinha, K. K. (1996a). Impact of work teams on manufacturing performance: A longitudinal field study. *Academy of Management Journal, 39*, 867–890.

Banker, R. D., Lee, S. Y., Potter, G., & Srinivasan, D. (1996b). Contextual analysis of performance impacts of outcome based incentive compensation. *Academy of Management Journal, 39*, 920–948.

Bartel, A. P. (1994). Productivity gains from the implementation of employee training programs. *Industrial Relations, 33*, 411–425.

Batt, R. (2002). Managing customer services: Human resource practices, quit rate and sales growth. *Academy of Management Journal, 45*, 587–598.

Beatty, R. W., & Schneier, C. (1997). New roles to impact organizational performance – from partners' to players'. *Human Resource Management, 36*, 29–37.

Beatty, R. W., Huselid, M., & Schneier, C. (2003). Scoring in the business scorecard. *Organizational Dynamics*, 32, 107–121.

Becker, B., & Gerhart, B. (1996). The impact of human resource management on organizational performance: Progress and prospects. *Academy of Management Journal, 39*, 779–801.

Becker, B. E., & Huselid, M. A. (1998). High performance work systems and firm performance: A synthsesis of research and managerial implications. *Research in Personal and Human Resource Management, 16*, 53–101.

Becker, B. E., & Huselid, M. A. (1999). Strategic human resource management in five leading firms. *Human Resource Management, 38*, 287–301.

Becker, B. E., Huselid, M. A., & Beatty, R. W. (2004). *Workforce success metrics: Creating a human capital scorecard for the CEO*. Boston, MA: Harvard Business School Press.

Becker, B. E., Huselid, M. A., Pickes, P., & Sprott, M. (1996). HR as a source of shareholder value: Research and recommendations. *Human Resource Management, 36*, 39–47.

Becker, B. E., Huselid, M. A., & Ulrich, D. (2001). *The HR scorecard: Linking people, strategy and performance*. Boston, MA: Harvard Business School Press.

Blanton, J. S. (2000). Why consultants don't apply psychological research. *Consulting Psychology Journal: Practice and Research, 52*, 235–247.

Boehm, V. R. (1980). Research in the "real-world": A conceptual model. *Personnel Psychology, 33*, 495–504.

Bowen, D. E., & Ostroff, C. (2004). Understanding HRM firm performance linkages: The role of the "strength" of the HRM system. *Academy of Management Review, 29*, 203–221.

Burke, R. J., & Cooper, C. L. (2005). *Reinventing human resources management: Challenges and new directions*. London: Routledge.

Cameron, K. S., Dutton, J., & Quinn, R. (2003). *Positive organizational scholarship*. San Francisco: Berrett-Koehler.

Cappelli, P. (1999). *The new deal at work*. Boston, MA: Harvard Business School Press.

Carpenter, M. A., Sanders, W. G., & Gregersen, H. B. (2001). Bundling human capital with organizational context: The impact of international assignment experience on multinational firm performance and CEO pay. *Academy of Management Journal, 44*, 493–511.

Cascio, W. F. (2002). *Responsible restructuring: Creative and profitable alternatives to layoffs*. San Francisco: Berrett-Koehler.

Cooke, W. (1994). Employee participation, group-based incentives, and company performance: A union–nonunion comparison. *Industrial and Labor Relations Review, 47*, 595–609.

Cutcher-Gershenfeld, J. (1991). The impact of economic performance of a transformation in workplace relations. *Industrial and Labor Relations Review, 44*, 241–260.

Datta, D. K., Guthrie, J. P., & Wright, P. M. (2005). Human resource management and labor productivity: Does industry *Academy of Management Journal, 48*, 135–145.

Davidson, W. N., Worrell, D.L., & Fox, J. B. (1996). Early retirement programs and firm performance. *Academy of Management Journal, 39*, 970–984.

Delaney, J. T., & Huselid, M. A. (1996). The impact of human resource management practices on perceptions of organizational performance. *Academy of Management Journal, 39*, 949–969.

Delery, J. E., & Doty, D. H. (1996). Modes of theorizing in strategic human resource management: Tests of universalistic, contingency and configurational performance predictions. *Academy of Management Journal, 39*, 802–835.

Dossahoy, N. S., & Berger, P. D. (2002). Business school research: Bridging the gap between producers and consumers. *Omega, 30*, 201–314.

Druckman, D., Singer, J. E., & VanCott, H. (1997). *Enhancing organizational performance*. Washington, DC: National Academy Press.

Dyer, L., & Reeves, T. (1995). Human resource strategies and firm performance: What do we know and where do we need to go? *International Journal of Human Resource Management, 6*, 656–670.

Ferraro, F., Pfeffer, J., & Sutton, R. I. (2005a). Economics language and assumptions: How theories can become self-fulfilling. *Academy of Management Review, 30*, 8–24.

Ferraro, F., Pfeffer, J., & Sutton, R. I. (2005b). Prescriptions are not enough. *Academy of Management Review, 30*, 32–35.

Ferris, G. R., Arthur, M. M., Berkson, H. M., Kaplan, D. M., Harrell-Cook, G., & Frink, D. D. (1998). Toward a social context theory of the human resource management-organizational effectiveness relationship. *Human Resource Management Review, 8*, 235–264.

Fulmer, I. S., Gerhart, B., & Scott, K. S. (2003). Are the 100 Best better?: An empirical investigation of the relationship between being a "great place to work" and firm performance. *Personnel Psychology, 56*, 965–993.

Galbraith, J. R., Lawler, E. E., & Associates (1993). *Organizing for the future: The new logic for managing complex organizations.* San Francisco: Jossey-Bass.

Gelade, G. A., & Ivery, M. (2003). The impact of human resources management and work climate on organizational performance. *Personnel Psychology, 56*, 383–404.

Goldsmith, M., Gandossy, R. P., & Efron, M. S. (2003). *HRM in the 21st century.* New York: Wiley.

Gratton, L., & Truss, C. (2003). The three-dimensional people strategy: Putting human resources policies into action. *Academy of Management Executive, 17*, 74–86.

Guthrie, J. P. (2001). High-involvement work practices, turnover, and productivity: Evidence from New Zealand. *Academy of Management Journal, 44*, 180–190.

Heskett, J. L., Sasser, W. E., & Schlesinger, L. A. O(1997). *The service profit chain: How leading companies link profit and growth to loyalty, satisfaction and value.* New York: Free Press.

Heskett, J. L., Sasser, W. E., & Schlesinger, L. A. (1997). *The service profit chain: How leading companies link profit and growth to loyalty, satisfaction and value.* New York: Free Press.

Horibe, F. (1999). *Managing knowledge workers: New skills and attitudes to unlock the intellectual capital in your organization.* Toronto: Wiley.

Huselid, M. A. (1995). The impact of human resource management practices on turnover, productivity, and corporate financial performance. *Academy of Management Journal, 38*, 635–672.

Huselid, M. A., Jackson, S. E., & Schuler, R. S. (1997). Technical and strategic human resource management effectiveness as determinants of firm performance. *Academy of Management Journal, 40*, 171–188.

Ichniowski, C., Kochan, T. A., Levine, D., Olson, C., & Strauss, G. (1996). What works at work: Overview and assessment. *Industrial Relations, 35*, 299–333.

Ichniowski, C., Shaw, K., & Prennushi, G. (1997). The effects of human resource management practices on productivity: A study of steel finishing lines. *American Economic Review, 87*, 291–313.

Kaplan, R. S., & Norton, D. P. (1996). *The balanced scorecard: Translating strategy into action.* Boston, MA: Harvard Business School Press.

Katzenbach, J. R. (2000). *Peak performance: Aligning the hearts and minds of your employees.* Boston, MA: Harvard Business School Press.

Kling, J. (1995). High performance work systems and firm performance. *Monthly Labor Review, 118*, 29–36.

Koch, M. J., & McGrath, R. G. (1996). Improving labor productivity: Human resource management policies do matter. *Strategic Management Journal, 17*, 345–354.

Konrad, A., & Linnehan, F. (1995). Formalized HRM structures: Coordinating equal opportunity or concealing organizational practices? *Academy of Management Journal, 38*, 787–820.

Konrad, A. M., & Mangel, R. (2000). The impact of work-life programs on firm productivity. *Strategic Management Journal, 21*, 1225–1237.

Koys, D. J. (2001). The effects of employee satisfaction, organizational citizenship behavior, and turnover on organizational effectiveness: A unit-level, longitudinal study. *Personnel Psychology, 54,* 101–114.

Lado, A. A., & Wilson, M. C. (1994). Human resource systems and sustained competitive advantage: A competency-based peerspective. *Academy of Management Review, 19,* 699–727.

Lawler, E. E. (1992). *The ultimate advantage: Creating the high involvement organization.* San Francisco: Jossey-Bass.

Lawler, E. E. (2003). *Treat people right.* San Francisco: Jossey-Bass.

Lawler, E. E., Mohrman, S. A., & Ledford, G. F. (1995). *Creating high performance organizations: Practices and results of employee involvement and total quality management in Fortune 1000 companies.* San Francisco: Jossey-Bass.

Liker, J. K. (2003). *The Toyota way.* New York: McGraw-Hill.

MacDuffie, J. P. (1995). Human resource bundles and manufacturing performance: Organizational logic and flexible production systems in the world auto industry. *Industrial and Labor Relations Review, 48,* 197–221.

McKinsey & Company. (1998). *The war for talent.* New York: McKinsey & Company.

McWilliams, A., Van Fleet, D. D., & Wright, P. M. (2001). Strategic management of human resources for global competitive advantage. *Journal of Business Strategy, 18,* 1–14.

Mohrman, S. A., Gibson, C. B., & Mohrman, A. M. (2001). Doing research that is useful to practice: A model and empirical exploration. *Academy of Management Journal, 44,* 357–376.

Nadler, D. A., Shaw, R. B., Walton, A. E., & Associates (1995). *Discontinuous change: Leading organizational transformation.* San Francisco; Jossey-Bass.

O'Reilly, C. A. III, & Pfeffer, J. (2000). *Hidden value: How great companies achieve extraordinary results with ordinary people.* Boston, MA: Harvard Business School Press.

Osterman, P. (2005). Skill, training, and work organization in American establishments. *Industrial Relations, 44,* 125–146.

Perry-Smith, J. E., & Blum, T. C. (2000). Work-family human resource bundles and perceived organizational performance. *Academy of Management Journal, 43,* 1107–1117.

Pfeffer, J. (1994). *Competitive advantage through people.* Boston, MA: Harvard Business School Press.

Pfeffer, J. (1998). *The human equation: Building profits by putting people first.* Boston, MA: Harvard Business School Press.

Pfeffer, J., & Sutton, R. I. (2000). *The knowing-doing gap: How smart companies turn knowledge into action.* Boston, MA: Harvard Business School Press.

Pil, F. K., & MacDuffie, J. P. (1996). The adoption of high-involvement work practices. *Industrial Relations, 35,* 423–455.

Ramsay, H., Scholarios, D., & Harley, B. (2000). Employees and high performance work systems: Testing inside the black box. *British Journal of Industrial Relations, 38,* 501–531.

Risher, H., & Fay, C. (1995). *The performance imperative: Strategies for enhancing effectiveness.* San Francisco: Jossey-Bass.

Sanchez, J. I., Kraus, E., White, S., & Williams, M. (1999). Adopting high-involvement human resource practices. *Group & Organizational Management, 24,* 461–478.

Schneider, B., Hanges, P. J., Smith, D. B., & Salvaggio, A. N. (2003). Which comes first: Employee attitudes or organizational financial and market performance? *Journal of Applied Psychology, 88,* 836–851.

Skaggs, B. C., & Youndt, M. (2004). Strategic positioning, human capital, and performance in service organizations: A customer interaction approach. *Strategic Management Journal, 25,* 85–99.

Stewart, T. (1997). *Intellectual capital.* New York: Doubleday-Currency.

Terpstra, D. E., & Rozell, E. J. (1993). The relationship of staffing practices to organizational level measures of performance. *Personnel Psychology, 46,* 27–48.

Tsui, A. S., Pearce, J. L., Porter, L. W., & Tripoli, A. M. (1997). Alternative approaches to the employee–organization relationship: Does investment in employees pay off? *Academy of Management Journal, 40*, 1089–1121.

Tushman, M., & O'Reilly, C. O. (1997). *Winning through innovation: A practical guide to leading organizational change and renewal.* Boston, MA: Harvard Business School Press.

Ulrich, D. (1997). *Human resource champions.* Boston, MA: Harvard Business School.

Ulrich, D., & Beatty, R. W. (2001). From partners to players: Extending the HR playing field. *Human Resource Management, 40*, 293–308.

Watson Wyatt (1999). *Work USA 2000: Employee commitment and the bottom line.* Bethesda, MD: Watson Wyatt.

Way, S. A. (2001). High performance work systems and intermediate indicators of firm performance within the US small business sector. *Journal of Management, 28*, 765–785.

Welbourne, T. M., & Andrews, A. O. (1996). Predicting the performance of initial public offerings: Should human resource management be in the equation? *Academy of Management Journal, 39*, 891–919.

Whitener, E. M. (2001). Do "high commitment": Human resource practices affect employee commitment? A cross-lagged analysis using hierarchical linear modeling. *Journal of Management. 27*, 515–535.

Way, S. A. (2001). High performance work systems and intermediate indicators of firm performance within the UIS small buisiness sector. *Journal of Management, 28*, 765-785.

Wright, P. M., Dyer, L., & Takla, M. G. (1999). What's next? Key findings from the 1999 state-of-the-art and practice study. *Human Resources Planning, 22*, 12–20.

Wright, P. M., Gardner, T. M., & Moynihan, L. M. (2003). The impact of HR practices on the performance of business units. *Human Resource Management Journal, 13*, 21–36.

Wright, P. M., McCormick, B., Sherman, W. S., & McMahan, G. C. (1999). The role of human resources practices in petro-chemical refinery performance. *International Journal of Human Resources Management, 10*, 551–571.

Wright, P. M., & McMahan, G. C. (1992). Theoretical perspectives for strategic human resource management. *Journal of Management, 18*, 295–320.

Wright, P., McMahn, G. C., & McWilliams, A. (1994). Human resources and sustained competitive advantage: A resource-based perspective. *International Journal of Human Resource Management, 56*, 301–327.

Youndt, M. A., Snell, S. A., Dean, J. W., & Lepak, D. P. (1996). Human resource management, manufacturing strategy, and firm performance. *Academy of Management Journal, 39*, 836–866.

Zacharatos, A., Barling, J., & Iverson, R. D. (2005). High-performance work systems and occupational safety. *Journal of Applied Psychology, 90*, 77–93.

CHAPTER 3

Emerging Perspectives on the Relationship between HRM and Performance

David P. Lepak, Riki Takeuchi, Niclas L. Erhardt and
Saba Colakoglu

Over the past couple of decades, researchers in the field of strategic human resource management (SHRM) have made considerable progress with respect to understanding the relationship between human resource management (HRM) and performance. The growing popularity of SHRM has grown, at least in part, due to rapid changes in the business landscape, including globalization, creation and diffusion of technological innovation, and worldwide search for global talent that have increased the potential role of employee contributions as a source of competitive advantage for organizations (DeNisi, Hitt, & Jackson, 2003; Jackson, Hitt, & DeNisi, 2003). As a field of research, SHRM can be distinguished from more traditional HRM research in several ways.

First, a major focus of SHRM research involves an emphasis on organizational performance. While HRM researchers have a long tradition examining the impact of HRM practices on individual-level outcomes, SHRM researchers have placed primary emphasis on macro-level performance outcomes (cf. Rogers & Wright, 1998; Wright, 1998). For instance, Delery and Doty (1996) used return on asset (ROA) and return on equity (ROE) and Huselid (1995) used gross return on assets (GRATE) and a variant of Tobin's Q (i.e., firm market value/book value) as their dependent variables. In contrast, traditional HRM research generally focused on individual outcomes such as task performance (cf. Locke & Latham, 1990), absenteeism (cf. Harrison & Martocchio, 1998), withdrawal behaviors (cf. Hulin, 1991), and turnover (cf. Griffeth, Hom, & Gaertner, 2000).

Second, there is a growing consensus that a system of HRM practices, rather than HRM practices in isolation, is a more appropriate focus for understanding how HRM impacts important performance outcomes. This focus is understandable as individuals are typically exposed to multiple practices simultaneously. And conceptually, the impact of one practice is dependent on the other practices in place. Implementing an individual level pay for performance plan, for example, might not prove effective in a team-based work environment.

As a result, the notion of synergy or complementarity among HRM practices has gained considerable importance in the SHRM literature (Becker & Huselid, 1998; Huselid, 1995; Wright & Snell, 1998).

Third, SHRM researchers typically focus on higher-level contingency variables. Underlying this perspective is the argument that the effectiveness of HRM practices and/or systems depend on their alignment with external variables to the HRM system such as strategy, technology, environmental conditions, and the like (e.g. Wright & Snell, 1998). While examining moderators or contingency factors are not new to HRM research, the focus on higher-level factors such as business strategy and capital intensity, or environmental and industry factors, marks a notable emphasis on more macro oriented contingencies. These basic distinctions between traditional HRM and SHRM are highlighted in Table 1.

As noted above, one of the most defining attributes of SHRM research is that it places renewed importance in the role of HRM and performance. And while there is a growing body of research demonstrating that HRM can serve as a value-creating function within organizations, there remains considerable room for improvement in our understanding of the HRM–performance linkage. The purpose of this chapter is to review the literature

Table 1: Strategic HRM perspective and more traditional HRM perspectives.

	Traditional HRM	**Strategic HRM**
Focus	Individual HRM practices (e.g. staffing practices [Terpstra & Rozell, 1993], training practices [Russell, Terborg, & Powers, 1985], and compensation practices [Gerhart & Milkovich, 1990])	System or configuration of HRM practices (e.g. "commitment" [Arthur, 1994], "human capital enhancing" [Youndt, Snell, Dean, & Lepak, 1996], "High Performance Work Systems"[Becker & Huselid, 1998; Huselid, 1995])
Contingencies	Person-environment fit (e.g. Dawis, 2000; Edwards & Van Harrison, 1993), Person-organization fit (e.g. Kristof, 1996; Van Vianen, 2000), Person-job fit (e.g. Kristof-Brown, 2000)	External fit (Industry characteristics-HRM & firm characteristics-HRM), Internal fit (HRM-HRM)
Outcomes	Individual-level outcomes (e.g. task performance [cf. Locke & Latham, 1990], absenteeism [cf. Harrison & Martocchio, 1998], withdrawal behaviors [cf. Hulin, 1991], and turnover [cf. Griffeth, Hom, & Gaertner, 2000])	Firm-level performance outcomes (e.g. ROA & ROE [Delery & Doty, 1996], GRATE & Tobin's Q [Huselid, 1995])

examining the HRM–performance relationship. In doing so, we place primary emphasis on some exciting and promising emerging areas of research that provide new and innovative ways to examine this relationship. The structure of this chapter is as follows. First, we review the theoretical perspectives that permeate the literature and examine the empirical studies that relate to each domain briefly. Then, drawing from a wide range of theoretical perspectives, we explore potential avenues for future research that might help to provide conceptual insights into the HRM –performance relationship.

Theoretical Perspectives of the HRM–Performance Relationship

Before we discuss the actual HRM–performance relationship, a brief discussion of the construct of performance is warranted. As shown in Figure 1, performance is a multi-dimensional construct and researchers have examined many different aspects of perform-ance. Dyer and Reeves (1995) noted different types of performance measures that are most appropriate for SHRM research. They proposed four effectiveness measures: (1) human resource outcomes such as absenteeism, turnover, job satisfaction, and individual or group performance, (2) organizational outcomes such as productivity, quality, and service, (3) financial or accounting outcomes such as profitability, return on assets, and return on invested capital, and (4) stock market performance (stock value or shareholder return).

As noted by Wright (1998), SHRM researchers tend to focus on maximizing organiza-tional performance, particularly financial performance, as the major goal to be achieved. This preference for financial measures of performance has been shown by Rogers and Wright (1998) who reviewed the literature and noted that out of 80 dependent variables included in SHRM studies up to that point in time, accounting measures such as return on asset, return on equity, profits, and sales and market measures such as stock price and Tobin's Q were used in more than half of the research.

While examining which performance measures are more or less appropriate is beyond the scope of this chapter, and may warrant an entire chapter in itself, we believe that it is important to acknowledge that there is no single performance measure that is most impor-tant; rather, many different performance measures deserve investigation, and have been examined, in the literature (Dyer & Reeves, 1995; Way & Johnson, 2005). And conceptu-ally, these multiple performance measures are related. Improved HR outcomes, for exam-ple, would logically be related to organizational and financial outcomes, which in turn, may help improve market performance. Regardless of the specific performance measure studied, there are some dominant theoretical perspectives regarding the role of HRM in improving, or diminishing performance. We now turn our discussion to these relationships.

Dominant Theoretical Perspectives in the HRM–Performance Relationship

Ten years ago, Delery and Doty (1996) developed a framework for organizing research examining the relationship between HRM and performance into one of several theoretical perspectives — the universal approach, also referred to as the best practice approach, the contingency perspective, and the configurational perspective. Figure 1 provides a graphic illustration of these different perspectives.

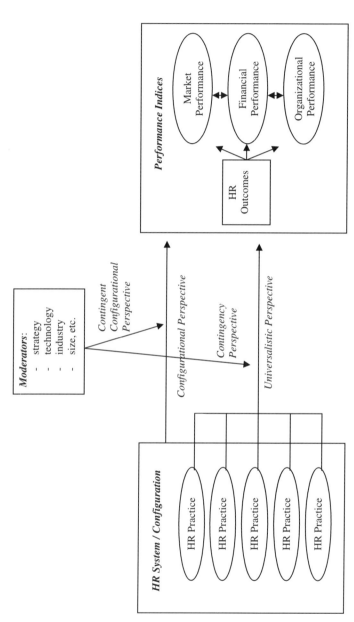

Figure 1: Universalistic, contingency, configurational, and contingent configurational perspectives for the HRM–performance relationship.

The universalistic perspective   The universalistic perspective is a conceptual vantage point based on the logic that there are a certain HRM practices related to recruitment, selection, training, job design, compensation, performance appraisal, and the like that have the potential to have a positive impact on firm effectiveness. Pfeffer (1995), for example, explored the notion of HR best practices by identifying successful companies and what specific HR practices they used. He found that these companies (with different strategies and in different industries) shared certain practices; namely employment security, selectivity in recruiting, high wages, incentive pay, employee ownership, information sharing, participation and empowerment, self-managed teams, training and skill development, cross-utilization and cross-training, symbolic equalitarianism, wage compression, and finally promotion from within, that were associated with overall performance.

The key point of this perspective is that certain HRM practices are expected to positively impact individual and/or organizational outcomes universally — regardless of the context in which they are utilized. For example, Terpstra and Rozell (1993) identified five staffing practices (follow-up on recruiting sources, conduct validation studies on selection tests, structured interviews, intelligence tests, biographical information blanks) that were positively linked with annual profit. Russell, Terborg, and Powers (1985) found that training practices (e.g. essential policies, stocking and transaction procedures, customer relations, customer service, customer satisfaction information, and basic sales techniques) were positively correlated with retail store sales volume and store image. Gerhart and Milkovich (1990) provided evidence that differences in compensation practices had a positive impact on financial firm performance. Perry-Smith and Blum (2000) found that the presence of work-family bundles of policies (e.g. on-site day care, help with day care costs, paid parental care, flexible schedule) were positively associated with greater firm-level performance.

The configurational perspective   The configurational approach extends the universalistic perspective and suggests that the combination of HRM practices, rather than any single practice is what drives organizational performance. The central tenet of the configurational perspective is that a bundle of HRM practices must be adopted that compliments each other to achieve greater performance. The degree of this internal or horizontal alignment among HRM practices influences whether or not companies realize a synergistic effect on firm effectiveness (Baird & Meshoulam, 1988). For example, Huselid (1995) found that high-performance work systems were related to turnover rate and labor productivity, which in turn, were related to two financial indicators of firm performance. Way (2002) and Batt (2002) found significant relationships between high performance work systems and labor productivity and turnover rate for small companies and service companies, respectively. Similarly, Ichniowski, Shaw, and Prennushi (1997) found a positive relationship between innovative work practices and labor productivity for steel-finishing lines.

Despite differences in the terms used to denote which practices comprise an HRM system, a consistently positive relationship between high-performance work systems (Becker & Huselid, 1998; Huselid, 1995), high involvement (Guthrie, 2001), human capital enhancing (Youndt, Snell, Dean, & Lepak, 1996), commitment-based HRM systems (Arthur, 1994), or innovative employment practices (Ichniowski et al., 1997) and aggregate performance measures such as plant (e.g. Arthur, 1994; Ichniowski et al., 1997; Youndt et al., 1996), business-unit (e.g. Delery & Doty, 1996; Koch & McGrath, 1996) and corporate perform-ance (e.g. Becker & Huselid, 1998; Huselid, 1995) has been found.

The contingency perspective   While the universalistic perspective focuses on HRM practices that are espoused to be beneficial in all circumstances, contingency perspectives are based on the logic that the impact of any HRM practice, or configuration of HRM prac-tices, on organizational outcomes is contingent upon the alignment of HRM practices with contextual factors such as strategy (Arthur, 1992; Youndt et al., 1996), technology (e.g. Snell & Dean, 1992), industry (e.g. Datta, Guthrie, & Wright, 2005; Jackson, Schuler, & Rivero, 1989), firm size (Davis-Blake & Uzzi, 1993), and life cycle stage (Baird & Meshoulam, 1988), to name a few. Conceptually, the logic for a contingency approach is straightforward. For example, 3M, a firm competing on knowledge and innovative prod-ucts (the strategy), would likely need a set of HRM practices that enables and promotes employee creativity. Another company such as Wal*Mart that competes based on effi-ciency and cost minimization may focus on HRM practices such as hourly pay, paying a relatively low wage and enforcing adherence to pre-established behaviors, in an attempt to minimize labor costs and to maximize labor productivity and efficiency.

Within the contingency perspective, there are two forms of this relationship. First, researchers may focus on whether or not there are contingencies that impact the effective-ness of *specific HRM practices* (contingent perspective). For example, does the impact of a certain type of selection or training practice on business unit performance depend on business strategy? Second, researchers may extend the configurational perspective and examine whether or not the benefits of *internally aligned systems or bundles of HRM prac-tices* depend on some contextual factor (contingent configurational perspective). Both forms are illustrated in Figure 1. Baird and Meshoulam (1988) suggested that to be most effective, HRM systems must be comprised of HRM practices that are mutually reinforc-ing with one another (internal fit) as well as in alignment with organizational factors (external fit). Related, MacDuffie (1995, p. 198) noted that "an HR bundle or system must be integrated with complementary bundles of practices from core business functions" and examined the interaction between flexible production and human resource capabilities that included HRM practices such as recruitment and hiring, contingent compensation, status differentiation, and training.

While the conceptual logic for a contingency perspective is persuasive, the empirical results are mixed. For example, Youndt et al. (1996) examined the relationship between manufacturing strategy, HRM, and operational performance (employee productivity, machine efficiency, and customer alignment) and found a moderating effect of a quality strategy on the relationship between the use of a human-capital-enhancing HR system and operational performance and a moderating effect of a cost strategy on an administrative HR system and operational performance. Arthur (1994) examined the relationship between commitment- and control-oriented HR systems, employee turnover, and labor productivity in steel mini-mills following different business strategies. As expected, the results sup-ported differences in the relationship between control HR system and performance versus a commitment HR system and performance. Similarly, Guthrie (2001, p. 180) tested whether Arthur's (1994) results about "the interactive effects of human capital investments (through the use of a "commitment" human resource system) and employee retention (turnover) on firm productivity" could be generalized beyond the small U.S. single indus-try to New Zealand. The results suggested that a firm's competitiveness can be enhanced by utilizing high-involvement work practices.

In contrast, in a study examining high-performance work systems, Huselid (1995) failed to find support for organizational benefits associated with the alignment between HRM systems and business strategy. Delery and Doty (1996) also examined the interac-tion between innovation strategy and seven HRM practices — results-oriented appraisals, profit sharing, job descriptions, employment security, internal career opportunities, train-ing, and participation/voice — on indicators of firm financial performance (ROA & ROE) but did not find the interaction step to explain incremental variance in ROA or ROE at the conventional level of 0.05. However, they did find significant betas for the interaction between results-oriented appraisal and innovation strategy on ROA and ROE, internal career opportunities and innovation strategy on ROA and ROE, and participation/voice and innovation strategy on ROA.

Looking across these studies, most of the research examining the impact of HRM on performance fits within one or more of these theoretical perspectives or modes of theoriz-ing (Delery & Doty, 1996). Moreover, it is fair to say that the results of these studies demonstrate that HRM matters for multiple indicators of performance ranging from HR outcomes to market-related indicators of performance. However, researchers continue to grapple with "how" HRM relates to performance.

Emerging Perspectives for the HRM–Performance Relationship

In the past several years there has been a flurry of activity related to examining how HRM relates to performance. In the remainder of this chapter, we examine some of these emerg-ing theoretical perspectives and offer some suggestions that will hopefully stimulate addi-tional research to provide insights into the HRM–performance relationship. Specifically, we focus on two broad categories of theoretical perspectives — investigating the black box and adopting an architectural perspective — that may impact what we know about the HRM–performance relationship.

The "Black Box" Perspective

Perhaps the greatest opportunity for understanding the relationship between HRM and per-formance lies in the identification of the intermediate linkages through which HRM relates to performance measures. This concern has been voiced fairly strongly as a need to open up the "black box" as a critical area of investigation (e.g. Becker & Gerhart, 1996; Delery, 1998), although empirical research has not followed suit. The relationship of this black box in existing conceptualizations of the HRM–performance relationship is depicted in Figure 2.

As shown in Figure 2, intervening mechanisms serve a fundamental role in translating HRM practices into performance outcomes. The importance of mediating factors should not be understated. As suggested by Delery (1998, p. 290), "a firm does not gain a com-petitive advantage from HRM practices, *per se*, but from the human resources that the firm attracts and retains." Collins and Clark (2003, p. 740) echoed this sentiment when they

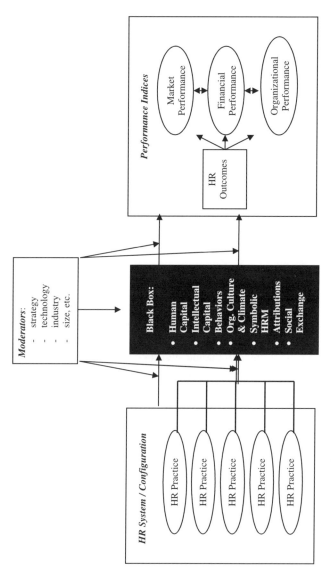

Figure 2: The "black box" in the HRM–performance relationship.

noted, "HR practices can only be a source of sustained competitive advantage when they support resources or competencies that provide value to a firm." Consequently, understanding the factors that exist between HRM and performance are of important concern. The challenge is to clarify what is in this black box.

Austin, Villanova, Kane, and Bernardin (1991), noted that (individual) performance is a function of ability (or in an aggregate form, human capital) and motivation (or in an aggregate form, behavioral norms) and both are needed for higher performance. In other words, human capital may provide the potential for higher firm performance while norms regarding the appropriate employee behaviors are instrumental in realizing that potential (cf. Wright & Snell, 1991; Huselid, 1995). Looking across the literature, a focus on abilities and attitudes/behaviors is consistent with two theories that have received considerable attention in SHRM — the resource-based view of the firm and the behavioral perspective. Beyond these two more established perspectives are issues relating to organizational climate and culture, symbolic and substantive perspective of HRM practices, HR attributions, and social exchange theories. We discuss these below.

The resource based view of the firm   Putting the resource-based view (RBV) of the firm in a section of this chapter entitled "emerging perspectives" may seem a bit awkward considering that this theoretical framework has been around for many years. And, it has certainly been invoked within the SHRM literature extensively. The logic of a RBV emphasis in SHRM is understandable as the RBV provides a broad argument as to why HRM practices and employees may be a potential source of value creation (Barney, 1991; Wright, Dunford, & Snell, 2001). Barney argued that a firm's resources (physical, organizational, and human) might generate a sustained competitive advantage when it possesses four attributes: (1) value, (2) rarity, (3) inimitability, and (4) nonsubstitutability. A firm resource adds value when it exploits opportunities and/or neutralizes threats in a firm's environment. It is rare when only a small number of current and potential competitors have it. A firm resource must be imperfectly imitable where other firms that do not possess these valuable and rare resources cannot obtain them easily. Finally, a firm resource needs to be imperfectly substitutable where other firms cannot use strategically equivalent resources to conceive and implement certain strategies. As noted by Wright, McMahan, and McWilliams (1994), employees have the potential to meet these four requirements.

Human capital   While this logic has been referred often, researchers have not historically tested this full argument. Conceptually, the underlying logic is that the use of certain HRM practices may result in human capital that is valuable, rare, inimitable, and non-substitutable that, in turn, facilitates competitive advantage. Empirically, within SHRM research, the focus of RBV has been predominantly on examining the linkage between employee competencies and firm performance (e.g. Lado & Wilson, 1994). For example, Hitt, Bierman, Shimizu, and Kochhar (2001) examined the relationship between human capital (articulable and tacit knowledge as measured by the quality of education and organizational tenure, respectively) and firm performance (return on sales) and found a positive, curvilinear association between the two. Similarly, Pennings, Lee, and Van Witteloostuijn (1998, p. 426) noted that "professionals endowed with a high level of human capital are more likely to deliver consistent and high-quality services" and the contribution of human capital investment to firm survival is critical. Similarly, Snell and Dean (1992) noted that human capital adds value to the firm because of enhanced potential for productivity provided by higher knowledge and skills. In other words, the higher the level of knowledge, skills, and abilities of employees, the more potential impact of human capital on performance.

Intellectual capital   Recently, several scholars have expanded the focus of the RBV in SHRM research to examine the broader notion of intellectual capital rather than focus solely on human capital. As noted by Youndt, Subramaniam, and Snell (2004, p. 337), intellectual capital can be broadly conceptualized as "the sum of all knowledge an organization is able to leverage in the process of conducting business to gain competitive advantage." More specifically, intellectual capital is comprised of three forms of capital — human, social, and organizational (Sullivan, 2000; Youndt et al., 2004). As noted above, human capital refers to individual employee capabilities — their knowledge, skills, and abilities. Social capital, in contrast, does not reside with any individual. Rather, it reflects knowledge in groups and networks of people. Nahapiet and Ghoshal (1998) define social capital as the aggregate of resources embedded within, available through, and derived from the network of relationships possessed by an individual or organization (Brass, Galaskiewicz, Greve, & Tsai, 2004). Finally, organizational capital refers to "institutionalized knowledge and codified experience stored in databases, routine, patents, manuals, structures, and the like" (Youndt et al., 2004, p. 338).

Subramaniam and Youndt (2005) examined the relationships between these three types of intellectual capital and innovation, and found that organizational capital was positively associated with incremental innovative capability and social capital was related to both incremental and radical capabilities. Interestingly, they also found that human and social capital interacted positively to influence radical innovative capability. One direct implication of this is that it suggests that the value of human capital is closely linked to social capital. As noted by Subramaniam and Youndt (2005, p. 459), "unless individual knowledge is networked, shared, and channeled through relationships, it provides little benefit to organizations in terms of innovative capabilities."

Drawing on the RBV and the growing importance of social capital, Collins and Clark (2003) explored the relationships among network-building HRM practices, internal and external social networks of top management teams, and firm sales growth and stock growth. Their results provide support for a mediating effect of top managers' social networks. Also focusing on the importance of social capital, Shaw, Duffy, Johnson, and Lockhart (2005) examined the influence of social capital losses on store performance, including productivity, change in productivity, and change in sales. They found that social capital losses accounted for additional variance in store performance above and beyond the effects of human capital losses and performance losses. In addition, they found that turnover rate acted as a moderator on the relationship between social capital losses and performance such that performance reduction due to network disruptions was more apparent when the overall turnover rate was low. Kang, Morris, and Snell (in press) suggest success in creating customer value requires that firm's are successful in both exploitation and exploratory innovation based on employee knowledge. Leveraging that knowledge requires that organizations design HRM systems in a way to encourage entrepreneurial activity among employees for exploratory innovation as well as cooperative activity among employees to exploit and extend existing knowledge for competitive advantage.

While still in its infancy, this growing focus on social and organizational capital in conjunction with human capital highlights a potentially fruitful avenue for understanding the HRM–performance relationship. Certainly more research is needed but these findings seem to suggest that HRM practices that facilitate the development of human capital, as well as the creation and effective utilization of social capital, may help organization outperform their competitors. Future SHRM research that focuses on identifying the HRM practices that bolster human capital and lead to network and social capital formation would prove beneficial.

The behavioral perspective As in the case with the resource-based view of the firm, placing the behavioral perspective as an emerging perspective may seem out of place. After all, the behavioral perspective has had a significant impact on SHRM researchers for a number of years (cf. McMahan, Virick, & Wright, 1999; Wright & McMahan, 1992). However, as we discuss below, while the theoretical arguments for this perspective have been clearly articulated, empirical tests of the behavioral perspective are limited.

The behavioral perspective suggests that firms design HRM practices in an attempt to elicit needed role behaviors for given organizational contingencies such as strategy, technology, and the like (Jackson et al., 1989; Schuler & Jackson, 1987). The central argument underlying this perspective is that HRM practices are one of the primary means to encourage employees to display appropriate role behaviors that contribute to organization success. As noted by Jackson et al. (1989, p. 728), "A behavioral perspective assumes that employers use personnel practices as a means for eliciting and controlling employee attitudes and behaviors." A closely related example of the behavioral perspective is Miles and Snow's (1984) description of the employee behaviors needed for different strategic business types: defender, prospector, analyzer, and reactor.

Given the clearly articulated argument that needed role behaviors for employees depend on the strategic objectives of the company, many researchers have invoked the behavioral perspective as support for a contingency perspective on the HRM–performance relationship. Our view on this is that while this is correct, an additional step is needed; that is, research is needed to identify the specific mediating components of this relationship. Existing empirical research acknowledges the importance of employee attitudes and behaviors for effective implementation of strategy and/or organizational functioning, but those that explicitly recognize and identify the necessary behaviors are rare.

For instance, Arthur (1994) suggested that a commitment HRM system is associated with employee motivation and organization citizenship behaviors, which in turn, are critical to organizational success. MacDuffie (1995) argued that innovative HRM practices influences the discretionary behaviors of employees, which, if aligned with the firm's interests, contributes to higher firm performance. Tsui, Pearce, Porter, and Hite (1995, p. 135) suggested, "organizations seeking an innovative [differentiation] strategy would use practices that encourage the exchange of ideas through cooperative, interdependent behaviors among employees." However, less common is the empirical testing of these employee behaviors as mediators (McMahan, Virick, & Wright, 1999). Rather, the logic of the behavioral perspective is imposed but employee attitudes and behaviors are not typically measured or tested. We strongly encourage additional research that places focus on the "how" component of the HRM–performance relationship. For example, researchers focusing on psychological contracts (e.g. Rousseau, 1995) have demonstrated that the nature and strength of the obligations felt by employees toward their organization are influenced by the HRM practices to which they are exposed. Thus, future studies need to investigate "what" employee attitudes and behaviors are critical as mediators and "how" HRM practices affect the nature of these employee attitudes and behaviors.

Organizational climate and culture   An additional avenue that has received increased attention in terms of explaining the intermediate linkages through which HRM relates to performance is the study of organizational culture and climate. Organizational culture is a complex set of values, beliefs, assumptions, and symbols that define the way in which a firm conducts its business (Barney, 1986; Schein, 1985), and is manifested in the behavior of its members as well as how the company interacts with its customers, suppliers, and employees. Wilderom, Glunk, and Maslowski (2000) reviewed a dozen of empirical studies on the link between culture and performance, and documented that various dimensions of organizational culture such as culture strength, strategy-culture fit, involvement, adaptability, consistency, and various organizational values were linked with performance measures such as return of investment, stock price, and market share (Denison, 1990; Kotter & Heskett, 1992; Zimmerman & Tregoe, 1997).

Another closely related but distinct construct is organizational climate, which is defined as the incumbents' perceptions of the routines and rewards that characterize an organizational setting (Schneider & Reichers, 1990). Climate research generally has a strategic focus of interest (such as service or safety), and attempts to identify those elements of the work environment, as described by employees, that correlate, or link, to critically important organizational outcomes such as customer satisfaction and business performance. Studies that indicate a significant and positive relationship between how favorably members of an organization describe their work environment and customer satisfaction levels and various business performance measures are numerous. Wiley and Brooks (2000) reviewed the literature on this type of linkage research and reported that various dimensions of work climate, such as customer orientation, quality emphasis, teamwork/cooperation, involvement/ empowerment, have been found to correlate with overall customer satisfaction and business performance.

Other than demonstrating that organizational culture and climate can indeed be another source of competitive advantage, this literature stream suggests that culture and climate of an organization are in part shaped by the HRM system and also help shape the HRM system (Way & Johnson, 2005). For example, Ostroff and Bowen (2000) proposed that researchers analyze the psychological and collective climate as a mediating variable between the HRM system and firm performance. They argue that when the HRM system creates a strong situation for the employees, individuals share a common interpretation of what behaviors are important, expected, and rewarded. According to their model, this strong organizational climate in turn, collectively guides the behaviors of individuals toward the business objective of the firm leading to increased firm performance.

Wright, Dunford, and Snell (2001) argued that rather than simply positing a relationship between HRM practices and sustained competitive advantage, one must realize that people management systems might impact this advantage in a variety of ways: creating cultures, mindsets that enable the maintenance of unique competencies, or they may promote socially complex relationships characterized by trust, knowledge sharing, and teamwork. Denison (1990) argued that only by placing value on the interactive characteristics of organizations — the systems of norms, beliefs, and patterns of behavior that forms the core of an organization's culture — can the true contribution of human resources to an organization's ultimate effectiveness be determined. As a result, the merger between organizational culture and climate and SHRM can certainly lend important insights into how HRM relates to performance.

Symbolic view of HRM   Another perspective that may provide insights into the mediating mechanisms linking HRM and performance is a symbolic approach to HRM (Ferris, Hochwarter, Buckley, Harrell-Cook, & Frink, 1999). As noted by Pffefer's (1981) symbolic action perspective, it may be possible to view HRM systems from two different perspectives: a symbolic content which sends signals and messages to employees and other parties about the value the organization places on them, and a substantive content which communicates information about the desired role behaviors from employees. Though not explicitly noted, we agree with Ferris et al. (1999) that the substantive perspective dominates the SHRM literature. While this is certainly a viable perspective, it is conceivable that HRM systems operate at a symbolic level as well. For example, while an HRM practice such as "selective recruitment" can ensure that hired employees are capable of displaying attitudes and behaviors in line with the strategy of the organization, organizational messages such as the value placed on the employees or the image of the employer are also embedded in how these practices are designed and how they are delivered. Individuals who are exposed to these practices perceive and interpret these symbolic cues, which in turn, shape their opinions about the organization, as well as the attitudes, and behaviors they choose to display.

In addition to highlighting a secondary mechanism through which HRM may influence performance, this perspective may provide depth into the external fit or the contingency argument. As noted above, despite being one of the core modes of theorizing in SHRM, empirical support for the contingency argument for the importance of fit between HRM systems and strategy has been somewhat mixed. Applying the symbolic action perspective, one may argue that the alignment between HRM system and strategic contingencies has been dominated by the substantive elements of HRM systems. For example, external fit may be assessed by examining the criteria used to select employees or the number of training hours employees' receive. While these are certainly critical elements to understanding HRM effectiveness, it is conceivable there may be different implications when we examine the fit between HRM and strategy from a symbolic perspective. For example, several researchers have suggested that companies pursuing a low cost strategy may de-emphasize employment security, participation, and investments in employees in an attempt to ensure employees are able to perform narrow tasks in a manner that keeps mistakes and costs to a minimum while maximizing productivity. From a substantive view, this is a logical argument. From a symbolic perspective, however, these diminished investments in employees may send signals to employees, and other relevant parties that employees are not valued. If this is the case, it could result in diminished performance, even though there is substantive alignment between the system and the strategy.

An attribution approach   Closely related to a symbolic perspective, examining employee attributions of the HRM practices to which they are exposed is an emerging body of research that may shed light on the HRM–performance relationship. Attribution theory suggests that individuals have a tendency to derive causal explanations about the events, occurrences, and individuals surrounding them (Heider, 1958; Kelley, 1967). Moreover, attribution theory may be able to provide insights into SHRM and explain how these interpretive mechanisms work in an organizational setting. For example, although employees may have a certain level of understanding about how they are expected to act (attitudes and behaviors) in response to exposure to HRM practices (Bowen & Ostroff, 2004), they may also have a tendency to derive causal attributions, as suggested by attribution theory, about the intent of organizations in implementing these practices. Several researchers (Koys, 1988; Nishii, 2003) have suggested that employees may make external attributions (out of the control of management) or internal attributions (within the control of management) regarding the motivation for implementing HRM practices.

If employees conclude that the implementation of HRM practices is due to some external factors beyond the control of a company, these attributions may not impact employee behaviors (Koys, 1988). However, when employees make internal attributions of HRM practices, these attributions will likely affect how they react in response to those practices. For example, if an employee perceives that the reason why their company implements an HRM practice is because it values the contribution of its employees, the employee may reciprocate by engaging in positive employee behaviors and attitudes. Conversely, when internal attributions for HRM practices used are more negative, such as viewed as an attempt to exploit the workforce, they may respond in a dramatically different and potentially negative manner than what HRM practice was originally designed to achieve. In an empirical investigation, Nishii (2003) found that such negative attributions of HR practices were negatively related to employee satisfaction, and positive attributions were positively related to both affective commitment and employee satisfaction in a large supermarket chain.

Social exchange   Social exchange theorists (e.g. Gouldner, 1960) examine the exchanges that occur between employers and employees regarding perceptions of reciprocity at an individual level of analysis. The essence of the norm of reciprocity is that employees feel obligated to respond equitably to treatments from others (including one's employer). As Wayne, Shore, and Liden (1997, p. 83) noted, "employees seek a balance in their exchange relationships with organizations by having attitudes and behaviors commensurate with the degree of employer commitment to them as individuals."

Though the exact focus of social exchange theorists may vary, a common theme is that the perceived balance of organizational inducement for employee contributions has performance implications. Based on this logic, HRM practices and systems may be viewed as an organization's inducement to realize some desired employee contributions (e.g. employee attitudes and behaviors) that, ultimately, influence company performance. For instance, Wayne et al. (1997) found that the use of HRM practices that were developmental in nature was positively related to perceived organizational support. Perceptions of organizational support, in turn, have been found to be positively associated with affective organizational commitment and constructive suggestions (Eisenberger, Fasolo, & Davis-LaMastro, 1990) as well as citizenship behaviors (Wayne et al., 1997). In addition, perceived organizational support is negatively associated with absenteeism (Eisenberger et al., 1990) and turnover intentions (Guzzo, Noonan, & Elron, 1994). Building on this logic, we view research that adopts a social exchange perspective to hold particular promise to provide greater insights into "how" HRM practices influence employees and their subsequent attitudes and behaviors.

While, at least from a SHRM perspective, these areas of research are still in their infancy, we encourage additional research that more directly examines the role of intellectual capital, employee behaviors, organizational climate and culture, symbolic interpretations of HRM as well as employee attribution and social exchange mechanisms to understand "how" HRM systems relate to multiple measures of performance. Beyond these mediating mechanisms, however, a second growing area of research focuses on the complexity of HR system use within organizations as well as the growing reliance on virtual organizations and the use of internal and external employment simultaneously to achieve organizational objectives.

The Architectural Perspective

Recently, several researchers have adopted an architectural perspective that extends the contingent configuration perspective by suggesting that not all employees within a single organization are managed by the same HRM practices or systems, but rather multiple HRM systems are likely to simultaneously exist within organizations (Delery & Shaw, 2001; Lepak & Snell, 1999; Tsui, Pearce, Porter, & Hite, 1995). There are three primary arguments for this assertion. First, not all employees are equally valuable to a company's success — different employees within an organization contribute toward company goals in different ways. Second, companies rely on external labor — temporary employees, contractors, and other contingent workers — in conjunction with a full time workforce to meet their strategic needs. Third, differences in the role of employees as well as whether or not they are internal or external may account for variability in the use of different HR systems within companies. Viewed broadly, this perspective highlights two primary issues that may provide insights into the HRM–performance relationship — multiple HRM systems within organizations and the growing presence of externalization of labor and virtual organizations.

Multiple HRM systems within organizations   Although, firms often differentiate the HRM practices used for exempt versus non-exempt workers (Huselid, 1995) or management versus non-managerial workers (Jackson et al., 1989), researchers do not typically capture these differences. Rather, different groups of employees are often aggregated or combined into a single workforce (e.g. Huselid, 1995; Snell & Dean, 1992) or only those workers deemed most critical to a firm's success are examined (e.g. Arthur, 1992; Delery & Doty, 1996).

Using the dimensions of strategic value and uniqueness, Lepak and Snell (1999) proposed four employment modes (internal development or knowledge-based, acquisition or job-based, alliances/partnership, and contract work) that are likely to be used by firms. In addition, they propose that each employment mode is likely to be accompanied by a particular HRM configuration. Lepak and Snell (2002) provide support for the argument that companies use different HRM systems to manage different employee groups, depending on the strategic value and uniqueness dimension. In a study of 375 companies in Spain,

Gonzales and Tacorante (2004) provide additional support for an architectural perspective. Their results indicate that over 70% of the companies in their sample relied on all four distinct modes of employment in their companies, 27% used three of the four employment modes, and 2% used only two employment modes. Consistent with Lepak and Snell (2002), Gonzales and Tacorante (2004) also found consistent differences in the HRM practices used among for each employee group.

While it is useful to understand the use of different HRM systems within organizations, an architectural perspective may also have two direct implications for the HRM–performance relationship. First, although not all employees may be of equal strategic importance (Stewart, 1997), all employees have the potential to impact a firm's bottom line — either positively or negatively. And while it is clearly important to understand the performance implications that stem from the way firms manage their core employees or their general approach toward managing their aggregate workforce, we would be remiss to assume that other workers within a firm, and how they are managed, are not important. In fact, the manner in which these other groups of workers are managed might be as important, and possibly even more important, for a firm's effectiveness. This may be particularly relevant in firms where core workers comprise a limited proportion of their workforce (Delery, 1998), or when firms use a wide assortment of employee groups. In the former case, the opportunity for non-core workers to influence firm performance may be greater as these workers may represent a significant proportion of a firm's overall workforce. Extending this logic, one implication may be that the relationship between HRM practices and performance may vary depending on which employee group is of focus. That is, there may be different types of relationships between HRM and performance depending on which employee group is examined.

Second, it may also be the case that the profile of HRM systems used for different employee groups, rather than any single HRM system, impacts performance. One of the underlying arguments for an architectural perspective is that companies may adjust their level of investment in different employee groups based on their potential contribution toward competitive advantage. To date, however, researchers have not examined if there are tangible organizational benefits (or costs) to adopting a more differentiating approach to managing employee groups. While a differentiation approach for HRM systems within firms may result in improved performance, it is also possible that such an approach may trigger equity concerns among different groups. Groups that receive lower levels of investment, though possibly justified in terms of their potential strategic contributions, may experience inequity and display less than desired attitudes and behaviors as a result. Unfortunately, the performance implications stemming from using multiple HRM systems within organizations have not been empirically investigated. This is certainly an area of research that warrants investigation to provide greater insights into how HRM practices and/or systems are related to performance.

Virtual organizations   With the growing use of external labor as a part of the production process (Matusik & Hill, 1998), a number of questions emerge regarding the relationship between HRM and performance. For example, Lepak, Takeuchi, and Snell (2003) examined the firm-level performance benefits associated with how firms structure their portfolio of employment arrangements in their HR architecture. The results indicate that a more extensive reliance on core knowledge-based employees and/or short-term contract workers is positively associated with enhanced firm performance (ROA and market-to-book value). Interestingly, these results indicate that an increased reliance on non-core job-based employees and long-term external workers is associated with diminished firm performance. While this study emphasized the firm-level performance benefits associated with internal and external employment arrangements, Way, Lepak, Fay, and Thacker (2005) examined if the underlying strategic motivation for using contingent employees alongside full-time employees influences the turnover and absenteeism of full-time employees. Their findings indicate that reasons for contingent labor use, more so than simply their use, are important factors to understand their influence on full time employees. We encourage additional research that examines how the use of external labor impacts important performance measures.

There are additional issues related to the notion of virtual organizations that may play a role in the HRM–performance relationship. Desanctis and Monge (1999) define a virtual organization as a collection of geographically distributed, functionally and culturally diverse people or units who are linked by technology and electronic forms of communication with the degree to which an organization is virtual varies on dimensions of temporal, spatial, cultural, and organizational dispersion (Shin, 2004). Compared to more traditional forms of organizations, virtual ones typically rely on virtual teams to accomplish certain goals, adopts work practices such as telecommuting or telework that support virtual work arrangements, emphasize self-managed teams, broad-based duties, cross-functional skills, and a network orientation (Wallace & Crandall, 2002).

These emerging forms of organizations present some interesting challenges for SHRM research. For example, how should HRM systems be structured to maximize the performance of virtual teams and virtual work arrangements (Hamilton & Scandura, 2003; Hertel, Geister, & Konradt, 2005)? To date, this literature stream has mostly taken the traditional micro-HRM approach such that it is largely focused on the effects of specific types of virtual work arrangements (e.g. telework or telecommuting) on employee morale and productivity (DiMartino & Wirth, 1990; Igbaria & Guimaraes, 1999) or the individual characteristics necessary for employees to be effective in virtual teams (Shin, 2004).

SHRM research can extend previous work on virtual organizations and practices by exploring questions such as whether HRM practices such as the use of virtual teams, or telecommuting can be included in the system of high performing practices, where virtual teams would fall within a firm's HR architecture, the requirements for an effective HRM system to manage virtual teams, as well as focusing beyond the organization's internal boundaries. For example, if a company relies on external business partners for the seamless production or delivery of its products and services, to what extent does it needs to be involved in the HRM practices of its partnering organizations, do the HRM systems of different partners within an organizational network need to match each other, and would alliances among the HR managers of the organizations provide better results for organizational performance? These questions can stimulate further research that takes the degree of virtuality as one important factor in the HRM–performance relationship.

Construct Clarification: HRM and Performance Measures

There is one final issue that we believe should receive additional attention to provide greater insights into the HRM–performance relationship. We would encourage researchers to focus more attention on the actual constructs of HRM and performance. As we briefly discussed earlier in this chapter, performance measures may range from HR outcomes to organizational to financial and market outcomes and may be assessed at multiple levels of analysis such as at the individual, team, unit, establishment, plant, division, organization, and corporation level of analysis. While these are all valid measures of performance that may be related to HRM research, the "appropriate dependent variable will vary with the level of analysis" and "the focus should be on variables that have inherent meaning for a particular context" (Becker & Gerhart, 1996, p. 791).

Given different conceptualizations of performance and an existence of multiple levels, it is important to clearly differentiate these outcomes and investigate the impact of human capital, employee attitudes and behaviors as well as other potential mediating factors and HRM for multiple outcomes if we are to fully understand the HRM–performance relationship. Perhaps, the outcome measures can be ordered from proximal to distal with employees as an anchor. Hence, HR outcomes would be the most proximal, which leads to organizational outcomes. Organizational outcomes, in turn, may lead to financial or accounting outcomes and, ultimately, market measures (cf. Becker & Huselid, 1998). Alternatively, certain performance measures may be more or less important in different contexts. For instance, turnover or retention rates may be more important for knowledge based companies than for manufacturing companies with high levels of pre-programmed tasks and activities. Similarly, the productivity of research and development personnel or their turnover rate may be more important for firms pursuing a differentiation strategy whereas the productivity of a firm's production staff may be more critical for firms following cost leadership strategy. Using a single performance measure to assess the benefits of HRM in different types of companies may mask the relative importance of different performance measures for those companies. We encourage future research to examine the relationship among these performance outcomes, as well as if there are certain contexts in which different performance measures have more or less importance, to provide insights into the HRM–performance relationship.

Related, there is a need for theory and research regarding what HRM practices should be included in HRM systems. This is certainly not a new issue in the literature, but this issue continues to plague this field of research. For example, Dyer and Reeves (1995) noted that incentive bonus was considered a component of the "control" HRM system in Arthur (1994) but part of the "flexible" production scheme in MacDuffie (1995). Similarly, Becker and Gerhart (1996) noted differences in the use of variable pay in Arthur (1994), Huselid (1995), and MacDuffie (1995). A low emphasis on variable pay was included as part of high-performance employment or "commitment" system in Arthur (1994) whereas a high emphasis on variable pay was included in the high-performance work systems in Huselid (1995) and MacDuffie (1995). Another example noted is the use of internal promotions and access to formal grievance procedures. Huselid (1995) and Pfeffer (1994) described such practices as part of high-performance HRM system. However, Arthur (1994) and Ichniowski et al. (1997) included these as elements of more rigid HRM systems. Becker and Huselid (1998) termed these two practices as component of "bureaucratic HR" system.

Unfortunately, we do not have the answer as to what practices should comprise these systems. We do believe, however, that without greater conceptual clarity into these systems, we will continue to struggle to build a cumulative body of research that helps clarify the relationship among HRM and performance measures.

Conclusion

In this chapter we have reviewed research findings in SHRM, which predominantly focuses on the link between HRM practices and performance. We reviewed the theoretical foundations underlying this link, the empirical evidence that supports it, and the challenges related to conducting research and interpreting the results of this field of study. Our review shows that SHRM researchers have come a long way in terms of demonstrating the potential effects of HRM practices in improving performance. Still, there is room for both theoretical advancement, which in turn will help organizations improve the effectiveness of their HRM practices and utilize their human capital in the most efficient way possible. Fortunately, researchers have made great progress building on the strategic foundation of SHRM research to explore additional theoretical perspectives for understanding how HRM relates with performance measures. And while we focused on some of the most promising perspectives, we hope that this review helps stimulate novel insights into how HRM may be used to improve employee and organizational performance.

References

Arthur, J. B. (1992). The link between business strategy and industrial relations systems in American steel mini mills. *Industrial and Labor Relations Review, 45*, 488–506.

Arthur, J. B. (1994). Effects of human resource systems on manufacturing performance and turnover. *Academy of Management Journal, 37*, 670–687.

Austin, J. T., Villanova, P., Kane, J. S., & Bernardin, H. J. (1991). Construct validation of performance measures: Definitional issues, development, and evaluation of indicators. In: G. R. Ferris (Ed.), *Research in personnel and human resource management* (Vol. 9, pp. 159–233). Greenwich, CT: JAI Press.

Baird, L., & Meshoulam, I. (1988). Managing two fits of strategic human resource management. *Academy of Management Review, 13*, 116–128.

Barney, J. (1996.) The resource-based theory of the firm. *Organization Science, 7*, 469–501.

Barney, J. (1991). Firm resources and sustained competitive advantage. *Journal of Management, 17*, 99–120.

Batt, R. (2002). Managing customer services: Human resource practices, quit rates, and sales growth. *Academy of Management Journal, 45*, 587–597.

Becker, B., & Gerhart, B. (1996). The impact of human resource management on organizational performance: Progress and prospects. *Academy of Management Journal, 39*, 779–801.

Becker, B. E., & Huselid, M. A. (1998). High performance work systems and firm performance: A synthesis of research and managerial implications. In: G. R. Ferris (Ed.), *Research in personnel and human resource management* (Vol. 16, pp. 53–101). Greenwich, CT: JAI Press.

Bowen, D. E., & Ostroff, C. (2004). Understanding HRM-firm performance linkages: The role of "strength" of the HRM system. *Academy of Management Review, 29*, 203–221.

Brass, D. J., Galaskiewicz, J., Greve, H. R., & Tsai, W. (2004). Taking stock of networks and organizations: A multilevel perspective. *Academy of Management Journal, 47*, 795–817.

Collins, C. J., & Clark, K. D. (2003). Strategic human resource practices, top management team social networks, and firm performance: The role of human resource practices in creating organizational competitive advantage. *Academy of Management Journal, 46*, 740–751.

Datta, D. K., Guthrie, J. P., & Wright, P. M. (2005). Human resource management and labor productivity: Does industry matter? *Academy of Management Journal, 48,* 135–145.

Davis-Blake, A., & Uzzi, B. (1993). Determinants of employment externalization: A study of temporary workers and independent contractors. *Administrative Science Quarterly, 38,* 195–223.

Dawis, R. V. (2000). P-E fit as paradigm: Comments on Tinsley. *Journal of Vocational Behavior, 56,* 180–183.

Delery, J. E. (1998). Issues of fit in strategic human resource management: Implications for research. *Human Resource Management Review, 8,* 289–309.

Delery, J. E., & Doty, D. H. (1996). Modes of theorizing in strategic human resource management: Tests of universalistic, contingency, and configurational performance predictions. *Academy of Management Journal, 39,* 802–835.

Delery, J. E., & Shaw, J. D. (2001). The strategic management of people in work organizations: Review, synthesis, and extension. In: G. R. Ferris (Ed.), *Research in personnel and human resources management* (Vol. 20, pp. 165–197). New York: JAI Press.

DeNisi, A. S., Hitt, M. A., & Jackson, S. E. (2003). The knowledge-based approach to sustainable competitive advantage. In: S. E. Jackson, M. A. Hitt & A. S. DiNisi (Eds), *Managing knowledge for sustained competitive advantage: Designing strategies for effective human resource management* (pp. 3–33). San Francisco, CA: Jossey-Bass.

Denison, D. R. (1990). *Corporate culture and organizational effectiveness.* New York: Wiley.

Desancits, G., & Monge, P. (1999). Introduction to the special issue: Processes for virtual organizations. *Organization Science, 10,* 693–702.

DiMartino, V.,& Wirth, L (1990). Telework: A new way of working and living. *International Labour Review, 5,* 529–555.

Dyer, L., & Reeves, T. (1995). Human resource strategies and firm performance: What do we know and where do we need to go? Paper presented at the 10th world congress of the International Industrial Relations Association (May). Washington, DC.

Edwards, J. R., & Van Harrison, R. (1993). Job demands and worker health: Three-dimensional reexamination of the relationship between person-environment fit and strain. *Journal of Applied Psychology, 78,* 628–648.

Eisenberger, R., Fasolo, P., & Davis-LaMastro, V. (1990). Perceived organizational support and employee diligence, commitment, and innovation. *Journal of Applied Psychology, 75,* 51–59.

Ferris, G. R., Hochwarter, W. A., Buckley, M. R., Harrell-Cook G.,& Frink, D. D. (1999). Human resources management: Some new directions. *Journal of Management, 25,* 385–415.

Gerhart, B., & Milkovich, G. T. (1990). Organizational differences in managerial compensation and financial performance. *Academy of Management Journal, 33,* 663–691.

Gonzalez, S. M., & Tacorante, D. V. (2004). A new approach to the best practices debate: Are best practices applied to all employees in the same way? *International Journal of Human Resource Management, 15,* 56–75.

Gouldner, A. W. (1960). The norm of reciprocity. *American Sociological Review, 25,* 161–178.

Griffeth, R. W., Hom, P. W., & Gaertner, S. (2000). A meta-analysis of antecedents and correlates of employee turnover: Update, moderator tests, and research implications for the next millennium. *Journal of Management, 26,* 463–488.

Guthrie, J. P. (2001). High-involvement work practices, turnover, and productivity: Evidence from New Zealand. *Academy of Management Journal, 44,* 180–192.

Guzzo, R. A., Noonan, K. A., & Elron, E. (1994). Expatriate managers and the psychological contract. *Journal of Applied Psychology, 79,* 617–626.

Hamilton, B. A., & Scandura, T. A. (2003). E-mentoring: Implications for organizational learning and development in a wired world. *Organizational Dynamics, 31,* 388–402.

Harrison, D. A., & Martocchio, J. J. (1998). Time for absenteeism: A 20-year review of origins, off-shoots, and outcomes. *Journal of Management, 24*, 305–350.Heider, F. (1958). *The psychology of interpersonal relations.* New York: Wiley.

Hertel, G., Geister, S., & Konradt, U. (2005). Managing virtual teams: A review of current empirical research. *Human Resource Management Review, 15*, 69–95.

Hitt, M. A., Bierman, L., Shimizu, K., & Kochhar, R. (2001). Direct and moderating effects of human capital on strategy and performance in professional service firms: A resource-based perspective. *Academy of Management Journal, 44*, 13–28.

Hulin, C. (1991). Adaptation, persistence, and commitment in organizations. In: M. D. Dunnette & L. M. Hough (Eds), *Handbook of industrial and organizational psychology* (2nd ed., Vol. 2, pp. 445–505). Palo Alto, CA: Consulting Psychological Press.

Huselid, M. A. (1995). The impact of human resource management practices on turnover, productivity, and corporate financial performance. *Academy of Management Journal, 38*, 635–672.

Ichniowski, C., Shaw, K., & Prennushi, G. (1997). The effects of human resource management practices on productivity: A study of steel finishing lines. *The American Economic Review, 87*, 291–313.

Igbaria, M., & Guimaraes, T. (1999). Exploring differences in employee turnover intentions and its determinants among telecommuters and non-telecommuters. *Journal of Management Information Systems, 16*, 147–164.

Jackson, S. E., Hitt, M. A., &. DeNisi, A. S. (2003). The knowledge-based approach to sustainable competitive advantage. In: S. E. Jackson, M. A. Hitt & A. S. DiNisi (Eds), *Managing knowledge for sustained competitive advantage: Designing strategies for effective human resource management* (pp. 399–428). San Francisco, CA: Jossey-Bass.

Jackson, S. E., Schuler, R. S., & Rivero, J. C. (1989). Organizational characteristics as predictors of personnel practices. *Personnel Psychology, 42*, 727–786.

Kang, S. C., Morris, S., & Snell, S. A. (in press). Relational archetypes, organizational learning, and value creation: Extending the human resource architecture. *Academy of Management Review.*

Kelley, H. H. (1967). Attribution theory in social psychology. In: D. Levine (Ed.), *Nebraska symposium on motivation* (Vol. 15, pp. 192–238). Lincoln: University of Nebraska Press.

Koch, M. J., & McGrath, R. G. (1996). Improving labor productivity: Human resource management policies do matter. *Strategic Management Journal, 17*, 335–354.

Kotter, J. P. & Heskett, J. L. (1992). *Corporate culture and performance.* New York, NY: Free Press.

Koys, D. J. (1988). Values underlying personnel/human resource management: Implications of the Bishops' economic letter. *Journal of Business Ethics, 7*, 459–467.

Kristof, A. L. (1996). Person-organization fit: An integrative review of its conceptualizations, measurement, and implications. *Personnel Psychology, 49*, 1–49.

Kristof-Brown, A. L. (2000). Perceived applicant fit: Distinguishing between recruiters' perceptions of person-job and person-organization fit. *Personnel Psychology, 53*, 643–671.

Lado, A. A., & Wilson, M. C. (1994). Human resource systems and sustained competitive advantage: A competency-based perspective. *Academy of Management Review, 19*, 699–727.

Lepak, D. P., & Snell, S. A. (2002). Examining the human resource architecture: The relationships among human capital, employment, and human resource configurations. *Journal of Management, 28*, 517–543.

Lepak, D. P., & Snell, S. A. (1999). The human resource architecture: Toward a theory of human capital allocation and development. *Academy of Management Review, 24*, 31–48.

Lepak, D. P., Takeuchi, R., & Snell, S. A. (2003). Employment flexibility and firm performance: Examining the moderating effects of employment mode, environmental dynamism, and technological intensity. *Journal of Management, 29*, 681–703.

Locke, E. A., & Latham, G. P. (1990). *A theory of goal setting & task performance*. Englewood Cliffs, NJ: Prentice-Hall.

MacDuffie, J. P. (1995). Human resource bundles and manufacturing performance: Organizational logic and flexible production systems in the world auto industry. *Industrial and Labor Relations Review, 48*, 197–221.

Matusik, S. F., & Hill, C. W. L. (1998). The utilization of contingent work, knowledge creation, and competitive advantage. *Academy of Management Review, 23*, 680–697.

McMahan, G. C., Virick, M., & Wright, P. M. (1999). Alternative theoretical perspectives for strategic human resource management revisited: Progress, problems, and prospects. In: P. M. Wright, L. Dyer, J. Boudreau & G. Milkovich (Eds), *Research in personnel and human resources management* (Vol. 4, Suppl. pp. 99–122). Greenwich, CT: JAI Press.

Miles, R. E., & Snow, C. C. (1984). Designing strategic human resources systems. *Organizational Dynamics,* (summer), *13*(1), 36–52.

Mincer, J. (1974). *Schooling, experience, and earnings*. New York: Columbia University Press.

Nahapiet, J., & Ghoshal, S. (1998). Social capital, intellectual capital, and the organizational advantage. *Academy of Management Review, 23*, 242–266.

Nishii, L. H. (2003). *The psychology of Strategic Human Resource Management: The effect of employee attributions for HR practices on unit commitment, satisfaction, organizational citizenship behaviors, and customer satisfaction.* Unpublished Doctoral Dissertation.

Ostroff, C., & Bowen, D. E. (2000). Moving HR to a higher level: HR practices and organizational effectiveness. In: K. J. Klein & S. W. Kozlowski (Eds), *Multilevel theory, research, and methods in organizations: Foundations, extensions, and new directions* (pp. 211–266). San Francisco, CA: Jossey-Bass.

Pennings, J. M., Lee, K., & Van Witteloostuijn, A. (1998). Human capital, social capital, and firm dissolution. *Academy of Management Journal, 41*, 425–440.

Perry-Smith, J. E., & Blum, T. C. (2000). Work-family human resource bundles and perceived organizational performance. *Academy of Management Journal, 43*, 1107–1117.

Pfeffer, J. (1981). Management as symbolic action: The creation and maintenance of organizational paradigms. *Research in Organizational Behavior, 3*, 1–52.

Pfeffer, J. (1994). *Competitive advantage through people: Unleashing the power of the work force.* Boston: Harvard Business School Press.

Pfeffer, J. (1995). Producing sustainable competitive advantage through the effective management of people. *Academy of Management Executive, 9*, 55–69.

Rogers, E. W., & Wright, P. M. (1998). Measuring organizational performance in strategic human resource management: Problems, prospects, and performance information markets. *Human Resource Management Reviews, 8*, 311–331.

Rousseau, D. M. (1995). *Psychological contracts in organizations: Understanding written and unwritten agreements.* Thousand Oaks, CA: Sage.

Russell, J. S., Terborg, J. R., & Powers, M. L. (1985). Organizational performance and organizational level training and support. *Personnel Psychology, 38*, 849–863.

Schein, E. (1985). *Organizational culture and leadership*. San Francisco, CA: Jossey-Bass.

Schneider, B., & Reichers, A. E. (1990). Climate and culture: An evolution of constructs. In: B. Schneider (Ed.), *Organizational climate and culture*, San-Francisco, CA: Jossey-Bass.

Schuler, R. S., & Jackson, S. E. (1987). Linking competitive strategies with human resource management practices. *Academy of Management Executive, 1*, 207–219.

Shaw, J. D., Duffy, M. K., Johnson, J. L., & Lockhart, E. (2005). Turnover, social-capital losses, and performance. *Academy of Management Journal, 48*, 594–606.

Shin, Y. (2004). A person-environment fit model for virtual organizations. *Journal of Management, 30*, 725–744.

Snell, S. A., & Dean, J. W. Jr. (1992). Integrated manufacturing and human resource management: A human capital perspective. *Academy of Management Journal, 35*, 467–504.

Stewart, T. A. (1997). *Intellectual capital: The new wealth of organizations*. New York: Currency and Doubleday.

Subramaniam, M., & Youndt, M. A. (2005). The influence of intellectual capital on the types of innovative capabilities. *Academy of Management Journal, 48*, 450–463.

Sullivan, P. H. (2000). *Value-driven intellectual capital: How to convert intangible corporate assets into market value*. New York: Wiley.

Terpstra, D. E., & Rozell, E. J. (1993). The relationship of staffing practices to organizational level measures of performance. *Personnel Psychology, 46*, 27–48.

Tsui, A. S., Pearce, J. L., Porter, L. W., & Hite, J. P. (1995). Choice of employee-organization relationship: Influence of external and internal organizational factors. In: G. R. Ferris (Ed.), *Research in personnel and human resources management* (Vol. 13, pp. 117–151). Greenwich, CT: JAI Press.

Van Vianen, A. E. M. (2000). Person-organization fit: The match between newcomers' and recruiters' preferences for organizational cultures. *Personnel Psychology, 53*, 113–149.

Wallace, M. J., & Crandall, N. F. (2002). HR strategy in virtual organizations. In: R. L. Henaman & D. B. Greenberger (Eds), *Human resource management in virtual organizations*. CT: Information Age Publishing.

Way, S. A. (2002). High performance work systems and intermediate indicators of firm performance within the US small business sector. *Journal of Management, 28*, 765–785.

Way, S. A., & Johnson, D. E. (2005). Theorizing about the impact of strategic human resource management. *Human Resource Management Review, 15*, 1–19.

Way, S. A., Lepak, D. P., Fay, C. H., & Thacker, J. W. (2005). Contingent labor strategies and the HR outcomes of full time employees: The moderating influence of high performance work systems. Paper presented at the 65th annual conference of the academy of management. Honolulu, HI.

Wayne, S. J., Shore, L. M., & Liden, R. C. (1997). Perceived organizational support and leader-member exchange: A social exchange perspective. *Academy of Management Journal, 40*, 82–111.

Wilderom, P. M., Glunk, U., & Maslowwski, R. (2000). Organizational culture as a predictor of organizational performance. In: N.M. Ashkanasy, C. Wilderom & M.F. Peterson (Eds), *Handbook of organizational culture and climate*. Thousand Oaks, CA: Sage.

Wiley, J. W., & Brooks, S. M. (2000). The high-performance organizational climate: How workers describe top-performing units. In: N. M. Ashkanasy, C. Wilderom & M. F. Peterson (Eds), *Handbook of organizational culture and climate*. Thousand Oaks, CA: Sage.

Wright, P. M. (1998). Introduction: Strategic human resource management research in the 21st century. *Human Resource Management Review, 8*, 187–191.

Wright, P. M., Dunford, B. B., & Snell, S. A. (2001). Human resources and the resource based view of the firm. *Journal of Management, 27*, 701–721.

Wright, P. M., & McMahan, G. C. (1992). Theoretical perspectives for strategic human resource management. *Journal of Management, 18*, 295–320.

Wright, P. M., McMahan, G. C., & McWilliams, A. (1994). Human resources and sustained competitive advantage: A resource-based perspective. *International Journal of Human Resource Management, 5*, 301–326.

Wright, P. M., & Sherman, W. S. (1999). Failing to find fit in strategic human resource management: Theoretical and empirical problems. In: P. M. Wright, L. Dyer, J. Boudreau & G. Milkovich (Eds), *Research in personnel and human resource management* (Vol. 4, Suppl. pp. 53–74). Greenwich, CT: JAI Press.

Wright, P. M., & Snell, S. A. (1991). Toward an integrative view of strategic human resource management. *Human Resource Management Review, 1,* 203–225.

Wright, P. M., & Snell, S. A. (1998). Toward a unifying framework for exploring fit and flexibility in strategic human resource management. *Academy of Management Review, 23,* 756–772.

Youndt, M. A., Snell, S. A., Dean, J. W. Jr., & Lepak, D. P. (1996). Human resource management, manufacturing strategy, and firm performance. *Academy of Management Journal, 39,* 836–866.

Youndt, M. A., Subramaniam, O., & Snell, S. A. (2004). Intellectual capital profiles: An examination of investments and returns. *Journal of Management Studies, 41,* 335–361.

Zimmerman J., & Tregoe, B. B. (1997). *The culture of success: Building a sustainable competitive advantage by living your corporate beliefs.* New York, NY: McGraw-Hill.

CHAPTER 4

Designing Effective HRM Systems: The Issue of HRM Strategy

Sven Kepes and John E. Delery

As competitive pressures continue to increase, organization leaders have been pushed to look beyond traditional sources of competitive advantage and many have focused on human resources and the systems used to manage these resources. Based on the work of Barney and his colleagues, the resource-based view provides additional insight into the dynamics of competitive advantage and potential sources of such an advantage. Human resources, or human capital, and the organizational systems used to manage them have been theorized to have the potential for competitive advantage. Wright, McMahan, and McWilliams (1994), for instance, argued that human capital may be one of the few forms of capital that truly meets the resource-based view criteria of value, rareness, in-imitability, and non-substitutability. At the same time, the academic literature in strategic human resource management (SHRM) has produced theoretical and empirical advances that support the importance of effectively managing human capital. There is still, however, much disagreement about the exact nature of and relationships between human resource management (HRM) systems, human capital, and organizational effectiveness.

In this chapter, we try to add to the discussion of HRM strategy by more clearly articulating the components of HRM systems and how these can be used to achieve organizational objectives. We start by briefly reviewing the literature on HRM strategy and system typologies. We use this review as a starting point to discuss the HRM architecture of a firm. Different authors have discussed the HRM architecture in differing ways, clouding the picture of one of the focal constructs in the SHRM literature. Following this, we propose HRM strategies and the HRM practices associated with each. Finally, we discuss the implications of our new framework for both the practice and research of HRM.

HRM Strategies

Over the past 20 years a number of authors have attempted to articulate systems of internally consistent HRM practices that are representative of HRM strategies. Some of these have focused only on particular aspects of HRM (e.g. career systems), while others have attempted to incorporate a more complete array of HRM practice areas. These works have served as the foundation for the field of SHRM; therefore, we provide a brief review.

Although it is clear that academics and practitioners were cognizant of strategic issues in the management of human resources early last century (Taylor & Russell, 1939), it was not until the late 1970s and early 1980s that researchers began to more completely develop the notion of HRM strategy. In one of the early attempts at explicating HRM strategies, Miles and Snow (1984) developed HRM systems to match their business strategy typology. The three basic HRM strategies outlined in their work were (1) building human resources, (2) acquiring human resources, and (3) allocating human resources. In essence, the first two strategies were opposite ends on a continuum with the third being somewhere in the middle. The "Building HR" strategy was predictably associated with HRM practices focused on developing talent inside the organization, and included such practices as extensive training and a focus on internal equity in compensation. The "Acquiring HR" strategy, on the other hand, was described as one where the organization focuses much more on the labor market for skill acquisition and was clearly more focused on external than internal equity in compensation. Virtually identical HRM strategies were presented a few years later by Sonnenfeld and Peiperl (1988), although, they chose to present them as career systems rather than HRM strategies.

Around the same time period, Kerr and Slocum (1987) presented a framework of reward systems in organizations. Their two systems or strategies, labeled hierarchy-based and performance-based, were also essentially very similar to the "Building HR" and "Acquiring HR" strategies outlined earlier by Miles and Snow (1984). Also consistent with the Miles and Snow (1984) typology, Delery and Doty (1996) presented a typology of HRM systems/strategies that focused on whether organizations had an internal focus fostering longer-term attachment or whether they used the labor market as the primary means of attainment of human capital.

Taking a slightly different approach, Arthur (1992, 1994) presented a typology of HRM/Industrial Relations strategies that focused more attention on the design of work and employee voice mechanisms. His two HRM strategies were labeled "cost reduction" and "commitment maximizing." These general strategies have often been referred to as the "low road/low commitment" and the "high road/high commitment" strategies. Arthur's work was extremely important for two reasons. First, he began the development of conceptual arguments that predicted that "high commitment" systems would result in superior organizational performance. Many of the earlier writers (e.g. Miles & Snow, 1984) had developed contingency arguments that predicted higher organizational performance when HRM strategy matched business strategy. Second, Arthur (1992, 1994) was one of the first to actually measure HRM strategy and conduct an empirical test of the relationship between business strategy, HRM strategy, and productivity.

Building on the idea that there was a single best way to manage human resources, Huselid and colleagues (Becker & Huselid, 1998; Huselid, 1995) developed the concept of the "high performance work system" (HPWS). This system of HRM practices is very similar to the "high commitment" HRM system, although it goes beyond it to include several additional HRM practices that might be considered "best" practices. For instance, the use of formal job analyses, valid selection devices, and conducting selection validation studies are practices included in the HPWS. Becker and Huselid (1998) present relatively strong evidence that the greater use of HPWSs in organizations is associated with greater overall organizational performance. Their conclusion is that there is one "best" system for managing employees. Delery and Doty (1996) labeled this the universalistic perspective because of the argument that the system's effectiveness was not contingent on other factors, such as business strategy.

This brief and selective review shows that there have been many perspectives on HRM strategy presented in the literature. Although we have highlighted some common themes, no two authors have presented HRM strategy in the same way, and the measurement of HRM strategies and their HRM systems in empirical studies has varied greatly. Nearly all empirical studies have measured different HRM practices and constructed HRM strategy and system measures in different ways. One possible reason for this has been the lack of clear theory and construct definition (Delery, 1998). This situation was highlighted by Becker and Gerhart (1996) nearly a decade ago, however, the situation is no better today than it was at that time.

What can be concluded from the literature on HRM strategy is that most authors view HRM strategies as coherent systems of HRM practices, and that there are at least two such coherent systems at either end of a continuum. It also appears that while different authors have provided different names to the two ideal HRM strategies and have included discussions of different HRM practices as components of these systems, the systems share some logic. At one end of the continuum is what we will identify as the "high commitment" system and at the other end is better termed the "low commitment" system. Some authors (e.g. Arthur, 1992, 1994) have used similar terminology. In most cases, researchers have labeled the "high commitment" system as such because they believe that it brings about higher commitment levels from employees. We believe an equally — and possibly more appropriate — reason is that it signals higher commitment from the employer to the employee. These systems are characterized by promotion-from-within, extensive training, and usually higher pay levels. These are clearly signals from the employer to the employee that influence his or her psychological contract as well as his or her attitudes and behaviors.

From the empirical literature (e.g. Arthur, 1992, 1994; Bae & Lawler, 2000; Guthrie, 2001; Huselid, 1995; MacDuffie, 1995), it can be concluded that these "high commitment" HRM strategies and systems are associated with lower turnover rates and greater employee productivity. Nearly all of the empirical research into the link with financial performance is also positive. Cappelli and Neumark (2001) are among the only studies finding no such link; however, their study methodology has been questioned (Delery & Shaw, 2001). The conclusion then is that organizations that use "high commitment" systems more completely throughout their workforce are likely to see many gains. Although this may seem like a logical conclusion, we believe that it is still too premature, particularly given the substantial potential weaknesses of most of the empirical studies to date (Gerhart, Wright, McMahan, & Snell, 2000; Wright et al., 2001), and the lack of strong conceptual logic in SHRM in general.

More recent conceptual work (Delery & Shaw, 2001; Lepak & Snell, 1999) may give rise to a new and more complete understanding of HRM strategy. While much of the previous work has been based on the idea that all employees are managed similarly throughout the organization, or that a "high commitment" system is appropriate for all employees in the organization, there are compelling theoretical arguments that different employees contribute in different ways to an organization's objectives. Employees performing different jobs in the organization should, therefore, be managed differently. A more complete understanding of HRM strategy, we believe, starts with an understanding of the HRM architecture as the foundation for the discussion of the relationship between HRM systems and organizational performance. In the following sections, we attempt to bring greater clarity to this construct and discuss implications for research and practice.

HRM Architecture

There is some confusion regarding the term "HRM architecture." Becker and Gerhart (1996) were among the first authors to use the term in the context of HRM systems. In their discussion, it referred to the linking of HRM philosophy, HRM policy, and HRM practice. Using the term somewhat differently, Lepak and Snell (1999) spoke about the overall picture of how a firm manages the various types of human resources it uses to accomplish its goals. Lepak and Snell (1999), building on work by Osterman (1987), noted that organizations may employ different HRM systems for different types of employees (see also Pfeffer & Baron, 1988). In their view, these different HRM systems throughout the organization constitute the HRM architecture. Their framework acknowledges that different employee groups contribute to the organization's objectives differently. For instance, the strategic core workforce of an organization may be managed differently than peripheral employees (Delery & Shaw, 2001; Rousseau & Wade-Benzoni, 1994). Lepak and Snell referred to the existence of different HRM systems within an organization as the HRM architecture. We want to integrate both conceptualizations and expand the concept of the HRM architecture.

HRM Architecture vs. HRM System

For the purpose of this chapter, we define HRM architecture as the HRM activities (philosophy, policies, practices, and processes) within different HRM systems that organizations must do today to manage and prepare themselves to develop the human capital required for achieving a competitive advantage in current or emerging opportunity areas. This conceptualization is aligned with Hamel and Prahalad's (1996) definition of strategic architecture.

An HRM architecture is, therefore the organization of several different HRM systems within the organization, targeted at different types of employees. Both, Lepak and Snell (1999) and Osterman (1987) identified four different types of employment modes and HRM systems. According to Lepak and Snell (1999), the choice of a particular employment mode depends on two factors derived from transaction cost economics (e.g. Williamson, 1975), human capital theory (e.g. Becker, 1975), and the resource-based view of the firm (e.g. Barney, 1991); the *value* and the *uniqueness* of the human capital to the organization. The former factor considers the costs and benefits of the human capital to the organization (an employee must add enough value to the organization to justify organizational expenditures related to him/her) while the later factor refers to the specificity or idiosyncrasy of the asset 'human capital' (unique human capital should be internally developed while "generic" human capital should be acquired in the open market).

Based on these factors, Lepak and Snell (1999) label the four HRM systems "creating human capital alliances" (high uniqueness, low value), "contracting human capital" (low uniqueness, low value), "developing human capital" (high uniqueness, high value), and "acquiring human capital" (low uniqueness, high value). Different employees, thus, fall into distinct HRM systems based on their individual value and uniqueness to the firm. A given system within the architecture is comprised of several components that we will describe next in some detail (see Figure 1).

Components of the HRM Architecture

The components of an HRM architecture are the different HRM systems employed in the organization, guided by the overall organizational climate. Organizational climate is often equated with the overall HRM philosophy since both communicate the same issues (Schuler, 1992). We use the term climate in this chapter to distinguish it from the HRM system philosophies. Organizational climate communicates the guiding principles that define the values of the organization with regard to its human resources and its HRM systems (Schuler, 1992). Each HRM system itself is divided into its philosophy, policies, practices, and processes (Becker & Gerhart, 1996; Schuler, 1992). While the most widespread distinction is between philosophy, policies, and practices (e.g. Becker & Gerhart, 1996), we feel that the consideration of processes is critical, especially when focusing on the implementation of HRM systems and the effects on employee attitudes such as commitment.

Organizational climate Climate is defined as the perception of formal and informal organizational policies, practices, and processes, and affects the perceived beliefs and values of the organization (Reichers & Schneider, 1990; Schneider, Brief, & Guzzo, 1996). This definition of climate is equivalent to conceptualizations of psychological collective climate (e.g. Jones & James, 1979) and is based on *shared* perceptions among employees within an organization (e.g. Schneider, Salvaggio, & Subirats, 2002).

We propose that the climate of an organization can serve as the glue that holds an organization together (Zamanou & Glaser, 1994) despite the use of differential HRM systems for distinct groups of employees. An organizational climate can unify a workforce and create a deep emotional commitment that makes employees believe that they are part of a unique bond with other employees and the whole organization (Clark, 1972). Climate can be seen as the interface between an organization's strategy and its HRM architecture. It provides guidance for the behavior and actions carried by both managers and lower level employees. Hence, it sets the tone for what HRM activities (e.g. HRM system philosophies, policies, practices, and processes) are appropriate and is simultaneously and successively shaped by them.

HRM system components The components of each HRM system include philosophy, policies, practices, and processes and the relationships among these components are depicted in Figure 1. An *HRM system philosophy* is a statement of the guiding principles that defines the values of the organization with regard to its human resources within a

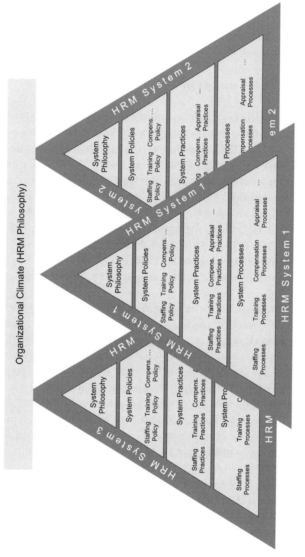

Figure 1: The HRM architecture.

particular system. It is thus an expression of how employees are valued, treated, and managed and their role in the success of an organizational unit (Schuler, 1992). System policies, practices, and processes communicate this "expression" and influence the perceived beliefs and values of the organizational unit covered by a particular HRM system (Reichers & Schneider, 1990; Schneider et al., 1996). To separate the HRM system philosophy from the overall climate, the system philosophy represents the *shared* perceptions among employees within an organizational unit covered by a particular HRM system while the climate is determined by all employees within an organization. A similar distinction is made in the climate research between "molar" and specific types of climate (e.g. Carr, Schmidt, Ford, & DeShon, 2003).

HRM system policies are the driving force for the selection of specific HRM practices (e.g. staffing, training, compensation) to make up a system. Every set of HRM practices needs an employee-related statement providing guidelines for the development of specific practices and processes. This statement severs as a goal or benchmark. An example from the staffing sub-system would be if the organization wishes to be very selective and hire only the best employees who fit the organization's culture (values and beliefs). Policies do not explain *how* an organization achieves its HRM goals but only *what* it is trying to achieve (e.g. hire the best employees). One level below the policies, *HRM system practices* identify broad techniques to ensure that the respective policy is put in place. Practices should ensure that the desired actions for achieving an HRM policy (e.g. select the best employees possible) are carried out (Schuler, 1992). For example, the general usage of some assessment procedures, job previews, and interviews would be practices to ensure that selective staffing takes place. Below the HRM practice level, the *HRM system processes*, is where the practices are implemented. Hence, detailed explanations of *how* the practices are executed are part of HRM processes. A certain personality test with instructions of how to administer it or a behavioral interview with structured questions and scoring guidelines would be part of the process of the HRM practice "assessment."

The distinctions between the components of the HRM architecture are important for two reasons. First, they highlight the fact that there is not only external fit between practices and business strategy and internal fit between different practices (Delery, 1998) but also *internal vertical fit* between each component of the HRM system. For instance, the HRM components of the staffing system must fit together to achieve consistency with the overall policy. Second, these distinctions highlight that organizations with the same policies but different practices and/or processes may reach the same result if these policies, practices, and process are aligned, which is consistent with the configurational perspective of SHRM and the concept of equifinality (Delery & Doty, 1996; Doty, Glick, & Huber, 1993).

The multi-dimensionality of the HRM architecture brings with it several critical issues. While it has been established that HRM systems affect organization level outcomes through their impact on KSAs (knowledge, skills, and abilities), motivation, and opportunity to decide and act (i.e., empowerment) of the workforce (Delery & Doty, 1996; Delery & Shaw, 2001; MacDuffie, 1995; Wright & Boswell, 2002), a uniform approach to HRM strategies (e.g. "low commitment"–"high commitment" HRM strategy) throughout the entire organization may not be appropriate (Delery & Shaw, 2001). The costs of such an approach may outweigh the benefits because it is likely to increase the costs (e.g. recruitment, compensation, and training costs) for an organization and possibly reduce the organization's flexibility in the marketplace to adjust to new economic circumstances (Cappelli & Neumark, 2001; Pfeffer & Baron, 1988). Specifically, Cappelli and Neumark (2001) concluded that while "high commitment" HRM systems improve workforce productivity, these systems also increase labor costs, possibly offsetting any gains in overall efficiency and effectiveness. Hence, high productivity in a peripheral area of the organization is only of limited effectiveness for the organization as a whole. Productivity gains in non-core areas "are likely equal to or greater then the benefits obtained" (Delery & Shaw, 2001, p. 179).

The most important workforce for an organization is its strategic core, the group of employees who represent the distinct core competencies of an organization (Delery & Shaw, 2001). This employee group is comprised of the employees who are both high in value and uniqueness for the organization (Lepak & Snell, 1999). Consequently, this core group of employees is likely to be managed with a "high commitment" approach to HRM. Other, more peripheral workgroups are not likely to receive the same treatment, and different HRM systems may be used to manage those groups to reduce costs and allow for greater flexibility (Lepak & Snell, 1999; Pfeffer & Baron, 1988).

It can be concluded that different types of HRM systems have different advantages and disadvantages, and any HRM strategy needs to address workforce differences in terms of the value and uniqueness of the human capital created by the HRM system. Different employee groups should thus be managed in distinct ways, depending on their value and uniqueness. This differential management, however, has the potential to create tension between different groups of employees, cause severe management problems, and reduce organizational effectiveness (Coff, 1997; Skarlicki & Folger, 1997). The HRM architecture is, therefore, of great strategic importance. Jobs need to be placed into HRM systems within the architecture, each HRM system needs to be internally consistent, and the systems need to be aligned to minimize the possibility of moral hazards and other management problems that can arise (Coff, 1997).

Strategies for Managing the HRM Architecture

We have now presented the basic logic explaining why organizations may use different HRM systems to manage various employee groups. Strategies for the design and management of the HRM architecture are thus critical for two reasons — they affect the desired characteristics of the workforce (e.g. KSAs, motivation, and empowerment) and the pool of human capital; and they determine and reinforce the organizational climate, which may be one way to avoid dysfunctional consequences associated with differential treatment of employees. Before conceptualizing possible strategies for managing the HRM architecture, it is necessary to discuss the importance of workforce characteristics and climate.

Workforce characteristics and organizational climate can play a critical role in the success of an organization. For instance, there is some evidence that workforce characteristics mediate the relationship between HRM systems and organizational effectiveness (e.g. Becker & Gerhart, 1996; Delery & Shaw, 2001; Huselid, 1995; MacDuffie, 1995). Also, there is preliminary support for the proposition that organizational climate and HRM philosophies mediate the relationship between HRM systems and firm performance (Gelade & Ivery, 2003) and that the fit between climate and organizational strategy may play a critical role (Burton, Lauridsen, & Obel, 2004). Organizational climate also influences a variety of individual level variables (e.g. job satisfaction, organizational commitment, and organizational identification) that affect outcomes critical to organizational effectiveness (e.g. Ashforth & Mael, 1989; Carr et al., 2003; Lindell & Brandt, 2000; Rousseau, 1998; Tyler, 1999).

The vital question then becomes how to develop a coherent HRM architecture — with different HRM systems for different types of employee groups — that develops the desired and necessary workforce characteristics and results in valuable organizational outcomes without creating dysfunctional consequences in the workplace associated with differential treatment of employee groups (e.g. Coff, 1997; Skarlicki & Folger, 1997). In answering this question, we propose two general strategies that link the overall organizational climate and individual HRM systems philosophies. In doing so, we associate particular HRM systems philosophies with a specific climate (e.g. safety, innovation, cost, efficiency, and citizenship behavior climate). Climate research has shown that organizational or "molar" climate is the overriding framework that influences broad outcomes whereas the philosophy of a particular system affect specific outcomes (Carr et al., 2003; Ostroff & Bowen, 2000). These specific strategies are presented below.

Strategy 1: Unifying Organizational Climate/HRM Philosophy

Studies have shown that broad climate perceptions affect job satisfaction, organizational commitment, organizational identification, other attitudinal outcomes, job performance, and retention (e.g. Carr et al., 2003; Rousseau, 1998). The first strategy, a unifying climate/HRM philosophy, calls for a unifying organizational climate that embraces and addresses all workgroups within an organization and creates shared perceptions and a unified workforce. If every employee, regardless of the HRM system associated with his/her workgroup, shares the same perceptions of the organization's goals and the appropriateness of the HRM policies, practices, and processes to achieve them, feelings of inequity and dysfunctional behavior associated with them are less likely to arise (Skarlicki & Folger, 1997). Instead, a positive climate is reinforced and organizational effectiveness enhanced (Bowen, Gilliland, & Folger, 1999; Rousseau, 1998; Schneider et al., 1996). This reinforcement, partly through social interaction, results in a strong organizational climate (González-Romá, Peiró, & Tordera, 2002) that creates a "strong situation" (Mischel, 1976) or "cultism" (Collins & Porras, 1994; Ouchi, 1980), which guides employee behavior.

HRM policies and practices need to be perceived as fair to achieve this (Bowen et al., 1999) — and be aligned with the climate and organizational strategy (González-Romá et al., 2002). Staffing, socialization, and training might be the most critical HRM practice areas to create and reinforce a strong climate across all employee groups. Compensation, appraisal, and other HRM practice areas are likely to be relatively distinct across different HRM systems and thus less useful in creating a unified workforce. Similar practices for staffing, socialization, and training, on the other hand, can be utilized across the board. *Recruitment and selection processes* can serve to select individuals "whose values are comparable with organizational values and screening out those whose values are incompatible" (Chatman, 1991, p. 461). Value congruence, an indicator of a strong climate, can be assessed during recruitment activities such as realistic job previews, personality tests, or selection interviews. Recruiters can assess the congruence between applicant characteristics and successful employees who embody the values of the organization (Rothstein & Jackson, 1980). These practices help to create, develop, and reinforce a strong climate, holding an organization together; all employees, despite being in different HRM systems, identify themselves with the organization as a whole and work together.

Organizational socialization has at its main objective to develop new organizational members' understanding of the organizational climate and the HRM architecture, including the system of shared values and beliefs (Bauer, Morrison, & Callister, 1998). Socialization often starts before an individual enters the organization. Company and product information, for example, influence individual beliefs about the climate of an organization (Cable, Aiman-Smith, Mulvey, & Edwards, 2000). After an applicant enters an organization, socialization practices can create perceptions of person–organization fit and value congruence (Cable & Parsons, 2001; Chatman, 1991), which are critical when creating a strong culture (Bauer et al., 1998). Extensive socialization also affects the accuracy of psychological contracts held by employees (De Vos, Buyens, & Schalk, 2003) and their identification with and commitment to the organization (Kammeyer-Mueller & Wanberg, 2003; Rousseau, 1998). Moreover, intensive socialization or "heavy-duty indoctrination" (Collins & Porras, 1994, p. 122) serves as a filter that ejects individuals that do not fit with the organization "like a virus" (Collins & Porras, 1994, p. 121) and can give an organization control over its employees (Rousseau, 1998). Socialization, therefore, can help unify an entire workforce despite the fact that different work groups are managed in distinct ways. *Formal training* can serve as an extension to initial socialization and ensure an ongoing process that reinforces the climate of an organization (Van Maanen, 1977).

In sum, HRM practices such as staffing, socialization, and training can create a strong organizational culture that ensures the entire workforce, despite being managed by different HRM systems, is integrated and united. The practices to achieve this should not be viewed as substitutes for each other, but rather as complements that have strong synergetic effects (Chatman, 1991). New employees will align their individual values with the ones of the organization or exit the organization (Schneider, 1987). This creates a strong climate, which unifies the workforce and can substitute for other types of control (Ouchi, 1980). That is, employees may choose to adhere to the organization's values, beliefs, and norms, and not act opportunistically.

Strategy 2: Buffering the Strategic Core

The second strategy to manage the HRM architecture is to buffer the strategic core workforce. This approach mirrors Thompson's (1967) conceptualization of buffering the technological core from environmental uncertainty to achieve rationality and control. According to Thompson (1967), the managerial level mediates between the institutional level (external environment) and the technological core (the actual operations that create value). Pfeffer and Baron (1988) were among the first to indirectly transfer Thompson's concept to the structuration of employment relations. They suggested that organizations may externalize the peripheral workforce to preserve the boundaries between the strategic core and other employee groups. This can be done by establishing distinct HRM systems with separate HRM system philosophies. As Klein and Sorra (1996) pointed out, distinct HRM system philosophies of equal strength may emerge from different HRM systems.

To achieve this, separate, strong, and specific system philosophies need to be developed and reinforced through distinct HRM policies, practices, and processes within every HRM system. Bowen and Ostroff (2004), relying on Kelley's (1967) attribution theory, proposed that HRM systems that are distinct (capture attention), consistent (reliable over time), and create consensus among employees can create a strong situation that guides individual behavior and may prevent dysfunctional employee behavior. HRM policies, practices, and processes thus need to be aligned within the individual HRM systems, highly distinctive, very consistent, and create consensus among the employees covered under a certain HRM system. Under these circumstances, individual HRM systems create a buffer between each workforce unit that ensures effective management of the overall workforce.

Social interaction within a workgroup, leader support and information sharing, and work design are three general management practices that have been found to predict the strength and quality of distinct HRM systems and their philosophies (i.e., specific climate types) (González-Romá et al., 2002; Lindell & Brandt, 2000). They are thus critical in ensuring that specific HRM systems are distinctive, consistent, and create consensus. A *reward system* that is well communicated and explained, fair, consistently applied by every manager within a work unit, and aligned with other HRM policies and practices is distinctive, consistent, and likely to create consensus among the employees covered by it. In addition, *work design* policies and practices that create physical barriers between different workgroups reinforce distinctiveness, consistency, and consensus. Since social interaction is a prime determinant of climate, employees that are covered under different HRM systems should interact as little as possible. This could distort the strong situation created by individual HRM systems and may cause feelings of inequity resulting in dysfunctional behavior in the workplace and diluting any possible competitive advantage (González-Romá et al., 2002; Skarlicki & Folger, 1997).

As with the other strategy (unifying HRM system), staffing, socialization, and training practices can be used to strengthen and reinforce each individual HRM system philosophy. Instead of focusing on organizational values and the organizational climate, system specific climates and their distinct values and beliefs need to be targeted with these practices. The goal must be to establish strong person-workforce fit in addition to person-organization fit. Specific values and beliefs at the occupational level (instead of values and beliefs at the organizational level) should be the focal point of these practices (Mortimer & Lorence, 1979). As with the unifying strategy, the buffering of the strategic core, if done effectively, may prevent the emergence of dysfunctional consequences in the workplace associated with differential treatment of different employee groups, which is associated with a decrease in organizational effectiveness (e.g. Coff, 1997; Skarlicki & Folger, 1997).

Integrating both Strategies

While it may appear as if these strategies are distinct options, we believe they should not be viewed as opposites. Certain elements of the overall climate are likely to be broad enough to cover all employee groups and their respective HRM systems. Values, beliefs, and norms for goal attainment, competitiveness, honesty, and cooperation could be characteristics of an organization climate and apply to all employee groups. Other values, beliefs, and norms are more specific (e.g. values for self-responsibility and accountability, ambitions, competencies, professionalism, etc.) and may differ highly across HRM systems and workforce groups. If this is the case, individual HRM systems may reinforce both sets of values, organization-wide and workgroup specific ones. As a result, synergistic effects may evolve that reinforce both organizational climate and HRM system philosophies. It is, therefore, quite possible for organizations to attempt both strategies simultaneously by unifying the entire workforce on some dimensions, while also buffering the core workforce.

Contingency Factors

When choosing a strategy for managing the HRM architecture, there are a number of contingency factors that must be taken into consideration. Delery and Shaw (2001) highlighted three such factors and suggested that they influence the design of HRM systems for non-strategic core employee groups. Extending their suggestions, we believe that the entire HRM architecture, including the HRM system for the strategic core workforce, will be influenced by those and other factors. If the management of the HRM architecture is to lead to organizational effectiveness, it must be aligned with other functions, strategies, and organizational design elements.

Functional strategies   Every function (e.g. manufacturing, marketing, finance, and human resources) in an organization has and follows a respective strategy. These strategies must be aligned with the competitive strategy of the business and with each other. A competitive strategy cannot be effectively adopted and executed without an integration of the capabilities of the organizational functions (Munive-Herandez, Dewhurst, Pritchard, & Barber, 2004). Research in various areas has shown that alignment between functional and organizational strategies enhances organizational effectiveness (e.g. Delery & Doty, 1996; Jayaram, Droge, & Vickery, 1999; McDonald, 1996; Ward, Bicklord, & Leong, 1996). As a result, functional strategies should reinforce each other and, from an HRM perspective, the design of the HRM architecture and each HRM system must fit with other functional strategies. For example, a research and development extensive marketing strategy calls for different HRM configurations than a marketing strategy that focuses on extensive advertising and selling. The value and uniqueness of certain employee groups is likely to be different under both scenarios. The different HRM systems in the HRM architecture need to be targeted at the diverse demands of the functional strategies of an organization.

Technology   Technology can be used to empower or control employees (Zuboff, 1985), and it can directly influence the required characteristics of the employees who deal with it (Osterman, 1987). It, therefore, has an indirect influence on the HRM architecture of organizations (Walton & Susman, 1987). Extensive research in the fields of operations management and HRM illustrates how diverse technologies, in particular manufacturing technologies, affect the design of the organization and the HRM architecture (e.g. Kathuria & Partovi, 2000; Shaw, Gupta, & Delery, 2001; Snell & Dean, 1992; Zammuto & O'Connor, 1992). Distinct manufacturing and process technology priorities (e.g. cost, quality, flexibility, and time) call for different HRM configurations (Jayaram et al., 1999; Kathuria & Partovi, 2000).

Since technology can be used to de-skill or increase skill requirements of employees (Zuboff, 1985), different types of technologies seem to be suitable for different types of employees. For example, highly automated technological systems with limited need for coordination and human interaction seem to be suitable for employee groups that are low in uniqueness and value to an organization. This would minimize the human element and possible errors that could result from less skilled employees. Technological systems that provide information to employees and require human interaction (e.g. integrated manufacturing, advanced customer relationship management systems) call for more skilled employees that are also motivated and empowered to use their KSAs in making day-to-day decisions (e.g. problem removal or prevention) (Black & Gregersen, 1997; Karuppan & Ganster, 2004). These employee groups are certainly of value to an organization but the technological requirements will determine the uniqueness and, thus, the appropriate HRM system. In fact, technology is likely one of the most powerful determinants of the value and uniqueness of differing work groups. As technology is introduced that removes KSA needs from certain jobs, it directly influences the characteristics of workers required for those jobs.

Workforce interdependence   The degree of workforce interdependence is an important contingency factor influencing the design of the HRM architecture. The more interdependent different workgroups within an organization, the less distinct different HRM systems should be because of the possibility of perceived inequity and its consequences (Skarlicki & Folger, 1997). Symbolic management practices such as a unified socialization and training process, a reduction of status distinctions, and profit- or gain-sharing programs can be used to counter possible feelings of inequity. High degree of workforce independence, on the other hand, allows for more distinct HRM systems since different types of employee groups are physically "buffered" from each other — making intense interaction across workforce types almost impossible.

Shaw, Gupta, & Delery. (2002), for example, found that individual rewards are only related to organizational effectiveness if the workforce is independent. Other authors have made similar claims (Gerhart & Rynes, 2003), indicating that workforce interdependence moderates the relationship between HRM systems and organizational performance. Hence, when designing the HRM architecture, the degree of interdependence between employee groups must be taken into consideration. It is easier to implement "high" *and* "low commitment" HRM systems under an HRM architecture if different employee groups do not interact much with each other and are independent.

These three factors are by no means exhaustive. Other external and internal factors such as national culture (individualistic vs. collectivistic), industry environment, organizational structure, leadership style, and institutionalized dynamics are also important contingencies that need to be considered when designing the HRM architecture.

Implications for Practice and Future Research

Despite the growing interest in the strategic management of human resources, our theoretical knowledge is still limited. In this chapter, we tried to advance the concept of the HRM architecture and illustrate strategies for managing it. This framework has many implications for practice as well as for future research. We will address both of these areas in the next sections.

Implications for Future Research

By integrating past research on HRM strategy, climate, and the HRM architecture, we emphasized two facts. First, organizations are unlikely to have a single HRM system that covers their entire workforce. Second, any HRM system is comprised of several layers, ranging from the system-specific philosophy at the highest level to particular processes at the lowest level. Both of these facts have implications for research.

Methodologically, we feel the need to reiterate previous calls for more theoretically grounded measures of elements of the HRM architecture and HRM systems (Becker & Gerhart, 1996; Delery, 1998; Delery & Shaw, 2001). Survey research often uses a dichotomous (yes/no) response format or estimations of the percentage of employees covered by a certain HRM policy or practice (e.g. Arthur, 1992; Becker & Huselid, 1998; Guthrie, 2001; Huselid, 1995). If firms have different workgroups with distinct HRM systems, global questions (e.g. "Are your employees covered by a pay-for performance plan?" or "What percentage of employees received training beyond that mandated by government regulations in the last 12 months?") that do not address a specific workforce are inappropriate and yield misleading results. Empirical studies to date have directed their survey questions at either the entire organization (e.g. Cappelli & Neumark, 2001; Huselid, 1995), the largest group of non-managerial employees (e.g. Arthur, 1992; Batt, 2002; Shaw, Delery, Jenkins, & Gupta, 1998), or employees performing a particular job (Delery & Doty, 1996). Several carefully constructed questions on Likert-type scales that assess a single HRM practice area (e.g. taffing, compensation, and training) collected for each particular workforce appear to be a more suitable approach to measuring the constructs of interest.

Identifying workforce characteristics and the uniqueness and value of them to the organization is another, maybe more difficult challenge. Until now, most studies ignore workforce characteristics, and the few that assessed them typically measure employee attitudes such as various facets of satisfaction, organizational commitment, and turnover intentions (e.g. Meyer & Smith, 2000; Schneider, Hanges, Smith, & Salvaggio, 2003; Vandenberg, Richardson, & Eastman, 1999) rather than KSAs, the degree of motivation, or the level of empowerment. While the measurement of these more "hard" workforce characteristics is a very difficult task (Delery & Shaw, 2001), the value and uniqueness of groups of employee groups could be more easily assessed and may serve as an indicator for more detailed workforce characteristics. After identifying several employee groups and their value and uniqueness, surveys could be targeted at them, individually. This would also help to test the proposition that different employee groups are covered by distinct HRM systems.

Another critical methodological aspect pertains to the construct definition and the level of analysis. Today, most studies measure either HRM policies or practices (or something in-between the two). Researchers often combine these measures by creating an index or scale, which is purported to capture the entire HRM system. Our discussion of the HRM architecture, however, pointed out that a coherent HRM system is comprised of far more levels than just policies or practices. It follows logically that current measures cannot accurately represent HRM systems and their alignment or fit. To measure entire systems, system philosophies, policies, practices, and processes need to be assessed. From an organizational effectiveness perspective, processes might be the most critical level of analysis. A policy that stresses pay-for-performance is likely to be ineffective (and maybe even counterproductive) without proper processes that implement that policy. Processes directly affect employees, their behaviors and attitudes. Careful definitions of the constructs and their relationships with organization level variables, including the mediating variables, is thus warranted and necessary (Delery, 1998). Simple abstractions from lower level to higher level relationships and vice versa are likely to be inappropriate (Klein & Kozlowski, 2000).

Implications for Practice

Managers must make choices about the adoption of HRM strategies. To better understand this process, it is important to focus on the main goals of the HRM system (Delery & Shaw, 2001). The strategic core workforce might be the most central, but other parts of the workforce are also important. All workgroups need to be managed with systems that create the KSAs, motivation, and empowerment desired by the organization for each particular workgroup. Peripheral workers low in value and uniqueness most likely will be managed in a way to limit empowerment and focus little on new skill development. The HRM systems that cover these employees have to ensure that this takes place. Additionally, HRM managers must focus on effectively managing the employee flow in and out of the organization that will likely be very high for this type of workforce. Efficiencies in the processing of applications, new hires, separations, and the paperwork associated with each must be sought.

Traditionally, job analysis has been used to do identify workforce characteristics. Job analysis, however, focuses on the characteristics that are needed today for a particular job. Competency modeling offers an alternative approach (Shippmann et al., 2000). A competency can be defined as an underlying characteristic of an employee (i.e., motive, trait, skill, aspect of one's self-image, social role, or body of knowledge) which results in effective and/or superior performance (Boyatzis, 1982, p. 21). Competency modeling also places a greater emphasis on long-term organizational fit instead of short-term job fit when compared to the traditional job analysis (Shippmann et al., 2000). According to the United States Office of Personnel Management, competency modeling is especially useful to "strengthen the link between organizational culture, results, and individual performance by emphasizing competencies that are needed [...]" (OPM, 1999, p. 8), and, thus, perfectly suited for identifying workforce characteristics to design and manage the HRM architecture.

After the characteristics of groups of employees have been identified, managers need to develop an overall HRM architecture that encompasses all possible workgroups in terms of their uniqueness and value. Specific HRM systems (e.g. HRM philosophies, policies, practices, and processes) can then be designed to target and develop the characteristics of each workforce. Organizations should be careful that HRM policies, usually set by higher level managers, are actually translated into the required HRM practices and processes, usually done by lower level managers and supervisors, to achieve the objectives of their

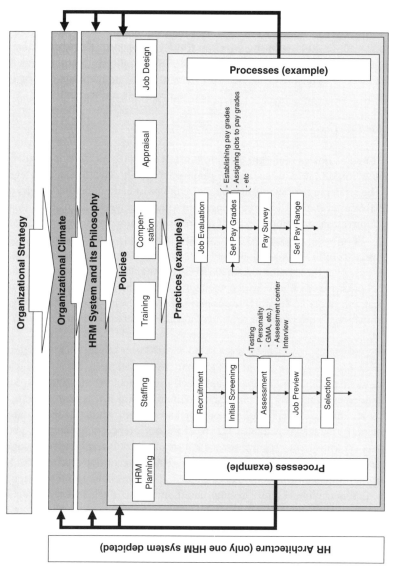

Figure 2: The HRM architecture as a process: Relationships between strategy, climate, and HRM system components.

respective HRM policy. If proper care is not taken during the implementation processes, a mismatch between higher and lower level HRM elements within the HRM system may occur and employees may feel inequitably treated, jeopardizing organizational effectiveness (Skarlicki & Folger, 1997). Designing processes and practices that fit system policies and philosophies is as critical as alignment with different HRM systems. Figure 2 summarizes the complexities of the HRM architecture from a process perspective.

Conclusion

As the competitive environment makes it increasingly difficult to achieve a competitive advantage, organizational climate and the management of human resources are two promising resources that could be sources of sustainable organizational effectiveness (e.g. Barney, 1986; Schneider, 2000; Wright et al., 1994). The management of human resources has gained attention over the past few decades and much progress has been made in both research and practice. With this chapter, we have integrated research in the fields of SHRM and climate to help explain the importance and complexities of managing the HRM architecture. We have attempted to clarify this construct and illustrate critical issues in the design and implementation of HRM systems.

We provided a brief overview of HRM strategies, and used it as a catalyst to discuss the complexities of the HRM architecture. Our conceptualization of the HRM architecture shows that it is far more complex than previously acknowledged and has high strategic value for an organization. Distinguishing between organizational climate and the individual HRM system philosophies, policies, practices, and processes is not only theoretically, but also practically important. While most researchers have only attempted to measure HRM policies or practices, processes directly influence employees and are likely to have a profound impact on workforce characteristics (e.g. KSAs, motivation, empowerment, behaviors, and attitudes) and ultimately organizational effectiveness.

Consistent with the arguments of other researchers (e.g. Delery & Shaw, 2001; Lepak & Snell, 1999), it appears to be inefficient to have a "high commitment" HRM system for the entire workforce. Our discussion of the HRM architecture has shown that different workforces are likely to be managed with different HRM systems. While the strategic core workforce most likely should be managed under a "high commitment" HRM system, peripheral groups of employees might be managed more effectively under other HRM systems. The management of employee groups less central to an organization is nonetheless critical. As Coff (1997, p. 393) stated, "firms can only generate rent if they have systems to cope with the associated dilemmas" of managing human resources. We developed two strategies to manage the HRM architecture to minimize these potential dysfunctional consequences. First, a strong, unifying organizational climate can serve as the glue that holds the organization together (Zamanou & Glaser, 1994) despite distinct HRM systems for various employee groups. Second, the strategic core workforce, the most valuable group of employees to an organization, can be physically and managerially buffered from other employee groups. Less interaction between employees within different HRM systems is likely to cause fewer human asset dilemmas or problems. Finally, both strategies can be integrated, which might be the most appropriate and practical management solution in many organizations.

We identified HRM practices associated with each of these strategies. HRM practices such as staffing, socialization, and training seem most influential in developing a strong, unifying climate, while other practices, such as compensation and work design, may be most helpful in creating "strong situations" within each workforce group. The first strategy requires a strong person-organization fit while the later one calls for a strong person-workforce fit. Studies in this area of research (e.g. Kristof, 1996; Kristof-Brown, Zimmerman, & Johnson, 2005) are likely to identify additional HRM practices appropriate for either strategy or the integration of both.

It has been our goal in this chapter to stimulate more thoughtful theoretical and empirical work into HRM systems. SHRM research can be greatly helped by more organized and methodical thinking in the design, implementation, and management of effective HRM systems. By focusing on established concepts, integrating them, and presenting them in a new light, we attempted to bring attention to the complexities of effective management of human resources.

References

Arthur, J. B. (1992). The link between business strategy and industrial relations systems in American steel minimills. *Industrial and Labor Relations Review, 45*(3), 488–506.

Arthur, J. B. (1994). Effects of human resource systems on manufacturing performance and turnover. *Academy of Management Journal, 37*(3), 670–687.

Ashforth, B. E., & Mael, F. (1989). Social identity theory and the organization. *Academy of Management Review, 14*(1), 20–39.

Bae, J., & Lawler, J. J. (2000). Organizational and HRM strategies in Korea: Impact on firm performance in an emerging economy. *Academy of Management Journal, 43*(3), 502–519.

Barney, J. B. (1986). Organizational culture: Can it be a source of sustained competitive advantage? *Academy of Management Review, 11*(3), 656–665.

Barney, J. B. (1991). Firm resources and sustained competitive advantage. *Journal of Management, 17*(1), 99–120.

Batt, R. (2002). Managing customer services: Human resource practices, quit rates, and sales growth. *Academy of Management Journal, 45*(3), 587–597.

Bauer, T. N., Morrison, E. W., & Callister, R. R. (1998). Organizational socialization: A review and directions for future research. In: G. R. Ferris (Ed.), *Research in personnel and human resource management* (Vol. 16, pp. 149–214). Greenwich, CT: JAI Press.

Becker, B. E., & Gerhart, B. (1996). The impact of human resource management on organizational performance: Progress and prospects. *Academy of Management Journal, 39*(4), 779–801.

Becker, B. E., & Huselid, M. A. (1998). High performance work systems and firm performance: A synthesis of research and managerial implications. In: G. R. Ferris (Ed.), *Research in personnel and human resources management* (Vol. 16, pp. 53–101). Greenwich, CT: JAI Press.

Becker, G. S. (1975). *Human capital: A theoretical and empirical analysis, with special reference to education* (2nd ed.). Chicago, IL: University of Chicago Press.

Black, J. S., & Gregersen, H. B. (1997). Participative decision-making: An integration of multiple dimensions. *Human Relations, 50*(7), 859–878.

Bowen, D. E., Gilliland, S. W., & Folger, R. (1999). HRM and service fairness: How being fair with employees spills over to customers. *Organizational Dynamics, 27*(3), 7–23.

Bowen, D. E., & Ostroff, C. (2004). Understanding HRM-firm performance linkages: The role of the "strength" of the HRM system. *Academy of Management Review*, 29(2), 203–221.

Boyatzis, R. E. (1982). *The competent manager: A model for effective performance*. New York, NY: Wiley.

Burton, R. M., Lauridsen, J., & Obel, B. (2004). The impact of organizational climate and strategic fit on firm performance. *Human Resource Management*, 43(1), 67–82.

Cable, D. M., Aiman-Smith, L., Mulvey, P. W., & Edwards, J. R. (2000). The sources and accuracy of job applicants' beliefs about organizational culture. *Academy of Management Journal*, 43(6), 1076–1085.

Cable, D. M., & Parsons, C. K. (2001). Socialization tactics and person–organization fit. *Personnel Psychology*, 54(1), 1–23.

Cappelli, P., & Neumark, D. (2001). Do "high-performance" work practices improve establishment-level outcomes? *Industrial & Labor Relations Review*, 54(4), 737–775.

Carr, J. Z., Schmidt, A. M., Ford, J. K., & DeShon, R. P. (2003). Climate perceptions matter: A meta-analytic path analysis relating molar climate, cognitive and affective states, and individual level work outcomes. *Journal of Applied Psychology*, 88(4), 605–619.

Chatman, J. A. (1991). Matching people and organizations: Selection and socialization in public accounting firms. *Administrative Science Quarterly*, 36(3), 459–484.

Clark, B. R. (1972). The organizational saga in higher education. *Administrative Science Quarterly*, 17(2), 178–184.

Coff, R. W. (1997). Human assets and management dilemmas: Coping with hazards on the road to resource-based theory. *Academy of Management Review*, 22(2), 374–402.

Collins, J. C., & Porras, J. I. (1994). *Built to last: Successful habits of visionary companies*. New York, NY: HarperBusiness.

De Vos, A., Buyens, D., & Schalk, R. (2003). Psychological contract development during organizational socialization: Adaptation to reality and the role of reciprocity. *Journal of Organizational Behavior*, 24(5), 537–559.

Delery, J. E. (1998). Issues of fit in strategic human resource management: Implications for research. *Human Resource Management Review*, 8(3), 289–309.

Delery, J. E., & Doty, D. H. (1996). Modes of theorizing in strategic human resource management: Tests of universalistic, contingency, and configurational performance predictions. *Academy of Management Journal*, 39(4), 802–835.

Delery, J. E., & Shaw, J. D. (2001). The strategic management of people in work organizations: Review, synthesis, and extension. In: G. R. Ferris (Ed.), *Research in personnel and human resource management* (Vol. 20, pp. 167–197). New York: JAI Press.

Doty, D. H., Glick, W. H., & Huber, G. P. (1993). Fit, equifinality, and organizational effectiveness: A test of two configurational theories. *Academy of Management Journal*, 36(6), 1196–1250.

Gelade, G. A., & Ivery, M. (2003). The impact of human resource management and work climate on organizational performance. *Personnel Psychology*, 56(2), 383–404.

Gerhart, B., & Rynes, S. L. (2003). *Compensation: Theory, evidence, and strategic implications*. Thousand Oaks, CA: Sage.

Gerhart, B., Wright, P. M., McMahan, G. C., & Snell, S. A. (2000). Measurement error in research on human resources and firm performance: How much error is there and how does it influence effect size estimates? *Personnel Psychology*, 53(4), 803–834.

González-Romá, V., Peiró, J. M., & Tordera, N. (2002). An examination of the antecedents and moderator influences of climate strength. *Journal of Applied Psychology*, 87(3), 465–473.

Guthrie, J. P. (2001). High-involvement work practices, turnover, and productivity: Evidence from New Zealand. *Academy of Management Journal*, 44(1), 180–190.

Hamel, G., & Prahalad, C. K. (1996). *Competing for the future.* Boston, MA: Harvard Business School Press.

Huselid, M. A. (1995). The impact of human-resource management-practices on turnover, productivity, and corporate financial performance. *Academy of Management Journal, 38*(3), 635–672.

Jayaram, J., Droge, C., & Vickery, S. K. (1999). The impact of human resource management practices on manufacturing performance. *Journal of Operations Management, 18*(1), 1–20.

Jones, A. P., & James, L. R. (1979). Psychological climate: Dimensions and relationships of individual and aggregated work environment perceptions. *Organizational Behavior & Human Decision Processes, 23*(2), 201–250.

Kammeyer-Mueller, J. D., & Wanberg, C. R. (2003). Unwrapping the organizational entry process: Disentangling multiple antecedents and their pathways to adjustment. *Journal of Applied Psychology, 88*(5), 779–794.

Karuppan, C. M., & Ganster, D. C. (2004). The labor-machine dyad and its influence on mix flexibility. *Journal of Operations Management, 22*(6), 533–556.

Kathuria, R., & Partovi, F. Y. (2000). Aligning work force management practices with competitive priorities and process technology: A conceptual examination. *Journal of High Technology Management Research, 11*(2), 215–234.

Kelley, H. H. (1967). Attribution theory in social psychology. In: D. Levine (Ed.), *Nebraska symposium on motivation.* Lincoln, NE: University of Nebraska Press.

Kerr, J., & Slocum, J. W. (1987). Managing corporate culture through reward systems. *Academy of Management Executive, 1*(2), 99–107.

Klein, K. J., & Kozlowski, S. W. J. (2000). *Multilevel theory, research, and methods in organizations: Foundations, extensions, and new directions.* San Francisco, CA: Jossey-Bass.

Klein, K. J., & Sorra, J. S. (1996). The challenge of innovation implementation. *Academy of Management Review, 21*(4), 1055–1080.

Kristof, A. L. (1996). Person-organization fit: An integrative review of its conceptualizations, measurement, and implications. *Personnel Psychology, 49*(1), 1–49.

Kristof-Brown, A. L., Zimmerman, R. D., & Johnson, E. C. (2005). Consequences of individuals' fit at work: A meta-analysis of person-job, person-organization, person-group, and person-supervisor-fit. *Personnel Psychology, 58*(2), 281–342.

Lepak, D. P., & Snell, S. A. (1999). The human resource architecture: Toward a theory of human capital allocation and development. *Academy of Management Review, 24*(1), 31–48.

Lindell, M. K., & Brandt, C. J. (2000). Climate quality and climate consensus as mediators of the relationship between organizational antecedents and outcomes. *Journal of Applied Psychology, 85*(3), 331–348.

MacDuffie, J. P. (1995). Human-resource bundles and manufacturing performance: Organizational logic and flexible production systems in the world auto industry. *Industrial and Labor Relations Review, 48*(2), 197–221.

McDonald, M. (1996). Strategic marketing planning: Theory, practice and research agendas. *Journal of Marketing Management, 12*(1–3), 5–27.

Meyer, J. P., & Smith, C. A. (2000). HRM practices and organizational commitment: Test of a mediation model. *Canadian Journal of Administrative Sciences, 17*(4), 319–331.

Miles, R. E., & Snow, C. C. (1984). Designing strategic human resources systems. *Organizational Dynamics, 13*(1), 36–53.

Mischel, W. (1976). Towards a cognitive social model learning reconceptualization of personality. In: D. Magnusson (Ed.), *Interactional psychology and personality* (pp. 166–207). New York, NY: Wiley.

Mortimer, J. T., & Lorence, J. (1979). Work experience and occupational value socialization: A longitudinal study. *American Journal of Sociology, 84*(6), 1361–1385.

Munive-Herandez, E. J., Dewhurst, F. W., Pritchard, M. C., & Barber, K. D. (2004). Modelling the strategy management process: An initial BPM approach. *Business Process Management Journal*, *10*(6), 691–711.

OPM (1999). *Looking into the future: Human resource competencies. An occupation in transition; Part 2* (MSE-99-6). Washington, DC: United States Office of Personnel Management.

Osterman, P. (1987). Choice of employment systems in internal labor markets. *Industrial Relations*, *26*(1), 46–67.

Ostroff, C., & Bowen, D. E. (2000). Moving HR to a higher level: HR practices and organizational effectiveness. In: K. J. Klein & S. W. J. Kozlowski (Eds), *Multilevel theory, research, and methods in organizations: Foundations, extensions, and new directions* (pp. 211–266). San Francisco, CA: Jossey-Bass.

Ouchi, W. G. (1980). Markets, bureaucracies, and clans. *Administrative Science Quarterly*, *25*(1), 129–141.

Pfeffer, J., & Baron, J. N. (1988). Taking the workers back out: Recent trends in the structuring of employment. In: B. M. Staw & L. L. Cummings (Eds), *Research in organizational behavior* (Vol. 10, pp. 257–303). Greenwich, CT: JAI Press.

Reichers, A. E., & Schneider, B. (1990). Climate and culture: An evolution of constructs. In: B. Schneider (Ed.), *Organizational climate and culture* (pp. 5–39). San Francisco, CA: Jossey-Bass.

Rothstein, M., & Jackson, D. N. (1980). Decision making in the employment interview: An experimental approach. *Journal of Applied Psychology*, *65*(3), 271–283.

Rousseau, D. M. (1998). Why workers still identify with organizations. *Journal of Organizational Behavior*, *19*(3), 217–233.

Rousseau, D. M., & Wade-Benzoni, K. A. (1994). Linking strategy and human resource practices: How employee and customer contracts are created. *Human Resource Management*, *33*(3), 463–489.

Schneider, B. (1987). The people make the place. *Personnel Psychology*, *40*(3), 437–453.

Schneider, B. (2000). The psychological life of organizations. In: N. M. Ashkanasy, C. P. M. Wilderom & M. F. Peterson (Eds), *Handbook of organizational culture and climate* (pp. xvii–xxii). Thousand Oaks, CA: Sage

Schneider, B., Brief, A. P., & Guzzo, R. A. (1996). Creating a climate and culture for sustainable organizational change. *Organizational Dynamics*, *24*(4), 6–19.

Schneider, B., Hanges, P. J., Smith, D. B., & Salvaggio, A. N. (2003). Which comes first: Employee attitudes or organizational financial and market performance? *Journal of Applied Psychology*, *88*(5), 836–851.

Schneider, B., Salvaggio, A. N., & Subirats, M. (2002). Climate strength: A new direction for climate research. *Journal of Applied Psychology*, *87*(2), 220–229.

Schuler, R. S. (1992). Strategic human resources management: Linking the people with the strategic needs of the business. *Organizational Dynamics*, *21*(1), 18–32.

Shaw, J. D., Delery, J. E., Jenkins, G. D., & Gupta, N. (1998). An organization-level analysis of voluntary and involuntary turnover. *Academy of Management Journal*, *41*(5), 511–525.

Shaw, J. D., Gupta, N., & Delery, J. E. (2001). Congruence between technology and compensation systems: Implications for strategy implementation. *Strategic Management Journal*, *22*(4), 379–386.

Shaw, J. D., Gupta, N., & Delery, J. E. (2002). Pay dispersion and workforce performance: Moderating effects of incentives and interdependence. *Strategic Management Journal*, *23*(6), 491–512.

Shippmann, J. S., Ash, R. A., Battista, M., Carr, L., Eyde, L. D., Hesketh, B., Kehoe, J., Pearlman, K., Prien, E. P., & Sanchez, J. I. (2000). The practice of competency modeling. *Personnel Psychology*, *53*(3), 703–740.

Skarlicki, D. P., & Folger, R. (1997). Retaliation in the workplace: The roles of distributive, procedural, and interactional justice. *Journal of Applied Psychology*, *82*(3), 434–443.

Snell, S. A., & Dean, J. W. (1992). Integrated manufacturing and human resource management: A human capital perspective. *Academy of Management Journal, 35*(3), 467–504.

Sonnenfeld, J. A., & Peiperl, M. A. (1988). Staffing policy as a strategic response: A typology of career systems. *Academy of Management Review, 13*(4), 568–600.

Taylor, H. C., & Russell, J. T. (1939). The relationship of validity coefficients to the practical effectiveness of tests in selection. *Journal of Applied Psychology, 23*, 565–578.

Thompson, J. D. (1967). *Organizations in action: Social science bases of administrative theory.* New York, NY: McGraw-Hill.

Tyler, T. R. (1999). Why people cooperate with organizations: An identity-based perspective. In: B. M. Staw (Ed.), *Research in organizational behavior* (Vol. 21, pp. 201–246). Greenwich, CT: JAI Press.

Van Maanen, J. (1977). Toward a theory of the career. In: J. Van Maanen (Ed.), *Organizational careers: Some new perspectives.* New York, NY: Wiley.

Vandenberg, R. J., Richardson, H. A., & Eastman, L. J. (1999). The impact of high involvement work processes on organizational effectiveness: A second-order latent variable approach. *Group & Organization Management, 24*(3), 300–339.

Walton, R. E., & Susman, G. I. (1987). People policies for the new machines. *Harvard Business Review, 65*(2), 98–106.

Ward, P. T., Bicklord, D. J., & Leong, G. K. (1996). Configurations of manufacturing strategy, business strategy, environment and structure. *Journal of Management, 22*(4), 597.

Williamson, O. E. (1975). *Markets and hierarchies, analysis and antitrust implications: A study in the economics of internal organization.* New York, NY: Free Press.

Wright, P. M., & Boswell, W. R. (2002). Desegregating HRM: A review and synthesis of micro and macro human resource management research. *Journal of Management, 28*(3), 247–276.

Wright, P. M., Gardner, T. M., Moynihan, L. M., Park, H. J., Gerhart, B., & Delery, J. E. (2001). Measurement error in research on human resources and firm performance: Additional data and suggestions for future research. *Personnel Psychology, 54*(4), 875–902.

Wright, P. M., McMahan, G. C., & McWilliams, A. (1994). Human resources and sustained competitive advantage: A resource-based perspective. *International Journal of Human Resource Management, 5*(2), 301–326.

Zamanou, S., & Glaser, S. R. (1994). Moving toward participation and involvement: Managing and measuring organizational culture. *Group & Organization Management, 19*(4), 475–501.

Zammuto, R. F., & O'Connor, E. J. (1992). Gaining advanced manufacturing technologies' benefits: The roles of organization design and culture. *Academy of Management Review, 17*(4), 701–728.

Zuboff, S. (1985). Automate/Informate: The two faces of intelligent technology. *Organizational Dynamics, 14*(2), 5–18.

PART **II**

Human Resources Management in the International Context

Human Resources Management in Europe and North America: Similarities and Differences

Bas van Diepen, Ad van Iterson and Robert A. Roe

Although the term human resources management (HRM) is equally popular in Europe and North America it carries different meanings and covers different practices. This chapter aims to describe similarities and differences in the meaning, function and content of HRM in Europe and North America. Rather than merely listing and comparing present features of HRM at the two sides of the Atlantic we will try to make these features understood by linking them to the societal contexts in which HRM has developed. More specifically, we will place HRM against the background of national cultures and societal institutions and show how its current forms can be seen as the outcomes of path-dependent developments in the respective contexts (see also Brewster, 1994). The apparent diversity of HRM policies and practices should not conceal that there is essentially one core function HRM should fulfil, i.e. to draw together people who are willing and able to perform the work from which the organization derives its existence. HRM must, on a continuous basis, attract, retain, utilize and develop 'human resources' in order for organizations to compete and survive. This implies that HRM has to find new ways to perform this core function while coping with the challenges posed by the ever-changing organizational environment.

When comparing Europe and North America we acknowledge that there are cultural and institutional differences as well as similarities, and that both continents display a certain degree of heterogeneity (Brewster, 1994). We also take into consideration that technological, economic and social changes are constantly modifying the European and North American contexts. Among those changes are globalization, which is bringing the North American, European and other economies into closer contact, and the social and economic integration in the European Union, which is reducing diversity within Europe. We will sketch the main aspects of diversity and change, which we believe are relevant for our understanding of present-day HRM. Our description will mainly be in terms of clusters of countries and we will only occasionally refer to individual countries. We will not consider regional differences within countries or differences between industrial sectors or segments of the labour market.

This chapter is structured in the following way. First, we will discuss the notion of HRM as it is conceived and turned into practice in Europe and North America. Second, we will depict the cultural and institutional contexts in which European and North American organizations and management are embedded, and highlight some general implications for the way in which HRM developed. This will include both structural and functional aspects of HRM. Third, we will identify some major technological, economic and social trends that organizations have to accommodate, and the way the issues emerging from them are reflected in European and North American HRM practices. We will conclude the chapter with a discussion of HRM's future development, addressing, amongst other questions, whether we can expect European and North American HRM to ultimately converge.

Views of HRM

In spite of the now global adoption of the term HRM, a generally agreed upon definition is impossible to find. For the authors who have introduced and promoted the term (e.g. Beer, Spector, Lawrence, Quin Mills, & Walton, 1984; Frombrun, Tichy, & Devanna, 1984) HRM has a very specific meaning derived from the view that personnel is a 'resource' that requires a particular way of management in order for the organization to achieve its strategic objectives. According to Frombrun et al. (1984), the management of the human resources should be guided by a strategy derived from the firm's general business strategy, just as is the case for other resources. For Beer et al. (1984), human resources have unique qualities that require special care to ensure that they display the commitment necessary for their utilization by the firm. Thus, HRM can help to shape and support the business strategy, rather than merely follow from it. These American views of HRM combine two contrasting elements: first, a call for a strategic approach driven by business goals and, second, a utilitarian conception of employees. The underlying idea is that of a temporary relationship between the firm and the employee, based on a *contract*, in which the employee's capabilities are maximally utilized or exploited. This is a view that presupposes a well-functioning external labour market and places a strong emphasis on recruitment and selection, flexible contracting, training and development, all driven by short-term business needs. Its practices aim at the enhancement of employee commitment and performance as well as at easy transfer and dismissal of employees (e.g. in the context of outsourcing and downsizing). HRM conceived in this way aims for optimal results and searches for 'best practices', designated with such notions as 'high-performance work system' or 'high-involvement human resource system', that create added value at the firm level (Ichniowski & Shaw, 1999; Pfeffer, 1994).

In Europe a different conception seems to prevail, in which HRM is just a fashionable label to designate any activity in the field of personnel management, regardless of whether it is practice or strategy oriented. Although it has become customary to speak of 'strategic HRM', the outlook in Europe is not confined to the strategic-utilitarian view dominant in the US but also includes elements of social responsibility, industrial democracy and worker protection (cf. Schneider & Barsoux, 2003). The resulting blend is often still designated as 'personnel policy'. While regional differences in emphasis exist, which will be explained more fully later, the underlying idea is that of a long-term relationship between the firm and the employee, based on a *covenant* that binds the employer and the employee, and obliges them to a fair exchange of efforts based on an understanding of mutual interests. It is a view which places a greater weight on the internal labour market, a balance of business and employee interests, training and development, transparent appraisal and promotion, and employee protection. Performance and performance commitment are to some degree implied in the relationship between the employee and the organization, and hence do often not receive special emphasis.

We perceive an interesting paradox in ways of describing HRM. In North America, the practice of instrumental, contract-based employee relations is complemented with rhetoric of employee devotion and loyalty to the company. In Europe, on the contrary, protracted employee relations are so self-evident that no special emphasis on positive employee attitudes and behaviours is needed. To many Europeans, the American rhetoric sounds exaggerated or shallow, while the European reluctance to be outspoken about the particular qualities of employee relations may puzzle American observers.

Cultural and Institutional Contexts

From the early 1990s on, various studies have suggested that the meaning, role and content of HRM reflect the national cultural and institutional environment in which it is embedded (e.g. Boxall, 1995; Brewster, 1994; Forster & Whipp, 1995). This applies to the full range of HRM practices, including recruitment and selection, appraisal and remuneration, training and development, etc. Following this perspective, we will try to understand differences and similarities in HRM, by distinguishing a number of clusters (see Ronen & Shenkar, 1985), i.e. (i) the Anglo-American cluster (US, Canada, UK, and Ireland), (ii) the Germanic cluster (Germany, the Netherlands, Austria, and Switzerland), (iii) the Latin cluster (France, Italy, Spain, and Portugal) and (iv) the Nordic cluster (Denmark, Sweden, Norway, and Finland). Of course, there are differences between the countries in these clusters, but putting them together means that there are significant commonalities as well as contrasts to countries in other clusters. Given our aim, to compare North America and Europe, it is important to note that the US and Canada are in the same cluster as the UK and Ireland. The reasons for this grouping will become clear in the following sections, which show that differences to the other European countries are indeed much greater than to the UK and Ireland.

Many researchers have adopted a *culturalist approach*, drawing on societal values, beliefs and norms to explain national differences in organization and management when studying cross-national phenomena such as different HRM practices. They mostly rely on the work of Hofstede (2001), Trompenaars and Hampden-Turner (1997) or the GLOBE Research Team (2002). Thus, they draw on individual data aggregated at the national level on the assumption that the nation circumscribes a relatively unitary culture — an assumption that does not fully account for the cultural diversity within countries and changes due to acculturation. Under these assumptions, it has been repeatedly recognized that US culture is considerably more individualistic and achievement-oriented than most other countries (cf. Gannon, 1994; Guest, 1990), which lowers the universal applicability of US-originated HRM concepts and practices across the globe (Erez & Earley, 1993;

Purcell, 1999). For instance, Western Europe is also characterized by a high level of indi-vidualism, but the Germanic, Latin and Nordic countries are much less achievement-oriented — either because of their high scores on 'femininity' (Hofstede, 2001) such as the Nordic cluster and the Netherlands, or because of the weight attached to ascription, as in France, the Mediterranean countries and rural parts of the Germanic countries. This may explain why individual performance-based rewards, cherished in the US, often do not 'work' in these parts of Europe.

Power distance is the cultural dimension that separates the Latin cluster (with high acceptance of power differences in society and in organizations) from the three others (low acceptance). For instance, the centralization of authority in French organizations is gener-ally seen as a reflection of the high power distance that characterizes French society (Calori, Lubatkin, Very, & Veiga, 1997; d'Iribarne, 1989; Hofstede, 2001). Similarly, con-sensus building in Dutch firms is seen as a reflection of the balancing of interests and the compromising attitude that is typical for Dutch society with its low power distance and high femininity (d'Iribarne, 1989; Van Iterson & Olie, 1992). These contrasts can explain differences in the roles of managers and relationships between managers and employees within Europe. In countries with high power distance human resources tend to be managed in a centralized, authoritarian way, whereas in countries with low power distance decen-tralization and participation prevail.

Other researchers in comparative HRM employ an *institutional perspective*, inspired by the assumption that firms seek to align resources with their institutional environments (Meyer & Rowan, 1977), i.e. the legal, political, economic and social arrangements in a society 'that promote certain types of behaviors and restrict others' (Scott, 1995). In this approach, cross-national variations in HRM policies, and the place of HRM in the organi-zation's structure, are largely attributed to nation-specific institutions such as legislation and regulations, and systems of corporate governance, finance, labour relations, and edu-cation (e.g. Maurice, Sorge, & Warner, 1980; Whitley, 1992, 1999).

A major institutional difference between HRM in the US and in Western Europe is the extent to which HRM is defined by *legislation and regulations* (Pieper, 1990). For exam-ple, regulations regarding employment protection (Blanchard, 1999), hours of work (Bielenski, Bosch, & Wagner, 2002), minimum levels of expenditure on training (for France see: Bournois, 1991) are much stricter in the *non*-Anglo-American clusters. Also, social security arrangements are far more developed in continental Europe, notably the Nordic and Germanic cluster and Belgium. On the other hand, in the US there is an empha-sis on issues of discrimination and equal employment opportunities.

Another important institutional factor comprises *corporate governance*. Corporate gov-ernance systems differ significantly in how they balance the interests of the firm's stake-holders (Albert, 1993; Lorsch & Graff, 1996; Yoshimori, 1995). Across North America and Europe, we find two contrasting stakeholder systems: the Anglo-American, in which the shareholder is pre-eminent, and the continental-European system, in which other stake-holders, such as the employees and the state, but also suppliers, creditors and customers are considered. Within Europe, these two systems are exemplified by the UK and Germany, respectively. The contrasting models of stakeholder relationships are reflected in specific board arrangements, which have ramifications vital for HRM. Characteristic of the Anglo-American model is the one-tier board consisting of both executive directors, employed by the company, and independent non-executive directors. The board of directors is the legal and accountable group responsible for all the corporation's actions and results. It is elected by the shareholders and serves as trustee of the shareholder's interest (Dalton, Kesner, & Rechner, 1988). The focus on increasing shareholder's wealth occurs to the detriment of the interests and development of other stakeholding parties, notably the employees. Unsurprisingly, in the Anglo-American model, formal worker participation institutions are largely absent. In the UK works councils, were not mandatory, until 2005 when new legislation based on the EU Directive on European Works Councils was introduced.

The other main board configuration is the two-tier system, which a growing number of European countries are adopting. Here, executives and non-executives are split into two different legal bodies. An overlap in membership between the executive board, responsible for the day-to-day running of the business, and the supervisory board which appoints and removes the executive board, exerts control and offers guidance regarding long-term policy-making, is not allowed. In a number of continental-European countries legislation requires employee involvement in the form of representation on the supervisory board, in most cases with representation via works councils (Brewster, 1995). Most far-reaching is the German co-determination system. Employee representatives hold one-third or one-half of the seats of the supervisory board in limited liability companies, depending on the size of the company.

Whereas governance of managers by shareholders is strongly developed in the Anglo-American model, managerial discretion is high compared to other stakeholders (Gedajlovic & Shapiro, 1998). US managers enjoy a high degree of freedom with regard to human resources, including employment and reward policies (Brewster, 1995). Characteristic of the US model is a flexible labour market combined with low job security (Gelauff & Den Broeder, 1996). If firm performance weakens and share prices fall, managers are tempted to lay off employees (Ahmadjian & Robinson, 2001). In continental-European countries, managerial discretion in the HR domain is far more restricted. Radical employment policies of termination and redundancy are of almost no avail in view of restrictive government legislation, stronger unionization and institutional democracy (Brewster, 1995; Gooderham, Nordhaug, & Ringdal, 1999; Pieper, 1990).

The *financial system* supports the system of corporate governance. The financial system of the Anglo-American cluster helps to put the interests of shareholders above those of other potential stakeholders. It is an integral element of the way in which capital providers control and monitor organizational policy (cf. Gelauff & Den Broeder, 1996). Capital mobilization takes place via stock markets and large powers are given to shareholders. In the US, 99% of the top 400 companies are publicly quoted on a stock exchange, as opposed to only 54% on average in EU countries. In these 'capital-based' countries (Zysman, 1983), the market for corporate control is strongly developed, leading to high turnover levels, and hence, shorter management tenures, which limits the chances of developing a long-term HRM policy. In contrast, German companies are legally defined as social institutions with public responsibilities to a range of stakeholders, including employees and the local community (Lorsch & Graff, 1996; Rubach & Sebora, 1998). In the 'credit-based' financial system of the Germanic cluster (Zysman, 1983) large banks have a prominent role in financing and controlling corporate firms. These banks and other financial institutions often become involved in the long-term development of companies, including HR development. Next to the 'capital-' and 'credit-based' financial system, the Latin cluster is characterized by widespread family control, considerable state ownership, large stocks of shares owned by financial holdings, weak disclosure regulation and government interference with mergers and acquisitions (Gelauff & Den Broeder, 1996; Mayer & Whittington, 1999; Pedersen & Thomsen, 1997). In this cluster, the development of such a long-term HRM policy is mired by the reticence that typifies family and state involvement.

National *labour relations* systems affect HRM practices in a variety of ways (cf. Brewster, 1995; Tayeb, 1994). If unions are weak, as in Spain (Baruel, 1996), or to some extent marginalized, as in the Anglo-American cluster (on the UK: Edwards et al., 1992), managerial discretion in administering employee relations is high, often leading to the adoption of 'innovative' HR concepts and practices. In Germany or Austria, where unions tend to be recognized as 'partners', or in France, where unions take an antagonistic stance (Gooderham et al., 1999), the power of the HR function is lower. In the Germanic and Nordic clusters, union demands are presented in collective bargaining with employers' federations and the government (cf. Hollingsworth, 1997). On account of these aggregated negotiations, employment and working conditions tend to be more uniform across firms, leaving only limited autonomy to company managers (Gooderham et al., 1999). In the UK, where unions are organized according to craft or profession, and defend the rights and identity of the skilled employees they represent, managerial discretion in HRM is also limited. Flexibility in responding to market demands is more easily established in countries with industry-based or general unions. Obviously, works councils and other forms of industrial democracy embody the idea of a covenant that binds employer and employee and thereby limit managerial discretion.

Important features of national systems of *education, training and development* are the weight of formal academic standards, the degree to which technical training is separated from academic education and the significance of publicly certified and professional expertise (Sparrow, 1995; Whitley, 1992). These features affect the levels and nature of employee qualifications, but also influence employee identity and value orientations. When formal academic standards enjoy high prestige and technical training is stringently separated from academic education, we speak of a unitary system of education, whereas the contrary is labelled as a dual system. In Europe, France is the best example of a unitary system (Calori et al., 1997). Large firms prefer to recruit pristine graduates to their own lower and middle echelons. The status of the academic institution defines an additional success criterion. Graduates of the three top *Grandes Écoles* who chose an industrial career have a 90% chance of becoming a president of a company (Evans, 1995; Lawrence, 1993).

Whereas in most unitary systems of education, practical training is weakly developed and enjoys low esteem, in dual systems the academic and practical orientation are more balanced. Germany provides a good example of this dual system. Promoted by German law, there is a well-developed system of vocational education and training offering standardized education for employment needs at diverse levels within the firm. Especially, the German association for personnel management (DGFP) plays a decisive role in postgraduate training, in cooperation with most large German companies (Wachter & Stengelhofen, 1992). Vocational qualifications, at all levels, are widespread among German employees. Despite signs of this system being under pressure, these qualifications still have prestige and foster occupational pride. In addition to theoretical qualifications, such as engineering and economics, practical skills are valued. It is not unusual for German managers to have served an apprenticeship. A further characteristic that distinguishes most of continental Europe from France as well as from the US and UK is the lack of differentiation between higher institutions of education. Elite institutions such as the *Grandes Écoles* in France, the university colleges of Oxford and Cambridge, in the UK or the Ivy League in the US are virtually unknown.

Variations in education and training systems have momentous implications for corporate HRM. In countries with unitary educational systems, firms will rely principally on the external labour market, applying externally defined standards for recruitment and selection. Development in firms employs standardized bought-in training programmes. In countries with dual educational systems, firms tend to focus on the internal labour market, establishing distinctive patterns of development and training (Evans, Lank, & Farquhar, 1989; Whitley, 1992). Likewise, career patterns can be predominantly external or internal. In the Anglo-American cluster, for instance, management ability is seen to be a general and transferable skill (Barsoux & Lawrence, 1991). Promotion is gained by moving between organizations, and early promotion to higher echelon positions is possible, even without experience of lower line positions. By contrast, in the other clusters promotion is primarily based on functional expertise in combination with company loyalty (for Germany: Lane, 1992). Interorganizational mobility is not as frequent as in Anglo-American firms. In France, management is seen as an intellectually rather than an interpersonally demanding task (Barsoux & Lawrence, 1991; Lawrence, 1993), whereas in the other Latin countries the interpersonal character receives more emphasis. All this seems to produce different HR architectures in terms of social-economic background (elitist versus non-elitist), labour markets (external versus internal career paths), and professional competencies (specialists versus general knowledge and skills).

The cultural and institutional context also affects the *structural embedding of the HR function* in the organization's structure. The dominant conception of how stakeholders' interests are to be balanced is reflected in whether the HR function is represented at the management board level. But there are also differences with respect to the view of HRM as part of the line manager's job or as a specialized area of expertise. When considering national differences in the line management-specialist balance across North America and Europe, the Cranet survey (the world's largest ongoing HRM survey) shows that the Anglo-American and Latin clusters are on the side of the spectrum where little responsibility is assigned to the line. The Nordic cluster and the Netherlands have consistently devolved HR responsibility to line management, while Germany occupies a middle-ground position (Larsen & Brewster, 2003). A greater role for line management is typically associated with fewer people in central HR departments (Brewster et al., 2003; Larsen & Brewster, 2003; Ulrich, 1997). This does not necessarily lead to a loss of status of central HRM departments. Typically, in countries at the 'devolved' side of the spectrum, HR departments tend to be more integrated in corporate strategic management. This is even the case in countries where HRM is traditionally granted low status, such as the UK (Budhwar, 2000).

An overall trend affecting the structural embedding of HRM function is the *outsourcing* of HR functions. In the past, substantial outsourcing has already taken place in domains such as wages, benefits and health, which involved the handling of large numbers of administrative data. Further outsourcing of HRM is likely to take place in domains such as recruitment, selection, training and development. Outsourcing is likely to have a different impact on organizations where HRM has been devolved to the line and those where it has remained centralized. The impact on the latter organizations, which are mainly to be found in the Anglo-American and the Latin cluster is likely to be more profound.

HRM Practices

In spite of the differences noted in the previous section, all forms of HRM share one common objective, i.e. to ensure the availability of an adequate number of qualified and motivated workers. As was noted earlier, HRM's core function is attracting employees and contract workers who are ready to accept and fulfil the roles defined by organizations under a certain range of conditions and for a particular period of time. On top of this, HRM may have certain strategic objectives aiming at support for corporate strategy, which may be pursued along different ways in Europe than in North America. There are two major tasks for corporate HRM in meeting these objectives. One is to accommodate the variety of conditions resulting from national, sectoral, organizational and occupational differences. Although there is a certain technology, comprising techniques for recruitment, selection, training, etc. that may be drawn upon, HRM has to provide specific answers to local problems *taking the cultural and institutional setting into account*. This even applies to the so-called 'best practices' (Pfeffer, 1994), which may work less well beyond the setting in which they were identified. The second task is to *accommodate ongoing technological, economic and social changes*. While its core function remains the same, HRM has to come up with new answers as the global and local environment of the organization's changes and new generations of workers enter the labour market. Thus, HRM must constantly search for ways to attract and develop workers with changing expectations and qualifications for organizations that are in continuous re-adjustment in their drive towards survival.

The literature bears witness to how HRM struggles to cope with these tasks. On the one hand, there is a broad literature showing differences in HRM practices between regions, countries and sectors. On the other hand, there are numerous publications highlighting new trends in the organization's environment, challenges for HRM resulting from them and approaches to cope with these challenges. We will refer to these literatures below. The major trends and challenges discussed in the recent literature can be group into a number of categories.

1. Economy
   - Technological innovation, development of mobile- and network-based ICT, spread of e-business, process and product innovation
   - Globalization and increasing competition
2. Organization
   - Mergers, acquisitions, joint ventures downsizing, outsourcing, off-shoring and privatization
   - Changes in organizational forms, management philosophies, team work, worker roles, market and customer orientation
   - Flexible work, telecommuting, self-employment and small business activity

3   Labour market
   • Demographic shifts (aging, changing gender composition) and workforce diversity
   • Changes in demand and supply of labour, competition for critical competences and knowledge, skill shortages
4.   Employment
   • Alternative work arrangements, empowerment and changes in psychological contracts
   • Changes in careers, international assignments and expatriate experiences
   • Changes in social security, early retirement arrangements and forms of compensation
5.   Stakeholder relations
   • Accountability, social responsibility, ethics and stakeholder involvement
   • Justice, fairness and equal employment opportunity
   • Work-life balance, work-family conflict and dual careers
   • Safety, health and environment
6.   HRM profession
   • Accountability, professionalization of HRM, benchmarking, outsourcing HRM and E-HRM.

In our description of HRM practices that follows (below) we will indicate how these trends are accounted for in Europe and North America and at the same time show how practices reflect the cultural and institutional factors mentioned before. We think of the interaction of these various factors in terms of a metaphor in which culture and institutions represent a prism that breaks the light of an ongoing environmental change into a broad spectrum of practices (see Figure 1).

Our review of practices in Europe and North America concentrates on three groups of HRM practices: procurement, appraisal and remuneration, and training and development.

Procurement

Practices related to workforce procurement comprise practices for defining human resource needs and actual recruitment and selection. Human resource needs follow from

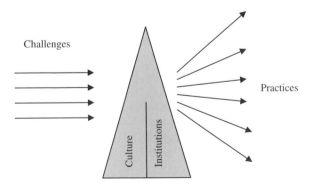

Figure 1: The spectrum of practices.

the organization's choices regarding the definition of its jobs, the deployment of the current workforce and from the conditions on the labour market. European firms are generally limited more in their room for strategic decisions than their American counterparts. These restrictive influences are clearly visible when it comes to efforts of European companies to increase the *numerical flexibility* of the workforce, e.g. by increasing the use of fixed-term contracts, part-time work, early retirement, outsourcing and downsizing, etc. Typically, some compensation for the impacts on employees is called for. For instance, outsourcing and downsizing have led to the development of outplacement programmes, an increasing number of part-time and temporary contracts and a combination of reduced working time and temporary job guarantees (i.e. the case of Volkswagen AG in Germany: Garnjost & Blettner, 1996). In Ireland and the UK, it has also led to multi-skilling and teamwork (Gunnigle, 1992; Richbell, 2001). In Northern Europe (Kjellberg, Soderstrom, & Svensson, 1998) and in the Germanic countries (Scholz, 1996; Wiersma & Van den Berg, 1999) there has been an increasing use of flexible work contracts and flexible working time. Altogether, numerical flexibility has remained rare. For instance, in the Germanic cluster there is a relatively stable core of employees with high job security and a variety of skills, which can be flexibly deployed from the internal labour markets. In the Latin-European numerical flexibility is low due to local regulations such as high severance pay levels (for Spain see: Baruel, 1996) and limitations of temporary work to non-managerial cadre employees (for France see: Cerdin & Peretti, 2001). In contrast, US companies are increasingly opting for outsourcing, contingent workforces and virtual organizations (Konrad & Deckop, 2001).

European *functional flexibility* patterns also reflect institutional patterns and different paths of industrial development. Countries in the Northern and Germanic clusters share an emphasis on job design and structuring work (e.g. autonomous working groups at Swedish Volvo and SAAB plants) and participative decision making (e.g. quality circles), particularly in relation to new technologies. Flexible specialization appears to have become a dominant market and production strategy, requiring higher levels of organizational trust and work involvement (Sparrow & Hiltrop, 1994). It seems that US companies emphasize quality circles, job rotation and TQM, with the use of teams remaining constant over recent years (Deshpande & Golhar, 1997; Konrad & Deckop, 2001), whereas Canadian companies also invest in employee participation.

Labour market conditions also influence human resource needs differently. In comparison to the US, Europe has witnessed relatively high unemployment levels due to high productivity levels in combination with high wage levels and social benefits resulting in relatively low labour mobility (Roe & Van den Berg, 2003). Moreover, due to diverging economic development, labour markets in Europe are frequently regionally determined (e.g. Norway, Sweden, Germany and the UK). National governments and the European Union have adopted policies specifically targeting at strengthening labour markets in remote areas by means of regulation and subsidizing.

The constraining influence of the European institutional environment applies to *staffing practices* as well, particularly in the Northern, Latin and Germanic clusters (Mabon, 1995; Roe & Van den Berg, 2003; Sparrow & Hiltrop, 1994). Thus, there are rules regarding employment protection (e.g. in Germanic and Nordic countries), the use of recruitment agencies (e.g. in Norway, Germany and Italy) and the staffing process (e.g. in Latin countries such as France and Spain). These rules derive from constitutional rights (e.g. in

Norway and Italy), collective agreements (e.g. in France) or the rulings of representative bodies (e.g. in Germany, Norway and Denmark). Staffing practices differ with regard to recruitment criteria, recruitment methods and selection methods. As for *recruitment criteria*, different emphases are put on ability versus achievement. In Latin-European countries, the emphasis is mainly on achievement. For instance, French employers are most interested in employees who have attended *Grandes Écoles* for business or engineering, while university graduates are considered second best. In contrast, ability is the dominant criterion in the Anglo-American cluster. In the other clusters, a variable mix of achievement and ability is found. Wachter and Stengelhofen (1992) have noted that Germanic countries emphasize a combination of ability and achievement criteria. Some interesting differences in the mix of ability and achievement criteria have been observed in the Nordic countries (Tixier, 1996), i.e. Sweden (ability to adapt to the group and to manage a diverse team), Denmark (educational levels and capabilities to manage and motivate), Norway (prior experience) and Finland (specialization and years of education, charisma and initiative). For instance, there is a thorough selection of recruits at Ikea (Swedish, home furnishing) on the basis of their value fit with the organization (e.g. humility, modesty and respect for other persons) (Schneider & Barsoux, 2003).

European *recruitment methods* bear the marks of internal labour markets and legal restrictions. As a result, recruitment is usually based on advertisements, job interviews and personal contacts (e.g. in Latin-European countries and Ireland) as well as school and college recruitment (e.g. in Denmark and France). Anglo-American countries appear less restricted and more creative in responding to labour supply changes, by proposing new recruitment sources and methods and more favourable labour conditions (e.g. sign-on bonuses). For instance, both US and Canadian manufacturing companies use job posting and bidding as a recruitment source, and Canadian companies frequently make use of laid-off workers and are less likely to turn to temporary employees (Deshpande & Golhar, 1997).

Similar differences show up in the choice of *selection methods*. Overall, in Europe the most popular selection method is the unstructured interview or interview panel, despite poor reliability and predictive validity, followed by the application form and references. Currently, the use of psychological tests is becoming more widespread in European countries, following the empirical tradition in the Anglo-American cluster that favours the use of validated selection tools and techniques. Personality tests appear to be somewhat more popular than cognitive tests in European companies (Roe & Van den Berg, 2003). The Latin-European countries (through disapproval by the Roman Catholic Church) and Nordic countries (due to veto-right by Swedish trade unions and on social and ethical grounds) have both been late adopters of these psychometric tests. In some countries (e.g. Spain), structured interviews have also become popular. The comparative study by Roe and Van den Berg (2003) shows that the use of curriculum vitae (resumes) is particularly common in countries such as Spain, France, Belgium, and Denmark, while the Nordic countries, the Netherlands, the UK and Ireland also include application forms, reference checks, tests and assessment centres. German companies seem to dislike the use of tests for selection purposes, contrary to Dutch firms, which have focused on personality traits and less on skills and (job specific) knowledge allowing for easy intra-firm transfer (Wiersma & Van den Berg, 1999).

Appraisal and remuneration

Appraisal systems show differences in focus, method and purpose between Europe and North America as well as within Europe. An important distinction regarding the *focus of appraisal* is between performance, behaviour at the work place and personal attributes such as work styles, attitudes, skills, etc. While North American companies have traditionally stressed individual performance, including the fulfilment of targets (Belout, Dolan, & Saba, 2001; Konrad & Deckop, 2001), the emphasis in Europe has been on the way of working and on a variety of attributes considered relevant for performance and/or development. In recent years, the focus of appraisal has changed, when the notion of competence was embraced as means to achieve greater competitiveness and accountability (Spencer & Spencer, 1993). Interestingly enough, there is a discrepancy between Europe and the US in the view of competences. In continental Europe, the predominant focus is on competen*ce* as mastery of a particular type of task in a specific work situation, which is in line with the tradition of vocational training (Roe, 2002). In contrast, the Anglo-American focus is on competen*cy*, that is any personal attribute (ability, skill, attitude and personality trait) associated with good performance (Spencer & Spencer, 1993). The growing adoption of these competence notions has broadened the scope of appraisal, with competen*cies* supplementing performance in North America, and competen*ces* supplementing work behaviour and personal attributes in Europe.

Apart from a difference in focus, there are also differences in *appraisal methods*, e.g. in the degree of subjectivity–objectivity and the involvement of different types of raters. Generally speaking, European countries have been slow in adopting objective rating scales, such as BOS or BES, which have gained considerable popularity in North America. Similarly, they have been slow in using multi-rater (360°) systems. These differences may have to do with the fact that Europeans tend to conceive appraisal as an instrument in a personal relationship of the employee with the manager, which is part of the (often durable) covenant with the employing organization. This suggests that new appraisal instruments are only adopted when they fit into the existing cultural and institutional context. Of course, there are differences between the clusters. For instance, in Latin-European countries there is not much place for objective performance appraisal systems because appraisal is seen as a prerogative of the manager. In the Germanic cluster, a form of appraisal has developed which is more like a dialogue between the supervisor and the subordinate about the way in which the work role is fulfilled and about hindering conditions (e.g. Nagel, Oswald, & Wimmer, 2002). In formal appraisals, subordinates have a right to contest or complement the view of the manager.

The specific appraisal techniques used depend on the *appraisal purposes*, i.e. performance enhancement, personal development, promotion, remuneration, etc. The way in which HRM responds to economic, organizational and employment related challenges, determines the emphasis on these purposes and hence the choice of techniques. The strong performance orientation of North American HRM is clearly visible in such techniques as management by objectives and goal setting, which have been advocated in connection with performance appraisals. Although these techniques and the results of research on goal setting (Locke & Latham, 1990) are well known in Europe, their direct application appears to be rare. While the idea of evaluating employee behaviour with regard to standards is generally accepted, other aspects of employee behaviour are often seen as equally important as performance *per se*, and the enhancement of performance is seen as requiring much more than setting particular types of performance goals by the manager. The broader focus of appraisals, including competences and other attributes, makes it possible for appraisals to serve as a basis for personal development and promotion at the same time.

A major difference between Europe and North America exists in remuneration practices. Generally speaking, *compensation* in Europe is still mainly collectively determined, in spite of pressures such as international competition, limited economic growth, shifting demographics and social values towards greater flexibility. Presently, all European countries have collective negotiations in wage setting (e.g. Denmark, Germany, Ireland and Italy) and minimum wage legislation (e.g. France, Spain, the Netherlands and the UK) or both. Conversely, American and Canadian companies can more easily match compensation to specific employee demands and characteristics of local labour markets towards more flexible and strategically aligned pay systems (Belout et al., 2001; Konrad & Deckop, 2001).

In Europe, the use of *performance related pay* has spread unevenly due to legislative restrictions and union resistance (Wiersma & Van den Berg, 1999). Merit rating has gained little popularity, except for the UK and Ireland (Gunnigle, 1992; Richbell, 2001). In the Latin-European countries (Cerdin & Peretti, 2001; Negrelli & Treu, 1995; Valle, Martin, & Romero, 2001), the use of pay for performance is traditionally not regarded highly since these countries feature a relatively high demand for equity. In France, the use of performance appraisals (for instance by means of MBO, see Hofstede, 2001) for remuneration purposes is not popular; collective variable pay (e.g. through gain sharing or profit sharing) is preferred (Cerdin & Peretti, 2001). The Nordic countries, traditionally hesitant in using individual performance measures due to the relative power of unions (Berglund & Löwstedt, 1996; Mabon, 1995; Scheuer, 1996), now use merit pay more frequently. Changes in appraisal and remuneration systems are slow. For instance, in Germany, the implementation of new appraisal and reward systems meant to improve customer service and quality performance is restrained since such systems are bound to collective agreements which are the subject of work council activity.

As pay levels also signify the differences between hierarchical levels in organizations (Lane, 1989), it is interesting to note that US firms display large *pay differentials* between executives and workers (Konrad & Deckop, 2001) and that differentials have particularly increased in some parts of Europe (e.g. Italy and the UK). Nordic countries with their egalitarian mindset have the most uniform pay policies and only modest increases for experienced and skilled employees. Fringe benefits (e.g. pension contributions and medical insurance) have spread over the pay packages of many European employees, not only in management but also in public institutions. However, the resulting pay packages diverge considerably. For instance, Swedish employees have a preference for non-financial incentives (time off) over financial incentives (bonus). Cafeteria compensation systems have gained some acceptance in Europe, but they are less frequently used than in the US, where they include a wider array of rewards (e.g. bonuses, gain sharing, profit sharing and stock-based plans).

Training and development

Approaches to training and development reflect differences in existing educational and vocational systems, labour markets and their deficiencies and assumptions regarding the nature of management. Moreover, countries have pursued different trajectories of industrial development that have also had implications for training and development, and still determine how management in different countries react to labour market changes. Broadly speaking, two *models of training and development* can be distinguished (Sung, Turbin, & Ashton, 2000). The first is the *'state corporatist model'* of the Germanic cluster and Denmark, where governments, employees and employers work closely together and have created apprenticeship systems. For instance, in the German apprenticeship system, companies have always been concerned with investing in human capital whereas in Denmark the publicly funded system is based on a traditional apprenticeship system in craft schools (Madsen & Larsen, 1998). The second is the Anglo-American *'market model'*, which is characterized by employers accepting responsibility for mainly in-company training and where HRM is challenged to provide training and develop employee commitment (Richbell, 2001).

Organisation for Economic Co-operation and Development (OECD) comparisons reveal a growing *degree of training and development* activity in Europe when compared to the US, with the greatest participation in the Nordic countries and the UK, and the smallest in the countries of the Latin cluster. A common reason for this intensified training and development in Europe is the recognition of the importance of training and development as a basis for individual employability (which reduces calls upon unemployment benefits), the qualification level of the labour force and long-term economic prosperity. In France, legal regulations force companies with 10 or more employees to spend at least 1.5% of the wage bill on training (Cerdin & Peretti, 2001). In Norway, there is an extensive collective fund to cover company-based training activities (Skule, Stuart, & Nyen, 2002). In North America such approaches are uncommon. The US seems to experience bifurcation of training and development with a minority of organizations leading training practices and the majority following at a distance (Marquardt, Nissley, Ozag, & Taylor, 2000).

There is some diversity in the way in which training is conducted. Although a strategic approach to the determination of *training needs* is generally recommended, practice in Europe is often different. Training needs are often determined in a bottom-up manner; i.e. they are established in yearly performance appraisals (e.g. in Sweden, Denmark and the UK) or originate from line managers' demands (see for France: Tregaskis & Dany, 1996). They are tailored to company needs rather than derived from these. As for *training methods*, informal, company related, on-the-job-training seems to be most popular, and internal instructors focusing on technical and operational skills are used rather than classroom training. This seems to be true for Europe and North America alike. Outsourcing of training is common in the Nordic and Germanic clusters, and also frequently occurs in Canada (Deshpande & Golhar, 1997) and the US (Marquardt et al., 2000), where training and development often becomes housed within a corporate university (performance-based learning).

Evaluation of training is not very popular in most European companies and is more common in the UK than in for instance Latin or Nordic countries. In these latter countries (e.g. France and Sweden) companies often rely on informal feedback from line management. In contrast, training evaluation is common in the US where HRM faces increased pressure to demonstrate return on investment thereby consistently responding to trends in labour and stakeholder relations.

Training and development practices clearly relate to *career development* conceptions in respective countries. For instance, German titles, skills and experience are often job-specific and at the same time company- or at least industry-specific. Employees are supposed to have the necessary technical competences (facilitated by the apprenticeship system) but also knowledge and skills relating to the company. By the same token, senior managers are expected to be technically competent and to have in-depth understanding of the company and the business. Hence, German managers typically develop competences in-house. A more generalist view is common in the UK, where managers' job mobility is more frequent and managers may be found leading in areas where they have limited expertise. Here, broad skills and experience (e.g. in interpersonal relations and communication) are perceived as the most important determinants of career progress (Laurent, 1989). However, the situation in Europe may be changing. A recent comparative study of France, Germany and the UK (Klarsfeld & Mabey, 2004) has revealed that the distinctions in management development that existed between the Latin cluster, the Germanic cluster and the UK are partly disappearing. In particular, succession planning, internal promotion, and importance given to job experience gained at the workplace (managerial track records), and insistence on formal qualifications were found to be equally dominant in the three areas. Similarly, it has been found that management development in Italy is moving from seniority-based careers to ability-based progression (Sirianni, 1992).

Future Developments

Although the core function of HRM seems to be universal, the foregoing review has shown that the way in which HRM is conceived and practised shows substantial differences between Europe and North America (and particularly the US) and, to a lesser degree, within Europe. As our review was based on the literature of the past 20 years, one might wonder whether and how the situation is changing. After all, there is an intense and large-scale communication and interaction between the US, Canada and Europe, partly in the context of globalization, and one might expect that organizations will learn from each other as to how to conduct HRM and mutually adapt their practices. Our impression is that in the area of HRM, unlike in areas such as finance, marketing or information technology, the dissemination of models and techniques does not readily result in mutual adoption or adaptation. The evidence gathered so far is in support of institutional theory, showing that organizations tend to incorporate structures and practices that are consistent, or 'isomorphic', with the regulatory and normative institutions operating in their environment (Powell & DiMaggio, 1991). The same can be said about the fit with the cultural environment. Thus, in spite of the common vocabulary of HRM that has developed in North America and Europe, and the availability of techniques for assessing and training employees, discrepancies prevail.

As a matter of fact, the very notion of HRM as propagated in the US has found little acceptance in Europe. Vice versa, there is little evidence of North American HRM adopting principles and methods of European origin. The reason seems to lie in the divergence in assumptions regarding the employment relationship and the roles of the parties involved.

The very conception of people as 'resource' and the instrumental approach based on it leads to practices that do not fit very well in the European environment, except perhaps for the UK and Ireland. Conversely, the idea of employee and employer as two parties in their own right, having diverging interests but also mutual responsibilities, seems not to fit well in the North American society.

Three questions emerge. First, what position is taken by 'transnational companies' (Bartlett & Goshal, 1989) which operate in North America and Europe, and often also in other parts of the world? How do they accommodate the demands and constraints of their environment in shaping HRM? One might hypothesize that in the case of these firms homogenizing pressures would be generated by international competitors, international financial capital markets, multinational consultancy firms and international media. Yet, it should be noted that homogeneity is difficult to achieve (Briscoe & Schuler, 2004) and that strategies of even the largest multinational companies reflect their national administrative heritage (cf. Calori et al., 1997; Lane, 2000). Most multinational companies still have a national centre of gravity (Hu, 1996), and have boards that are firmly uni-national and are composed of managers and employees who have received their education, training and socialization in their home country (Glunk, Heijltjes & Olie, 2001).

Second, what developments are to be expected as the cultural and institutional environment is changing over time? This question is particularly pertinent for European organizations as the European Union is in the process of developing a new legislative, normative and regulatory environment in which national institutions of education, labour market, corporate governance, etc. are transformed into European ones. It seems very likely that European HRM practices will somehow be affected by these developments (e.g. Brewster, Mayrhofer & Morley, 2004). In this respect, we should mention the European Social Charter, which provides protection and opportunities for development to employees. We can also point at the increasing adoption of the two-tier system of corporate governance in mid-European and East-European countries, with the subsequent positive effect on the position of employees. It is difficult to predict the speed at which HRM practices will change and to what degree cultural differences will remain visible. But it is possible that growing convergence of national systems results in a more homogeneous European approach to HRM that can constitute an alternative to the neo-liberalist, US-based and internationally exported notion of HRM (Brewster et al., 2004).

Third, what will happen in the long term and how will the process of Europeanization and the wider changes subsumed under the label of globalization interact with each other? Although we can see some further exchange of models and techniques for HRM across the globe, we consider it unlikely that North American and European HRM will come close to each other. In view of what history has taught us so far, we rather expect the existence of two (or more) parallel approaches to HRM in the long run.

References

Ahmadjian, C. L., & Robinson, P. (2001). Safety in numbers: Downsizing and the deinstitutionalization of permanent employment in Japan. *Administrative Science Quarterly*, *46*(4), 622–654.

Albert, M. (1993). *Capitalism against capitalism*. London: Whurr Publishers.

Barsoux, J. L., & Lawrence, P. (1991). *Countries, cultures and constraints.* London: Sage.

Bartlett, C. A., & Goshal, S. (1989). *Managing across borders: The transnational solution.* Cambridge: Harvard Business School Press.

Baruel, J. (1996). *Spain in the context of European human resource management.* Oxford, UK: Basil Blackwell.

Beer, M., Spector, B., Lawrence, P., Quin Mills, D., & Walton, R. (1984). *Managing human assets.* Glencoe, Il: Free Press.

Belout, A., Dolan, S. L., & Saba, T. (2001). Trends and emerging practices in human resource management. *International Journal of Manpower, 22*(3), 207.

Berglund, J., & Löwstedt, J. (1996). Sweden: The fate of human resource management in a 'folkish' society. In: T. Clark (Ed.), *European human resource management* (pp. 215–243). Oxford, UK: Basil Blackwell.

Bielenski, H., Bosch, G., & Wagner, A. (2002). *Working time preferences in sixteen European countries.* Luxembourg: Office for Official Publications of the European Communities.

Blanchard, O. (1999). *European unemployment: The role of shocks and institutions.* Boston: MIT.

Bournois, F. (1991). Gestion des RH en Europe: donnees comparees. *Revue Francaise de Gestion*(mars-avril-mai), *17*, 68–83.

Boxall, P. (1995). Building the theory of comparative HRM. *Human Resource Management Journal, 5*(5), 5–17.

Brewster, C. (1994). Human resource management in Europe: Reflection of, or challenge to, the American concept? In: P. Kirkbride (Ed.), *Human resource management in Europe: perspectives for the 1990s* (pp. 56–89). London: Routledge.

Brewster, C. (1995). Towards a 'European' model of human resource management. *Journal of International Business Studies, 26*(1), 1.

Brewster, C., Carey, L., Dowling, P., Grobler, P., Holland, P., & Warnich, S. (2003). *Contemporary issues in human resource management: Gaining a competitive advantage* (2nd ed.). South Africa, Cape Town: Oxford University Press.

Brewster, C., Mayrhofer, W., & Morley, M. (Eds). (2004). *European human resource management — convergence or divergence?* London: Butterworth-Heinemann.

Briscoe, D., & Schuler, R. H. (2004). *International human resource management.* London: Routledge.

Budhwar, P. S. (2000). Strategic integration and devolvement of human resource management in the UK manufacturing sector. *British Journal of Management, 11*(4), 285.

Calori, R., Lubatkin, M., Very, P., & Veiga, J. F. (1997). Modelling the origins of nationally-bound administrative heritages: A historical institutional analysis of French and British firms. *Organization Science, 8*(6), 681–696.

Cerdin, J.-L., & Peretti, J.-M. (2001). Trends and emerging values in human resource management in France. *International Journal of Manpower, 22*(3), 216.

Dalton, D. R., Kesner, I. F., & Rechner, P. L. (1988). Corporate governance and board directors: An international, comparative perspective. *Advances in International and Comparative Management, 3*, 95–105.

Deshpande, S. P., & Golhar, D. Y. (1997). HRM practices of Canadian and US manufacturing firms: An empirical investigation. *Production Planning and Control, 8*(3), 208–212.

d'Iribarne, P. (1989). *La logique de l'honneur. Gestion des entreprises et traditions nationales.* Paris: Seuil.

Edwards, P., Hall, M., Hyman, R., Marginson, P., Sisson, K., Waddington, J., et al. (1992). Great Britain: Still muddling through. In: A. Ferner & R. Hyman (Eds), *Industrial relations in the New Europe* (pp. 1–68). Oxford: Blackwell.

Erez, M., & Earley, P. C. (1993). *Culture, self-identity and work.* Oxford: Oxford University Press.

Evans, P. A. L. (1995). Managing human resources in the international firm. In: C. A. B. a. S. Goshal (Ed.), *Transnational management*. Boston: McGraw-Hill.

Evans, P. A. L., Lank, E., & Farquhar, A. (1989). Managing human resources in the international firm: lessons from practice. In: P. Evans, Y. Doz & A. Laurent (Eds), *Human resource management in international firms: Change, globalization and innovation*. London: Macmillan.

Forster, N., & Whipp, R. (1995). Future of European human resource management: A contingent approach. *European Management Journal, 13,* 434–442.

Frombrun, C. J., Tichy, N., & Devanna, M. A. (Eds). (1984). *Strategic human resource management*. New York: Wiley.

Gannon, M. J. (1994). *Understanding global cultures: Methaphorical journeys through 17 countries*. Thousand Oaks, CA: Sage.

Garnjost, P., & Blettner, K. (1996). Volkswagen: Cutting labour costs without redundancies. In: J. Storey (Ed.), *Blackwell cases in human resource and change management* (pp. 86–99). Oxford, UK: Basil Blackwell.

Gedajlovic, E. R., & Shapiro, D. M. (1998). Management and ownership effects: Evidence from five countries. *Strategic Management Journal, 19*(6), 533.

Gelauff, G. M., & Den Broeder, C. (1996). *Governance of stakeholder relationships: The German and Dutch experience*. The Hague: CPB Netherlands Bureau for Economic Policy Analysis.

GLOBE Research Team (2002). *Culture, leadership, and organizational practices: The GLOBE findings*. London: Sage.

Glunk, U., Heijltjes, M. G., & Olie, R. (2001). Design characteristics and functioning of top management teams in Europe. *European Management Journal, 19*(3), 291.

Gooderham, P. N., Nordhaug, O., & Ringdal, K. (1999). Institutional and rational determinants of organizational practices: Human resource management in European firms. *Administrative Science Quarterly, 44*(3), 507.

Guest, D. E. (1990). Human resource management and the American dream. *Journal of Management Studies, 27*(4), 377.

Gunnigle, P. (1992). Human resource management in Ireland. *Employee Relations, 14*(5), 5.

Hofstede, G. H. (2001). *Culture's consequences: International differences in work-related values* (2nd ed.). Beverly Hills: Sage Publications.

Hollingsworth, J. R. (1997). Continuities and changes in social systems of production: The cases of Japan, Germany, and the United States. In: J. R. H. a. R. Boyer (Ed.), *Contemporary capitalism: The embeddedness of institutions*. Cambridge, MA: Cambridge University Press.

Hu, Y. S. (1996). Globalization and corporate nationality. In: M. Warner (Ed.), *International encyclopedia of business and management* (pp. 1664–1672).

Ichniowski, C., & Shaw, K. (1999). The effects of human resource management systems on economic performance: An international comparison of U.S. and Japanese Plants. *Management Science, 5*(45), 704–721.

Kjellberg, Y., Soderstrom, M., & Svensson, L. (1998). Training and development in the Swedish context: Structural change and a new paradigm? *Journal of European Industrial Training, 22*(4/5), 205.

Klarsfeld, A., & Mabey, C. (2004). Management development in Europe: Do national models persist? *European Management Journal, 22*(6), 649–658.

Konrad, A. M., & Deckop, J. (2001). Human resource management trends in the USA. *International Journal of Manpower, 22*(3), 269.

Lane, C. (1989). *Management and labour in Europe: The industrial enterprise in Germany, Britain, and France*. Aldershot Hants, UK: E. Elgar.

Lane, C. (1992). European business systems: Britain and Germany compared. In: R. D. Whitley (Ed.), *European Business Systems. Firms and Markets in their National Contexts*. London: Sage.

Lane, C. (2000). Understanding the globalization strategies of German and British multinational companies: is a 'societal effects' approach still useful? In: M. Maurice & A. Sorge (Eds), *Embedding organizations*. Amsterdam: John Benjamins Publishing Company.

Larsen, H. H., & Brewster, C. (2003). Line management responsibility for HRM: what is happening in Europe? *Employee Relations, 25*(3), 228–244.

Laurent, A. (1989). A cultural view of change. In: P. Evans, Y. Doz & A. Laurent (Eds), *Human resources management in international firms: Change globalization, innovation*. London: Macmillan.

Lawrence, P. (1993). Management development in Europe: A study in cultural contrasts. *Human Resource Management Journal, 3*, 11–23.

Locke, E., & Latham, G. P. (1990). *A theory of goal-setting and task performance*. Englewood Cliffs, NJ: Prentice-Hall.

Lorsch, J., & Graff, S. K. (1996). Corporate governance. In: M. Warner (Ed.), *International encyclopdia of business and management* (pp. 772–782).

Mabon, H. (1995). Human resource management in Sweden. *Employee Relations, 17*(7), 57.

Madsen, P., & Larsen, H. H. (1998). Training and development in the Danish context: Challenging education? *Journal of European Industrial Training, 22*(4/5), 158.

Marquardt, M. J., Nissley, N., Ozag, R., & Taylor, T. L. (2000). International briefing 6: Training and development in the United States. *International Journal of Training and Development, 4*(2), 138.

Maurice, M., Sorge, A., & Warner, M. (1980). Societal differences in organizing manufacturing units: A comparison of France, West Germany. *Organization Studies, 1*(1), 59.

Mayer, M. C. J., & Whittington, R. (1999). Strategy, structure and 'systemness': National institutions and corporate change in France. *Organization Studies, 20*(6), 933.

Meyer, J. W., & Rowan, B. (1977). Institutionalized organizations: Formal structure as myth and ceremony. *American Journal of Sociology, 83*, 340–363.

Nagel, R., Oswald, M., & Wimmer, R. (2002). *Das Mitarbeitergespräch als Führungsinstrument*. Stuttgart: Klett-Cotta.

Negrelli, S., & Treu, T. (1995). Human resource management and industrial relations in Italy. *International Journal of Human Resource Management, 6*(3), 720.

Pedersen, T., & Thomsen, S. (1997). European patterns of corporate ownership: A twelve-country. *Journal of International Business Studies, 28*(4), 759.

Pfeffer, J. (1994). *Competitive advantage through people*. Boston, MA: Harvard Business School Press.

Pieper, R. (1990). *Human resource management: An international comparison*. Berlin: Walter De Gruyter.

Powell, M. E., & DiMaggio, P. J. (1991). *The new institutionalism in organizational analysis*. Chicago: University of Chicago Press.

Purcell, J. (1999). Best practice and best fit: chimera or cul-de-sac? *Human Resource Management Journal, 9*(3), 26–41.

Richbell, S. (2001). Trends and emerging values in human resource management. *International Journal of Manpower, 22*(3), 261.

Roe, R. A. (2002). Competenties — Een sleutel tot integratie in theorie en praktijk van de A&O-psychologie/Competences — A key towards the integration of theory and practice in work and organizational psychology. *Gedrag & Organisatie, 15*(4), 203–224.

Roe, R. A., & Van den Berg, P. T. (2003). Selection in Europe: Context, developments and research agenda. *European Journal of Work and Organizational Psychology, 12*(3), 257.

Ronen, S., & Shenkar, O. (1985). Clustering countries on attitudinal dimensions: A review and synthesis. *Academy of Management Review, 10*, 435–454.

Rubach, M. J., & Sebora, T. C. (1998). Comparative corporate governance: Competitive implications of an emerging convergence. *Journal of World Business, 33*(2), 167.

Scheuer, S. (1996). *Denmark: Human resource management under collective bargaining, the sociological perspective.* Oxford, UK: Basil Blackwell.

Schneider, S. C., & Barsoux, J.-L. (2003). *Managing across cultures* (2nd ed.). Harlow, UK: Financial Times/Prentice Hall.

Scholz, C. (1996). Human resource management in Germany. In: T. Clark (Ed.), *European human resource management* (pp. 118–155). Oxford, UK: Basil Blackwell.

Scott, W. R. (1995). *Institutions and organizations.* Thousand Oaks: Sage.

Sirianni, C. A. (1992). Human resource management in Italy. *Employee Relations, 14*(5), 23.

Skule, S., Stuart, M., & Nyen, T. (2002). International briefing 12: Training and development in Norway. *International Journal of Training & Development, 6*(4), 263–276.

Sparrow, P. R. (1995). Towards a dynamic and comparative model of European human resource management: An extended review. *The International Journal of Human Resource Management, 6*(4), 935–953.

Sparrow, P. R., & Hiltrop, J.-M. (1994). *European human resource management in transition.* London, UK: Prentice Hall.

Spencer, L. M., & Spencer, S. M. (1993). *Competence at work: Models for superior performance.* New York: Wiley.

Sung, J., Turbin, J., & Ashton, D. (2000). Towards a framework for the comparative analysis of national systems of skill formation. *International Journal of Training and Development, 4*(1), 8.

Tayeb, M. (1994). Japanese managers and British culture: A comparative case study. *International Journal of Human Resource Management, 5*(1), 145.

Tixier, M. (1996). Cross-cultural study of managerial recruitment tools in Nordic countries. *International Journal of Human Resource Management, 7*(3), 753.

Tregaskis, O., & Dany, F. (1996). A comparison of HRD in France and the UK. *Journal of European Industrial Training, 20*(1), 20.

Trompenaars, F., & Hampden-Turner, C. (1997). *Riding the waves of culture.* London: Nicholas Brealey.

Ulrich, D. (1997). *Human resource champions: The next agenda for adding value and delivering results.* Boston (Mass): Harvard Business School.

Valle, R., Martin, F., & Romero, P. M. (2001). Trends and emerging values in human resource management: The Spanish scene. *International Journal of Manpower, 22*(3), 244.

Van Iterson, A., & Olie, R. L. (1992). European business systems: The Dutch case. In: R. Whitley (Ed.), *European business systems. Firms and markets in their national contexts.* London: Sage.

Wachter, H., & Stengelhofen, T. (1992). Human resource management in a unified Germany. *Employee Relations, 14*(4), 21.

Whitley, R. D. (1992). Societies, firms and markets: The social structuring of business systems. In: R. D. Whitley (Ed.), *European business systems. Firms and markets in their national contexts.* London: Sage.

Whitley, R. D. (1999). *Diverging capitalisms: The social structuring and changes of business systems.* Oxford: Oxford University Press.

Wiersma, U. J., & Van den Berg, P. T. (1999). Influences and trends in human resource practices in the Netherlands. *Employee Relations, 21*(1/2), 63.

Yoshimori, M. (1995). Whose company is it? The concept of the corporation in Japan and the West. *Long Range Planning, 28*(4), 33–44.

Zysman, J. (1983). *Government, markets and growth: Financial systems and the politics of industrial change.* Ithaca: Cornell University Press.

CHAPTER 6

Globalizing HRM: The Growing Revolution in Managing Employees Internationally

Paul Sparrow and Chris Brewster

Introduction: A Changing Context for International Human Resource Management

It is important from the outset in a chapter like this to establish some important principles. First, there are currently few organizations that would be described as being truly global. Second, the concept of globalization is itself somewhat fuzzy and needs to be studied at many levels of analysis.

Stateless organizations operating independently of national borders under global rules of economic competition are few and far between (Ferner, 1997; Ferner & Quintanilla, 1998). Multinational corporations (MNCs) continue to have assets, sales, ownership of workforces and control concentrated in home countries or regions. In an analysis of the 500 largest MNCs Rugman and Verbeke (2004a, b) found that 84% had an average of just over 80% of their sales concentrated in one of the three regional trade blocks (EU, Asia or North America). Only 11 of the 500 MNCs could be deemed to have truly penetrated markets across the globe. Few firms are considered to have developed an effective capability to locate, source and manage human resources anywhere in the world (Lewin & Volberda, 2003). There are then in practice US-, European- and Japanese-global firms, each operating in distinctive national business systems with their own patterns of corporate governance and human resource management (HRM) (Sparrow, Brewster, & Harris, 2004). The strategies that they pursue towards globalization of HRM, and the associated shifts in centralization and decentralization, are therefore bounded by this inheritance. Moreover, strategic decision making inside these firms has elements that are driven simultaneously by global, regional and national logics and these logics may not always be mutually supportive. However, there is a trend towards globalization and as a process it is clearly exerting an effect inside organizations. For example analyses by the United Nations Conference on Trade and Development (UNCTAD, 2001) at the beginning of the decade showing a clear trend towards increasing globalization (as measured by the average of the ratios of foreign to total assets, sales and employment) driven primarily by an expansion of foreign direct investment (FDI) and an enlargement of international production in the world economy. In all, 63,000 transnational corporations shaped trade patterns account for about two-thirds of all world trade. Indeed the top 100 of these corporations (just 0.2% of the total number of such corporations) account for 14% of worldwide sales, 12% of assets and 13% of employment (UNCTAD, 2004). We need to understand better how this process operates in relation to the HRM inside organizations.

This is evidently the case given the confusion over what is implied by globalization and the different levels of analysis that might be used explore its consequences. The main models and frameworks that have been used in the field concentrate on:

• the globalization of industries;
• relative levels of internalization of the firm;
• the progressive building of international capabilities within firms; and
• functional realignment taking place in response to globalization.

Globalization of industries. Global industries are ones in which a firm's competitive position in any particular country is dependent upon competition that might exist in other countries (Makhija, Kim, & Williamson, 1997). The level of international trade, intensity of international competition, worldwide product standardization and presence of international competitors in all key international markets are all high (Morrison & Roth, 1992) and firms can only achieve efficiencies through global scale, local responsiveness and world-wide learning (Bartlett & Ghoshal, 1989).

Relative levels of internationalization of the firm. Estimating the degree of internationalization of the firm is still an arbitrary process and both the choice of constructs to evidence it and the actual measures used are contentious (Sullivan, 1994; Ramaswamy, Kroeck, & Renforth, 1996; Sullivan, 1996). The most popular single measures used as a proxies of are things like: foreign subsidiaries' sales as a percentage of total sales; export sales as a percentage of total sales; foreign assets as a percentage of total assets, as an estimate of the material international character of an organization; number of foreign subsidiaries, to distinguish the degree of foreign investment and attitudinal perspectives that exist within the firm such as a tally of the cumulative duration of top managers' international assignments as summarized in company-reported career histories or the dispersion of subsidiaries across cultural groupings and zones in the world.

Progressive building of international capabilities within firms. The concept of organizational capability focuses on the ability of a firm's internal processes, systems and management practices to meet customer needs and to direct both the skills and efforts of employees towards achieving the (in this context global) goals of the organization (Prahalad & Doz, 1987). The focus on capabilities does not emphasize the importance of the organization's position in relation to its industry, but rather the way in which it manages the resources that enable it to develop core competences and distinctive capabilities (Stonehouse, Hamill, Campbell, & Purdie, 2000). Capabilities reflect "… a firm's capacity to deploy resources, usually in combination, applying organizational processes to effect a desired end" (De Saá-Pérez & García-Falcón, 2002, p. 124). International expansion is only possible when firms can transfer their distinctive knowledge-assets abroad into new international markets (Dunning, 1993; Caves, 1996). Models of international organizational design have been developed to suggest a sequence of evolutionary stages through which firms have to evolve — variously called international, multinational, global and transnational/network/heterarchy (Bartlett & Ghoshal, 1989). Organization structures have to respond to a series of strains faced by the process of globalization (e.g. growth, increased geographical spread and the need for improved control and co-ordination across business units) and organizations have to build capability in each stage sequentially in order to maintain integrated standards for some business lines but remain locally responsive in others (Hamel & Prahalad, 1985; Yip, 1992; Ashkenas, Ulrich, Jick, & Kerr, 1995).

Functional realignment within globalizing organizations. At this level of analysis it is argued that globalization within organizations is driven by what happens within business functions as they seek to co-ordinate (develop linkages between geographically dispersed units of a function) and control (regulate functional activities to align them with the expectations set in targets) their activities across borders (Kim, Park, & Prescott, 2003). Malbright (1995, p. 119) argued that true "…Globalization occurs at the level of the function, rather than the firm". We therefore need to understand how organizations enhance the ability of specific functions to perform globally.

Picking up this latter issue — understanding how organizations in practice attempt to globalize key functions inside the firm — it is now possible to discern some clear developments that have taken place. Findings from our recent study — henceforth called the Chartered Institute of Personnel and Development (CIPD) Globalization Project (see Sparrow et al., 2004; Brewster, Sparrow, & Harris, 2005) — will be drawn upon throughout this chapter to outline the new focus in global HRM. This study examined the globalization process at the level of functions within organizations and applied a dynamic capability perspective as applied to the field of international human resource management (IHRM) and aimed to understand the ways in which the human resource (HR) function itself is responding and contributing to the process of globalization. It reported on a number of issues facing MNCs: the need to build a global presence, centralization or decentralization of decision making, creating centres of excellence on a global basis, facilitating knowledge transfer, designing core business processes, outsourcing business processes, e-enabling management, forging strategic partnerships, engaging in industry wide convergence of practice, rationalizing costs and maximizing shareholder value. Empirical analysis of these pressures revealed five factors driving the organizational strategy of globalizing firms, each associated with different combinations of the above issues (Brewster et al., 2005):

- Efficiency
- Information exchange/organizational learning
- Global provision
- Core business process convergence
- Localization

The need for efficiency comprised two main elements — high outsourcing of business processes and high levels of centralization. In turn this strategy is associated with three key delivery mechanisms for global HRM: a focus on shared service structures, the e-enablement of many HR processes on a regional or global scale, and the pursuit of centres of excellence. These three elements are highly interconnected — e-enablement allows many HR processes to be automated and devolved to line managers, which in turn suggests the development of centralized service centres to handle informational and transactional needs, which then leads to a separation out of specialized, expert and value-added HR services.

Information exchange and organizational learning as a driver of organizational strategy follows on from the changes being wrought in the interests of efficiency. The strategy comprises two key elements — knowledge transfer/knowledge management and forging strategic partnerships. Knowledge management is linked to the objective of improving organizational capability. So far, largely perhaps because much of this debate has been driven by the technical specialists, the possibilities of using global HRM as a process which adds to and helps exploit the knowledge stock of the organization (particularly the more powerful intrinsic knowledge stock) have not been fully developed. This situation is changing. The need to capture and share explicit knowledge is putting pressure on company intranets and on the information technology infrastructure. For the HR function, however, the challenge is also to make sense of the intrinsic knowledge that is held in people's heads, yet is often the key to competitive advantage. Hence, HR departments are taking on responsibility for the conscious development of operating networks, both as practitioners within the HR community and as facilitators elsewhere in the organization. Forging strategic partnerships is a second important factor related to the issue of information exchange and organizational learning, where the objective is to learn from the new partnerships arrangements and internalize the learned capabilities rapidly.

The need to have a much wider global presence has become important for many organizations. Their markets have become more international and they have to set up operations closer to these key markets, and their customers expect them to provide the same level of capability whatever the geography they operate in. This global provision comprises two key elements — rapidly building a global presence through joint ventures, acquisitions and organic growth, and e-enabling management in order to reduce the cost of such expansion.

Global HRM is also being pursued inside organizations as a response to the creation of core business processes and the movement away from country-based operations towards business-line-driven organizations. It would be wrong to assume that convergence around core business processes is automatically associated with centralization of management — it can also be associated with decentralization and devolvement of decision making closer to customer bases. Moreover, the HR function does more than just respond to this phenomenon and can play a key part in managing the re-orientation of the organization's strategy, structures and processes entailed by this change.

Finally, for a significant minority of organizations, localization of management is an important drive. This tends to be important where key markets are in countries where there is now a high level of skill in local labour markets and cost pressures dictate more efficient use of resources, where government or institutional pressures are forcing higher levels of local activity, and where organizations operate through other local partners.

It is interesting to note that across the above five organizational driver strategic recipes, Brewster et al. (2005) found that efficiency, core business process convergence and global provision were the dominant pressures. However, this global reconfiguration of activity has extensive ramifications for the field of IHRM and will also have a significant effect on the roles and career paths of HR professionals. A move to shared service provision often entails the creation of a three-tier system of expertise, which has clear implications in terms of the level of HR expertise (and the level of internationalization of knowledge and experience) sought at point of selection and the amount of training given by the organization, including the professional qualification standards of institutions such as strategic human resource management (SHRM) and CIPD.

Historically much IHRM was the preserve of those professionals who dealt with managers who had to work on overseas postings. Attention was therefore given, for example, to the need to identify the particular skills and competencies that were important to be an effective manager in this context. However, as the years have passed the focus of attention has shifted to the need not just to have separate HR for a dedicated group of managers, but to internationalize all of the fundamental HR processes of an organization. HR is being applied to an ever more diverse and global workforce and the key challenge is to be able to ensure that HR professionals, who might work in a specific domestic setting, nonetheless operate HR processes that are robust enough to operate across cultures and diverse labour markets. HR professionals need to have a much broader international education. Sparrow et al. (2004) surveyed the role and knowledge base needed by UK and Irish HR professionals and found that more than 40% of professionals now needed to have international insights in areas such as communication processes, recruitment and selection and pay and benefits.

Building on the Past: A Review of the Previous International HRM Literature

So, to what extent does the existing IHRM literature reflect and explain these developments on the ground and facilitate a more global understanding of HR processes? It would be fair to say — though we know this is a contentious statement — that the IHRM literature in the main has not really caught up with work in the broader field of international management (which does incorporate many of the above issues). However, the early IHRM literature has expanded from a narrow focus on the practical issues raised by moving people around the world to a more ambitious attempt to understand the strategic deployment of HR policies and practices within international organizations. Thus the field has developed from a focus on the management of expatriates (see, for example, early work by Ivancevich, 1969; Tung, 1981; Torbiorn, 1982; Mendenhall & Oddou, 1985) into a growing literature on international business strategy (again with early work by Porter, 1986; Prahalad & Doz, 1987; Bartlett & Ghoshal, 1989), examining issues of managing people in international organizations. This literature has been based in the main on the differences between countries in the way that people are and can be managed.

The stream of literature exploring comparative HRM (Pieper, 1990; Sparrow & Hiltrop, 1994; Brewster, Tregaskis, Hegewisch, & Mayne, 1996; Brewster, Mayrhofer, & Morley, 2004) has noted two general explanators of these differences: cross-cultural and institutional factors. Essentially this literature has tried to ask whether differences in HRM are "sustained because people find it repulsive, unethical or unappealing to do otherwise … [or] … because a wider formal system of laws, agreements, standards and codes exist" (Sorge, 2004)?

Boyacigiller et al. (2004) has delineated three streams of research from a cultural perspective, each making its own assumptions: cross-national comparisons of workplace values; studies of inter-cultural interactions and more recently the ways in which firms can carry multiple cultures. The first of these has proved to be dominant in the literature with the last now becoming a more accepted view (Sparrow, 2006). Cross-national comparisons of workplace values (see, for example, Hofstede, 1980, 1991, 2001; Laurent, 1983, 1986; Trompenaars, 1993; House, Hanges, Javidan, Dorfman, & Gupta, 2004) assume that variations in practices will be in line with different cultural contexts. Most of these studies conflate "national culture" and nation state boundaries and cultures may vary within national boundaries or cut across them. Within this tradition, a range of researchers have found geographically based, usually national, differences in deep-seated values about what is good or bad, honest or dishonest, fair or unfair and so forth. These perceptions of the world inevitably affect the way people in a country, especially for us here, perhaps, managers and employees, view the world. The result is to "cast serious doubt on the universality of management and organizational knowledge and praxis" (Laurent, 1983, p. 95). Schwartz (1992, 1994) points to the inter-relation between cultural- and individual-level values and offer a model of the interaction between personality and cultural factors that was tested in an empirical study including 88 samples in 40 countries.

The "culturalist" school is a broad one but what these approaches have in common is that they treat culture as a given; while it may be possible for a society to enhance its "social capital", it is not possible to develop social trust deliberately and systematically, or radically depart from established rules and norms. Culture is seen as a specific component of reality, shared by individuals as a means of conferring meaning, and adding sense to social interactions. While its composition may be relatively fluid and subjective, it provides a persistent boundary, horizon or "segment" to the life-world of individuals and clusters thereof (Brewster, 2005). These are, therefore, rather static explanations of the way the world is (however, see Erez & Gati, 2004 and Sackmann & Phillips, 2004 for more dynamic conceptualizations of culture).

By contrast, the institutional perspective sees the institutions of a nation state (usually) as being the environmental structures that keep them distinctive (DiMaggio & Powell, 1983). There is a version of this theory (the "North-American phenomenological neo-institutionalism", Djelic & Bensedrine, 2001) that argues that institutions reflect power relationships. Therefore, economic and technological pressures will ensure that similar structures and practices are adopted throughout the world (such as the de-regulation "strings" typically tied to International Monetary Fund (IMF) loans to underdeveloped countries); normative pressures (from professional bodies, international associations and the growing internationalization of executive education) and cognitive isomorphism (as international organizations attempt to spread their policies and cultures around the world). It has been argued that one effect of this global institutional isomorphism is that the role of nation states becomes less significant.

The alternative institutional approach (DiMaggio & Powell, 1983; Meyer & Rowan, 1983; Hollingsworth & Boyer, 1997) emphasises the distinctiveness of the social arrangements in a nation and examines some of the institutions likely to shape the social construction of an organization. Among the institutions examined are the general and vocational education system and the industrial relations system. The institutional approach postulates that the structure of organizations in a country reflects a 'societal effect' reflected in the country's particular institutional arrangements. National differences in ownership, structures, educational systems and laws all have a significant effect on the architecture and the practices of employing organizations. This literature has been synthesized in the work of such authors as Hall and Soskice (2000) who draw a sharp distinction between "co-ordinated market economies" of say Germany and Sweden and "liberal market" (Anglo-American) ones. Whitley (1999) proposes a more nuanced version, with six different possible varieties of capitalism (fragmented, co-ordinated industrial district, compartmentalized, state organized, collaborative and highly co-ordinated — according to HRM a distinctive role in creating the difference between these systems).

Both the cultural and institutional perspectives, of course, recognize the relevance of the other perspective. While many of the "cultural" writers see institutions as being key artefacts of culture reflecting deep underlying variations in values that they see between societies, many "institutional" writers include culture as one of the institutional elements explaining differences (DiMaggio & Powell, 1983; Scott, 1995). Giddens (1986) put forward the concept of structuration theory: individual behaviour and social structures are reciprocally constituted. Thus, institutions cannot survive without legitimacy, but individuals' perspectives are partially created and sustained by the institutional context. Arguably, the two explanations simply explore the same factors from different points of view.

So, how has the literature on IHRM attempted to understand the ways in which international companies will manage their workforces across these nationally different contexts? Much of the early work in the field was essentially concerned with information gathering. The limited early theoretical work in IHRM focused on the role of MNCs; arguing that finding and nurturing the people able to implement international strategy is critical for such firms. IHRM was considered to have the same main dimensions as HRM in a national context but to operate on a larger scale, with more complex strategic considerations, more complex co-ordination and control demands and some additional HR functions. Additional HR functions were considered necessary to accommodate the need for greater operating unit diversity, more external stakeholder influence, higher levels of risk exposure, and more personal insight into employee's lives and family situation (Dowling, Welch, & Schuler, 1999). The research focused on understanding those HR functions that changed when the firm went international. The research also began to identify important contingencies that influenced how certain HR functions were internationalized (countries, the size and life cycle stage of the firm, types of employee, etc.).

Among recent trends, the IHRM has explored the link between HR policies and practices and organizational strategy, resulting in a literature on strategic IHRM — termed SIHRM (see, for example, Schuler, Dowling, & De Cieri, 1993). The ways in which MNCs organize their operations globally has been the subject of extensive research by international management scholars. Early work (see, for example Prahalad & Doz, 1987; Bartlett & Ghoshal, 1989; Porter, 1990) has been developed more recently by examinations of the role of HRM within MNCs pursuing a global/transnational SIHRM orientation (see, for example, DeCieri & Dowling, 1997; Egelhoff, 1999; DeCieri, Cox, & Fenwick, 2001 and Schuler, Budwhar, & Florkowski, 2002).

One recurring theme in this literature has been the link between strategy-structure configuration in MNCs and the competing demands for global integration (see, for example, Levitt, 1983; Hamel & Prahalad, 1985; Bartlett & Ghoshal, 1989; Adler & Ghader, 1990; Hu, 1992; Sera, 1992; Yip, 1992; Ashkenas et al., 1995; Birkinshaw & Morrison, 1995; Evans, Pucik, & Barsoux, 2002). This has been opposed to the need for local responsiveness (see for example, Whitley, 1992; Rosenzweig & Nohria, 1994; Sparrow & Hiltrop, 1994).

Clearly, an element of both is required in most organizations and international organizations have to be good at both ends of this spectrum simultaneously (Evans et al., 2002). However, it is likely that where global integration and co-ordination is important, subsidiaries need to be globally integrated with other parts of the organization or/and strategically co-ordinated by the parent. In such circumstances, HRM too will have to be more integrated In contrast, where local responsiveness is important, subsidiaries will have far greater autonomy and there is less need for integration.

There have also been attempts to offer an integrative framework for the study and understanding of SIHRM that include exogenous and endogenous factors (Schuler et al., 1993). Exogenous factors would include industry characteristics and technology, the nature of competitors and the extent of change; and country/regional characteristics such as political, economic and socio-cultural conditions and legal requirements Endogenous factors cover such features as the structure of international operations, the international orientation of the organization's headquarters, the competitive strategy being used, and the MNC's experience in managing international operations. Others (Taylor, Beechler, & Napier, 1996) have applied the resource-based theory of the firm to SIHRM: identifying three international HRM orientations — the adaptive, exportive and integrative — to corporate, affiliate and employee group level HR issues, functions, policies and practices.

These models demonstrate the complexity of HR decisions in the international sphere and the broad scope of its remit. In this SIHRM perspective, HR practitioners in international organizations are seen to be engaging in every aspect of international business strategy and adopting HR policies and practices aimed at the most effective use of the HR in the firm. Even these integrative models, however, do not fully answer some of the criticisms that have been levelled against the fields of IHRM and SIHRM. These criticisms run broadly as follows.

The issue of cultural relativity has tempted researchers to focus on the 'hard' or 'core' HR functional processes (Easterby-Smith, Malina, & Yuan, 1995). Researchers from the "universalist" tradition (Brewster, 1999) invoke idealized HRM systems, such as the western view of HRM, which emphases what has become known as high performance work systems (HPWS), as a basis of comparison. The field tends to ignore the subtle ways in which cultural and institutional differences influence the experienced reality of HRM (Earley & Singh, 2000).

The wider convergence–divergence debate (see Brewster, 2005) tends to assume that the HRM system as a whole has to converge or remain divergent, rather than considering whether some parts of the overall HR system might be converging, in some regions or geographies, while other parts might be diverging. Moreover, even within a single HR function there might be convergence at one level but divergence at another. An HR function operates at multiple levels that Schuler (1992) called the 5Ps: philosophy, policy, programme, practice and process.

Sparrow and Hiltrop (1997) argued therefore that any analysis of IHRM must consider three competing dynamics:

- *The range of factors that engender distinctive national and local solutions to HRM issues.* This requires insight into the institutional influences on the employment relationship, the nature of national business systems, modernization processes within these national business systems, the structure and operation of labour markets, differences in the historical role and competence of the HRM function, the way such factors are reflected in the cognitive mindsets of HR professionals from specific countries, and the role of cultural value orientations and their subsequent impact on behavioural processes within employees.

- *The strategic pressures that make these national models more receptive to change and development.* This requires insight into the ways in which the adoption of global line of business structures can override the role of country level HR managers, the ways in which new forms of work organization create convergent HR needs, the impact that FDI has on organizations and its associated effects on local labour markets; the role that technology has (such as shared service structures, or e-enabled HR) in reshaping national HRM systems, and the impact that best practice benchmarking and optimization has on HRM system change.

- *The firm-level processes through which such change and development in actual HRM practice will be delivered.* These are important for two reasons. First, they provide insight into the complex patterns of continuity and change that exist at this level. Second, they help reveal how firms can move beyond the constraints of the national business system within which they operate. Analysis at this level requires insight into the role of political opportunism and the ways in which various potential integration mechanisms in the organization can be mobilized to support the introduction of new policies and practices, the nature of mergers and acquisitions and the impact that they have on the conduct of HRM, the nature of knowledge transfer and the role that global expertise networks and forum can have in facilitating this, and the role of new cadres of like-minded internationalists within the organization and the spread of such internationalism through alternative forms of international working.

The Growing Revolution: A New Focus

To summarize, then, the literature to date has made an extraordinary contribution to our understanding but, to draw on the title of this volume, we can see the beginnings of a revolution in the research and practice of HRM in the international context. In particular, we see a new focus on three areas:

- IHRM is now more explicitly focused on all the human resources of the organization, not just on the highly paid, internationally mobile, ones. In this respect IHRM is moving towards the critical literature informing the debates about what has come to be known as the new international division of labour (Henderson, 1986, 1997; Standing, 1997; DiMartino, 2000). How are companies to ensure a common philosophy and coherent practice across disparate countries and workforces? What capabilities enable this to happen? This presents major challenges for research and theory.

- More practically, IHRM, at the level of both theory and practice, is beginning to adjust to the opportunities and challenges presented by new technologies of e-enabled HRM and a new focus on the benefits of knowledge transfer.

- Linked to these developments, the pressure to ensure the affordability of staff (and the affordability of the function) have moved centre-stage.

In the introduction we outlined the organizational capability perspective on globalization. Tallman and Fladmoe-Lindquist (2002) noted that current models of MNCs can be
seen as having a *"capability-recognizing"* perspective. The models demonstrate that firms
must possess some unique knowledge-based resources. These resources are typically
treated as being home country based or somehow belonging to the corporate function and
top team. They argued however that we now need a *"capability-driven"* perspective: an
understandable theory of MNC strategy based on how they attempt to build, protect and
exploit a set of unique capabilities and resources. This is also known as the *"dynamic capability"* perspective. In order to understand how organizations develop, manage, and deploy
capabilities to support their business strategy (Montealegre, 2002) we generally have to
conduct longitudinal studies. Only a handful of strategists have considered specifically
how MNCs develop organizational capability (see, for example. Collis, 1991; Fladmoe-
Lindquist & Tallman, 1994; Hedlund & Ridderstråe, 1997; Kogut, 1997). Grasping which
overall business- and corporate-level capabilities are relevant to the particular international
strategy of their organization remains an important task for international HR managers.

Given the complex strategic execution issues facing global HRM functions, attention
now needs to be given to: the rationale and thought process behind their interventions and
the criteria for success; the political, process and technical skills that have to be brought to
bear to manage these interventions; contrasting stakeholder expectations of the intervention role; and the link back to organizational strategy and effectiveness. When this is done,
a clear picture of the new focus of global HRM functions emerges. Figure 1 outlines the
model of factors shaping the conduct of global HRM. Empirical support for this has been
reported by Brewster et al. (2005). In this chapter we link these themes back to the literature and identify the key messages that are emerging about global HRM.

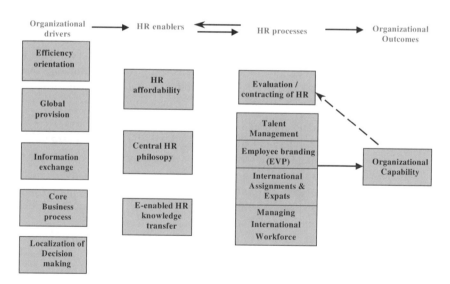

Figure 1: Factors driving Global HRM. *Source*: Brewster et al. (2005).

Building Organizational Capability through Global HRM

Organizational capability may be established as a general consequence of a long and slow internationalization process within an organization or as part of a deliberate part of organization design where HQ managers decide to grant autonomy to units that have also been given a specific strategic mandate. Capability is often created out of the international networking that surrounds building specific new co-ordination activities on a global scale inside globalizing organizations, such as research and development or production centres, logistic networks or indeed the development of new HR structures, networks, systems and processes. The conduct of these activities in global context generally requires the mobilization of several streams of activity. For example, in one of the case studies examined by the CIPD Globalization Project, Diageo, a global consumer organization, it entailed the alignment of strategic planning, investment decisions, management development activity and executive rewards to the single governing objective of building global brands. The development of strong management teams with world-class brand management and international management skills was an important way in which this capability was to be realized.

When organizations build capabilities, then, these tend to be generated internally. However, they may also be shared or created across organizational boundaries, between an organization and one or more of its suppliers, distributors or customers (Stonehouse et al., 2000). From a resource-based view of strategy, there are often advantages for MNCs of more collaboration between themselves and other organizations, especially if they have mutually complementary competences (Sanchez & Heene, 1997). This observation applies to several types of global organization, not just the MNCs. For example, the CIPD Globalization Project also studied non-governmental organizations. In the late 1990s the charity ActionAid undertook a strategic review of its work, aware that the external environment was changing rapidly and that the organization was in need of a new direction. The outcome of the exercise was a new strategy document, *Fighting poverty together*, which set out ActionAid's understanding of the causes of poverty and strategic priorities for action for 1999–2005. The strategy had four main goals, one of which involved working in partnership with others to achieve greater impact. ActionAid worked with over 2000 organizations that have a deep knowledge of local conditions, customs and politics in poor communities, from local support groups for HIV-positive people in Africa to national workers' movements in Latin America. Local people and partners in 24 countries helped review the effectiveness of the work, enabling ActionAid to hold itself accountable to them and to their donors. These alliances helped it to work more effectively with poor people as well as strengthening the global anti-poverty movement.

Knowledge Transfer

We noted the need for information exchange and organizational learning earlier in the chapter. Strategists point out that organization-level skills can be developed through a number of channels such as international diversification into multiple markets, collaborating with organizations that have mutually complementary competences, emphasizing strategic leadership roles for national subsidiaries and gaining access to foreign-based clusters of excellence (Tallman & Fladmoe-Linquist, 2002). The last two of these approaches have become increasingly important. MNCs have relied on specialized and often network-based structures to coordinate their activities for many years, but given their increasingly dispersed activities, the response of the corporate headquarters in recent years has been to adjust its level of co-ordination and control to reflect the role of the subsidiary and the strategic importance of the mandate that it has. As MNCs change their organization design in response to the need to build more international capability, then as part of their natural development they often establish centres of excellence (Ohmae, 1990, 1996). The role of centres of excellence (COEs) has been considered in the context of national or regional clusters of skills and capability — such as the location of IS work in India or in Ireland — but also increasingly in the context of small teams or units within subsidiaries that take a lead COE role in one area, with other units taking the lead in different areas of capability (Holm & Pedersen, 2000). A COE is then best considered as an organizational unit that embodies a set of organizational capabilities. The capabilities inherent in a COE must be explicitly recognized as an important source of value creation (Frost, Birkinshaw, & Prescott, 2000).

A number of general management principles have been discussed in the literature. Leadership of these centres may be vested in a physical location or vested within the dynamics that exist within emergent networks and teams in different geographies. Ideally COEs should only be loosely tied into the organization and co-ordinated with other units if they are to help search for new knowledge and augment the capability of the MNC (Hansen, 1999). Control may be categorized as being centralized and personal, formal and bureaucratic, based on output, or exerted through socialization and networks (Harzing, 1999).

Various labels other than that of COE are now used to describe the organizational forms that are being used to facilitate a process of progressive global knowledge transfer: centres of competence, centres of expertise or communities of practice (COPs). Common to all these forms is that in order to endure they must (Sparrow, 2005):

- take on a strategic role in the global organization that reaches beyond local undertakings (these strategic remits may include the intention to leverage or disseminate the capabilities within the centre to other parts of the firm),
- have to be tightly integrated with their surrounding technical or professional communities,
- be able to maintain one or several critical fields of knowledge that have a long-term impact on the development of activity in the other subsidiaries and units of the MNC and
- must have both high competence *and* high use of this competence throughout surrounding units.

Helping the organization understand the role, design, competence and leadership needs of its own COEs is a major challenge and opportunity for global HR functions. Currently, our understanding of the managerial issues involved is rudimentary:

> … a growing body of anecdotal evidence suggests that the COE phenomenon is increasing amongst the world's major MNCs, at the same time that this evidence also suggests that many firms are struggling with the managerial issues involved (Frost et al., 2000, p. 1016).

The role of the global HR function initially has been reactive — coping with the need to relocate staff into new countries, considering the special terms and management conditions that should surround such units, and eventually applying the concept of COEs to its own structures (Sparrow et al., 2004). The global HR function has to help devise roles and performance management systems that clarify the mandate and ensure that the design enables the unit and its key actors to act as a:

* focal point for knowledge development that serve people with related skills or disciplines,
* conduit for the dissemination of knowledge within the firm and
* problem-solving unit that provides advice and fosters new competences within the firm.

An important research priority therefore is to now understand what is necessary to build globally distributed COEs into viable operations (Sparrow, 2005). IHRM researchers now need to consider more pertinent questions. What activities, processes and capabilities might constitute a COE and how should such units be mandated (i.e. what has to happen in terms of capability building investments are needed, decision-making autonomy, requisite levels of connectivity to other sources of competence inside the organization, leadership and processes of knowledge management)? What are the indicators of success under what contingencies? To what extent do the institutional factors alluded to earlier in the chapter preclude or support long term survival and contribution of COEs?

In addition to the development of COEs, there are a series of other integration mechanisms that are necessary to assist in the acquisition, capture and diffusion of knowledge in international organizations. Sparrow (2005) has outlined five main forms of global knowledge management, or integration mechanisms that are currently dominating organizational action, namely:

* organizational design and the specific issue of COEs,
* managing systems and technology-driven approaches to global knowledge management systems,
* capitalizing on expatriate advice networks,
* co-ordinating international management teams and
* developing COPs or global expertise networks.

HR Affordability

A critically important enabling force behind most global HR functions' recent restructuring efforts has been the need to deliver global business strategies in the most cost efficient manner possible. Both people and activities are now examined to identify their added value and organizations are devoting much attention to ensuring that people are operating where they can be most cost-effective and that central overheads are as low as possible. The increased interest in metrics to demonstrate this reflects the need to be able to deliver proven cost reductions and ensure HR affordability. The HR enabling recipes examined by Brewster et al. (2005) showed there were high pressures on HR affordability for 53% of organizations — only 15% seemed to be immune to these pressures. Importantly, pressure on HR affordability was *not* automatically associated with strong e-enablement — the cluster of organizations that were strongly e-enabling actually had no pressures on HR affordability placed upon them. Instead, the factor of HR affordability consisted of two elements: maximizing shareholder value and rationalization of costs. In some cases maximizing shareholder value is an implicit business objective while in others it is more plainly stated.

Behind most global HR functions' recent restructuring efforts, then, has been the need to deliver global business strategies in the most cost efficient manner possible. This is not to be confused with "cheapest possible" — although to many HR practitioners it sometimes feels that way — because many of the organizations are making substantial investments in getting this global restructuring right. Using the terminology adopted by Ulrich (1997), they are assessing their activities to cut out duplication and waste, to ensure added value and to move away from purely transactional and informational work, which can often be delivered directly by new technology. At an international level this is reflected in a move towards those activities that deal with capability and business development. There is an increased interest in an organization's ability to measure the output of the HR function, reflecting the need to be able to deliver and prove cost reductions to ensure HR affordability.

Conclusion: Understanding the New Role of Global HR Professionals

The CIPD Globalization project, detailed throughout much of this chapter, has examined new developments in the IHRM field. However, there remains a significant gap in our understanding about the way HRM is managed in international organizations. The original research examined the globalization process in Anglo Saxon organizations and broader and more generalizable insight is now needed. Many of the initiatives explored such as e-enabled HRM were still in their infancy and more considered learning can now be found inside organizations. Such geographical broadening aside, we believe that there are four underlying research issues that need to be addressed, concerning:

- Evolving global HRM structures and strategies
- The role of line managers in global HRM
- E-enabled HRM
- Networking, social capital and knowledge transfer

If we examine the first research need, which is to understand evolving global HRM structures and processes, it would be fair to say that the CIPD Globalization Project demonstrated that largely as a result of technology "a new line in the sand" was being drawn between standardized and localized HR practices. Indeed, there was considerable debate within organizations about the difference between standardized and optimized HR processes. In *IHRM* there is a continual tension between the requirement to standardize and the requirement to be sensitive to local circumstances. It is widely accepted that within international business, HRM is the most likely activity to be localized (Rosenzweig & Nohria, 1994). This is one area where, as Evans and his colleagues (Evans & Lorange, 1989; Evans & Doz, 1992; Evans & Genadry, 1999; Evans et al., 2002) have put it, organizations are faced with a "duality": they have to be good both at standardizing and at respecting the local environment. Even this may understate the complexity that they face.

Organizations often split HR responsibilities in these areas between a global HR department, country management and business stream leaders. The CIPD Globalization Project identified a trend towards the regionalization of businesses and HRM, but we believe that there is yet another layer of complexity in the mix. Definitions of the geographical nature of regions, their scope, their resources and their capabilities vary from organization to organization. An important research contribution still to be made is to explain *how* organizations manage this complexity. The CIPD Globalization Project helped establish the direction that global HR functions had to follow. What is needed now is a study that signposts which particular route organizations should follow.

Global organizations today are presented with multiple choices as how to structure and organize their HR organizations. There is a need for research to provide guidance as to the best and most appropriate solutions. The answer to such questions is unlikely to be a case of identifying simple contingencies, but will rather need us to understand what pushes organizations in one direction or pulls them in another and with what practical implications? We need to help global HR functions position themselves inside the rest of the organization so that they can best achieve the needs of their (many and diverse) stakeholders. The requirement then is to understand and advise on the positioning of global HR functions generates a series of operational, but challenging, questions. At a pragmatic level we need to help advise on:

- Who should have the responsibility for the HR policies and the practice?
- How should such responsibility be integrated with the organizational strategy at a global and local level?
- What conflicts of interest can be expected between these areas and how can they be resolved?
- How should HR specialists manage their multi-line reporting relationships and what is really meant by the business partner role in global context?
- What is the role of the regional co-ordination processes and structures in the way people are managed within global organizations?

One of puzzles however still facing HR functions is how to achieve the HR business partner role. Despite there being clear specifications about the nature of this role, " … the challenge lies in creating the contexts and practices through which the strategic partner role can be realized" (Smethurst, 2005, p. 25). In his original conception, Ulrich (1997) outlined four HR roles of employee champion (which was later split into two roles of employee advocate and human capital developer), administrative expert (later re-termed functional expert), strategic partner and change agent (later combined into a broadened strategic partner role and accompanied by a new leader role). In all of these roles HR acted as a business partner but the practical realization of the job title "business partner" became that of "strategic partner" or "strategic business partner". Exactly what was involved in this role was unclear. The boundaries between the attention given simply to business issues (i.e. working with line management but with an HR background, and focusing therefore on strategic execution) as opposed to higher level strategy formulation advice has once more become vague. The strategic business partner role has become opportunistic in its delivery. While the complexities and strategic centrality of the international business partner role often affords the necessary context to create understanding, demonstrate value and relevance and acquire support from line managers, it also risks removing strategic influence of HR previously exerted by a central board-level role and subsuming it in a decentralized and more anonymous line relationship, dependent on the idiosyncratic skills and unplanned opportunities negotiated by HR practitioners.

The *role and responsibility of the line manager* has also been much debated over the years (Guest, 1987; Schuler, 1990; Blyton & Turnbull, 1992; Harris, Brewster, & Sparrow, 2003). Moreover, there is now considerable evidence that this role varies in a significant and consistent manner across countries (Brewster & Larsen, 1992; Brewster & Soderstrom, 1994; Paauwe, 1995; Brewster & Mayne, 1995; Brewster, Larsen, & Mayrhofer, 1997; Gennard & Kelly, 1997; Brewster & Larsen, 2000; Larsen & Brewster, 2003). The opportunities and the difficulties this creates for organizations are obviously magnified across international boundaries. There are many unresolved questions about the distinctions about HR work is conducted within the "line management" category: responsibilities at the different levels will vary considerably; there may well be HQ/subsidiary differences. Clearly there is an opportunity now for research to address a number of important questions:

- Who has the responsibility, authority and accountability to set HR policies, and at what level?
- Who is responsible for carrying out the policies through into practice?
- How are we to understand the responsibilities of the different levels of line management that may be involved in these processes?

Sparrow et al. (2004) found that e-enabled HRM is a significant and developing trend in international organizations. It is already evident that there will undoubtedly be a considerable impact on the role and activities of global HR departments, centrally and locally. This will likely affect the credibility and authority of such departments, in turn having significant implications for the roles and activities of line managers. This comment shows of course that the four research needs that we discuss here are highly interrelated, hence our view that they need to be addressed in a coherent and integrated manner. There will also be extensive resourcing implications for global HR functions given that e-enablement is often associated with shared service structures and adjustments in terms of global outsourcing or in-sourcing of HR activity. Indeed, subsequent to the original research by Sparrow et al. (2004) developments in one of the case studies, BOC, draws attention to three areas in which significant progress in globalizing HR service delivery can be made: technology; process streamlining and sourcing. Developing a global HR and technology strategy and implementation plan covers everything from the information management of data, to global appraisal systems, to compensation and benefits management, to a knowledge base with a single global Internet feel and look, and to a knowledge management system. However, effective technology-based solutions are to a large extent dependent on process streamlining. Global HR functions aim to have, for example, the same resourcing and recruiting process in Europe as in the South Pacific unless there are extremely good reasons for there being a difference. So, for example, if one area has the best approach and technology for a graduate training programme, they should be able to carry out the global management of graduates. In the same way, if for example, most of the expatriate managers work in Asia, it may be cheaper and easier to administer them from Asia. With a technology base, time zones are becoming less important. The final element of a global agenda is sourcing and the sourcing strategy for HR services. This involves making decisions about the possible centralization or outsourcing of some areas of activity.

However, Sparrow et al. (2004) found that no organization had managed to develop a fully effective way of exploiting these possibilities. Indeed, global organizations are only at the early stages of realizing the benefits of this change and are therefore just coming to terms with the implications of the use of information technology in global HRM. Most organizations are struggling to understand what possibilities the new technology gives them. We therefore now need research to address the following questions:

- What is the extent of usage of e-enabled HRM?
- What are the implications of technical developments and process streamlining for the design and conduct of international activity?
- What are the specific challenges of operating shared services on a regional or a global basis?
- What are the implications for the role of HR departments and line managers?

The fourth and final research need results from the growth of *networking* as a way of managing the extensive demands of HRM in international organizations. This too was identified by the CIPD Globalization Project. It is clear that network and project-based structures have had a significant impact on the conduct and quality of international HR interventions and on the career trajectories of HR professionals. However, there is little clarity about the extent to which these networks can be local as well as global; external as well as internal. The development of (both real and/or virtual) shared service centres and COEs provides global organizations with two distinct models of how these networks might work. From a knowledge management perspective, there are important questions to be resolved as to the location and input of resources necessary for HR COEs (Sparrow, 2005). Similarly, the ways in which network- and project-based activity can best be used to build social capital within the HR function needs to be investigated (Sparrow & Braun, 2005).

Harvey and Novicevic (2004) have observed that global leaders must possess a complex amalgamation of technical, functional, cultural, social and political competencies. They made a distinction between human, social and political capital. Human capital leads to competencies. This is an area that is well researched and is quite well understood. Less well understood are the areas of social and political capital. Social capital leads to trust. It is typically reflected in the standing the manager has in the organization and his or her ability to use that standing to influence others. It helps build on and meld the many cultural norms that exist in a foreign subsidiary. Political capital by contrast leads to legitimacy. Global leaders have to accumulate political capital, which as subsets includes reputational capital (i.e. being known in the network for getting things done) and representative capital (the capacity to effectively build constituent support and acquire legitimacy by using traditional forms of power) simply in order to be in a position to remove obstacles to co-operation. An important new direction for researchers therefore is to advise firms on how they can use expatriation and inpatriation processes to develop and exploit these different forms of capital. The implication of this is that we need more research on new assessment methods that are more closely aligned to the strategic requirement of knowledge transfer and the development of an international mindset (Sparrow, 2006). Building an international mindset provides a fundamental basis for overcoming inadequate political and social capital development. Research therefore needs to address the following questions:

- How much is networking used by international organizations?
- How do they conceive of and use networks?
- Can the different types of networks be categorized and can protocols for managing the networks be established?
- How does the configuration of networks change in relation to the concentration of expertise into COEs?
- How do the various COEs in HR activity broker their expertise throughout the organization successfully?
- How does the operation of networks and COEs help address the needs of line management for effective HR management?

Clearly, these four issues are not discrete and, as indicated above, interact with each other. For example, the linkages between regionalization, e-enabled HRM and networking are likely to have a significant effect on the internal discussion about, and the practicality of, increasing line managers' responsibility for HRM. It is therefore important that research is not based on over-confident assumptions about the roles of rationality and logic in these matters. Experience shows that opportunism and emotion are frequently as powerful as, or more than, careful planning. For these reasons as researchers we need to study these issues holistically using multiple research techniques.

References

Adler, N. J., & Ghadar, F. (1990). Strategic human resource management: A global perspective. In: R. Pieper (Ed.), *Human resource management in international comparison* (pp. 235–260). Berlin: de Gruyter.

Ashkenas, R., Ulrich, D., Jick, T., & Kerr, S. (1995). *The boundaryless organization.* San Francisco, CA: Jossey-Bass.

Bartlett, C. A., & Ghoshal, S. (1989). *Managing across borders: The transnational solution.* Boston, MA: Harvard Business School Press.

Birkinshaw, J. M., & Morrison, A. J. (1995). Configurations of strategy and structure in subsidiaries of multinational corporations. *Journal of International Business Studies, 4*, 729–753.

Blyton, P., & Turnbull, P. (1992). *Reassessing human resource management.* Sage: London.

Boyacigiller, N. A., Kleinberg, J., Phillips, M. E., & Sackmann, S. (2003). Conceptualizing culture: Elucidating the streams of research in international cross-cultural management. In: B. J. Punnett & O. Shenkar (Eds), *Handbook for international management research* (2nd ed.). pp. (99–167). Michigan: University of Michigan Press.

Brewster, C. (1999). Different paradigms in strategic HRM: Questions raised by comparative research. In: P. Wright, L. Dyer, J. Boudreau & G. Milkovich (Eds), *Research in personnel and HRM* (pp. 213–238). Greenwich, CT: JAI Press, Inc.

Brewster, C. (2005). Comparing HRM policies and practices across geographical boundaries. In: I. Björkman & G. Stahl (Eds), *Handbook of research into international HRM*. London: Edward Elgar.

Brewster, C., & Larsen, H. (1992). Human resource management in Europe: Evidence from ten countries. *International Journal of Human Resource Management, 3*(3), 409–434.

Brewster, C., & Larsen, H. H. (2000). *Human resource management in Northern Europe*. Oxford: Blackwells.

Brewster, C., Larsen, H. H., & Mayrhofer, W. (1997). Integration and assignment: A paradox in human resource management. *Journal of International Management*, *3*(1), 1–23.

Brewster, C., & Mayne, L. (1994). The changing relationship between personnel and the line: The European dimension. *Report to the Institute of Personnel and Development*. Wimbledon: IPD.

Brewster, C., Mayrhofer, W., & Morley, M. (Eds). (2004). *Human resource management in Europe: Evidence of convergence?* London: Elsevier.

Brewster, C., & Soderstrom, M. (1994). Human resources and line management. In: C. Brewster & A. Hegewisch (Eds), *Policy and practice in European human resource management*. London: Routledge.

Brewster, C., Sparrow, P., & Harris, H. (2005). Towards a new model of globalizing HRM. *International Journal of Human Resource Management*, *16*(6), 953–974.

Brewster, C., Tregaskis, O., Hegewisch, A., & Mayne, L. (1996). Comparative research in human resource management: A review and an example. *International Journal of Human Resource Management*, *7*(3), 585–604.

Caves, R. E. (1996). *Multinational enterprise and economic analysis*. Cambridge: Cambridge University Press.

Collis, D. J. (1991). A resource-based analysis of global competition: The case of the bearings industry. *Strategic Management Journal*, *12*, 49–68.

DeCieri, H., Cox, J. W., & Fenwick, M. (2001). Think global, act local: From naïve comparison to critical participation in the teaching of strategic international human resource management. *TAMARA Journal of Critical Postmodern Organization Science*, *1*(1), 68–78.

DeCieri, H., & Dowling, P. J. (1997). Strategic international human resource management: An Asia-Pacific perspective. *Management International Review*, *37*(1), 21–42 (special issue).

DeMartino, G. F. (2000). *Global economy, global justice: Theoretical objections and policy alternatives to neo-liberalism*. London and New York: Routledge.

De Saá-Pérez, P., & García-Falcón, J. M. (2002). A resource-based view of human resource management and organisational capabilities development. *International Journal of Human Resource Management*, *13*(1), 123–140.

DiMaggio, P. J., & Powell, W. W. (1983). The iron cage revisited: Institutional isomorphism and collective rationality in organizational fields. *American Sociological Review*, *48*, 147–160.

Djelic, M. -L., & Bensedrine, J. (2001). Globalisation and its limits: The making of international regulation. In: G. Morgan, P. H. Kristensen & R. Whitley (Eds), *The multinational firm* (pp. 258–280). Oxford: Oxford University Press.

Dowling, P. J., Welch, D., & Schuler, R. S. (1999). *International human resource management: Managing people in a multinational context* (3rd ed.). London: South Western College Publishing.

Dunning, J. H. (1993). *Multinational enterprises and the global economy*. Reading, MA: Addison-Wesley.

Earley, P. C., & Singh. (Eds). (2000). *Innovations in International and Cross-cultural Management*. Thousand Oaks, CA: Sage.

Easterby-Smith, M., Malina, D, & Yuan, L. (1995). How culture-sensitive is HRM? A comparative analysis of practice in Chinese and UK companies. *International Journal of Human Resource Management*, *6*(1), 31–59.

Egelhoff, W. G. (1999). Organizational equilibrium and organizational change: Two different perspectives of the multinational enterprise. *Journal of International Management*, *5*, 15–33.

Erez, M., & Gati, E. (2004). A dynamic, multi-level model of culture: From the micro level of the individual to the macro level of a global culture. *Applied Psychology: An International Review*, *53*(4), 583–598.

Evans, P., & Doz, Y. (1992). Dualities: A paradigm for human resource and organisational development in complex multinationals. In: V. Pucik, N. Tichy & C. Barnett (Eds), *Globalising management: Creating and leading the competitive organization*. New York: Wiley.

Evans, P., & Genadry, N. (1999). A duality-based prospective for strategic human resource management. In: P. M. Wright, L. D. Dyer, J. W. Boudreau & G. T. Milkovich (Eds), *Strategic human resource management in the twenty-first century* (Vol. 4, Research in personnel and human resource management). Stamford, CT: JAI Press.

Evans, P., & Lorange, P. (1989). The two logics behind human resource management. In: P.A.L Evans, Y. Doz & P. Lorange (Eds), *Human resource management in international firms, change, globalization, innovation* (pp. 144–161). London: Macmillan.

Evans, P., Pucik, V., & Barsoux, J. L. (2002). *The global challenge: frameworks for international human resource management*. London: McGraw-Hill.

Ferner, A. (1997). Country of origin effects and HRM in multinational companies. *Human Resource Management Journal, 7*(1), 19–38.

Ferner, A., & Quintanilla, J. (1998). Multinational, national business systems and HRM: The enduring influence of national identity or a process of 'Anglo Saxonization'? *International Journal of Human Resource Management, 9*(4), 710–731.

Fladmoe-Lindquist, K., & Tallman, S. (1994). Resource-based strategy and competitive advantage among multinationals. In: P. Shrivastava, A. Huff & J. Dutton (Eds), *Advances in strategic management* (Vol. 10). Greenwich, CT: JAI Press.

Frost, A., Birkinshaw, J. M., & Prescott, C. E. (2002). Centers of excellence in multinational corporations. *Strategic Management Journal, 23*(11), 997–1018.

Gennard J, & Kelly, J. (1997). The unimportance of labels: The diffusion of the personnel/HRM function. *Industrial Relations Journal, 28*(1), 27–42.

Giddens, A. (1986). *The constitution of society*. Berkeley and Los Angeles: University of California Press.

Guest, D. (1987). Human resource management and industrial relations. *Journal of Management Studies, 24*(3), 503–522

Hall, P. A., & Soskice, D. (2000). *Varieties of capitalism: The institutional basis of competitive advantage*. Oxford: Oxford University Press.

Hamel, G., & Prahalad, C. K. (1985). Do you really have a global strategy? *Harvard Business Review, July/August*, 139–148.

Hansen, M. T. (1999). The search-transfer problem: The role of weak ties in sharing knowledge across organization subunits. *Administrative Science Quarterly, 44*, 82–111.

Harris, H., Brewster, C., & Sparrow, P. (2003). *International Human Resource Management*. Wimbledon: CIPD.

Harvey, M., & Novicevic, M. M. (2004). The development of political skill and political capital by global leaders through global assignments. *International Journal of Human Resource Management, 15*(7), 1173–1188.

Harzing, A. -W. K. (1999). *Managing the multinationals. An international study of control mechanisms*. Cheltenham: Edward Elgar.

Hedlund, G., & Ridderstråle, J. (1997). Toward a theory of self-renewing MNCs. In: B. Toyne & D. Nigh (Eds), *International business: An emerging vision*. Columbia, SC: University of South Carolina Press.

Henderson, J. (1986). The new international division of labour and urban development in the contemporary world-system. In: D. Drakakis-Smith (Ed.), *Urbanisation in the developing world*. London: Routledge.

Henderson, J. (1997). The changing international division of labour in the electronics industry. In: D. Campbell, A. Parisotto, A. Verma & A. Lateef (Eds), *Regionalization and labour market interdependence in East and Southeast Asia*. Geneva: MacMillan Press in association with International Institute for Labour Studies.

Hofstede, G. (1980). *Culture's consequences: International differences in work related values*. Beverly Hills, CA: Sage.

Hofstede, G. (1991). *Cultures and organizations: Software of the mind*. London: McGraw-Hill.

Hofstede, G. (2001). *Culture's consequences: Comparing values, behaviours, institutions, and organizations across nations* (2nd ed.). Thousand Oaks: Sage.

Holm, U. I. F., & Pedersen, T. (2000). *The emergence and impact of MNC centre of excellence*. London: Macmillan Press.

Hollingsworth, J. R., & Boyer, R. (Eds). (1997). *Contemporary capitalism*. Cambridge: Cambridge University Press.

House, R. J., Hanges, P. J., Javidan, M., Dorfman, P. W., & Gupta, V. (2004). *Culture, leadership and organizations: The GLOBE study of 62 societies*. New York: Sage

Hu, Y. -S. (1992). Global or stateless corporations are national firms with international operations. *California Management Review, 34*(2), 107–126.

Ivancevich, J. M. (1969). Selection of American managers for overseas assignments. *Personnel Journal, 18*(3), 189–200.

Kim, K., Park, J. -H., & Prescott, J. E. (2003). The global integration of business functions: A study of multinational businesses in integrated global industries. *Journal of International Business Studies, 34*, 327–344.

Kogut, B. (1997). The evolutionary theory of the multinational corporation: Within and across country options. In: B. Toyne & D. Nigh (Eds), *International business: An emerging vision*. Columbia, SC: University of South Carolina Press.

Larsen, H. H., & Brewster, C. (2003). Line management responsibility for HRM: What's happening in Europe? *Employee Relations, 25*(3), 228–244.

Laurent, A. (1983). The cultural diversity of western conceptions of management. *International Studies of Management and Organization, 13*(1/2), 75–96.

Laurent, A. (1986). The cross-cultural puzzle of international human resource management. *Human Resource Management, 25*(1), 91–102.

Levitt, T. (1983). The globalization of markets. *Harvard Business Review, May/June*, 92–102.

Lewin, A. Y., & Volberda, H. W. (2003). Beyond adaptation–selection research: Organizing self-renewal in co-evolving environments. *Journal of Management Studies, 40*(8), 2109–2110.

Makhija, M. V., Kim, K., & Williamson, S. D. (1997). Measuring globalization of industries using a national industry approach: Empirical evidence across five countries and over time. *Journal of International Business Studies, 28*(4), 679–710.

Malbright, T. (1995). Globalization of an ethnographic firm. *Strategic Management Journal, 16*, 119–141.

Mendenhall, M., & Oddou, G. (1985). The dimensions of expatriate acculturation. *Academy Of Management Review, 10*, 39–47.

Meyer, J. W., & Rowan, B. (1983). The structure of educational organisations. In: J. W. Meyer & W. R. Scott (Eds), *Organisational environments: Ritual and rationality* (pp. 179–197). Beverly Hills, CA: Sage.

Montealegre, R. (2002). A process model of capability development: Lessons from the electronic commerce strategy at Bolsa de Valores de Guayaquil. *Organization Science, 13*(5), 514–531.

Morrison, A. J., & Roth, K. (1992). A taxonomy of business-led strategies in global industries. *Strategic Management Journal, 13*(6), 399–418.

Ohmae, K. (1990). *The borderless world*. New York: Harper Collins.

Ohmae, K. (1996). *The end of the nation state*. Cambridge, MA: Free Press.

Paauwe, J. (1995). Personnel management without personnel managers: Varying degrees of outsourcing the personnel function. In: P. Flood, M. Gannon & J. Paauwe (Eds), *Managing without traditional methods*. Wokingham: Addison-Wesley.

Pieper, R. (Ed.). (1990). *Human resource management: An international comparison*. Berlin: Walter de Gruyter.

Porter, M. E. (1986). Changing patterns of international competition. *California Management Review, 28*(2), 29–40.

Porter, M. E. (1990). *The competitive advantage of nations*. London: Macmillan.

Prahalad, C. K., & Doz, Y. (1987). *The multinational mission: Balancing local demands and global vision*. New York: The Free Press.

Ramaswamy, K., Kroeck, K. G., & Renforth, W. (1996). Measuring the degree of internationalization of a firm: A comment. *Journal of International Business Studies, 27*(1), 167–177.

Rosenzweig, P. M. V., & Nohria, N. (1994). Influences on human resource development practices in multinational corporations. *Journal of International Business Studies, 251*, 229–251.

Rugman, A., & Verbeke, A. (2004a). A perspective on regional and global strategies of multinational enterprises. *Journal of International Business Studies, 35*, 3–18.

Rugman, A., & Verbeke, A. (2004b). Regional transnationals and triad strategy. *Transnational Corporations, 13*(3), 1–20

Sackmann, S. A., & Phillips, M. E. (2004). Contextual influences on culture research: Shifting assumptions for new workplace realities. *International Journal of Cross Cultural Management, 4*(3), 370–390.

Sanchez, R., & Heene, A. (1997). *Strategic learning and knowledge management*. New York: Wiley.

Schuler, R. S. (1990). Repositioning the human resource function: Transformation or demise? *Academy of Management Executive, 4*(3), 49–60.

Schuler, R. S. (1992). Linking the people with the strategic needs of the business. *Organizational Dynamics, Summer*, 18–32.

Schuler, R. S., Budhwar, P. S., & Florkowski, G. W. (2002). International human resource management: Review and critique. *International Journal of Management Reviews, 4*(1), 41–70.

Schuler, R. S., Dowling, P., & De Cieri, H. (1993). An integrative framework of strategic international human resource management. *Journal of Management, 19*(2), 419–459.

Schwartz, S. H. (1992). Universals in the content and structure of values: Theoretical advances and empirical tests in 20 countries. In: M. P. Zanna (Ed.), *Advances in experimental social psychology* (Vol. 25). New York: Academic Press.

Schwartz, S. H. (1994). Beyond individualism/collectivism: New cultural dimensions of values. In: U. Kim, H.C. Triandis, C. Kagitcibasi, S. C. Choi & G. Yoon (Eds), *Individualism and collectivism*. London: Sage.

Scott, W. R. (1995). *Institutions and organizations*. Thousand Oaks, CA: Sage.

Sera, K. (1992). Corporate globalization: A new trend. *Academy of Management Executive, 6*(1), 89–96.

Smethurst, S. (2005). The long and winding road. *People Management, 11*(15), 25–29.

Sorge, A. (2004). Cross-national differences in human resources and organization. In: A.-W. Harzing & J. van Ruysseveldt (Eds), *International human resource management*. London: Sage.

Sparrow, P. R. (2005). Knowledge management in global organisations. In: I. Björkman & G. Stahl (Eds), *Handbook of research into international HRM*. London: Edward Elgar.

Sparrow, P. R. (2006). International management: Some key challenges for industrial and organizational psychology. In: G. P. Hodgkinson & J. K. Ford (Eds), *International review of industrial and organizational psychology* (Vol. 21). Chichester: Wiley.

Sparrow, P. R., & Braun, W. (2005). HR strategy theory in international context. In: M. Harris (Ed.), *The handbook of research in international human resource management*. Mahwah, NJ: Lawrence Erlbaum.

Sparrow, P. R., & Hiltrop, J. M. (1994). *European human resource management in transition.* Hempel Hempstead: Prentice-Hall.

Sparrow, P. R., & Hiltrop, J. M. (1997). Redefining the field of European human resource management: A battle between national mindsets and forces of business transition. *Human Resource Management, 36*(2), 1–19.

Sparrow, P. R., Brewster, C., & Harris, H. (2004). *Globalizing human resource management.* London: Routledge.

Standing, G. (1997). Globalization, labour market flexibility and insecurity: The era of market regulation. *European Journal of Industrial Relations, 3*(1), 7–37.

Stonehouse, G., Hamill, J., Campbell, D., & Purdie, T. (2000). *Global and transnational business: Strategy and management.* Chichester: Wiley.

Sullivan, D. (1994). Measuring the degree of internationalization of a firm. *Journal of International Business Studies, 25*(2), 325–342.

Sullivan, D. (1996). Measuring the degree of internationalization of a firm: A reply. *Journal of International Business Studies, 27*(1), 179–192.

Tallman, S., & Fladmoe-Lindquist, K. (2002). Internationalization, globalization and capability-based strategy. *California Management Review, 45*(1), 116–135.

Taylor, S., Beechler, S., & Napier, N. (1996). Toward an integrative model of strategic international human resource management. *Academy of Management Review, 21*(4), 959–985.

Torbiorn, I. (1982). *Living abroad: Personal adjustment and personnel policy in the overseas setting.* New York: Wiley.

Trompenaars, F. (1993). *Riding the waves of culture: Understanding cultural diversity in business.* London: Economist Books.

Tung, R. L. (1981). Selection and training of personnel for overseas assignments. *Columbia Journal of World Business, 16*(1), 57–71.

Ulrich, D. (1997). *Human resource champions: The next agenda for adding value to HR practices.* Boston: Harvard Business School Press.

UNCTAD. (2001). Foreign direct investment soars, but will decline this year. *UNCTD digital library.* TAD/INF/PR/21. http://www.unctad.org/Templates/webflyer.asp?docid=2544&intItemID=1397&lang=1.

UNCTAD. (2004). Research note: World Investement Report 2004: The shift towards services. *Transnational Corporations, 13*(3), 87–124.

Whitley, R. D. (1999). *Divergent capitalisms: The social structuring and change of business systems.* Oxford: Oxford University Press.

Whitley, R. D. (Ed.). (1992). *European business systems: Firms and markets in their national contexts.* London: Sage.

Yip, G. S. (1992). *Total global strategy,* Englewood Cliffs, NJ: Prentice-Hall.

CHAPTER 7

Developing the Global Manager

Maxine Dalton

This chapter presents the basic steps in an executive development program and describes what must be done differently when the Human Resources task is to develop global managers. Recent literature on the global manager is reviewed and integrated. The term, global manager, is defined and the skills that a manager needs to be effective in a global context are discussed. Finally, the argument is made that international experience and organizational support for experiential learning are the core to success in developing effective global managers.

In the history of modern commerce, organizational leaders have never faced more complex challenges. The conduct of business is enmeshed in the political relationships that exist between countries. Americans call for the boycott of French wines as a protest against certain actions by the French government and the French vandalize American fast food outlets as a protest against a perceived assault on deeply held cultural values. Job outsourcing provides work to millions of workers in poor countries but causes unemployment in the organization's county of origin. Income rises among certain foreign workers but this rise in the standard of living is coincident with the disruption of local communities and the exploitation of the natural environment. Globalization, itself, is suspect as activists around the world rise up to protest a perceived assault on their autonomy and values. Globalization is a grand experiment with an uncertain future.

The task of the Human Resources (HR) professional charged with developing managers to work effectively in this environment mirrors this complexity. In facilitating the development of global leaders, the HR professional must take into account how cultural values and societal practices will influence every step in the management development process. Laws, customs, beliefs, and values beyond the organization's boundaries will ultimately determine the success of the HR initiative and indeed, the success of the organization itself. This chapter is meant to provide some ideas for the global HR professional to consider as he goes about doing his work.

The Development Process

There is a standard process common to the design of any management or executive development initiative (e.g. Dalton & Hollenbeck, 1996; Sloan, Hazucha, & Katwyk, 2003):

- Clarify the business strategy.
- Engage and orient the stakeholders and decision makers.
- Determine the human resource requirements.
- Define the knowledge, skills, and abilities that will be needed, given the business strategy.
- Identify the pool of employees targeted for development.
- Choose the learning methodology (e.g. training programs, advanced university degrees, assignments).
- Implement the program.
- Evaluate the process.

This list of activities represents a broad initiative, a process and not an event. In the best organizations these activities are part of an ongoing effort in which the evaluation of one cycle feeds into the design and implementation of the next. Although the purpose of this chapter is to focus on the development of global managers, it is not necessary to create yet another list of steps. Instead we will concentrate on what is unique to the development of global managers within this established process.

Outline of the Chapter

This chapter is about the role of HR in developing global managers. In general, management development is a responsibility that is shared by the employee, his or her boss, the executive team and HR. We focus on HR in this chapter because the HR professional responsible for developing global talent needs a particular set of skills and abilities. The HR professional must understand the need to identify and develop global talent across the organization's many locations. The HR manager must understand how culture influences indicators of manager effectiveness. The HR professional must appreciate the need to constantly monitor and track the progress of potential global talent so that development efforts do not get lost in the press of business. Moreover, the HR professional must have the ability to sell a program of management development to other managers and senior executives world wide, many of whom will tend to believe that (1) an effective manager is an effective manager no matter where he works; (2) the cream will rise to the top; and (3) if you hire smart people from excellent schools; there is no need for development. Of course, only the first of these arguments is specific to the development of global managers.

   In this chapter we will first define the term, global manager. We will identify the knowledge, skills, and abilities that an effective global manager needs and discuss whether these skills appear to be developed or hard wired — the subject of selection. We will then discuss the factors that HR needs to take into account in tailoring a developmental process for global managers. Those facets of the development process that require comment include — identifying the knowledge, skills, and abilities that will be needed; identifying the employees targeted for development; choosing the learning methodology; and evaluation — the task of tracking and monitoring.

What is a Global Manager?

In order to understand the knowledge, skills, and abilities that an effective global manager will need, it is necessary to understand the nature of global managerial work. Gessner and Arnold (1999) define global leadership as influencing the thoughts and actions of others to achieve some set of … goals … in large multicultural contexts. They do not attempt to limit the definition to the particular number of cultures that someone must work in before the work becomes global.

We define a global manager by the work that he does. A global manager is someone who accomplishes his work across simultaneously interacting borders (Dalton, Ernst, Deal, & Leslie, 2002; Dalton, Ernst, Leslie, Deal & Ritter, 2002). These interacting borders include time zones, geography, countries, and culture. The global manager may be an expatriate in which case the challenge of personal and family adjustment may be added to the mix, but an expatriate is not necessarily a global manager. Indeed, a global manager may never relocate but instead manages complex operations by phone, e-mail, fax, and frequent short trips to destinations all over the world.

The work of the global manager is characterized by its complexity. McCall and Hollenbeck (2002) describe the work of the global manager as cognitively and emotionally complex. They note that working across business borders is a complex intellectual task but "working across countries and cultures is an assault on the identity of the person" (p. 22).

We characterize this complexity along a continuum. The work of a manager who is responsible for employees, services, operations, or specialized functions on one continent in one or two time zones does not face the same level of complexity as a manager responsible for multiple countries on more than one continent across multiple time zones.

There are three factors that make the work of the global manager so complex: the sheer inconvenience and potential for confusion and misunderstanding inherent in communicating across time zones; the concrete imperatives of country-based political and legal systems; and the abstract expectations of culture. While society dictates such rules and regulations as the role of unions, the relationship of the organization to the banking system and the government, the prescribed treatment of the disabled, etc.; culture dictates that which is unspoken — what employees and managers expect from one another; what customers, vendors, and competitors expect from the manager and his or her organization. The dictates of society can be learned in an international MBA program. The unacknowledged expectations of culture are learned elsewhere. Unfortunately, many aspiring managers believe that formal education is sufficient to prepare them for a global career. They fail to appreciate the need for focused developmental experiences in the workplace. In an article entitled Plain Talk (Business Week, 2004), Larry Summers comments, "Our country has never been so misunderstood. So we will create an expectation that all students will have an international experience in college". (p. 74) The same expectation must hold for development programs in business.

The business section of any major newspaper regularly provides illustrations of the complexities of global management. A recent story featured on National Public Radio in the United States described the following situation. A retail clothing store was being pressured by stockholders and protestors in the street to institute fair labor and environmental standards according to US standards in its Southeast Asia location. The US-based global manager had successfully introduced better safety and environmental practices at this location and these policies and practices did not cause any particular problems in the host country. But these actions were not sufficient for the activist stockholders. Instead, these stockholders continue to press for equal rights for women in the workplace. This story caused me to wonder if equal rights for women would receive the same positive reception in the host country as safety and environmental standards. Equal rights for women violate basic cultural assumptions about the role of women in the host country and instituting such policies may cause serious political and economic repercussions for the organization in the host country. On the other hand, not instituting such policies may cause serious political and economic repercussion in the home country.

On a lighter note, imagine the surprise of the Japanese manager who was called before the French agricultural minister for failing to provide wine in the company cafeteria!

The global manager must anticipate these Gordian knots and make the best decisions that he or she can. The global manager must constantly balance the wants, needs and expectations of the stakeholders and constituency groups in one location with the realities of the other. What kind of manager is able to do this?

The Knowledge, Skills, and Abilities of the Effective Global Manager

Given the complexity of the work, what does it take to be an effective global manager? If one presumes that the managers who are targeted for global development are competent in their own countries, then the effective global manager is the person who can adapt what he knows to the situation at hand. For example, the GLOBE project (Den Hartog, House, Hanges, Ruiz-Quintanilla, & Dorfman, 1999), an exemplary 62 country-based study, identified a set of leadership characteristics that were universally endorsed by employees in most of the countries in their sample, but GLOBE researchers also acknowledged that the relative importance of each of these characteristics — one to another — is different in different countries (Brodbeck, Frese, Akerblom, & GLOBE Associates, 2000) and the *behaviors that exemplify these characteristics differ from country to country.* In other words, effective decision-making may be central to being perceived as an effective leader in one country but only peripherally related to expectations of leadership in another country. Additionally, effective decision making in France, for example, is behaviorally not the same as effective decision-making in the US. Effective leaders in Singapore do not behave like effective leaders in Denmark. And yet, employees in France, the US, Singapore, and Denmark would agree that decision-making and leadership are essential managerial skills.

In our own research we found that managers must play the same roles, regardless of the global complexity of their work. They must be able to serve as leader, decision maker, negotiator, spokesperson, etc., but to be effective global managers; they must be able to play these roles within the shifting context of time, country, and cultural expectations. We call this concept, *the same but different*. In other words, playing the role of leader or decision maker is essential to the managerial task whether the work is global or domestic, but how the role is played is culturally contingent. We found that managers who are able to be the same but different have a certain skill set. We named this global skill set the pivotal skills.

The Pivotal Skills

Beginning in the mid-1990s, scholars began to address the skill set of the global manager as distinct from the skill set of the successful expatriate. Much of the work on expatriates had been conducted with missionaries and peace corps volunteers and scholars spent a great deal of time differentiating the skills needed to perform well on a job in another country from the skills needed to adjust to daily life in another country. They also addressed other topics such as the impact of the expatriate assignment on the family of the expatriate, his or her career, and the high failure rate of expatriates, especially from the US.

The position of global manager appeared on the scene coincident with major advances in communication and transportation and the desire of many organizations to reduce the costs associated with the use of expatriates. For the first time in history, it appeared to be possible to manage by e-mail, fax, conference call, and frequent travel. Since many of the skills found to be associated with expatriate effectiveness were related to adjustment to a foreign country rather than job performance, the stage was set for trying to understand the skill set of the effective global manager.

A project team led by Martin at Hay/McBer (1995) determined that the effective global manager demonstrated international adaptability while enacting universal competencies. Gregerson, Morrison, and Black (1998) identified personal character, the ability to embrace duality, savvy, and unbridled inquisitiveness as the essential characteristics of the effective global manager. Funakawa (1997) wrote of the need for high context and high content managers. McCall and Hollenbeck (2002) identified six themes cited by global executives as lessons they had to learn. These lessons were: (1) learning to deal with cultural issues and different cultures; (2) learning to run a business (global versus local); (3) learning to lead and manage others; (4) learning to deal with problematic relationships; (5) learning about the personal qualities required of a leader; (6) learning about self and career.

In our work, we wanted to identify the skills of the effective global manager and we also wanted to be able to identify how these skills were developed. Dalton et al. (2002), conducted a study with 194 managers — half with global responsibilities and half with domestics responsibilities. Global managers who received high performance ratings from their bosses shared four skills in common. We named these the pivotal skills, skills that allowed managers to adapt to time, place, and situation — to be the "same but different" as discussed in the previous section. The four pivotal skills are *international business knowledge*, *cultural adaptability*, *perspective taking*, and *innovativeness*. *International business knowledge* is defined as knowledge of one's own business (e.g. transportation, fast food, textiles) coupled with knowledge of how business is conducted in all the locations in which the organization operates. *Cultural adaptability* is defined as the ability to perform basic managerial tasks — selection, development, motivation, and information sharing, in a culturally appropriate fashion. *Perspective-taking* is defined as the ability to demonstrate appreciation of someone else's point of view. *Innovativeness* defines the global manager's ability to transform what he knows about a local culture into novel ideas, new approaches, new opportunities, and sometimes new goods and services.

Conceptually, the pivotal skills build on one another in a more or less hierarchical and cumulative fashion. *International business knowledge* constitutes what a manager needs to know about the cultural, political, regulatory, and financial framework of other countries. *Cultural adaptability* is the ability to use that knowledge in managing others. *Perspective-taking* describes the ability to understand and appreciate why customers, vendors, employees, etc. behave as they do. *Innovativeness* is the ability to apply this collective knowledge and understanding — to create new products, goods, and services.

It is encouraging to note the convergence of the research studies cited in this section. Although each of the studies that we have briefly reviewed was conducted independently using different methodologies and different populations — there is general agreement that the effective global manager is able to adapt what he knows. It is not so much that the effective global manager needs to acquire new managerial skills. Rather, the potential global manager must acquire the skills that under gird adaptability. This person must be able to escape from the symbolic and interpretive systems of his own culture (Gardner, 1983) and do work within the symbolic systems of others.

Choosing the Learning Methodology

When the HR professional is called upon to design a development process and choose the learning strategies that will be employed, it is helpful to understand whether a given skill or ability is likely to be hard wired of if it can be developed. If a skill represents an inborn trait or ability, it is a selection issue. If it can be learned, it is the work of development.

Personality

In our work we found that managers who displayed the four pivotal skills — international business knowledge, cultural adaptability, perspective taking, and innovativeness; shared certain personality traits and experiences in common. To investigate the role of personality in the development of global managers we used a five-factor model of personality as measured by the NEO PI-R (Costa & McCrae, 1992). The NEO PI-R characterizes personality as consisting of five traits: Emotional stability; Extraversion; Openness to experience; Agreeableness; and Conscientiousness. We chose the NEO PI-R because it has been demonstrated to have some degree of universal applicability (McCrae & Costa, 1997) and because certain traits measured by the five-factor model of personality are related to performance outcomes in the business context in North America and Europe (Barrick & Mount, 1991; Salgado, 1997). Indeed, in our own work we found that trait of Conscientiousness was related to higher performance ratings for the global manager.

But of greater interest to the topic of development is the relationship of certain personality traits to the pivotal skills. We found that the managers who possessed a high degree of international business knowledge and cultural adaptability were also more likely to have two personality traits, Conscientiousness and Emotional stability. These managers were more likely to be emotionally stable, meaning that they were relatively confident and did not experience excessive worry, stress, or self-doubt. They were also more likely to exhibit the trait of Conscientiousness which Costa and McCrae (1992) define as dependable, organized, disciplined, achievement oriented, and persevering. In other words, international business knowledge and cultural adaptability were directly related to performance ratings and Conscientiousness and Emotional stability were related to the presence or absence of these skills. This pattern continued for the other two pivotal skills. Managers who demonstrated perspective taking were more likely to exhibit the personality trait of Agreeableness — trusting, friendly, altruistic, and sympathetic. Managers who were innovative were more likely to be open to experience and extroverted. They were curious, open to new ideas and novel experiences and they could sell their novel ideas to others. These personality traits might be thought of as antecedent to or coincident with skill development.

Experience

We also found that the pivotal skills were related to certain experiences. Managers with a particular skill set were more likely to have had particular experiences. Managers who demonstrated international business knowledge and cultural adaptability were more likely to speak more languages, have lived in at least one other country, and have been expatriates. Managers with the skill of innovativeness were also more likely to speak more languages. In our study the skill of perspective taking was not related to any particular set of experiences.

McCall and Hollenbeck found similar results. The critical lessons learned by global executives in their study were learned in cultures other than their own. What are the implications of these findings for the global HR professional who must choose the learning strategies that will be the backbone of a global management development process?

Although personality and experience increase the probability that a manager will have a particular skill set, there are some limits to the application of these findings. First we turn to the relationship of personality to the pivotal skills. There are three important points here that the HR professional needs to understand in designing a process of global management development. The first point is related to the composition of the global talent pool.

Each of the five personality traits is related to different pivotal skills, Conscientiousness and Emotional stability are related to international business knowledge and cultural adaptability. The trait of Agreeableness is related to the skill of perspective taking; and the traits of Openness to experience and Extraversion are related to the skill of innovativeness. However, it is very unlikely that a single individual will demonstrate all of these traits — high scores on Emotional stability, Openness to experience, Conscientiousness, Agreeableness, and Extraversion. This suggests that a global talent pool needs to be comprised of a mix of people with different but complementary personality styles — some extraverts and some introverts; some empathetic people and some cynics, etc. This also means that HR will have to work hard to overcome an organization's bias to hire a certain 'type' of employee. For example, organizations who insist on hiring only those who are dominant and hard driving may not have anyone on the executive team capable of being a good listener and recognizing someone else's point of view. This also suggests that a program of development must include attention to the skill of getting along with and appreciating different others — not just culturally different others but of those with different personality styles.

The second critical point is cautionary. First, our findings are based on a response to paper and pencil ratings and the statistical findings are correlational. This means that one cannot assume cause and effect. A correlation statistic indicates that two things co-occur. Second, although the performance ratings of the global managers were made by the bosses of the research subjects, the personality ratings and skill ratings were completed by the subjects, themselves. Third, statistically, personality accounts for only a small portion of a particular skill or ability; somewhere between 5% and 15%. In other words, a person with a particular personality trait is only somewhat more likely to also display a particular skill than someone without that trait. The implication for HR is that personality testing to select employees who will become effective global managers can provide only modest incremental utility. Personality tests may be more useful as feedback for the aspiring global manager — to help him or her understand the kinds of people he may find it difficult to work with and to help him or her understand which skills seem to come more naturally than others.

As to the relationship of experience to the development of the pivotal skills, we again quote McCall and Hollenbeck (2002), "It is the lessons of culture that truly differentiate the global context". (p. 201) In their study of global executives, McCall and Hollenbeck found that global executives learned 19% of their cultural lessons from international experience, 76% from expatriate experience, and 5% from domestic experience. To reiterate our own work, we found that managers who demonstrated the four pivotal skills were more likely to have been expatriates, learned to speak other languages, and spent time living and working in other countries.

These results are in keeping with many years of work from The Center for Creative Leadership on management development (e.g. McCall, Lombardo, & Morrison, 1988; McCauley, Ruderman, Ohlott, & Morrow, 1994; Dalton, 1999). In this research effective senior managers identified challenging experience as the most critical component of their own development. Given this, we have come to think of development as helping people to become better learners and providing them with opportunities in which to learn.

In other words, the HR professional needs to recognize that there is no substitute for cross cultural experience as the centerpiece to any process of the development of effective global managers. This will be a hard sell when for example, companies are trying to save money by cutting down on expatriate assignments or when somewhat parochial managers insist that since English is the international language of business there is no need to learn another language. But if one adds the 5–20% likelihood that a person with various international experience will demonstrate a certain skill set to the 5–15% likelihood that a person with a particular personality trait will demonstrate a certain skill set, than identifying the right people for language training, international MBA support, and assignments in other countries starts to become worthwhile activity. There can be a payoff for purposefully selecting the right employees for the global talent pool and intentionally developing them to assume positions for global responsibility.

To conclude this section we suggest that the learning methodology for developing global managers will incorporate self-assessment opportunities, formal education, training programs, and assignments and will include the following:

- Personality assessment to help participants understand their natural tendencies: this will help them realize why some skills may be easier to acquire than others.
- Formal university courses in international finance, marketing, etc.
- Training programs about cultural differences: this will give participants a vocabulary within which to frame their experience.
- Language training.
- Graduated international assignments, e.g. business trips, working on cross-cultural teams; working with experienced internationalists; expatriate assignments; etc.

Identify the Pool of Employees Targeted for Development

One of the most critical steps in implementing a process of development for future global managers is the selection of the employees to be targeted for development. Some organizations do not specify a particular talent pool but rather, include everyone at a particular level. This strategy casts a very broad net and only the most prosperous organizations are in a position to afford such an investment — particularly if the process includes all of the activities listed at the end of the last section. For less prosperous organizations, the decision to include everyone can translate into providing less for more and the results may be disappointing.

Other organizations decide to focus their resources on those employees who are more likely to continue to advance. With this approach it is important not to make the talent pool too small as the competition for competent global executives is intense and an organization is always in danger of having some of its best people lured away.

A second selection issue is the problem of the glass ceiling. Organizational decision makers, particularly those who live in the country where headquarters is located, often inadvertently overlook valuable foreign employees that should have been selected into the global talent pool. Over the years I have had the occasion to observe this phenomenon many times. In developmental discussions with young managers about their career goals, aspirations, strengths, and developmental needs, the conversation inevitably turns to the place where a bright and effective young manager tells me that in a few more years he will have to either find a job with the competition or start his own business because his current organization will never promote a foreigner beyond the level of country manager. I have heard this statement in California, in Kuala Lumpur, in Tokyo, in Delhi, in Berlin. Unintentional ethnocentrism is not limited to a particular geography. Rather, senior executives have a tendency to hire and promote in their own image because they, like the rest of us, feel most comfortable with what is known and familiar.

This practice has serious implications for an organization's global strategy. There are three visible indicators of how serious an organization is about its global intentions — the composition of the Board of Directors, the composition of the Executive Team, and the composition of the talent pool. To the extent that the Board of Directors and Executive team are made up of people from only one country, the organization is not yet global. To the extent that the talent pool is made up of people from only one country, the company does not intend to be global in the future.

Therefore, a major HR task is to open the talent pool worldwide. The management development process should include candidates from every geographic location of strategic importance.

A third selection issue is when to start the process of global management development. McCall and Hollenbeck (2002) suggest that it is important to start early. It is easier for young people to accept expatriate assignments before they start families and become established in the routines and responsibilities of a community. We suggest starting early because international business trips and working on cross cultural teams will provide a job preview — it can help employees to decide if they have an interest in a global career path and if they are willing to make the sacrifices associated with this complex role. Of course, a part of the selection process is to note, which employees come to the work place already able to speak more than one language, with a history of travel and education in other countries. In our own work we found that managers who had spoken more than one language as a child and had been educated in more than one country were more likely to have the skill of cultural adaptability. While this may be a statement of the obvious, it suggests that in developing global executives, there is no substitute for experience.

But How to Identify that Talent — the Cultural Standards of Effectiveness

Even if a company is committed to creating an international talent pool, standards of effectiveness vary from country to country. The classic approach to designing management development programs is to come up with two lists of competencies — one that can be used as a criterion for selection into the development process and a second list of competencies that the participants in the program are expected to develop. Indeed, HR professionals spend many years and piles of money to develop the set of competencies that will serve as the criteria against which to identify employees for the talent pool. This is a thankless task under any set of circumstances. For the identification of potential global managers, it is particularly difficult because definitions of effectiveness are culturally contingent.

Derr and Laurent (1989) conducted a now classic study of what American and European managers believe constitutes effective managerial performance. They found that the Germans value managers who are technically creative and competent. The French value managers who have the ability to manage power relationships and work the system. The British value managers who create the right image. The Americans value entrepreneurial behavior. Undoubtedly this list of characterizations would be even more varied and complex if we were able to include studies from Africa, the Middle East, Asia, South America, etc.

For this reason, if the intention of the development process is provide effective managers with the opportunity to become effective global managers, we recommend that country managers simply nominate employees to participate in the process. If these employees do develop the pivotal skills, it should not matter that German managers are being nominated for technical competence and Americans are being nominated for their entrepreneurial behavior. The pivotal skills will help them adapt what they do best to the context in which they find themselves and to appreciate and learn from one another.

However, in addition to nominating employees to the process that are considered effective in their domestic jobs, the nominating manager should be looking for employees who have demonstrated the ability and willingness to learn from experience. If the key to development is experience, than those in the talent pool should be those who are willing to learn from experience. Evidence of the ability and willingness to learn from experience can be identified in an employee's work history. Learning behaviors include accepting or seeking out new and unfamiliar challenges, persistence in the effort to master a difficult task, the demonstration of a willingness to learn from the experience of others, a willingness to admit not knowing how to do something, an openness to feedback about one's efforts and impact. Of course, evidence of the willingness to learn is also culturally contingent. For example in countries characterized as egalitarian and individualistic, employees who enjoy learning might be those who *seek* novel opportunities and feedback. In countries characterized as more hierarchical or collectivist, the learner may be characterized as one who *accepts* challenging and novel assignments. In either case we would expect to see a persistent effort at mastery.

In summary, our advice is not to construct a universally applicable list of selection criterion for who should be in the global talent pool. Rather, we suggest that managers nominate employees who are good at their current jobs, willing to live in other countries, willing to learn another language, and willing and able to learn from experience. The goal of the developmental process is to develop the pivotal skills — the ability to be the same but different, to take what one does well and apply it appropriately in a different context. If the development process for global managers is to be primarily experiential — learning about international business, cultural adaptability, perspective taking, and innovation through the process of travel, living and working in other countries, working as a member of cross country team, then the HR professional wants to help managers select employees for these developmental assignments who are open to learning.

A Few More Words about Learning from Experience

As referenced earlier in this chapter, in the late 1980's some researchers at the Center for Creative Leadership demonstrated a relationship between development and work (McCall, Lombardo, & Morrison, 1988). They found that about 70% of the important lessons that effective managers had learned about how to do their work were developed from a variety of challenging experiences and critical relationships. This finding has been replicated with global managers by McCall and Hollenbeck (2002) and in our own work. Adults learn from doing the work and from observing and working with experts. However, these findings have often been misunderstood by management development professionals who interpret the findings to mean that development is like sheep dipping. You simply drop employees into an assignment and they automatically learn. This, of course, is not the case. Some employees learn from their experiences. Some do not. Secondly, these findings have been interpreted to mean that training has no value. This is not the case. Training can provide the knowledge, the understanding, and the self-awareness to help employees sort out what their strengths and weaknesses are; to articulate development goals; to recognize the kinds of experiences they need to accomplish these goals. Training in the form of education also provides content knowledge about a host of phenomenon. Training and education are necessary but not sufficient components of the development process.

To learn from experience in pursuit of global managerial effectiveness HR professionals need to work with managers to design a development process that includes the following components:

- Employees need to understand their strengths and development needs.
- They need to understand the kinds of experiences they need and what they can learn from these experiences.
- They need to understand that every work assignment combines both task and developmental components. The development challenge is to accomplish the task and learn from the challenges imbedded in the task itself.
- They need to be provided with ongoing feedback and support from a manager who supports this employee's development goals, understands what the manager is trying to learn, and recognizes progress.
- They need to be taught how to use a variety of tactics as part of their learning strategy — reflection, reading, seeking the advice of colleagues and experts, and sometimes, just jumping in.
- If these employees are truly on a path to global manager status, then when they have mastered a task, they need to be moved on to the next challenge — and the whole learning process of self-awareness, goal setting, learning from the experience, etc. starts again.

Evaluation: Monitoring and Tracking

It is fairly easy to make a list of how to build a development process around the naturally occurring demands and challenges of the workplace. It is very hard to actually accomplish such a process. Organizations have a mission and to accomplish this mission, work must get done. People cannot always be given an assignment just because they need it and they cannot always be taken off of an assignment just because they have mastered it. On the other hand, someone in the organization needs to track where the talented employees are, why they are there — what are they supposed to be accomplishing and what they are supposed to be learning, and facilitating the next step.

For example, one of the most powerful development experiences on the career path of a global executive is the expatriate experience and yet it is the norm that expatriates get lost while they are "out there," are miserably underutilized on their return to the home country, and more often than not — leave the organization because their career has reached a dead end. It is the job of HR to insure that this does not happen. The expatriate experience is the most visible example of the failure to leverage employee learning. The same thing happens on a smaller scale even when young professionals begin to travel internationally. The trip is not seen as a development opportunity and the learning is not harvested. HR must create a system to debrief employees on these development tracks, monitor their whereabouts, and help prepare for their homecoming. And HR must teach managers how to facilitate the development of their employees.

Facilitating Development

The most critical feature of any process of executive development is the help that HR can provide to employees and managers alike in teaching them how to learn from experience. Early pilot work on learning from experience (Lombardo, Bunker, & Webb, 1990) suggested that learning from experience only "came naturally" to about 10% of a group of highly young employees identified as high potentials. Another 20–30% seemed unable or unwilling to learn from novel experience and another 60–70% were able to learn with help. Therefore, the global HR professional must facilitate the learning process. This involves three major points: (1) helping employees and managers understand that development occurs as part of accomplishing work. Development is not simply a training program. It is not separate from work. It is the work; (2) learning requires a variety of approaches; (3) learners need feedback.

Summary

In many ways the work of developing managerial and executive talent is always the same — regardless of the nature of the work. The job responsibilities of the Human Resources professional who is charged with the task of developing global managers are clear. He or she must understand the organization's global business strategy and be able to translate this into numbers and skill sets — how many employees with what types of skills must be ready to assume global responsibilities by what point in time. The Human Resources professional must develop a plan to identify the talent pool of employees who will be the target for an organization's developmental initiatives. The HR professional must design, implement, and monitor an initiative that will help these managers develop the skill set to work in a global environment.

In developing global managers the focus is less on managerial and leadership skills and more on teaching already competent people how to adapt what they know for use in complex international environments. Adapt is probably too soft a word as this adaptation most likely requires a major shift in one's world view.

Managers are more likely to learn the pivotal skills described in this chapter — international business knowledge, cultural adaptability, perspective taking and innovation, by acquiring specialized knowledge and through engagement in a series of increasingly complex international experiences. HR may facilitate this learning by teaching these managers how to become better learners.

Finally, it is the HR responsibility to insure that the talent pool reflects the company's global strategy and that future global talent does not get lost or slip through the cracks in the press of work. This HR manager needs to be one of the more effective global managers in the organization.

References

Barrick, M. R., & Mount, M. K. (1991). The big five personality dimensions and job performance: A meta-analysis. *Personnel Psychology, 44*, 1–26.

Brodbeck, F. C., Frese, M., Akerblom, S., & GLOBE Associates. (2000). Cultural variation of leadership prototypes across 22 European countries. *Journal of Occupational and Organizational Psychology, 73*(1), 1–21.

Business Week (2004). Plain talk from Larry Summers. *Business Week*, November 8, p. 74.

Costa, P. T., & McCrae, R. R. (1992). *Revised NEO personality inventory and NEO five factor inventory professional manual*. Odessa, FL: Psychological Assessment Resources.

Dalton, M. (1999). *Learning tactics inventory: Facilitator's guide*. San Francisco, CA: Jossey-Bass/Pfeiffer.

Dalton, M., Ernst, C., Deal, J., & Leslie, J. (2002). *Success for the New Global Manager: How to work across distances, countries and cultures*. San Francisco, CA: Jossey-Bass.

Dalton, M., Ernst, C., Leslie, J., Deal, J., & Ritter, W. (2002). Effective global management: Established constructs and novel contexts. *European Journal of Work and Organizational Psychology, 11*(4) 443–468.

Dalton, M., & Hollenbeck, G. (1996). *How to design an effective system for developing managers and executives*. Greensboro, NC: Center for Creative Leadership.

Derr, C. B., & Laurent, A. (1989). The internal and external careers: A theoretical and cross cultural perspective. In: M. Arthur, D. T. Hall & B. S. Lawrence (Eds), *The handbook of career theory*. Cambridge, England: Cambridge University Press.

Den Hartog, D. N., House, R. J., Hanges, P. J., Ruiz-Quintanilla, S. A., & Dorfman, P. W. (1999). Culture specific and cross-culturally generalizable implicit leadership theories: Are attributes of charismatic/transformational leadership universally endorsed? *Leadership Quarterlyl, 10*(2), 219–256.

Funakawa, A. (1997). *Transcultural management: A new approach for global organizations*. San Francisco: Jossey-Bass.

Gardner, H. (1983). *Frames of mind: The theories of multiple intelligences*. New York: Basic Books.

Gessner, M. J., & Arnold, V. (1999). Introduction to conceptual perspectives. In: W. H. Mobley, M. J. Gessner & V. Arnold (Eds), *Advances in global leadership,* (pp.xiii-xviii). Stamford, CT: JAI Press.

Gregerson, H. B., Morrison, A. J., & Black, J. S. (1998). Developing leaders for the global frontier. *Sloan Management Review, Fall*, 21–32.

Lombardo, M. M., Bunker, K., & Webb, A. (1990). Learning how to learn. Paper presented at the fifth annual conference for the Society for Industrial and Organizational Psychology, Miami, Fl.

McCall, M. W., & Hollenbeck, G. P. (2002). *The lessons of international experience: Developing global executives*. Boston, MA: Harvard Business School Press.

McCall, M. W. Jr., Lombardo, M. M., & Morrison, A. M. (1988). *The lessons of experience: How successful executives develop on the job*. Lexington, MA: Lexington Books.

McCauley, C. M., Ruderman, M. N., Ohlott, P. J., & Morrow, J. (1994). Assessing the developmental components of managerial jobs. *Journal of Applied Psychology, 79*(4), 544–560.

McCrae, R. R., & Costa, P. T. Jr. (1997). Personality trait structure as a human universal. *American Psychologist, 52*, 509–516.

Martin, K. (1995). *Mastering global leadership (Tech Rep). Hay/McBer International CEO Leadership Study*. Philadelphia: Hay/McBer.

Salgado, Y. J. F. (1997). The five factor model of personality and job performance in the European Community. *Journal of Applied Psychology, 82*(1), 30–43.

Sloan, E. B., Hazucha, J. F., & Van Katwyk, P. T. (2003). Strategic management of global leadership talent. In: W. H. Mobley & P. W. Dorfman (Eds), *advances in global leadership* (pp. 231–274). Oxford, UK: Elsevier.

PART III

Human Resources Management and Employee Well-Being

CHAPTER 8

The Challenges of HRM in Managing Employee Stress and Improving Well-Being

Cary L. Cooper

Introduction

The "enterprise culture" of the 1980s and the "flexible workforce" of the 1990s helped to transform economies in Western Europe and North America. But as we discovered by the end of these decades, there was a substantial personal cost for many individual employees. This cost was captured by a single word, *stress*. Indeed, stress has found as firm a place in our modern lexicon as texting, emailing, fast food and junk bonds. We toss the term about casually to describe a wide range of "aches and pains", which result from our hectic pace of work and domestic life. "I really feel stressed", someone says to describe an acute sense of disquiet. "She's under a lot of stress", we say when we are trying to understand a colleague's irritability or forgetfulness. "It's a high-stress job", someone says, awarding an odd sort of prestige to his or her occupation. But to those whose ability to cope with day-to-day matters is at crisis point, the concept of stress is no longer a casual one; for them, stress can be translated into a four-letter word — pain. (Cartwright & Cooper, 1997; Cooper, Dewe, & O'Driscoll, 2001).

Costs Associated With Occupational Stress

Employees are becoming increasingly aware of the impact that occupational stress is having on their work, health and well-being. The International Social Survey Program, conducted in 15 OECD countries, found that 80 per cent of employees report being stressed at work (OECD, 1999). The collective cost of stress to US organizations in terms of absenteeism, reduced productivity, compensation claims, health insurance and direct medical expenses has been estimated at approximately $150 billion per year (Quick et al., 2002).

The UK Health and Safety Executive (HSE) estimates that 20 per cent of employees admit to taking time off work because of work-related stress and 8 per cent consult their general practitioner on stress-related problems (Earnshaw & Cooper, 2001). A survey on working conditions by the European Foundation for the Improvement of Living and Working Conditions showed that 57 per cent of European workers feel their health is negatively affected by work and 28 per cent felt that their health and safety was at risk (Paoli, 1997). Occupational or workplace stress accounts for a high proportion of sickness absence. The HSE estimates that 60 per cent of all work absences are caused by stress-related illnesses, totalling 40 million working days per year (Earnshaw & Cooper, 2001). Schabracq, Winnubst, and Cooper (1996) estimate that about half of all work absences are stress-related. The costs associated with sickness absence are high, for example, the Confederation of British Industry (CBI) estimates that in financial terms, sickness absence costs some £11 billion per year in the United Kingdom, of which it has been estimated that about 40 per cent is due to workplace stress. This amounts to approximately 2–3 per cent of Gross National Product (GNP), or £438 per employee per year (CBI, 2000).

It is also estimated that occupational stress is involved in 60–80 per cent of accidents at work (Sutherland & Cooper, 1991). When work accidents and injuries are included, the costs associated with occupational stress escalate further. Although in the United States alone, 65,000 people die each year from work-related injuries and illnesses (Herbert & Landrigan, 2000), work-related fatalities are relatively rare, compared to the numbers of employees injured at work, who subsequently take sickness absence. Dupre (2000) estimated that in approximately 50 per cent of work accidents that occurred in Europe (in 1996) absence from work ranged between two weeks and three months. In Australia, the average absence for compensated injuries was "two months" in the period 1998–1999 (National Occupational Health and Safety Commission, 2000). It is estimated that 80 million working days were lost in the United States due to workplace accidents in 1998 (US Bureau of the Census, 2000). Work accidents are damaging not only for those involved, but also for their employers. Work injuries cost Americans $131.2 billion in 2000, a figure that exceeds the combined profits of the top 13 Fortune 500 companies (National Safety Council, 2001). In the United Kingdom, it has been estimated that work accidents cost employers £3–7 billion per year, equivalent to approximately 4–8 per cent of all UK industrial and commercial companies' gross trading profits (Health and Safety Executive, 1999).

This brief overview indicates the enormity of the costs associated with stress-related illness and accidents, and highlights the potential benefits of successfully managing the risks of occupational stress. There are often hidden business costs that are incurred as a result of work-related illness and injuries, including the costs of training and recruitment of temporary cover for absent employees.

The Changing Nature of Work

Since the industrial revolution, every decade has had its unique defining characteristics. Innovation and challenging the established norms of society epitomized the 1960s; industrial strife and conflict between employer and employee the 1970s; the "enterprise culture", with its strategic alliances, privatizations and the like, the 1980s; and the short-term contract culture, with its outsource, downsizing and long working hours culture, the 1990s; and the undermining of the psychological contract, between employer and employee, the 2000s. In effect, we are beginning to see the Americanization of Europe, starting with the UK and spreading throughout the continent of Europe. It was logical that this trend, towards what is euphemistically called the "flexible workforce", should originate in the UK, given the fact that Britain led the way in Europe towards privatizing the public sector in the 1980s, downsizing its workforce substantially during the recession of the late 1980s and early 1990s and outsourcing many of its corporate functions as it left behind the recession in the 1990s faster than its European counterparts. However, this Americanized scenario of "leaner" organizations, intrinsic job insecurity and a longer working hours culture is beginning to have an adverse effect on employee attitudes and behaviour. For instance, in the CMI Quality of Working Life surveys, between 1997 and 2001, (Worrall & Cooper, 2001) of a cohort of 5000 British managers (from the level of Director to the junior manager), it was found that the changes towards downsizing, outsourcing, delayering and the like, led to substantially increased job insecurity, lowered morale and the erosion of motivation and, most important of all, loyalty. Although these changes were perceived to have led to an increase in profitability and productivity, decision-making was slower and the organization was deemed to have lost the right mix of human recourse skills and experience in the process.

What was more worrying about this trend was the major increase in working hours and impact of this on the health and well-being of managers and their families. It was found that over 80 per cent of executives work over 40 hours a week, a third of them over 50 and roughly 10 per cent over 60 hours, with a substantial minority of them also working frequently at the weekends. In addition, whereas a third of this cohort of executives in 1998 felt that their employer expected them to put in these hours, by 2001 this rose to nearly 60 per cent. What is also disturbing about this trend towards a "long hours culture", is the managers' perception of the damage it is inflicting on them and their families: around 70 per cent of these executives reported that these hours damaged their health, over 80 per cent reported that it adversely affected their relationship with their children, three-quarters reported that it damaged their relationship with their partner, and two-thirds that long hours reduced their productivity.

Another manifestation of the Americanization of the UK and other European workplaces other than the "long hours" culture is the increasing levels of job insecurity. Since the Industrial Revolution in Europe, few white collar, managerial and professional workers have experienced high levels of job insecurity. Even blue-collar workers who were laid off in heavy manufacturing industries of the past, were frequently re-employed when times got better. The question that we have to ask is "can human beings cope with permanent job insecurity, without the security and continuity of organizational structures, which in the past also provided training, development and careers? The European survey by ISR of 400 companies in 17 countries representing 8 million workers throughout Europe found most European countries showed a substantial decline from 1985 to 1995 in perceived job security, with the most Americanized, Britain, showing the worst decline in employee satisfaction in terms of employment security, dropping from 70 per cent who were job satisfied (in terms of security) in 1985 down to 48 per cent by 1995.

The big questions about this development are: is the trend towards a short-term contract, long hours and intrinsically job insecure workplace the way forward for us? How will this affect the health and well-being of employees? Can organizations continue to demand commitment from employees they do not commit to? What will these long-hours culture do to the two-earner family, which is now the majority family in most developed countries? In comparative terms, the UK, Ireland and a few other European countries are doing remarkably well during the early phases of Americanization, but the levels of job insecurity and dissatisfaction are high and growing. Developing and maintaining a "feel good" factor at work and in the economy generally is not just about bottom line factors such as profitability; in a civilized society it should be about quality of life issues as well, like hours of work, family time, manageable workloads, control over one's career and some sense of job security.

A Strategy For Managing Stress in a Changing Workforce

So how should HR manage the pressures currently experienced by their employees in a changing workplace culture? Cartwright and Cooper (1997) have come up with a three-prong strategy for stress management in organizations. For the prevention and management of stress at work, there are three approaches that should provide a comprehensive strategic framework: primary (e.g. stressor reduction), secondary (e.g. stress management) and tertiary (e.g. employee assistance programmes/workplace counselling) prevention.

Primary Prevention

Primary prevention is concerned with taking action to modify or eliminate sources of stress inherent in the work environment and so reduce their negative impact on the individual. The focus of primary interventions is in adapting the environment to "fit" the individual. Elkin and Rosch (1990) summarize a useful range of possible strategies to reduce workplace stressors:

- Redesign the task
- Redesign the work environment
- Establish flexible work schedules
- Encourage participative management
- Include the employee in career development
- Analyse work roles and establish goals
- Provide social support and feedback
- Build cohesive teams
- Establish fair employment policies
- Share the rewards.

Primary intervention strategies are often a vehicle for culture change. Obviously, as the type of action required by an organization will vary according to the kinds of stressors operating any intervention needs to be guided by some prior diagnosis or stress audit or risk assessment to identify the organizational, site or departmental, specific stressors responsible for employee stress (Clarke & Cooper, 2004). There are many psychometric audit instruments now available to carry out an appropriate stress risk assessment — the most widely used of which is ASSET (an organizational stress screening tool) (Faragher, Cooper, & Cartwright, 2004).

Secondary Prevention

Secondary prevention is essentially concerned with the prompt detection and management of experienced stress by increasing awareness and improving the stress-management skills of the individual through training and educative activities. Individual factors can alter or modify the way employees exposed to workplace stressors perceive and react to this environment. Each individual has their own personal stress threshold, which is why some people thrive in a certain setting and others suffer.

Secondary prevention can focus on developing self-awareness and providing individuals with a number of basic relaxation techniques. Health promotion activities and lifestyle-modification programmes also fall into the category of secondary-level interventions. Stress education and stress-management training serve a useful function in helping individuals to recognize the symptoms of stress, and to overcome much of the negativity and stigma still associated with the stress label. Awareness activities and skills-training programmes designed to improve relaxation techniques, cognitive coping skills and work/lifestyle modification skills (e.g. time management courses or assertiveness training) have an important part to play in extending the individual's physical and psychological resources. However, the role of secondary prevention is essentially one of damage limitation, often addressing the consequences rather than the sources of stress, which may be inherent in the organization's structure or culture. They are concerned with improving the "adaptability" of the individual to the environment. Consequently, this type of intervention is often described as "the band aid" or inoculation approach. Because of the implicit assumption that the organization will not change but continue to be stressful, the individual has to develop and strengthen his/her resistance to that stress.

Tertiary Prevention

Tertiary prevention is concerned with the treatment, rehabilitation and recovery process of those individuals who have suffered or are suffering from serious ill health as a result of stress. Interventions at the tertiary level typically involve the provision of counselling services for employee problems in the work or personal domain. Such services are either provided by in-house counsellors or outside agencies in the form of an Employee Assistance Programme (EAP). EAPs provide counselling, information and/or referral to appropriate counselling treatment and services. There is evidence to suggest that counselling is effective in improving the psychological well-being of employees and has considerable cost benefits (Berridge, Cooper, & Highley-Marchington, 1997).

Like stress-management programmes, counselling services can be particularly effective in helping employees deal with workplace stressors that cannot be changed and non-work-related stress (i.e. bereavement, marital breakdown, etc.), which nevertheless tends to spill over into work life.

The Future

For this millennium, the pressures on all of us are likely to get worse. Stress is primarily caused by the fundamentals of change, lack of control and high workload. Further developments within European Union, the rise of China and India, increasing cross-national mergers, increasing international competition and joint ventures between organizations across national boundaries will lead inevitably to a variety of corporate "re's": re-organizations, relocations of personnel, redesign of jobs and reallocations of roles and responsibilities. "Change" will be the by word of the first part of this new millennium, with its accompanying job insecurities, corporate culture clashes and significantly different styles of managerial leadership — in other words, massive organizational change and inevitable stress. In addition, change will bring with it an increased workload as companies try to create "in fighting machines" to compete in the European, Far East and other international economic arenas. This will mean fewer people performing more work, in more job insecure environments.

Finally, as we move away from our own internal markets and enter larger economic systems (e.g. EU), individual organizations will have less control over business life. Rules and regulations are beginning to be imposed in terms of labour laws; health and safety at work, methods of production, distribution and remuneration and so on all laudable issues of concern in their own right but, nevertheless, workplace constraints that will inhibit individual control and autonomy. Without being too gloomy, it is safe to say that we have in the start of this millennium all the ingredients of corporate stress, an ever-increasing workload with a decreasing workforce in a climate of rapid change, and with control over the means of production increasingly being exercised by bigger bureaucracies (Sutherland & Cooper, 2000; Cooper & Dewe, 2004). These are the real challenges for HRM over the next decade. It appears, therefore, that stress is here to stay and is not just a bygone remnant of the entrepreneurial 1980s, or as Woody Allen once reflected on the importance of "work". "I don't want to achieve immortality through my work — I want to achieve it by not dying".

References

Berridge, J. R. K., Cooper, C. L., & Highley-Marchington, C. (1997). Employee assistance programmes and workplace counselling.Chichester: Wiley.

Cartwright S., & Cooper C. L. (1997). *Managing workplace stress.* London: Sage.

Clarke, S., & Cooper, C. L. (2004). *Managing the risk of workplace stress.* London: Routledge.

Confederation of British Industry (CBI) (2000). *Focus on absence.* London: CBI.

Cooper, C. L., Dewe, P., & O'Driscoll, M. (2001). *Organizational stress.* California: Sage.

Cooper, C. L., & Dewe, P. (2004). *Stress: A Brief History.* Oxford & Malden, MA: Blackwell Publishers.

Dupre, D. (2000). Accidents at work in the EU in 1996. *Statistics in Focus: Population and Social Conditions. 3,* 1–7.

Earnshaw, J., & Cooper, C. L. (2001). *Stress and employer liability.* London: Institute of Personnel and Development (IPD).

Elkin, A., & Rosch, P. (1990). Promoting mental health at the workplace. *Occupational Medicine, 5*(4), 739–754.

Faragher, B., Cooper, C. L., & Cartwright, S. (2004). A structured stress evaluation tool. *Stress & Health*, *20*, 189–201.

Health and Safety Executive (1999). *The costs to Britain of workplace accidents and work related ill health in 1995/96*. Sudbury: HSE Books.

Herbert, R., & Landrigan, P. J. (2000). Work-related death: A continuing epidemic. *American Journal of Public Health*, *90*, 541–545.

National Occupational Health and Safety Commission (2000). *Compendium of Workers' Compensation Statistics, Australia, 1998–1999*. Canberra: Commonweath of Australia.

National Safety Council (2001). *Report on injuries in America* (2001). Available at: http://www.nsc.org/library/rept2000.htm.

OECD (1999). *Implementing the OECD job strategy: Assessing performance and policy*. Paris: OECD.

Paoli, P. (1997). *Second European survey for the European foundation for the improvement of living and working conditions*. Luxembourg: European Foundation.

Quick, J. C., Cooper, C. L., Quick, J. D., & Gavin, J. H. (2002). The Financial Times Guide to Executive Health. London: Prentice-Hall.

Schabracq, M., Winnubst, J., & Cooper, C. (1996). *Handbook of work and health psychology*. New York: Wiley.

Sutherland, V., & Cooper, C. L. (1991). *Stress and accidents in the offshore oil and gas industry*. Houston, TX: Gulf Publishing.

Sutherland, V., & Cooper, C. L. (2000). *Strategic stress management*. London: Macmillan.

US Bureau of the Census (2000). *Statistical Abstract of the United States*: (2000) Washington, DC: US Bureau of the Census.

Worrall, L., & Cooper, C. L. (2001). *Quality of working life survey*. London: Chartered Management Institute.

CHAPTER 9

Human Resource Policies for Work–Personal Life Integration

Evangelia Demerouti

The conclusion of a recent review on the work–family literature by Eby, Casper, Lockwood, Bordeaux, and Brinley (2005) that only 'few studies examined family-supportive organizational policies given practitioner interest in developing "family friendly" work environments' (p. 186) is quite disappointing. Even more disappointing is the conclusion of the meta-analysis by Kossek and Ozeki (1999) that HRM policies that aim to enhance work–family balance are often underutilized by employees, frequently unsupported by prevailing corporate cultures (Solomon, 1994), and may not result in reducing work–family conflict (Blum, Fields, & Goodman, 1994) or improving organizational effectiveness (Dunham, Pierce, & Castenada, 1987).

Therefore, it is not surprising that the forces for family responsiveness fall short. This is partly because the assumed benefits of many family-responsive policies have not been demonstrated either for productivity (the obvious selling point to business) or for the quality of workers' family lives (Kingston, 1990).

In order to encourage employers to improve the implementation of such policies, policy makers to facilitate and support policies' realization and researchers to investigate gaps in the knowledge concerning these policies using good methodological practices this chapter addresses the following questions: What does 'work–personal life integration' policies mean? Why do organizations apply work–life policies? What is the effectiveness of existing work–life policies? What additional policies can be suggested? What are the methodological/ theoretical deficiencies of the existing studies? Why don't work–life policies really work? The next section concerns the consideration of work–life policies as strategic HRM decisions. The final question addressed in this overview is what are the challenges for research and practice in the future?

What does 'Work–Personal Life Integration' Policies Mean?

Policies that are meant to help employees better manage their work and non-work times are called in the literature as work–family policies, family friendly or family-responsive policies. A problem with the use of these terms is that they restrict the attention to parenting and childcare issues ignoring several other activities in which people are involved, besides the time that they devote to their work and family. In the present review, I will use the term work–personal life integration policies (or shorter work–life policies). This term is more inclusive than the previous 'family-friendly' agenda, which focused primarily on the needs of working mothers. Therefore, the review is applicable to work–life integration policies that focus not only on the care of young children, but applies also to carers of older children and adults as well as to those without care responsibilities. Moreover, it applies to employees that are involved in voluntary work, community activities, politics, religion, physical exercise and other free time activities and social life.

Why do Organizations Apply Work–Life Policies?

To Increase Participation of Female Personnel and Make Use of their Capacities

If companies take a more active stance on providing career opportunities for women, they will be able to take advantage of a pool of qualified female personnel, since women are often those who make use of such policies. Indeed, Konrad and Mangel (2000) observed a positive association between the provision of work–life policies and the percentage of company's workers who are female. Additionally, firms with the most generous benefits for work–life balance — comprising such things as flextime, job sharing, telecommuting, elder care adaptation benefits and dependent childcare options — also tended in the study of Dreher (2003) to be the firms with the highest percentages of female senior management positions. As the percentage of women in managerial positions increases, they are able to form coalitions and exert political influence. This should work to increase the possibility that work–life policies are provided by the organization.

To Keep Employees Motivated and Well Performing

The recognition of the importance of family issues, particularly with respect to important technical outcomes such as firm performance, motivates greater organizational responsiveness (Goodstein, 1994). It has been argued that work–life programs generate performance by enhancing recruitment and by reducing absenteeism and turnover (Greenhaus & Parasuraman, 1999). When job demands interfere with family life, employees may try to reduce this tension by expending less time and effort on their jobs (Brett, 1997), by moving to a job that (presumably) generates less tension between both domains (Greenhaus, Collins, Singh, & Parasuraman, 1997), or by totally stop working (Klerman & Leibowitz, 1999). The assumption is therefore that the provision of work–life programs will increase the productivity of the organization since they will reduce absenteeism and turnover and they will encourage employees to put forth extra effort. Unfortunately, if the economic benefits were so obvious, widespread adoption should be expected (Kingston, 1990). The general absence of well-documented 'productivity benefits' in the research literature can do little to dispel the skepticism of organizations.

To Make the Organization more Attractive for the Employees

Organization's human resource (HR) systems are considered instrumental in staffing decisions made by the organizations and the choice decisions made by applicants (Rynes, 1992), which corresponds to the person–organization fit perspective. The provision of work–life benefits more clearly distinguishes an employer from its competitors and might have substantial effects on an organization's image as "good place to work" (Rynes, 1992). Indeed, Bretz and Judge (1994) found that relative older female applicants with high team orientation were attracted by organizations offering work–life policies, since this is the group that affords greatest weight in achieving work–life balance.

To have a Better Corporate Social Responsibility

Being socially responsible means not only fulfilling legal expectations, but also going beyond compliance and investing 'more' into human capital, the environment and the relations with stakeholders. The experience with investment in environmentally responsible technologies and business practice suggests that going beyond legal compliance can contribute to a company's competitiveness. Going beyond basic legal obligations in the social area, for example, training, working conditions, management–employee relations, can also have a direct impact on productivity. It opens a way of managing change and of reconciling social development with improved competitiveness (European Commission, 2001). Among the stakeholders of an organization i.e., the people or groups with an interest in the organizational activities and the outcome of those activities (Donalson & Preston, 1995), employees are important constituencies. If an organization does not provide policies that facilitate the balance between work and life, not only the quality of life of the individual is harmed, but also this creates problems in the social life since for instance, birth rates might be reduced, participation of women in the work force is diminished, cultural and voluntary activities deteriorate. Several of the policies known as work–life benefits are included in the list of typical corporate and stakeholder issues (Clarkson, 1995). Moreover, there is said to be strong evidence that the most successful firms adopt a stakeholder perspective (Greenley & Foxall, 1997).

What is the Effectiveness of Existing Work–Life Policies?

Flexible Working Times

The ways suitable for increasing flexibility of working hours can include several different interventions such as: compressed working weeks, seasonal work, bank of hours, gliding schedule, early retirement, etc. (Lewis, 2003). Though many forms have been proposed under the umbrella term of flexible working times (FWTs), the most well-known form is daily schedule flexibility, namely the core time during which all employees have to be present, and flexible periods at the beginning and the end of the working day (Van Rijswijk, Bekker, & Rutte, 2002). Daily schedule flexibility is now available to 27% of the US work force, compared to 15% in 1991 (Golden, 2001). The percentage of employees (excluding those in shiftwork) with variable start and end times (gliding schedules) ranges in the EU between 7% (Greece) and 30% (The Netherlands and UK) with an average of 22% (European Foundation for Improvement of Living and Working Conditions, 2001).

Perhaps, the reason why FWTs have become that popular is the advantages that are linked to them. Major advantages claimed include lowered stress, better work–family balance, increased job enrichment and autonomy and improved job satisfaction and productivity (Christensen & Staines, 1990; Golembiewski & Proehl, 1978; Pierce & Newstrom, 1983). However, there is another side of the coin, which concerns the disadvantages that have also been related to the FWTs. Major disadvantages identified include increased costs, problems with scheduling and work coordination, difficulties with supervising employees and changes in organizational culture (Christensen & Staines, 1990; Golembiewski & Proehl, 1978; Pierce & Newstrom, 1983).

Despite the fact that FWTs are widespread in practice, available research has several deficiencies. First, with few exceptions, research has not been based on theoretical models (Pierce, Newstrom, Dunham, & Barber, 1989). Second, results are inconclusive. The effects of FWT schedules on work-related criteria/outcomes (e.g. absenteeism, performance, work–family conflict) range from negative (Kluwer, Boers, Heesink, & van de Vliert, 1997; Pierce et al., 1989) to zero or positive effects (Lewis, 2003; Ronen & Primps, 1981). These mixed results may point to the existence of moderators (e.g. fairness) in the relationship between FWTs and outcomes (Baltes, Briggs, Huff, Wright, & Neuman, 1999). Third, much of the literature is dominated by anecdotal reports, non-standardized research methods and unsystematic data collection (Pierce & Newston, 1983), which make the validity of the studies questionable. Finally, most researchers have utilized their own definition of FWT, and have ignored the multidimensional (design) character of flexible work schedules (Pierce et al., 1989).

In general, two types of flexibility can be distinguished, employer flexibility and employee flexibility (Costa et al., 2003). *Employer flexibility* refers to conditions where customer demands, production goals or other organizational requirements determine the working times. In contrast, *employee flexibility* refers to conditions where individual employees' needs and preferences determine the working times. If the employer can flexibly appoint the working hours to the employees, this is basically done for economic reasons: it allows the company to lengthen or reduce the machine run times or the service schedules. Based on these definitions we can assume that employer flexibility will have favorable effects on organizational outcomes like productivity (at least in the short term) and unfavorable on employees' well-being and family life (Demerouti, Geurts, Bakker, & Euwema, 2004), while employee flexibility will be more beneficial for employees' well-being and family life. There are some first indications that this is the case (Demerouti, Kattenbach, & Nachreiner, 2003).

However, it can also be assumed that the most beneficial FWT arrangements would be those that involve control over the working times from both parties (employees and employers) — a so-called *win–win* situation. This contention that FWT arrangements should strive for a win–win situation for employees and employers is supported by the conclusion of Lewis (2003) that 'too much flexibility is a bad thing' (p. 8). Highly flexible FWT arrangements have diminished effectiveness (in terms of job performance, absenteeism and job attitudes) in comparison to less flexible programs (Baltes et al., 1999).

However, the policies (including FWT) reviewed by Kossek and Ozeki (1999) did not necessarily reduce work–family conflict in all circumstances, particularly if they did not enhance employee's control over their work schedules. In addition, Barling and Barenburg (1984) found that compared to their non-flexible counterparts, working mothers with FWT arrangements experienced significantly lower depression but not less conflict between the work (professional) and non-work (parent or spouse) roles, as was hypothesized. Interventions in which employees have been able to participate in the design of work schedules appear to have the potential to achieve highly workable, flexible arrangements and be associated with positive work-related attitudes (Rapoport, Bailyn, Fletcher, & Pruitt, 2002). Conversely, lack of consultation with management about the development of FWTs can contribute to feelings of (procedural) unfairness, which may undermine implementation (Lewis, 2003) and lead to negative affective, cognitive and behavioral responses (Cropanzano, Byrne, Bobocel, & Rupp, 2001) creating in the long term higher risk for health impairment. However, several researchers (e.g. Baltes et al., 1999; Lewis, 2003) speculate that one reason for the negative effects of high levels of flexibility in the studies that appear in reviews may be that more flexible policies on paper may result in managers clamping down flexibility in practice in order to sustain control.

Alternative Work Location, Teleworking, Telecommuting

Telework, remote work or telecommuting is the use of computers and telecommunications equipment to do office work away from a central, conventional office during regular office hours (Kraut, 1987). Telework replaces work done at a central office location. Employees who work at home might experience enhanced autonomy, more flexible working hours, fewer interruptions and reduction in costs for transportation (Zedeck & Mosier, 1990). They can also solve easier several family demands since they can take care of their children, such that less daycare is necessary or be with their child in case of sickness while they actually are working. Paradoxically, for those with childcare responsibilities working at home was found to be related to more conflict between work and family, while for those without childcare responsibilities telecommuting enhanced their work and family integration (Olson & Primps, 1984).

The predictions about the effectiveness of telecommuting in reducing problems with balancing work and family as well as the initial research findings were more positive (e.g. Gordon, 1976) than the results of recent investigations. For instance, Duxbury, Higgings, and Thomas (1996) found that users of telecommuting were more likely to report high overload, greater stress and more work–family interference. This is not surprising since the physical boundaries between the two environments are eliminated (Shamir & Salomon, 1985), and the beginning as well as end times of work are unclearly defined (Hamilton, 1987) and therefore extended. However, the biggest concern about telecommuting is the potential for exploitation by the organization (Zedeck & Mosier, 1990). According to Zedeck and Mosier (1990), telecommuting contains the danger to exploit the more vulnerable groups of the working population, like females with enhanced childcare responsibilities, elderly individuals and people with handicaps. The reason is that telecommuters are isolated from the organization and therefore their promotion possibilities might be impaired. Due to its attractiveness, telecommuting is expected to increase in the near future, therefore careful countermeasures should be applied, e.g. restrict telecommuting to one or two days per working week, open clear contact channels between telecommuters and the organization.

Voluntary Reduced Time and Part-Time Work, Job Sharing

Unlike most part-time employment, a permanent part-time position involves responsibility, the potential for upward mobility and rewards, as well as benefits that are proportionally comparable to employees with a full-time appointment (Kingston, 1990). Job sharing is a variant of permanent part-time work. Under this arrangement two employees jointly hold a position, giving both of them access to the responsibilities and rewards of a full-time position but involving a lesser time commitment (Kahne, 1985).

For organizations, permanent part-time jobs can solve scheduling problems such as fluctuations in required personnel by providing sufficient coverage for peak periods. Moreover, part-timers work more hours than formally required which enhances unpaid labor for organizations (Lee, MacDermid, Williams, Buck, & Leiba-O'Sullivan, 2002). For employees such arrangements give the chance to pursue working instead of leaving the work force. Particularly for women part-time work allows them to have sufficient time for the family (Zedeck & Mosier, 1990). However, empirical findings are not so straightforward.

A study by Higgins, Duxbury, and Johnson (2000) among employed women in career jobs (i.e., managerial or professional positions) and non-career jobs (i.e., clerical, administrative, retail or production jobs) showed that simply making part-time work available was not enough to help employed women to deal with high work and family responsibilities. Accordingly, although non-career women benefited from working part-time, career women did not. Whereas for non-career women, part-time work was associated with significant improvement of the work–non-work balance, career women reported high role overload and high family-to-work conflict regardless of their full-time or part-time status. As Higgins et al. (2000) conclude, in order to truly make a difference in the quality of life for employed women (especially working mothers) part-time work must also be made desirable and rewarding. The latter concerns again the informal organizational climate and the degree to which the different alternatives are incorporated in the daily practice and culture. Their research stresses the necessity for organizations to pay greater attention to some of the individual differences between career and non-career employed women in terms of the role that work plays in their lives and the rewards they are seeking through employment.

On the contrary, the study of Lee et al. (2002) among managers and professionals showed that individuals who used reduced-load work arrangements had better work–life balance and greater well-being and more positive evaluations of the relationship with their children. Participants believed that part-time work did not have negative consequences on one's career, although professionals were more likely to mention stifled career opportunities. Contextual factors that influenced the success of these work arrangements were management support and a supportive organizational culture, the presence of formal HR policies regarding reduced work arrangements and assistance in the implementation of such arrangements.

Barnett (1998) argues that the reduced amount of working hours alone is not enough to ameliorate problems with work–life balance. She believes that the nature of work (e.g. flexibility, schedule control and a supportive environment) is more important than the hours worked. An additional drawback of part-time work is the lower income that it brings, which certainly can have negative consequences to some families.

On-Site and Near-Site Childcare, Elder care

Developing childcare provision systems in the EU and in the US appears to have been an emerging priority for the past years. This concern is related to the need to promote equal opportunities for men and women in the labor pool. Despite discrepancies in statistics and information about childcare available across EU member countries, the EU does its best to gather information and recommend guidelines to benefit both working parents and children. Childcare subsidies are available throughout the EU, but the cost of childcare remains a controversial issue. The availability of childcare is not enough. Childcare should also be affordable to give parents more incentive to use it and improve parental choice. There is only limited information available on the amount of money spent on childcare services and on the most optimal division of childcare costs between the government, the employers and the individual parents. Evidence seems to suggest that in most states childcare services are not freely accessible. Parents pay an income-related fee, which, on average, amounts to 25–35% of childcare costs (Plantenga & Siegel, 2004). Moreover, an important issue for the coming years seems to be the streamlining of childcare services into one integrated system of services of care, education and leisure. Diversity, variety and parental choice are important issues when it comes to reconciling work and family. Fragmentation, and non-corresponding time schedules and difficulties in transitions from one service to another should be considered inefficiencies, which hinder the optimal use of services and the growth of female labor force participation (Plantenga & Siegel, 2004).

The involvement of organizations on child and dependent care can range between the provision of information (least costly provision) to payment for childcare and corporate sponsored daycare programs (most expensive commitment) (for more details, see in Zedeck & Mosier, 1990). Research about the effects of on-site care has produced mixed results. Although one study found that the existence of an on-site care center was positively associated with user's attitudes toward managing work and family life (Kossek & Nichol, 1992), another study found that an on-site care center had no effects on the experience work–family conflict (Thomas & Ganster, 1995). Eby, Casper, Lockwood, Bordeaux, and Brinley (2005) reviewed studies that examined issues relevant to childcare. In general, utilization of and satisfaction with on-site childcare was related to lower work–family conflict (Goff, Mount, & Jamison, 1990), fewer problems with childcare, and favorable attitudes about the ability to manage childcare (Kossek & Nichol, 1992). Besides these effects on attitudes, the provision of on-site childcare had no direct relationship to (lower) absenteeism (Goff et al., 1990; Kossek & Nichol, 1992), but only indirect via experienced work–family conflict. Not surprisingly, the preferred childcare assistance (e.g. voucher system, family daycare network) differs among employees as a function of family situation and sociodemographic characteristics (Kossek, 1990).

Elder care means providing some kind of assistance with the daily activities for an elderly relative who is chronically ill or disabled (Galinsky & Stein, 1990). While this is a low priority issue for organizations, it seems that many employees are involved in the care of an aged or sick parent, e.g. one out of ever five employees in the study of Friedman (1987). Moreover, employees who provide elder or ill care have also more depressive symptoms and declined emotional health than their counterparts without care giving obligations. In particular, women are more susceptible to the negative effects of care giving (Lee, Walker, & Schoup, 2001). Kossek, Colquitt, and Noe (2001) found that having to take care for an elder dependent at home was more detrimental for the well-being and family as well as work performance than when the dependent was a child. Having to provide family-based home care for an elder within a family that sharing of work concerns was discouraged was the most detrimental situation for employees' well-being and work performance.

Maternity, Paternity and Adoption Leave

Maternity leave is the time a mother takes off from work at the birth or adoption of a child. Actual paid maternity leave is unusual in the US, although some companies offer new parents some paid time off, up to six weeks in some cases. This law applies especially to medium or large firms (Zedeck & Mosier, 1990). Most likely, the employees use a combination of short-term disability, sick leave, vacation, personal days and unpaid family leave during their maternity leave. In Europe, the minimum maternity leave is 14 weeks allocated before and/or after confinement and without payment loss. In addition, it is compulsory a maternity leave to include at least two weeks allocated before confinement (European Community, 1992; Directive 92/85/EEC). Many organizations in the US do not guarantee that the employee will get the same job if she takes more than six weeks maternity leave. In Europe, the member states have to take the necessary measures to prohibit the dismissal of workers, during the period from the beginning of their pregnancy to the end of the maternity leave.

Paternity leave is a relatively new trend in some EU countries, but not in others. Such regulations have been refined to give fathers more rights in taking care of their children. The EU Directive on Parental Leave provides for two weeks paid paternity leave. In the US, family leave is not limited to care for young children but includes everyone in the family from the spouse to elderly relatives through the Family and Medical Leave Act.

Supervisory Training in Work–Family Sensitivity

Several scholars view supervisors as a crucial factor for the success of work–life policies. Supervisory support is an important resource that lowers stress and has been found to be more important than support from colleagues (Terry, Callan, & Sartori, 1996). Supervisors are the persons who represent the organization and stand between the organization and employees. They are often those who decide about which employee will get what policy and consequently supervisors are those who can fairly or unfairly distribute them. Therefore, supervisors (should) receive trainings in order to be aware of the company policies that apply to family issues, to consider as a part of their role the managing of family issues of employees, to be flexible when work–family problems arise and to treat employees fairly regarding the provision of work–family policies (Galinsky & Stein, 1990). Several studies examined how perceptions of organizational and supervisor support for work and family relate to employee outcomes. Supportive supervision and organizational support related to having more benefits available within the organization as well as more utilization of benefits (Allen, 2001). Clark (2001) found that (perceptions of) supportive supervision for family issues related to higher work functioning (organizational citizenship) and greater family functioning (in terms of cohesion). Counter to expectations, supportive supervision was not found to help individuals in dual-career partnerships, individuals with many dependents or individuals working long hours much more than it helps individuals without these characteristics (Clark, 2001). Perhaps those at risk for work–family conflicts (i.e., those with more than one dependent at home and in dual earner families) had other support channels than their supervisors.

Multiple Benefits

Grover and Crooker (1995) systematically assessed the effect of multiple family supportive benefits on employee organizational attachment and found that employees who worked for companies that applied multiple benefits had higher affective commitment and lower turnover intentions than employee who worked in companies without such policies. An interesting finding was though that the availability of family supportive policies had a positive impact of employee attachment, regardless of whether an employee individually could or could not directly benefit from the policies. Grover and Crooker explain that work–family benefits may have a symbolic value, because they signify corporate concern for employees' well-being.

What Additional Policies can be Suggested?

As has become clear from the description of the different human resource management (HRM) policies, the concept of family responsive policies corresponds to two main types of personnel policies: (1) additions to the provision of the corporate social welfare system, including support for childcare, accommodations to childbirth, cafeteria plans; (2) modifications in typical work schedules, e.g. flextime, part-time, job sharing other leave policies. This operational definition obscures the breadth of the ways, in which business practices can influence family life and restricts policy debates to a narrow range of modest policy reforms (Kingston, 1990). As Kingston (1990) argues the primary concern of employees with family responsibilities is the availability of a job with good security and adequate pay. These resources are essential for a stable family life. For example, a frequent cited problem is the lack of affordable childcare and thus the increasingly heard remedy is the provision of subsidized services. However, childcare is unaffordable because the wages are inadequate to pay for it. If organizations fail to deliver on this account, all other concerns about responsiveness are largely mooted. Additionally, the operational definition of responsiveness that we currently use may lead us to overlook fundamental ways, in which business policies are unresponsive to families.

Inspection of prior research (e.g. Frone, Russell, & Cooper, 1992) indicates that employees are better at managing the potentially disrupting influence of their home demands on work life than they are at managing the potentially disrupting influence of their job demands on home life. In other words, family boundaries are more permeable to job demands than are work boundaries to family demands (Eagle, Miles, & Icenogle, 1999). Nevertheless, to date, strategies implemented by employers have sought to mitigate the impact of Family-Work-Conflict (FWC) conflict in order to improve employee productivity while on the job, and have paid less attention to how work might be negatively affecting the employee's family life. Thus, the majority of employers seem to use family responsive policies such as maternity and parental leaves, childcare programs, alternative work schedules and employee assistance and relocation programs (Zedeck & Mosier, 1990), instead of reducing job demands, e.g. through job re-design, training and HR development (Bakker, Demerouti, & Dollard, 2005).

A further surprising observation is that while several work-related factors have been recognized as valid antecedents of work–family interference, the so-called family friendly policies fail to refer to them. Specifically, job demands and requirements that might be incompatible with the family role (Greenhaus & Beutell, 1985) have been related to work–family conflict. Among the job demands, work overload is consistently found to be the most robust antecedent of work–family conflict (for an overview see Geurts & Demerouti, 2003). Employees who experience a high level of work–family conflict are those who also report high work role conflict and work role ambiguity (Carlson & Perrewé, 1999; Grandey & Cropanzano, 1999), pressure at work (Grzywacz & Marks, 2000) and work overload (Geurts, Rutte, & Peeters, 1999). Thus, classical job (re) design approaches that are appropriate in promoting employee well-being are definitely applicable to work–family issues. It makes little sense to provide on-site childcare on the one hand and on the other to completely exhaust employee energy due to high work overload (cf. strain-based work–family interference).

In a similar vein, several job characteristics have been found to alleviate the degree of conflict between work and private life and to enhance work–life integration. Higher levels of decision latitude or job control are related to lower levels of work–family conflict (Kinnunen & Mauno, 1998; Demerouti & Geurts, 2004), to lower levels of family–work conflict (Parasuraman, Purohit, Godshalk, & Beutell, 1996), and to higher levels of positive spillover in both directions (Grzywacz & Marks, 2000). Similarly, social support at the workplace is negatively associated with work–family conflict (Moen & Yu, 2000). Higher levels of social support at the workplace have also been found to contribute to higher levels of positive interaction between both domains (Grzywacz & Marks, 2000; Demerouti, Geurts, & Kompier, 2004). In the study of Wallace (1997), motivators like promotion opportunities and the social value of work were negatively related to work–family conflict.

Consequently, the most important suggestion to policy makers, practitioners and researchers is to concentrate on the basic factor that inhibits employees from integrating work and life, namely the adverse working conditions. If work is designed in such a way that job demands (e.g. work pressure, emotional demands) are not too high and, at the same time, job resources (e.g. job control, developmental possibilities) are sufficiently provided, then the harmful potential of work on individual's well-being and private life will be minimized (Demerouti, Bakker, Nachreiner, & Schaufeli, 2001; Demerouti et al., 2004).

What are the Methodological/Theoretical Deficiencies of the Existing Studies?

The studies on the effectiveness of work–life balance policies have been criticized in terms of both quantity and quality (Raabe, 1990). A first criticism has been that only a few employers conduct evaluation studies to assess the effects of the implementation of work–life policies. Companies do not seem to monitor how many employees use the offered policies and the in-house company research is often restricted and the quality of such research is unknown. Second and similar to research on workplace interventions (Kompier, Geurts, Gründemann, Vink, & Smulders, 1998), the research design of evaluative research is inadequate. Policy implementations have lacked longitudinal and comparative research with pre- and post measures, as well as research including control groups. A further criticism is that the existing research on the effects of policy implementation has restricted itself in 'soft' rather than 'hard' data i.e., in perceptions of effects or satisfaction measures instead of real behavioral outcomes (Raabe, 1990). Enhanced satisfaction with a policy is not a sufficient argument for an organization to implement work–life policies. Rather, organizations can better be persuaded to introduce such policies when survey results show improvements in absenteeism rates, performance and work morale. However, organizations should also realize that outcomes like performance, absenteeism or work morale are affected by many other factors besides work–life policies and such factors should be included in the evaluation research design. Still, research indicates that selected working conditions together with measures of well-being explain a meager 4% in the variance of absenteeism (Bakker, Demerouti, De Boer, & Schaufeli, 2003) or 8% in the variance of in-role performance (Bakker, Demerouti, & Verbeke, 2004), implying that organizations should not expect spectacular results.

Another critic concerns the lack of theoretical understanding of the way in which work–life policy variables and parameters may be linked to desired outcomes specifying the mechanisms and the nature of the linkages (Bowen, 1988). Such an overarching model of work and life linkages should specify whether different policies have different effects on organizational variables for varying populations (e.g. parents vs. non-parents or male vs. female), whether there are intervening variables which modify the influence of the applied policies (cf. the role of a supportive supervisor), whether the effects of a policy are short- or long term, whether each policy has unique effects or whether the effects of different policies are interrelated and combined (cf. Raabe, 1990). Studies that overcome the discussed methodological deficiencies and that build upon conceptual refinements can uncover the complexity of the impact of work–life policies on organizational and family variables.

Why do not Work–Life Policies Really Work?

Kamerman and Kahn's (1987) case studies of diverse firms show that employees may not be consistently informed of their benefits, be pressured not to use all of them or be subject to inefficient and uncooperative administration. There are several factors that may inhibit the effectiveness of such policies and, therefore, they will be discussed in the following section.

Employees are Afraid to Participate due to Negative Career Consequences

A first reason why work–life policies may not work is that employees do not make use of them, because they are afraid of the negative career consequences these opportunities might bring them. A study by Galinsky, Bond, and Friedman (1993) in the US revealed that only 2% of the employees participated in work–family programs. In a study among university female employees, 77% thought that taking maternity leave would hurt their career, and only 30% of those who gave birth took the full leave allowed (Finkel, Oslwang, & She, 1994). Also engineers were reluctant to make use of work–life policies due to fears for negative consequences to their careers (Perlow, 1995).

Formal Policies vs. Informal Pressure not to Participate

The enactment of work–life policies that are inconsistent with a broader concern for employee well-being may well be wasted effort (Galinsky & Stein, 1990) and actually foretell that work–life policy implementation alone will fail to generate beneficial effects for either employees or organizations (Behson, 2005). As Thompson, Beauvais, and Lyness (1999) noted it appears that unsupportive cultures and managers who enforce norms that enact such cultures may undermine the potential effectiveness of these programs. Another example are organizational norms that the time visible at work is considered as an indicator of employees' dedication and investments (Lewis & Taylor, 1996), and these norms may inhibit employees to take off for non-work responsibilities. According to the findings of Dikkers, Geurts, Den Dulk, Peper, and Kompier (2005), more than half of their participants were incorporated in contradictory cultures reflecting perceptions of high organizational, supervisory and collegial support combined with high hindrance i.e., high time expectations and negative career consequences. Therefore, organizations can expect to see positive results from the implementation of work–life programs only when they are willing to invest time and effort to create workplace cultures and management styles that will be truly supportive for employees. Examples of such actions are to give employees autonomy on how they get their work done, encourage supervisors to be supportive of work–family issues and not to penalize employees for devoting attention to their family (Behson, 2005).

Fairness

There is ample evidence that at least some of the work–life policies are not equally distributed among employees. While policies that belong to the collective employment package are consistently accessible to all employees, e.g. daycare options, other policies are not formal and therefore they are subject to management discretion, e.g. FWTs (Golden, 2001). For instance, access to FWTs are less likely for individuals who are non-white, women, unmarried and young, who have short job tenure, have a low education and who are employed in the public sector (Golden, 2001; Young, 1999). Those who have more access to flexibility are men, parents of young children (Young, 1999) or highly skilled and veteran employees (Rousseau, 2001). Ironically, women who would mainly benefit from working time flexibility, given the double burden they experience (work demands and family demands), have less access to flexibility. These findings apply to both the US and many European countries. One

explanation is that such policies are often made available only, or at least at first, to a particular segment of an organization's force, typically to managerial and professional staff on a
case-by-case basis or only temporally, or experimentally. Thus, at the moment, several policies are viewed as idiosyncratic features of the employment package (i.e., unique to particular individuals) that are provided to individual employees, and not standardized features that
are offered to all employees (e.g. health care benefits) or position-based (e.g. wage rates for
professionals) features (Rousseau, 2001). This unequal distribution of some work–life policies can potentially create feelings of unfair treatment among employees (distributive unfairness), which may undermine implementation (Lewis, 2003) and lead to negative affective,
cognitive and behavioral responses (Cropanzano et al., 2001) diminished motivation
(Van den Bos, 2002) creating in the long-term higher risk for health impairment (De Boer,
Bakker, Syroit, & Schaufeli, 2002), thus undermining the success of work–life policies.

   People care about justice largely because of the tangible outcomes they receive. People
also are interested in predicting the course of events (cf. need for control; Thibaut &
Walker, 1975). Fair processes (or procedural fairness, i.e., the fairness of allocation
processes or the way superiors arrive at decisions in general; Cropanzano & Greenberg,
1997) allow people to foretell more accurately the allocation of rewards and punishments
(Cropanzano et al., 2001). Fair procedures may be instrumentally important so long as they
establish a foreseeable pattern of events, which persists even when desired outcomes are
not received. This implies that if some policies cannot be provided to every employee
within an organization (which is the case, at least at the moment) in order to create fairness in achieving both consistency and flexibility, it is important that there are clear criteria for allocating benefits such as FWT (Rousseau, 2001). For instance, interventions in
which employees have been able to participate in the design of work schedules appear to
have the potential to achieve highly workable, flexible arrangements and be associated
with positive work-related attitudes (Rapoport et al., 2002).

Misfit between Employee Needs and Available Policies

While individual and organizational effectiveness can be boosted by introducing greater
flexibility or dependent care supports, such programs are expensive and it is important that
they are well thought and that they fit with the needs of both employees and the organization (Kossek & Ozeki, 1999). For instance, instead of forcing everybody to change from
fixed working times to compressed working weeks (4/40 week) it makes more sense to
give the workers the choice to select among these possibilities. The bottom line is that
employees must experience a policy as enabling enhanced role integration before job performance and attitudes are favorably affected. This relationship is likely to vary among
employee groups and therefore, organizations are advised to avoid one-size-fits-all
approaches, while researchers should avoid making generalizations of findings for all
types of employees, jobs and families (Kossek & Ozeki, 1999).

Demographic Composition of the Employees

Whether work–life programs will be successful in terms of productivity depends additionally on the demographic composition of the employees. Konrad and Mangel (2000) found

that firms employing higher percentages of professionals and of women showed a stronger relationship between the provision of extensive work–life benefits and productivity. The specialized knowledge of professionals is difficult and costly to develop and therefore makes them precious for organizations. Therefore, organizations will be more inclined to provide professionals (as compared to low-skilled and hence easily replaceable employees) extensive work–life programs in order to keep them at the company. Moreover, due to their scarcity and transferability of their skills, professionals may have greater power to persuade firms to provide them with costly work–life benefits. For women things are different. They have more problems with combining work and non-work life due to double burden (Greenhaus & Parasuraman, 1999). Therefore, they are more on need and more willing to use work–life policies in comparison to men who are more reluctant to make use of them in order to achieve balance (Thomson et al., 1999). Consequently, they are better candidates to profit by them and to reciprocate the investment of the organization with investing more effort in their job (Blair-Loy & Wharton, 2002; Wise, 2003; Konrad & Mangel, 2000).

Thus, policies have the best chance of success if the people using them, employees and line managers are fully involved in their design. Lack of consultation can result in policies, which do not match individuals' needs or cannot be used because of operational constraints.

Work–Life Policies as Strategic HRM Decisions

During the last decades there have been dramatic changes in the field of HRM. The focus of HRM has been broadened from the microlevel to more macro- or strategic perspective, known as strategic HRM. The basic promise of this perspective is that organizations that achieve congruence between their HR practices and their strategies should enjoy superior performance (Delery & Doty, 1996). The strategic HRM perspective emphasizes that a workforce strategy should fit an organization's business goals, culture and environmental circumstances and that HRM practices should be interrelated and internally consistent (Dreher, 2003).

While the field has been criticized for lacking theoretical foundation, Delery and Doty (1996) recognized three theoretical modes that are utilized in strategic HRM to explain mainly financial performance. The first theoretical approach is the universalistic perspective, which assumes that some practices are always better than others (the so-called best practices) and if organizations adopt them this will result in productivity (Pfeffer, 1994). A second theoretical approach is the contingency perspective arguing that in order to be effective the organization's HRM policies must be consistent with aspects like the organization's strategy (Gomez-Mejia & Balkin, 1992). The third theoretical model is the configurational approach, which is guided by a holistic principle of inquiry, and identifies typologies — instead of unique factors — that are posited to be maximally effective (for performance) (Doty, Glick, & Huber, 1993).

The question is now, which of these approaches are relevant to the study of the effectiveness of work–life policies. The first problem that we encounter when answering this question is how to operationalize effectiveness. Does it refer to the smooth functioning of family life, or to positive organizational behavior i.e., job performance, or is it merely the answers on questions about the experienced conflict between work and private life?

Evidence provides strong support for the universalistic perspective and some support for both the contingency and configurational perspective, at least what concerns the prediction of company's performance (Delery & Doty, 1996). This means that some HR practices were more appropriate under specific strategic conditions and less appropriate in other conditions underlining the complexity of the HR manager's job. Interestingly, none of the universalistic strategies investigated by Delery and Doty (1996) belongs to the traditional work–life policies except of employment security, which has been proposed in this chapter.

Based on the discussion of the different work–life policies it can be concluded that day and elder care options and leave possibilities could be considered as universalistic policies that enhance *family functioning*. The other policies are effective for family life either when they are offered in combinations e.g. part-time work together with FWTs or when they fit the strategy of the organization e.g. supportive supervisor in work–life issues within organizations that place issues in the organizational goals. Predictions about universalistic approaches that are appropriate for improved work performance are hard to make. Actually, none of the known work–life policies has been consistently found as beneficial for *job performance*. Also Konrad and Mangel (2000) found no relationship between a composite measure of 19 work–life initiatives and productivity. While there is not strong evidence for the universalistic approach for work–life policies regarding their effects on job performance, Perry-Smith and Blum (2000) provide evidence for the configurational approach. Specifically, organizations with a greater range of work–family policies (including leave policies, traditional dependent care and less traditional dependent care) had higher organizational performance, market performance and profit–sales growth. Work–life policies have not been studied yet from a contingency perspective while this can be promising in terms of effectiveness.

While it seems logical that there should be a lot of research on the relationship between the provision of specific (combinations of) work–life policies and experienced *work–life balance or conflict*, the studies reviewed in this chapter as well as the overviews of Eby et al. (2005) and of Kossek and Ozeki (1999) do not confirm this. What can be concluded from the existing studies is that there are no universalistic policies that have been found to be beneficial in reducing conflict between work and non-work domain (Eby et al., 2005; Kossek & Ozeki, 1999). In a study among male executives, Judge, Boudreau, and Bretz (1994) found that the more the organizations provided comprehensive policies to accommodate work and family issues the less work–family conflict was experienced by these employees. However, the relationship was not so strong and Jugde et al. used a global scale to rate the provision of policies. While we cannot make any conclusion about which policies were supplied, this finding can be considered as an indication that it is the provision of constellations of work–life policies that matters and not a unique policy. This pleads for the configuration or contingency approach as more applicable for the reduction of conflict between work and life/family.

What are the Challenges for Research and Practice in the Future?

Based on the previous literature review, several suggestions can be made for research and practice in order to improve our understanding, choice, implementation and effectiveness of work–life policies.

Suggestions for Research

Understand the underlying mechanisms   A task for future research is to comprehend the mechanisms, through which work–life policies have impact on the outcomes that they are aimed to, i.e., the work functioning and in particular performance, family functioning and experienced work–family conflict. It is possible that their impact is indirect through intervening variables, like the evaluation of whether the policy is useful for a given individual, in a particular life stage and family status, and within specific working conditions. For instance, the mechanism for job performance could be that employees reciprocate the care of the organization by investing more effort and interest in their job, enhancing in that way their performance. Another possibility is that bundles of work–life policies create a competitive advantage in a business climate in which adaptation of such policies is limited (Perry-Smith & Blum, 2000). Moreover, it is possible that the effects of such policies appear with a time lag, since users of such policies might have to get used to them, or to make some adjustments to their work or family life before they profit by them. Therefore, the impact of work–life policies is more probable a long-term process which should be considered in studies on their effectiveness.

Together or in isolation   Another issue important for future research is to investigate whether there are best practices in the work–life policies (cf. universalistic approach), whether the most effective ones are those that fit to some characteristic(s) of the organization (cf. contingency approach) or whether there are clusters of policies who are more effective in specific situations (cf. configuration approach). Such theoretically driven research could uncover the way in which work–life policies come to positive effects for both the organizations and the employees. Moreover, such systemic and holistic thinking would motivate researchers and practitioners to consider and investigate policies other than childcare or FWTs, thus expanding their meaning.

Consideration of cross-cultural differences   Studies on the implementation and effectiveness of work–life policies should consider the cultural context of the country or society, the organization and even the work group in which the policies are applied. Policies should be consistent with the core characteristics of the specific country or society (which comes back to the legislation and the organization of working and family life), the specific organization (in particular to its strategy, products and competitive environment) and the work group (which can have the own subculture driven from the nature of work and the characteristics of its members). A particular (sub) culture may require the implementation of specific policies, which are then more effective than others. For instance, in individualistic societies struggling between work and personal life is most probably seen as an individual matter, therefore provision of individual autonomy and flexibility might be more helpful than a company childcare facility.

Improvement of research practices   As this review has shown, studies that investigate the impact of work–family policies on the work–life interface have been rather scarce. At this point Westman and Piotrkowski (1999, p. 304) seem to be right with their suggestion that 'we need to look for opportunities to conduct "natural experiments" when people are changing or starting jobs, or when corporate restructuring occurs'. Additionally studies on the work–life integration need to move toward better methodological and research design approaches. Instead of asking only employees themselves about their experiences and therefore running the danger of measuring cognitive consistencies in the response patterns, it is important to have multiple sources of information from both domains, family, e.g. the partner, adolescent child(ren) and work domain, e.g. supervisors or observers. The use of longitudinal designs can further improve our insight into the possible causal relationships of the policies and their consequences for organizations, employees and their families. Moreover, longitudinal studies could provide insight into the question whether the work–life policies are effective in the long run, which would explain the discouraging results of the existing studies.

Suggestions for Practice

Compatibility of policies with the HRM strategies   One of the most important tasks for HRM professionals is to view the work–life policies as a part of the organization's HRM practices. This will also increase the compatibility between work–life and other HRM policies and eventually enhance the integration of work–life policies in a company's strategy (which is probably the prerequisite of the effectiveness of such policies). Such compatibility between work–life policies and organizational strategy (and consequently the resulting HRM policies) will further ensure that work–life policies match to the company's environment and to the nature of the jobs, since these two should be closely related to an organization's strategy.

Legitimization of the problem   A further suggestion linked to the previous point is that organizations should enhance the realization that struggling between working life and personal life is not an individual problem but also a broader, organizational problem for which the organization shares responsibility. Employers should recognize that providing support to their employees for work–life matters by implementing work–life policies should be a main part of the employment issues.

Involve individual needs   Individual preferences and needs should be considered in the choice of the specific work–life policies. Important in this respect is to consider the impact of the various work–life interventions for different subgroups, because what is helpful for, for instance, working women with young children is not necessarily beneficial for working women without (young) children or for male workers. As stated before, individual preferences are by no doubt, again, a key factor and therefore they should be integrated in the process of selection of the most applicable policies. This means automatically that employees should be involved in the implementation process, which brings several advantages with itself. On the one hand, it facilitates the selection of potentially more effective policies and on the other, employees are better informed about such policies (since several studies mention inadequate information as a problem).

Combination of policies   What became clear from the previous overview is that single work–life policies are less probable to be effective. More possible seems the view that constellations of policies have more potential to enhance work–life integration. This makes the task of HRM managers extremely difficult and challenging but, at the same time, it emphasizes that organizations should not have high expectations from one single policy.

Supportive environment and managers   HRM managers should invest in creating a supportive organizational environment in which the utilization of work–life policies by employees is not seen as a deviant behavior. Moreover, attention should be devoted in the training of line managers, i.e., the key persons for practicing such policies, such that they can facilitate instead of inhibiting their implementation and operation. This means that line managers should be provided with the necessary resources like adequate knowledge about the policies, sufficient time to manage work–life policies.

More legislative basis   Given the slow progress of the work–life policies, more legislative stimulus may be needed to give such polices a stronger foothold in organizational life. Formal policies both at the organizational and national level are important for giving legitimacy, reducing the reliance on the sake of the good will of managers. The historical record on the provision of other worker benefits indicates that firms rarely take initiative to apply them except insofar as these benefits enhance control over employees (Kingston, 1990). More generally, businesses have responded when compelled to do so by law or collective bargaining or when 'concessions' were strategically opportune.

Concluding Remarks

To conclude, the value of these suggestions lies in their ability to provide guidelines for the design of effective strategies for improving the integration of work and private life (Lambert, 1990). Research on the interface between work and personal life has consistently shown that the influence of work on personal life is evaluated more often negatively, rather than positively (Grzywacz & Marks, 2000; Demerouti et al., 2004). Therefore, the most promising strategy to reduce conflict and facilitate integration between both domains is to create a healthy and motivational workplace that respects workers who have responsibilities and interests outside the workplace that they consider important for their quality of life (Geurts & Demerouti, 2003). This organizational strategy can be expected to have a positive and profound impact on people's functioning within and outside the workplace, which is beneficial not only for employees themselves, but also for their families, organizations and society.

References

Allen, T. D. (2001). Family-supportive work environments: The role of organizational perceptions. *Journal of Vocational Behavior, 58*, 414–435.
Bakker, A. B., Demerouti, E., & Verbeke, W. (2004). Using the job demands — resources model to predict burnout and performance. *Human Resource Management, 43*, 83–104.
Bakker, A. B., Demerouti, E., De Boer, E., & Schaufeli, W. B. (2003). Job demands and job resources as predictors of absence duration and frequency. *Journal of Vocational Behavior, 62*, 341–356.

Bakker, A. B., Demerouti, E., & Dollard, M. (2005). Do job demands influence one's partner's feelings of exhaustion? A study on spillover and crossover, manuscript submitted for publication.

Baltes, B. B., Briggs, T. E., Huff, J. W., Wright, J. A., & Neuman, G. A. (1999). Flexible and compressed workweek schedules: A meta-analysis of their effects on work-related criteria. *Journal of Applied Psychology, 84*, 496–513.

Barling, J., & Barenburg, A. (1984). Some personal consequences of 'flexitime' work schedules. *Journal of Social Psychology, 123*, 137–138.

Barnett, R. C. (1998). Toward a review and reconceptualization of the work/family literature. *Genetic, Social, and General Psychology Monographs, 124*, 125–182.

Behson, S. J. (2005). The relative contribution of formal and informal organizational work–family support, *Journal of Vocational Behavior, 66*, 487–500.

Blair-Loy, M., & Wharton, A. S. (2002). Employees' use of work–family policies and workplace social context. *Social Forces, 80*, 813–845.

Blum, T. C., Fields, D. I., & Goodman, J. S. (1994). Organizational level determinants of women in management. *Academy of Management Journal, 37*, 241–268.

Bowen, G. (1988). Corporate supports for the family and lives of employees: A conceptual model for program planning and evaluation. *Family Relations, 37*, 183–188.

Brett, J. M. (1997). Family, sex and career advancement. In: S. Parasuraman & J. H. Greenhaus (Eds), Integrating *work and family: Challenges and choices for a changing world* (pp. 143–153). Westport, CT: Quorum.

Bretz, R. D, & Judge, T. A. (1994). The role of human resource systems in job applicant decision processes. *Journal of Management, 20*, 531–551.

Carlson, D. S., & Perrewé, P. L. (1999). The role of social support in the stressor–strain relationship: An examination of work–family conflict. *Journal of Management, 25*, 513–540.

Christensen, K. E., & Staines, G. L. (1990). Flextime: A viable solution to work/family conflict? *Journal of Family Issues, 11*, 455–476.

Clark, S. C. (2001). Work cultures and work/family balance. *Journal of Vocational Behavior, 58*, 348–365.

Clarkson, M. B. E. (1995). A stakeholder framework for analyzing and evaluating corporate social performance. *Academy of Management Review, 20*, 92–117.

Costa, G, Akerstedt, T., Nachreiner, F., Frings-Dresen, M., Folkard, S., Gadbois, C., Grzech-Sukalo, H., Gärtner, J., Härmä, M., & Kandolin, I. (2003). *SALTSA: As time goes by — flexible work times, health and well-being*. Stockholm: National Institute for Working Life.

Cropanzano, R., Byrne, Z. S., Bobocel, D. R., & Rupp, D. E. (2001). Moral virtues, fairness heuristics, social entities, and other denizens of organizational justice. *Journal of Vocational Behavior, 58*, 164–209.

Cropanzano, R., & Greenberg, J. (1997). Progress in organizatinal justice: Tunnelling through the maze. In: C. Cooper & I. Robertson (Eds), *International review of industrial and organizational psychology* (pp. 317–372). New York: Wiley.

De Boer, E. M., Bakker, A. B., Syroit, J. E., & Schaufeli, W. B. (2002). Unfairness at work as a predictor of absenteeism. *Journal of Organizational Behavior, 23*, 181–197.

Delery, J. E., & Doty, D. H. (1996). Modes of theorizing in strategic human resource management: Tests of universalistic, contingency, and configurational performance predictions. *Academy of Management Journal, 39*, 802–835.

Demerouti, E., Bakker, A. B., Nachreiner, F., & Schaufeli, W. B. (2001). The job demands — resources model of burnout. *Journal of Applied Psychology, 86*, 499–512.

Demerouti, E., & Geurts, S. (2004). Towards a typology of work–home interference: The prevalence of work–home interference patterns under specific individual, job and home characteristics. *Community, Work & Family, 7*, 285–309.

Demerouti, E., Geurts, S. A. E., Bakker, A. B., & Euwema, M. (2004). The impact of shiftwork on work–home interference, job attitudes and health. *Ergonomics, 47*, 987–1002.

Demerouti, E., Geurts, S. A. E., & Kompier, M. A. J. (2004). Demands and resources as antecedents of positive and negative interference between work and home. *Equal Opportunities International, 23*, 6–35.

Demerouti, E., Kattenbach, R., & Nachreiner, F. (2003). Flexible working times: Consequences on employees' burnout, work–non-work conflict and performance. *Shiftwork International Newsletter, 20*, 61.

Dikkers, J., Geurts, S., Den Dulk, L., Peper, B., & Kompier, M. (2004). Relations among work–home culture, the utilization of work–home arrangements, and work–home interference. *International Journal of Stress Management, 11*, 323–345.

Donalson, T., & Preston, L. E. (1995). The stakeholder theory of the corporation: Concepts, evidence and implications. *Academy of Management Review, 20*, 65–91.

Doty, D. H., Glick, W. H., & Huber, G. P. (1993). Fit, equifinality, and organizational effectiveness: A test of two configurational theories. *Academy of Management Journal, 36*, 1196–1250.

Dreher, G. F. (2003). Breaking glass ceiling: The effects of sex ratios and work–life programs on female leadership at the top. *Human Relations, 56*, 541–562.

Dunham, R. B., Pierce, J. L., & Castenada, M. B. (1987). Alternative work schedules: Two field quasi experiments. *Personnel Psychology, 40*, 215–242.

Duxbury, L. E., Higgins, C. A., & Thomas, D. R. (1996). Work and family environments and the adoption of computer-supported supplemental work-at-home. *Journal of Vocational Behavior, 49*, 1–23.

Eagle, B. W., Miles, E. W., & Icenogle, M. L. (1997). Interrole conflicts and the permeability of work and family domains: Are there gender differences? *Journal of Vocational Behavior, 50*, 168–184.

Eby, L. T., Casper, W. J., Lockwood, A., Bordeaux, C., & Brinley, A. (2005). Work and family research in IO/OB: Content analysis and review of the literature (1980–2002). *Journal of Vocational Behavior, 66*, 124–197.

European Commission. (2001). Promoting a European framework for corporate social responsibility. Green paper. http://europa.eu.int/comm/employement_social/soc_dial/greenpaper_en.pdf.

European Community (1992). Council Directive 92/85/EEC of October 1992. http://europa.eu.int/smartapi/cgi/sga_doc? smartapi!celexplus!prod!DocNumber&lg=en &type_doc=Directive&an_doc=1992&nu_doc=85

European Foundation of the Improvement of Living and Working Conditions. (2001). *Third European survey on working conditions 2000*. Luxembourg: Office for Official Publications of the European Communities.

Finkel, S. K., Oslwang, S., & She, N. (1994). Childbirth, tenure, and promotion for women faculty. *Review of Higher Education, 17*, 259–270.

Friedman, D. E. (1987). Work vs. family: War of worlds. *Personnel Administrator, 32*, 36–39.

Frone, M. R., Russell, M., & Cooper, M. L. (1992). Prevalence of work–family conflict: Are work and family boundaries asymmetrically permeable? *Journal of Organizational Behavior, 13*, 723–729.

Galinsky, E., Bond, J. T., & Friedman, D. E. (1993). *Highlights: The national study of the changing workforce*. New York: Families and Work Institute.

Galinsky, E., & Stein, P. (1990) The impact of human resource policies on employees: Balancing work/family life. *Journal of Family Issues, 11*, 368–383.

Geurts, S. A. E., & Demerouti, E. (2003). Work/non-work interface: A review of theories and findings. In: M. Schabracq, J. Winnubst & C. L. Cooper (Eds), *The handbook of work and health psychology* (2nd ed., pp. 279–312). Chichester: Wiley.

Geurts, S. A. E., Rutte, C., & Peeters, M. (1999). Antecedents and consequences of work–home interference among medical residents. *Social Science & Medicine, 48*, 1135–1148.

Goff, S. J., Mount, M. K., & Jamison, R. L. (1990). Employer supported child care, work–family, and absenteeism: A field study. *Personnel Psychology, 43*, 793–809.

Goldon, L. (2001). Flexible work schedules: Which workers get them? *American Behavioral Scientist, 44*, 1157–1178.

Golembiewski, R. T., & Proehl, C. (1978). A survey of empirical literature on flexible workhours: Character and consequences of a major innovation. *The Academy of Management Review, 3*, 837–853.

Gomez-Mejia, L. R., & Balkin, D. B. (1992). *Compensation, organizational strategy, and firm performance.* Cincinnati: South-Western.

Goodstein, J. D. (1994). Institutional pressures and strategic responsiveness: Employer involvement in work–family issues. *Academy of Management Journal, 37*, 350–382.

Gordon, F. (1976). Telecommunications: Implications for women. *Telecommunications Policy, 1*, 68–74.

Grandey, A. A., & Cropanzano, R. (1999). The conservation of resources model applied to work–family conflict and strain. *Journal of Vocational Behavior, 54*, 350–370.

Greenhaus, J. H., & Beutell, N. J. (1985). Sources of conflict between work and family roles. *Academy of Management Review, 10*, 76–88.

Greenhaus, J. H., Collins, K. M., Singh, R., & Parasuraman, S. (1997). Work and family influences on departure from accounting. *Journal of Vocational Behavior, 50*, 249–270.

Greenhaus, J. H., & Parasuraman, S. (1999). Research on work, family, and gender: Current status and future directions. In: G. N. Powell (Ed.), *Handbook of gender and work* (pp. 391–412). Thousand Oaks, CA: Sage.

Greenley, G. A., & Foxall, G. R. (1997). Multiple stakeholder orientation in UK companies and the implications for company performance. *Journal of Management Studies, 34*, 258–282.

Grover, S. L., & Crooker, K. J. (1995). Who appreciates family-responsive human resource policies: The impact of family friendly policies on the organizational attachment of parents and non-parents. *Personnel Psychology, 48*, 271–288.

Grzywacz, J. G., & Marks, N. F. (2000). Reconceptualizing the work–family interface: An ecological perspective on the correlates of positive and negative spillover between work and family. *Journal of Occupational Health Psychology, 5*, 111–126.

Hamilton, C. (1987). Telecommuting. *Personnel Journal, 66*, 90–101.

Higgins, G., Duxbury, L., & Johnson, K. L. (2000). Part-time work for women: Does it really help balance work and family? *Human Resource Management, 39*, 17–32.

Judge, T. A., Boudreau, J. W., & Bretz, R. D. (1994). Job and life attitudes of male executives. *Journal of Applied Psychology, 79*, 767–782.

Kahne, H. (1985). *Reconceiving part-time work: New perspectives for older workers and women.* Totowa, NJ: Rowman & Allanheld.

Kamerman, S., & Kahn, A. (1987). *The responsive workplace.* New York: Columbia University Press.

Kingston, P. W. (1990). Illusions and ignorance about the family responsive workplace. *Journal of Family Issues, 11*, 438–454.

Kinnunen, U., & Mauno, S. (1998). Antecedents and outcomes of work–family conflict among employed women and men in Finland. *Human Relations, 51*, 157–177.

Klerman, J. A., & Leibowitz, A. (1990). Job continuity among new mothers. *Demography, 36*, 145–155.

Kluwer, E. S., Boers, S. A., Heesink, J. A. M., & van de Vliert, E. (1997). Rolconflict bij tweeverdieners: De invloed van een 'zorgvriendelijke' werkomgeving [Role conflict among dual-earners: The impact of a 'family-friendly' workplace]. *Gedrag en Organisatie, 10*, 223–241.

Kompier, M. A. J., Geurts, S. A. E., Gründemann, R. W. M., Vink, P., & Smulders, P. G. W. (1998). Cases in stress prevention: The success of a participative and stepwise approach. *Stress Medicine, 14*, 155–168.

Konrad, A. M., & Mangel, R. (2000). The impact of work–life programs on firm productivity. *Strategic Management Journal, 21*, 1225–1237.

Kossek, E. E. (1990). Diversity in child care assistance needs: Employee problems, preferences, and work-related outcomes. *Personnel Psychology, 43*, 769–791.

Kossek, E. E., Colquitt, J. A., & Noe, R. A. (2001). Caregiving decisions, well-being, and performance: The effects of place and provider as a function of dependent type and work–family climates. *Academy of Management Journal, 44*, 29–44.

Kossek, E. E., & Nichol, V. (1992). The effects of on-site child care on employee attitudes and performance. *Personnel Psychology, 45*, 485–509.

Kossek, E. E., & Ozeki, C. (1999). Bridging the work–family policy and productivity gap: A literature review. *Community, Work & Family, 2*, 7–32.

Kraut, R. (1987). Telework as a work style innovation. In: R. E. Kraut (Ed.), *Technology and the transformation of white collar work* (pp. 49–64). Hillsdale, NJ: Lawrence Erlbaum.

Lambert, S. (1990). Processes linking work and family: A critical review and research agenda. *Human Relations, 43*(3), 239–257.

Lee, J. A., Walker, M., & Shoup, R. (2001). Balancing eldercare responsibilities and work: The impact on emotional health. *Journal of Business and Psychology, 16*, 277–289.

Lee, M. D., MacDermid, S. M., Williams, M. L., Buck, M. L., & Leiba-O'Sullivan, S. (2002). Contextual factors in the success of reduced-load work arrangements among managers and professionals. *Human Resource Management, 41*, 209–223.

Lewis, S. (2003). Flexible working arrangements: Implementation, outcomes and management. In: C. L. Cooper & I. T. Robertson (Eds), *International review of industrial and organizational psychology* (Vol. 18, pp. 1–28). Chichester: Wiley.

Lewis, S., & Taylor, K. (1996). Evualuating the impact of family-friendly employer policies: A case study. In: S. Lewis & J. Lewis (Eds), *The work family challenge: Rethinking employment* (pp. 112–127). London: Sage.

Moen, P., & Yu, Y. (2000). Effective work/life strategies: Working couples, work conditions, gender, and life quality. *Social Problems, 47*, 291–326.

Olson, M. H., & Primps, S. B. (1984). Working at home with computers: Work and nonwork issues. *Journal of Social Issues, 40*, 97–112.

Parasuraman, S., Purohit, Y. S., Godshalk, V. M., & Beutell, N. J. (1996). Work and family variables, entrepreneurial career success, and psychological well-being. *Journal of Vocational Behavior, 48*, 275–300.

Perlow, L. A. (1995). Putting work back into work/family. *Group and Organization Management, 20*, 227–239.

Perry-Smith, J. E., & Blum, T. C. (2000). Work–family human resource bundles and perceived organizational performance. *Academy of Management Journal, 43*, 1107–1117.

Pfeffer, J. (1994). *Competitive advantage through people: Unleashing the power of the work force.* Boston: Harvard Business School Press.

Pierce, J. L., & Newstrom, J. W. (1983). The design of flexible work schedules and employee responses: Relationships and process. *Journal of Occupational Behavior, 4*, 247–262.

Pierce, J. L., Newstrom, J. W., Dunham, R. B., & Barber, A. E. (1989). *Alternative work schedules.* Needham Heights, MA: Allyn and Bacon.

Plantenga, J., & Siegel, M. (2004) *European childcare strategies* (114 pp.). Groningen/The Hague: CMK/Ministerie van Social Zaken en Wekgelegen.

Raabe, P. H. (1990). The organizational effects of workplace family policies: Past weaknesses and recent progress toward improved research. *Journal of Family Issues, 11*, 477–491.

Rapoport, R., Bailyn, L., Fletcher, J., & Pruitt, B. (2002). *Beyond work–family balance. Advancing gender equity and workplace performance.* San Francisco: Jossey-Bass.

Ronen, S, & Primps, S. B. (1981). The compressed workweek as organizational change: Behaviors and attitudinal outcomes. *Academy of Management Review, 6*, 61–74.

Rousseau, D. M. (2001). The idiosyncratic deal: Flexibility versus fairness? *Organizational Dynamics, 29*, 260–273.

Rynes, S. L. (1992). Recruitment job choice and post-hire consequences: A call for new research directions. In: M. D. Dunnette & L. M. Hough (Eds), *Handbook of industrial and organizational psychology* (2nd ed., Vol. 2., pp. 399–444). Palo Alto, CA: Consulting Psychologists Press.

Shamir, B., & Salomon, I. (1985). Work-at-home and the quality of working life. *Academy of Management Review, 10*, 455–464.

Solomon, C. (1994). Work/family's failing grade: Why today's initiatives aren't enough. *Personnel Journal, 73*, 72–87.

Terry, D. J., Callan, V. J., & Sartori, G. (1996). Employee adjustment to an organizational merger: Stress coping and intergroup differences. *Stress Medicine, 12*, 105–122.

Thibaut, J., & Walker, L. (1975). *Procedural justice: A psychological analysis.* Hillsdale, NJ: Lawrence Erlbaum.

Thomas, L. T., & Ganster, D. C. (1995). Impact of family-supportive work variables on work–family conflict and strain: A control perspective. *Journal of Applied Psychology, 80*, 6–15.

Thompson, C. A., Beauvais, L. L., & Lyness, K. S. (1999). When work–family benefits are not enough: The influence of work–family culture on benefit utilization, organizational attachment, and work–family conflict. *Journal of Vocational Behavior, 54*, 392–415.

Van den Bos, K. (2002). Assimilation and contrast in organizational justice: The role of primed mindsets in the psychology of the fair process effect. *Organizational Behavior and Human Decision Processes, 89*, 866–880.

Van Rijswijk, K., Bekker, M. H. J., & Rutte, C. G. (2002). Parttime werk, flexibele werktijden en de werk-familiebalans: een overzicht van de literatuur. *Gedrag & Organisatie, 15*, 320–333.

Wallace, J. E. (1997). It's about time: A study of hours worked and work spillover among law firm lawyers. *Journal of Vocational Behavior, 50*, 227–248.

Westman, M., & Piotrkowski, C. S. (1999). Introduction to the special issue: Work–family research in occupational health psychology. *Journal of Occupational Health Psychology, 4*, 301–306.

Wise, S. (2003). *Work life balance: Literature and research review.* Edinburgh: DTI and Fair Play.

Young, M. (1999). Work–family backlash. Begging the question, what's fair? *Annals of the American Academy of Political Science, 562*, 32–46.

Zedeck, S., & Mosier, K. L. (1990). Work in the family and employing organization. *American Psychologist, 45*, 240–251.

PART IV

Human Resources Management and Organizational Effectiveness

CHAPTER 10

HRM for Team-Based Working

Michael A. West, Lynn Markiewicz and Helen Shipton

Introduction

The activity of a group of people working co-operatively to achieve shared goals via differentiation of roles and using elaborate systems of communication is basic to our species. The fundamental human drive and pervasive motivation to form and maintain lasting, positive and significant relationships help us to understand the functioning of teams at work. There is a solid evolutionary basis to our tendency to form strong attachments and by extension to live and work in groups. Groups enable survival and reproduction (Ainsworth, 1989; Axelrod & Hamilton, 1981; Barash, 1977; Bowlby, 1969; Buss, 1990, 1991; Hogan, Jones, & Cheek, 1985; Moreland, 1987). By living and working in groups early humans could share food, easily find mates and care for infants. They could hunt more effectively and defend themselves against their enemies. Individuals who did not readily join the groups would be disadvantaged in comparison with group members as a consequence. The need to belong, which is at the root of our tendency to live and work in groups, is manifested most profoundly in the behaviour of children and infants. Children who stuck close to adults were more likely to survive and be able to reproduce, because they would be protected from danger, cared for and provided with food. And we see across all societies that when there is danger, illness or the darkness of night people have a desire to be with others, indicating the protection offered by group membership. Adults who formed attachments would be more likely to reproduce, and adults who formed long-term relationships would stand a greater chance of producing infants who would grow to reproductive age. 'Over the course of evolution, the small group became the survival strategy developed by the human species' (Barchas, 1986).

However, there has been an extraordinary change in the design of work organizations in the last 200 years. Prior to around 1800, apart from the religious and the military, there were virtually no organizations bigger than around 30 people. Indeed, the vast majority were small groups of 6, 7, 8, or 9 people working together in small craft or agricultural groups. Since then, organizations have expanded rapidly to hundreds and thousands of employees. This has proved difficult with many people finding themselves alienated in large social structures that they struggle to identify with or to achieve a sense of belonging.

How then can we recreate the basic form of human production in these large entities and enjoy the benefits of both team working and economies of scale? In this chapter, we suggest this requires a structure, culture and set of human resource management (HRM) processes that support team-based working. But first we briefly consider whether research evidence supports a move to build team-based organizations.

Are Team-Based Organizations Effective?

Applebaum and Batt (1994) reviewed 12 large-scale surveys and 185 consultants' reports and academic case studies of managerial practices. The authors conclude that team-based working leads to improvements in organizational performance on measures of both efficiency and quality. Similarly, Cotton (1993) reports on studies examining the effects of team working on productivity, satisfaction and absenteeism. He reviewed 57 studies that report improvements on productivity, seven that found no change and five that report productivity declines, following the implementation of self-directed teams. Even though the results of Cotton's review may overestimate the effect of team working due to heavy inclusion of case studies over quasi-experimental designs, the pattern of key findings is replicated by Macy and Izumi's (1993) more powerful meta-analysis.

Macy and Izumi investigated organizational change interventions involving 131 organizations. They report that the relationship between team working and organizational effectiveness was strongly significant. If the full sample of studies was considered and overall performance was used, the introduction of autonomous and semi-autonomous teams had the *strongest* effect size on overall company performance out of 18 different organizational interventions. In health care organizations, team working also contributes to performance by reducing errors and improving the quality of patient care (Edmondson, 1996; Dawson et al., 2004; West, Borrill, Carter, Dawson, & Scully, 2005; West & Borrill, 2005).

Furthermore, these findings are not restricted to self-report measures and soft outcomes, but extend to hard outcome criteria. West et al. (2002) examined the relationship between people management practices in hospitals and patient mortality, and found a strong negative relationship between HRM practices and patient mortality. One of the three practices most strongly associated with mortality was team working. Results showed that the higher the percentage of staff working in teams in hospitals, the lower the patient mortality. On an average, in hospitals where over 60% of staff reportedly worked in formal teams, mortality was around 5% lower than would be expected. Overall, despite the strain placed on team working by large organizational structures and complex processes, the results indicate the value of team working to the success of modern organizations.

In the last 20 years, there has been a shift in research towards understanding the organizational context within which teams perform (Guzzo & Shea, 1992; Hackman, 1990; Kolodny & Kiggundu, 1980; Mohrman, Cohen, & Mohrman, 1995; Pearce & Ravlin, 1987; Sundstrom, De Meuse, & Futrell, 1990). Hackman (1990), for example, has drawn attention to the influence of organizational reward, training and information systems in influencing team effectiveness. Campion, Medsker, and Higgs (1993), in a cross-sectional study of 80 work groups, found a significant correlation between organizational factors such as training and managerial support with work group effectiveness.

Building Team-Based Organizations

How can we build organizations that ensure the effectiveness of teams as a way of working? Efficiently introducing team-based working across organizations involves dramatic, deep and wide-ranging change to the organization's structure and culture. In traditional organizations, command structures include status levels representing points in the hierarchy — supervisors, managers, senior managers, assistant chief executives and so on. In team-based organizations, the structures are more collective (West & Markiewicz, 2004). Teams orbit around the top management team and other senior teams (which themselves model good team work), influencing and being influenced, rather than being directed or directive. The gravitational or inspirational force of different teams affects the performance of the teams around them. The traditional organization has a chart with lines of reporting and layers of hierarchy, but the team-based organization looks more like a solar system with planets revolving around each other and affected by the central force of the major planet (the top management team).

Figure 1 shows a fractured neck of femur patient pathway management team and the other teams that have contact with patients. All the associated teams revolve around the patient pathway management team and must interact effectively with each other.

The role of team leaders in such structures is to ensure that their teams work as powerful and effective parts of the solar system and that they think about how the system as a whole works, not just their particular planets. To do this they must continually emphasize integration and co-operation between teams. Team leaders must be clear about which other teams they need to have close and effective relationships with — identifying the precise

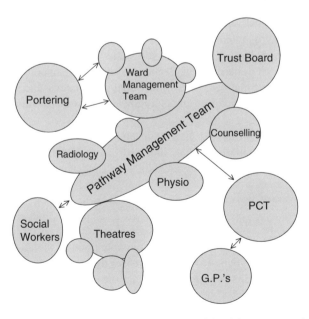

Figure 1: Organization chart in a team based health care organization.

ways in which each will contribute towards the effectiveness of the other. They must also ensure that the objectives of teams within the 'team community' are congruent and understood by all team members and, importantly they should keep asking leaders of the other teams 'How can we help each other more?', 'What are we doing that gets in the way of your effectiveness?' and 'Can we work together to come up with a radical new way of improving our products or services?'.

In traditional organizations, managers manage and control; whereas the role of the team leader in team-based organizations is to encourage teams in their organizations to be largely self-managing and take responsibility for monitoring the effectiveness of their strategies and processes. In one company we worked in, a production team videoed their performance in the production process and invited members of other teams to view the video and suggest ways in which they could dramatically improve the production process. This led to radical improvements in productivity, quality and time taken for goods to reach the customers.

HRM for Building Team-Based Working

We now describe the HRM systems and practices that are required to ensure the effectiveness of team-based organizations. Broadly, team performance must be monitored and managed to ensure effectiveness, reward systems must be correctly aligned, selection and assessment procedures must take into account the skills required for effective team working and good team-level communication systems must reinforce the principles of team-based working. Perhaps most important for organizational success is the extent to which teams cooperate and support each other across team boundaries. Putting effective team orientated systems in place means that team work is nourished and supported in the organization, team members will be motivated, the organization will become healthier and the roles of team leaders will be challenging, interesting and rewarding, since they will not always be dealing with the problems created by lack of support for team work.

HRM systems in team-based organizations serve and support teams rather than focussing primarily on the management of individual performance and satisfaction. This is a fundamental difference, which represents a radical challenge for human resource (HR) professionals.

Below we describe each of the nine main arenas of HRM practice in team-based organizations, beginning with the climate that HRM should nurture in team-based organizations.

Climate for Team-Based Working

Team-based working is a philosophy or attitude about the way in which organizations work, where decisions are made at the closest possible point to the client or customer by teams rather than by individuals. It is vital therefore that there is a general commitment within the organization to this way of working and the existence of an organizational climate that nurtures and promotes the growth of team-based working.

Supportive and challenging environments are likely to sustain high levels of team performance and creativity, especially those which encourage risk taking and idea generation

(West, 2002). Teams should frequently have ideas for improving their workplaces, work functioning, processes, products and services. Where climates are characterized by distrust, poor communication, personal antipathies, limited individual autonomy and unclear goals, the implementation of these ideas is inhibited. The extent to which teams in the organization are encouraged to take time to review their objectives, strategies and processes; plan to make changes and then implement those changes will also determine the effectiveness of the teams and their organizations. Such 'reflexivity' is a positive predictor of both team and organizational innovation (West, 2000). And innovation in turn predicts organizational performance. The HR function plays a key role in creating the organizational structures, strategies and processes, which enable such an ethos, and it is vital that HR strategies are orientated to supporting a team-based organization rather than an individually based organization. Members of the HR department need to be knowledgeable about all aspects of team working, including team composition, team development, team processes and team-performance management. They particularly need to have an understanding of inter-team processes and inter-team conflict in the organizations and how to manage these conflicts. Such knowledge should be augmented by an appreciation of what a team-based organization represents. Understanding the functioning of a team-based organization is much more than simply understanding what constitutes team working. Visits to team-based organizations to learn about good practice, hindrances and the processes involved in developing a team-based organization are therefore necessary.

Appraisal and Performance Review Systems

Team performance review   Considerable performance benefits result from the provision of clear, constructive feedback to teams, though this is often an area which team members report is neglected. Individuals get feedback on performance but team performance is rarely evaluated. In a team-based organization, attention is most appropriately focussed on the development of performance criteria against which teams can be measured. Such team-based working performance criteria need to reach further than simply evaluating team output. These could include the effectiveness criteria listed below.

- *Team outcomes* — the team's performance, be it producing parts, treating patients or providing customer service, likely to be best defined and evaluated by the 'customers' of the teams.
- *Team identification* — the extent of team members' sustained identification with and commitment to their teams. This will include their feelings of loyalty, belonging and pride in relation to the team and its work.
- *Team member growth and well-being* — the learning, development and satisfaction of team members. In well-functioning teams, members learn from each other constantly.
- *Team innovation* — the introduction of new and improved ways of doing things by the team. Teams, almost by definition, should be fountains of creativity and innovation since they bring together individuals with diverse knowledge, orientations, skills, attitudes and experiences in a collective enterprise, thus creating the ideal conditions for creativity (West, 2000).

- *Inter-team relations* — cooperation with other teams and departments within the organization. Teams must not only be cohesive; they must also co-operate with other teams and departments. Otherwise team cohesion may simply reinforce the steel walls of traditional silos within the organization, undermining collective efforts to achieve organizational goals. Evaluation of this dimension is best provided by the other teams with which the target team works most closely.

Goal setting   Perhaps the most powerful component of appraisal is goal setting and this applies no less to teams. The overall direction of a team's work — its purpose — should be clearly articulated by the team leader or the senior management team. This purpose should link tightly to the overall purpose of the organization. As with all performance-management systems, the way in which team goals are set can be a major motivating or de-motivating factor. In keeping with the nature of team-based working, goal-setting works best if all team members are involved in the process. This involves these goal-setting steps:

- develop a shared understanding among all team members of the needs of their 'customer' or 'customers'; their customer/s may be the organization, another part of the organization or an external customer
- describe the overall goal or purpose of the team's activity (the team task)
- define outcomes that will enable the achievement of the goal
- identify performance indicators
- establish measurement processes.

Teams should have the opportunity to review their performance against targets, whether set internally or by others within the organization. This enables learning to take place, which will enhance future team performance. It also prompts the review of team processes that will enable the team to grow and develop.

Individual performance review   Individuals also require regular, constructive feedback about their performance if they are to grow and develop in their jobs. Team-based organizations do not replace individual-performance management with team-performance management. Rather, team performance reviews become the key focus, which is augmented by individual performance review. Traditionally, this has taken place via the annual appraisal or review interview in which the individual's manager gives feedback on the year's performance. However, as flatter structures lead to larger spans of control and each employee's contact network becomes wider, this is an ineffective means of giving an individual the feedback they need. Moreover, it is consistent with a team-based working philosophy that the team, rather than the individual's manager, should be the primary agent that appraises team members. For example, many organizations respond to the challenge of providing more appropriate team-based working appraisal systems for individuals by using one of the two systems: 360 degree feedback, or peer assessment or review.

360-Degree feedback   360-degree feedback systems are being used at all levels within organizations. The mechanics of the system are straightforward: it consists of an audit of an individual's skills and performance, undertaken by collecting feedback (usually via a questionnaire) from his/her line manager and from a range of customers, employees and peers. The questionnaire usually assesses performance against predetermined competencies. Answers are then analysed and feedback is given to the individual. The process is designed to identify any gaps in performance and to provide support in developing improvement plans. Organizations where 360-degree feedback systems are in place report the following benefits:

- *Individuals take responsibility for their own development* — they are alerted to their development needs and take responsibility for them rather than relying on their supervisor or line manager.
- *The feedback is regarded as 'real'* — particularly if the organization climate is such that the system is used genuinely to improve the overall performance.
- *When enough people give the same feedback, it is seen as true* — the weight of numbers is convincing.
- *Individuals can have an impact* — people at all levels within the organization feel that they have the opportunity to comment upon the performance of those with whom they work.

The 360-degree feedback system is neatly in keeping with the concept of the team-based organization: it improves communication processes; extends ownership and involvement and enhances the concept of team feedback. It is important that the culture generally supports continuous improvement, training and development to meet gaps in skills and knowledge. And those introducing the system must be persistent, i.e. enough time is dedicated to setting up the system, and once established, it becomes integral to the normal performance-management system.

Peer review   Team peer review is a more informal version of the 360-degree feedback system described above. However, it may be more appropriate at team level where numbers are not so large and where the most potent feedback is from peers rather than managers. Team-based working peer review of an individual's performance achieves its effects by the following means. It …

- reviews an individual's contribution to the output of the team, measured against predetermined targets derived from the team's overall goals
- reviews the individual's performance in their team role
- reviews the team member's contributions in the areas of communication, goal setting, giving feedback to other team members; planning and co-ordination; collaborative problem-solving; conflict resolution; innovation, and supportiveness
- reviews the individual's contribution to the team climate or how the team works
- there are a number of different peer-review methods for team-based working
- the team leader collects team members' views on predetermined dimensions, collates the information and gives feedback to the individual
- at the time of the team performance review, the team also discusses individual performance, sometimes with the help of a facilitator from outside of the team
- a sub-group of the team is delegated to consider individual aspects of performance and give feedback to individuals on that area only.

Such reviews should take place regularly (at least annually) and be formally constituted since there is a danger that peer-review systems, which become informal will fall into disuse. Staff who have been accustomed to traditional forms of manager-led appraisal, or indeed have not been used to receiving any formal feedback at all, may take some time to feel comfortable with such participative processes. More anonymous feedback from team members presented in aggregated form may be appropriate early on. Later it should be possible to move to a system where the team meets as a whole to give feedback on performance and set goals with each individual in an open, supportive and professional manner. The important principles are that the process should help individuals clarify their work objectives, help them to feel valued, respected and supported and help them identify the means to achieve personal development.

Reward Systems

The implementation of team-based reward systems should be a careful, slow and incremental process. Quick arbitrary changes in the way people are rewarded can generate considerable discontent.

Reward systems can be focused on:

The individual: Here individual performance is appraised and rewarded. This can include individual rewards for contribution to team working where this is a specific target set for the individual. Performance-related pay can reflect individual contributions to the team's performance as rated by other team members.

The team: Here reward is related to the achievement of predetermined team goals. Reward may be distributed equally to each member of the team or it may be apportioned by senior management, by the team leader or in a manner determined by the team itself. It is important to note that when rewards are given equally to team members by an external party, this can lead to considerable resentment. Team members who do not pull their weight are seen as 'free riders' and their failures lead to resentment and demotivation among other team members (Rutte, 2003). This will be exacerbated if the distribution of team rewards is achieved in ways that do not mirror the effort or contribution made by individual team members. It is important therefore that the reward system for the team is seen as fair by team members and this may involve some process by which team members themselves determine the distribution of the team rewards. Or the organization may provide team-level rewards such as an away day in a luxury spa, dinner for the team, new office furniture or equipment or the devolution of a budget to the team.

The organization: The performance of either the total organization or the business unit is reflected in rewards allocated to individuals or teams. Incorporating all elements (individual, team and organizational) provides a well-rounded reward system. However, if the organization's aim is to introduce team-based working then there must be a strong emphasis on team-performance factors and as much delegation of decisions regarding team reward distribution as possible.

Reward systems to promote team-based working require an organization commitment to delegation of power to, and consultation with, teams — this commitment is demonstrated through:

- clear, achievable but challenging targets which team members understand, agree and ideally are involved in setting

- clear and fair means of measuring team outcomes
- team members working interdependently to achieve team goals
- allowing the team a considerable degree of autonomy in the way in which it manages its work
- giving the team access to the necessary materials, skills and knowledge to achieve the task
- providing a reward valuable enough to be worth having, and delivered soon after the achievement of the outcome.

How can organizations go about designing systems for rewarding teams while still rewarding individuals? Below we outline steps in the process, drawing on the excellent analysis of 27 team reward and recognition plans from top companies reviewed by Parker, McAdams, and Zielinski (2000).

1. Customize the plan. Ensure the reward system is customized to your organization rather than slavishly copying a scheme introduced elsewhere. The fit of the plan to the organization is clearly important.
2. Create many winners and few losers. Reward systems should leave most employees feeling pleased, recognized and motivated. There should be few losers, and those should be clear about why they have missed out.
3. Involve employees in the nomination of teams and individuals for awards. Reward plans command much more credibility if employees perceive that they have influence over the decisions rather than a select and remote group of managers making the nominations and decisions.
4. Use non-monetary as well as monetary awards — these can include a simple thank-you, letters of congratulations, time off with pay, a trophy, merchandise, gift certificates, a dinner for two, travel for business or on vacation. One company gives a reward of a free video rental a week for a year to employees (actually a relatively inexpensive reward).
5. Give a few big awards and lots of small ones. Lots of small awards given soon after a success or accomplishment have a more powerful impact than one or two large awards given to a select group of employees long after the event.
6. Communicate. Employees need to understand the reward plan and the reasons for it. Communication serves several purposes:

   (i) Education about how the measures work and what employees can do to improve performance.
   (ii) Feedback to employees on how they are doing.
   (iii) Rewarding frequently — feedback is more effective when attached to a reward.
   (iv) Message reinforcement — information about reward systems can reinforce the values of the organization. For example, performance in generating useful ideas for new and improved products or ways of working is rewarded because the organization has innovation as one of its core values.
   (v) Role modelling — information about successful teams that are rewarded offers role models to others.

The reward schemes should emphasize the core value of teamwork and this needs driving home repeatedly. Many managers make the mistake of assuming that employees understand the organization's core values. They need to be repeatedly affirmed and spelled out. Managers should also strive continually to tell employees how they are performing (with most information providing positive feedback) and to reinforce the messages about how the rewards link to the core values of the organization.

It also makes sense to create a smorgasbord of reward plans. Merck (a US company), for example, had an organizational-level incentive that paid rewards to employees for the achievement of annual organizational targets. This was augmented by a system whereby team members nominated each other for outstanding team performance, which earned non-monetary rewards. For high performing teams, there was a quarterly stock option reward plan. Another company (ASCAP) allowed all account services teams that met their targets to receive an award that represented a percentage of the individual's base pay. In addition, there was a sales team of the year ceremony to which all teams that exceeded their annual targets were invited. Although only one team won the big award, all the other teams received a plaque and merchandise in recognition of their achievement.

This means that senior managers have to budget for recognition activities in advance to make sure there are sufficient resources to ensure the systems really have an impact. That also means planning to collect, process and feedback performance data. Those data must be of high quality and perceived to be reliable and valid by employees. The rewards must also be sufficiently substantial to matter to the employees since the value of payoffs are in the eye of the beholder. Some organizations offer a variety of rewards from which employees can choose: travel passes, money, a case of wine, time off with pay, flexitime working, etc. Employees can then choose rewards that are most valuable to them.

The process of introducing reward systems in developing a team-based organization is also critical. There are six key principles:

1. Roll out the plan down through the normal line management chain. Managers must understand the plan and be able to communicate its detail effectively.
2. Keep the explanations simple even if the plans are not. How does the plan work? What can the team earn? What can the team do to affect its performance? What can management do to help the team achieve its targets?
3. Involve teams in projects that enable them to win rewards. In other words, give teams opportunities.
4. Communicate the plan repeatedly to all teams. They will forget the details so the content of the plan needs to be repeatedly stressed.
5. Get feedback on how it is going.
6. Do a formal evaluation that determines each plan's future and ensure this is related to the business strategy. If the plans are working there should be substantial changes in organizational performance in the areas that matter. If there are not, the plans should be scrapped or amended.

Recruitment, Selection and Succession Planning

In team-based organizations, recruitment and selection is focussed not only on the necessary individual and technical competencies. Account is taken also of previous experience in working in teams, team working competencies and the motivation to work in teams. Account may also need to be taken of the personality characteristics of applicants for positions since there is some evidence that certain personality constellations are more appropriate for particular types of teams. It is important to note that assessing candidates against generic team knowledge, skill and ability requirements (KSAs) has been found to be a relatively successful selection tool, and one which can enhance the effectiveness of teams (Campion et al., 1993). These team skills include goal setting, planning, conflict management, co-ordinating and communication.

So, personality factors are important. Teams composed of people high in conscientiousness appear to perform to a high level. There is some evidence that teams with high levels of extraversion among their members are better at decision-making than at planning and performance tasks, probably because the warmth and optimism associated with extraversion is important in persuading others to accept the decisions (Barrick & Mount, 1996). For decisions requiring creativity or adaptability in thinking, openness rather than conscientiousness or extraversion is most important. HRM functions need to gather data on which configurations of personality are most effective for the kinds of tasks their organizational teams perform.

Another consideration is who does the recruiting and selecting. In many team-based organizations, it is common practice (and consistent with the team-based working philosophy) that team members themselves recruit and select new members. Usually they have assistance from HR and an external participant to ensure probity and an alternative view so that team members do not select simply clones of themselves, thereby limiting potentially valuable diversity in the team.

On a wider organizational level, HR should consider how the succession planning process can support the development of team-based working; for example, by ensuring that selection criteria for development into senior positions include identification of the necessary attitudes and skills to manage team-based working at a strategic level. Team members should also be encouraged to develop succession-planning processes within the team and be involved in feedback to more senior levels of management in the identification of required skills and attributes for senior positions.

Education and Training Systems

Working in teams presents significant learning opportunities as well as challenges for individual team members, and the pace at which team working can be successfully implemented and embedded into the organization will vary in line with pre-existing knowledge and skills. In this section, we explore the role of training and development in promoting effective team working. We start by focussing on interventions at team level, and go on to consider the training implications of team working for three groups of employees: those outside immediate team boundaries, team leaders and individual team members. We conclude by briefly considering the importance of integrating any team training initiatives with existing HRM mechanisms in the wider organizational environment.

Interventions at team level

The start-up Team-building interventions can be divided into five main types, each requiring a very different approach. The start-up of teams presents particular challenges, and specific exercises are appropriate when a team is just beginning its work and needs to clarify its objectives, strategies, processes and roles. The beginning of a team's life has a significant influence on its later development and effectiveness, especially when crises occur. Start-up interventions can help create team ethos, determine clarity of direction and shape team working practices. They include:

- Ensuring the team has a whole and meaningful task to perform.
- Clarifying team objectives.
- Ensuring that each team member has a whole, meaningful and intrinsically interesting task to perform.
- Ensuring that team members' activities can be evaluated.
- Ensuring that team performance as a whole is monitored and that team members are given regular and clear feedback on individual and team performance.
- Establishing a means for regular communication and review within the team.

Specifying the way in which team members will work together — the 3 or 4 things the team should *always* do and the 3 or 4 things the team should *never* do.

The principle of 'guided growth' (Stern & Sommerlad, 1999) suggests that newly functioning teams benefit from working with facilitators (either from within or outside the organization) whose purpose it is to help teams develop the learning processes and methodologies that will serve to increase the efficiency of the whole system. Over time, and given appropriate support, team leaders as well as individual members will usually gain the collaborative and communicative skills necessary to self-regulate, but there is no immediate solution. One manager, responsible for leading a major team working initiative in a successful manufacturing organization, spoke eloquently on this point: 'when you say how long does it take to train somebody, I would say forever, I have said minimum six months, but we don't stop training…it is a continual renewal process…. it is a long, long haul.'

Many team-building interventions are based on the expectation that a day or two of team building will lead to dramatic improvements in team functioning. It is equivalent to hoping that one session of psychotherapy will change a person's life dramatically. The evidence suggests that it is continual interaction, and effort leads to improvements in functioning rather than any 'quick fix'.

Regular formal reviews   Formal reviews usually take the form of 'away days' of one or two days' duration during which the team reviews objectives, roles, strategies and processes in order to maintain and promote effective functioning.

As in any other area of human activity, regular review can lead to greater awareness of strengths, skills, weaknesses and problem areas and improvement in functioning (West, 2000). Within work teams, regular away days are a useful way of ensuring a team's continuing effectiveness. Indeed there is much evidence that teams which take time out to review processes are more effective than those which do not.

Topics to be covered in an away day can include:

- Team successes and difficulties in the previous six-months or one-year period and what can be learned from them
- A review of team objectives and their appropriateness. Their fit with the organization's overall purpose and with team members' values
- The roles of team members

- Quality of team communication
- Team member interaction frequency
- Team meetings and how they can be improved
- Team decision-making processes
- Excellence in the team's work
- Levels of innovation (both evolutionary and revolutionary)
- Team members mutual social support
- Team conflicts — value of limited task conflict
- Avoidance of interpersonal task conflict
- Errors and near misses — what can be learned from them
- Support for personal growth and development of team members
- Overall workload
- Work–personal life integration
- Time management.

Addressing known task-related problems   In order to deal with specific known problem issues (problems the team encounters repeatedly, for example), teams sometimes take time out to define carefully the task-related problem it is confronting. Then the team develops alternative options for overcoming the problem, and action plans for implementing the selected way forward.

Identifying unknown problems   Here the intervention focusses on the diagnosis of task-related problems in which the cause is not immediately obvious. For example, it might be that a piece of equipment malfunctions irregularly, or that important information is not acted upon by another team, despite the fact that it is transmitted. After the agreed identification of the nature of specific problems, the team goes on to use appropriate strategies to overcome them in future.

Social process interventions   Social interventions focus on the interpersonal relationships, social support, team climate, support for growth and development of team members and conflict resolution. They aim to promote a positive social climate and team member well-being. However, such interventions should be skilfully handled by those expert in conflict resolution since there is some evidence that many attempts to deal with interpersonal problems in teams often lead to the intensification rather than the resolution of those problems. A dinner out together for the whole team or a trip to some beautiful or exciting location is likely to be more beneficial. Whatever the intervention, it is essential that team leaders are clear that interpersonal problems should not be allowed to interfere with the team's performance. At the extreme, a team may need to be disbanded (e.g. where interpersonal problems inhibit the breast cancer care team's ability to provide good diagnosis and treatment for patients).

The blanket approach to team building often employed is unlikely to be effective for most teams. The first question to ask is 'What intervention is most appropriate, for which teams, and at which point in time?' The following checklist can be used to ensure appropriate focus for the intervention:

1. Are the objectives of the intervention clear?
2. Is the intervention appropriate for the particular issues facing the team?

3. Is the intervention appropriately timed?
4. Does the intervention attempt to cover too many areas?
5. Are means for sustaining change built in to the intervention?
6. Are facilitators employed who have the knowledge and skills required to conduct team-building interventions?
7. Will clear action plans emerge as a result of the team-building intervention?
8. Will regular reviews be instituted as a result of the team-building intervention?

Training for those outside immediate team boundaries   Team working presents a shift in the balance of power within organizations and for this reason may be regarded with some trepidation by those who are more accustomed to the traditional 'command and control' style of management. Because managers working alongside teams may find the process difficult or even threatening, it is important to involve them in decision-making surrounding all aspects of team functioning. Furthermore, managers are likely to need support themselves as they adjust to the different dynamics involved in acting as facilitators rather than allocating work tasks.

Mentoring presents a way in which individuals adjusting to a team working ethos can gain the guidance, support and advice of more experienced members of staff; 'off-line help by one person to another in making significant transitions in knowledge, work or thinking' (The European Mentoring Centre, 1998). Clutterbuck (2004) notes that 'the rapid rise of planned mentoring schemes…. has been one of the success stories of the late twentieth century'. Effective mentors will not only encourage individuals to reflect upon their career goals, thereby promoting a sense of purpose and control. They will also help individuals to acquire the skills necessary to operate within a less hierarchical structure. For example, managers familiar with issuing instructions controlling performance may need to learn how to listen actively, to plan time for reflection and to allow others to take responsibility for outcomes. Coaching — working alongside a facilitator or more experienced member of staff to develop a specific skill — is another valuable technique for promoting understanding of what team working represents. In line with the points made earlier concerning the importance of workplace climate, managers are far more likely to make the necessary adjustments where performance management and reward systems recognize the value and importance attached to doing so.

Training for team leaders   The success of the team frequently hinges upon the capability of the team leader. He or she will not only represent the team within the wider organization, enhancing its visibility and securing valuable resources, but also facilitate team functioning and help to create a shared sense of purpose. Again, both new and experienced team leaders will benefit from the support of a mentor. This may be a manager from another level of the organization or a team leader from another team who has more or different experience of working with teams.

Team leader training can include developing:

- awareness of the differences between leadership in a traditional and a team-based environment
- skills to identify team and team community boundaries

- increased awareness of personal leadership style — particularly in the areas of personal need for control, ability to trust and take risks, confidence to work across organizational levels and professional boundaries
- skills to facilitate team member involvement in task design, goal-setting, role clarification and problem solving
- understanding of team processes and their effect on team member relationships
- networking skills to ensure continued learning and development
- increased confidence to manage at the team community and organizational level.

Training for individual team members   A number of different options present themselves when contemplating ways in which to develop the team working skills of individual members. Research by Onstenk (1997), conducted in Dutch manufacturing firms, suggests that individual jobs should be designed to promote learning and knowledge sharing across the team as a whole. Thus, individual members of effective teams have their remit broadened to encompass new tasks through job rotation. Each team member is encouraged to coach and support others to facilitate this multi-skilling process. In this way, the team is able to respond more flexibly to external demands, while individuals develop the knowledge and skills necessary for effective team performance.

Individual team members working within successful teams may also take responsibility for activities previously outside their remit, such as repair work, quality or customer relationships. A Dutch textile printing company, for example, encouraged team members to liaise with customers and to make presentations on behalf of the team where appropriate. Through doing so, team members learned more about the challenges facing customers, while simultaneously developing their own interpersonal and communication skills and forging closer links with the end-users of their product.

In a similar vein, members of top performing teams are encouraged to create opportunities for discussion and collaboration with colleagues within and outside the team. Leonard and Swap (1999), in their vivid depiction of working practices within Chaparral Steel, describe how operators anticipate requests to implement improvements in working practices and have a regular forum to discuss the feasibility of ideas raised. The turnaround of Corus Steel in the UK can be attributed in part to the willingness of team members to make suggestions and to share with others their ideas about how to improve production and other processes. These and similar activities promote learning, communication and knowledge sharing both within and across team boundaries.

Team work training and work place climate   As we noted earlier in the chapter, the workplace climate plays a significant role in either impeding or facilitating team work training. Reward and performance management systems should be designed so that everyone concerned is clear that learning is recognized, valued and anticipated by those at senior levels in organizations. Supporting team members as they acquire new skills is important and HRM practitioners need to consider carefully what mechanisms can be implemented to facilitate this process (Shipton, West, Dawson Patterson, & Birdi, 2005). Recognizing achievement through praise and reinforcement can be as important as pay, although ideally there should be a way of combining both financial and non-financial elements (Armstrong, 2002). Given that reward is one of the key variables to influence perceptions of justice (Bowen, Gilliland, & Folger, 1999), the system should be transparent, well communicated and applied consistently.

Organizations committed to team working are likely to endorse a variety of methods designed to promote knowledge and skills in addition to those highlighted above. Work shadowing — working alongside a more experienced member to observe and imitate — is an effective method for transferring the unconscious, tacit skills that frequently underlie performance. Action learning — whereby individuals are brought together to share work-related problems and to consider alternative solutions — is a method that fits in well with many of the methods described above and builds upon the dynamics of effective team work. Other methods involving formal accreditation both in the workplace and outside have their place in creating a learning environment within which teams and the individuals within them can flourish. Thus, individuals can gain knowledge through participating in Modern Apprenticeships and National Vocational Qualifications or through engaging in post-experience professional training at colleges and universities. Knowledge acquired through such endeavour represents a resource that can be drawn upon by the team within which the individual operates.

Teams present powerful learning opportunities for teams members and those with whom they interact. Orr (1990) investigating the processes by which technicians achieve proficient performance, concluded that these employees learnt more from the colleagues with whom they worked closely than from any externally imposed training programmes or protocols. This approach holds that those closest to the task in hand are most able to provide support and guidance to new members of the community and to devise new and better ways of performing tasks. Those with responsibility for managing teams should be concerned first and foremost with providing support to teams, rather than controlling their performance. Their primary concern should be to create an environment within which each individual can achieve his or her potential with the auspices of the team and the wider organizaton.

Communication Systems

Effective communication systems are essential for team-based working to:

- ensure clarity of purpose and team processes throughout the organization
- constantly reinforce those purposes and processes
- check for common understanding.

In his lectures on team working based on his experiences as a mountaineer, Chris Bonington describes the importance of establishing and publicizing communication systems right at the start of a project. He points out that it is difficult to renegotiate the process with the team when you are half way up a mountain! Within organizations also, it is better to establish effective communication systems with teams before there is a problem, and to regularly review those systems with teams to ensure that they remain effective as the organization grows and changes. Many organizations carry out communication audits to ensure that their systems are working effectively.

There is an increasing variety of communication media available to even the smallest organization. Any form of face-to-face communication is likely to be more influential than written forms, because there will be more opportunity for checking understanding and clarifying issues as they arise. The choice of media and the route which will be used to communicate information, knowledge, norms and attitudes within organizations are influenced by a variety of important factors, as shown in Table 1:

Team-Process Support Systems

Teams need help and support to establish and maintain effective team working processes during various stages of their development. In team-based organizations, some teams will encounter difficulties in working effectively. This may arise because of lack of clarity over objectives, lack of clarity about roles or, much more rarely, personality problems. It is unrealistic to always expect team members to work these difficulties through to a satisfactory conclusion without support. Consequently, successful team-based organizations ensure there is an internal facilitator or external consultant who can provide assistance to teams that are having difficulty — in short 'process assistance' or 'process support'. Such support may be required at the following times:

- *The initial set-up stage* when both team leaders and team members may require training and support to establish appropriate working practices and to develop team working skills.
- *Periods of difficulty*, either in the achievement of tasks, where assistance may be provided in such areas as co-ordination of effort or skill sharing within the team, or in resolving conflict within the team.
- *Periods of growth and development* when team members are looking for new ways of working, external interventions can be used to challenge mind sets which have developed within the team and encourage appropriate risk taking.
- *Periods of review and evaluation* since teams should be encouraged to regularly review both their outcomes and the way in which they work. If this does not happen it may lead to the development of an introverted or stagnant team environment.
- *The closing stages of team life* when too little attention may be given to the ending of team relationships. Appropriate closing processes can enhance team-member learning, which will be applied in future teams. Also team members' self-esteem and motivation will be enhanced by the celebrations and leave-takings that should naturally occur at the end of a successfully completed project. Teams may be reluctant to disband when their job is really done so this process should be speedily and sensitively enabled.

Each team should have a 'sponsor', preferably a senior and influential staff member within the organization who has a particular interest in the success of the team (this may well be the team leader). This sponsor will provide general support and access to required resources. However, specific process support can only be provided by people skilled in team facilitation who are knowledgeable about empirically based theories of team working. This individual does not require a detailed knowledge of the content of the team's work. Such team facilitators must understand the role and the team(s) must be aware of the range of support the facilitator can provide.

   The team facilitator may be someone from outside the organization. This is often the case in which new team-based working systems are being implemented and a large amount of process support is required. Alternatively, organizations may establish a team of internal team facilitators. As team-based working systems mature and develop, many organizations

Table 1: Communication in team based organizations.

The culture of the organization	In a traditional hierarchical organization, major communications tend to take place by written instruction from a senior manager to other staff. If team-based working is to be successful, team briefings and lateral as well as vertical communications must be used.
Cultural differences between parts of the organization	In large, complex organizations or in partnership organizations, there is a tendency for communication to take place in the language and by the method preferred by the most powerful group or partner. If such organizations are to be successful they need to be sensitive to the nuances of language and process which impact on the way in which messages will be received by different parts of the organization.
The nature of the message to be communicated	Features of the message include its content, whether it is information, a directive, team or individual recognition, attitude, etc. Also, whether the news is good or bad may influence how an organization chooses to deliver a message (bad news is better delivered face-to-face).
The frequency of the communication	Routes will become established quickly for information that is transmitted frequently. It is important to check that these continue to be appropriate and that familiarity with the process does not 'breed contempt' in the target audience. Teams are likely to have high levels of intra-team communication and low levels of inter-team communication so it is important to develop the latter.
The skills of those who communicating	In team-based organizations, which will typically have more open communication systems, communication skills are an essential requirement for the team leader role. Training can improve personal skills, such as presentation and influencing, and also enable team leaders to use communication systems effectively. Every member of the team however will require good listening skills, the ability to interpret and use non-verbal signals and a commitment to plan for effective communication.

Table 1: Continued.

Geographical spread and the availability of communication technology	Many organizations today rely heavily on information technology to maintain regular communication links between both individuals and teams. Modern technology provides tremendous opportunities to create truly open access to information. These opportunities, however, need to be managed effectively if individuals are not to suffer from either information overload or the increasing feelings of isolation that are reported by some employees who spend the majority of their time working remotely. You simply have to work much harder at communicating when teams are geographically spread regardless of the sophistication of your communication technology.

find they have the appropriate skills internally, often using successful team leaders to provide process consultancy to other teams within the organization. Such team leaders, equipped with additional facilitation and consultancy skills training, form a core resource that can be called upon by any team requiring assistance.

Feedback Systems

As indicated above, feedback systems must be established which allow both individuals and teams to accurately assess their performance against targets and also to assess the impact of their working practices on others within the organization.

Each team needs to ensure that they are regularly engaging in effective feedback sessions with other mutually dependent teams — taking opportunities to celebrate success jointly and review learning from difficulties.

Within the effective team-based working organization, there will also be effectively functioning mechanisms to ensure that feedback travels upwards from teams and is incorporated into strategic decision-making. Organizations can use various techniques to facilitate this process. The essential criteria for their success are that the organization climate encourages honest welcoming of constructive feedback as a means of improving performance and that those giving feedback see that action is taken as a result. Techniques include:

(i) *Vertical review groups* — A number of individuals drawn from various levels, functions and teams within the organization and representing their peer groups meet at regular intervals to discuss key strategic issues. Such groups can also be used to ensure effective feedback between teams.

(ii) *Change management forums* — Senior managers hold open meetings or lunches at which honest and open feedback about organizational change from teams is encouraged.

(iii) *Staff surveys* — Questionnaires are distributed to all staff (or a random selection) on a regular (at least annual) basis. These questionnaires usually include a number of standard questions to highlight long-term trends but may also include questions about topical issues.

(iv) *Team reports* — Teams produce regular reports that represent team members' views on how the organization is working.

Inter-Team Processes

The strengths of team-based working in organizations are the involvement of all in contributing their skills and knowledge, in good collective decision-making and innovation. The fundamental weakness is the tendency of team-based organizations to be torn and damaged by competition, hostility and rivalry (sometimes called a silo mentality) between teams (Richter, Van Dick, & West, 2004).

Increasing intergroup contact   The best team-level strategy to reduce inter-team bias in organizations is to increase the quantity and quality of inter-team contact, for example by having the conflicting teams meet on a regular basis (Hewstone, 2002). Some experimental research also suggests that overcoming problems of inter-team bias when teams come into contact is *not* best achieved by having the teams work on a task together, but is better achieved by encouraging them to get to know each other on a personal level. Moreover, these effects tend to generalize to other out-team members. In this light, it is perhaps also not surprising that having friends who are members of the out-team also reduces bias.

Recategorization   The most common method of recategorization is termed the 'common in-group identity' model, in which the aim is to replace subordinate (us and them) categories with superordinate (we) categorizations. Social and health care workers in a geographical area may be encouraged to identify themselves as common members of the superordinate category of Arcadia Community and Health Action Group in addition to the subordinate teams with which they currently identify. Inter-team bias is reduced because former out-team members are now recategorized as in-team members. Moreover, inter-team relations improve because individuals tend to engage in more self-disclosing interactions with, and develop more differentiated representations of, former out-team members as a consequence of their recategorization.

Other research suggests that it is vital to encourage all team members to have strong identification and a sense of pride in their organization. A strong team and organizational identification (particularly among those who communicate or span the boundaries between teams) leads to more inter-team co-operation and less inter-team competition and conflict (Richter (in press)).

Such strategies are not simple fixes where categorizations are of long standing or are based on very strong categorizations such as the long-standing tensions between midwives and junior doctors in hospitals. In that circumstance, appealing to a common superordinate team identity (we are all employees of one hospital) may be ineffective.

Maintaining the salience of category distinctions   In some circumstances, teams should be encouraged to recognize and value differences between them. This can be accomplished by ensuring that when two teams co-operate, it is clear that they have separate roles that maintain their positive distinctiveness. Encouraging social services and health service workers to co-operate will be more effective if their distinct expertise is acknowledged and applied in interacting but distinct roles.

There is a danger that the development of a number of individually successful teams within an organization will lead to levels of inter-team competition, which could in the long term be detrimental to organization performance. The aim of the organization in establishing inter-team processes is therefore to allow the development of individual team identity while ensuring that communication and feedback flows between teams. This allows teams to avoid duplication of effort, to learn from each other's experiences and to co-ordinate efforts to achieve the broader goals of the organization.

Other practical techniques that can be used include:

(i) *Team representatives sitting on senior staff teams* — This requires the team representative to take on a wider organization role. They will not only represent their team's view but will be expected to consider the views of other teams when taking part in strategic decision-making. Representatives also fulfil an educational role in developing the knowledge and understanding of their own team members concerning the wider organization context.

(ii) *Team-member exchanges* — Team members can be seconded to work in other teams or visit as observers in order to increase mutual understanding and provide opportunities for individual development.

(iii) *Team news is publicized* — Internal organization newsletters are often a forum for providing information about both the successes of teams and team working processes. In one company in Scotland, teams regularly make presentations regarding their projects, which are videoed and distributed to all other teams within the organization.

(iv) *Benchmarking* — Processes and best practices are benchmarked within the organization and also with other organizations so that there is a sense of sharing best practice rather than competition to be the best team.

Conclusions

In this chapter, we have considered the organizational context for team-based working in relation to specific support systems available, and suggested that HRM should consider how these support systems can be strengthened before the wholesale introduction of teams is undertaken. Building team-based organizations is not simply a matter of introducing team building for selected teams of staff. It requires that organizations assess their cultures, structures and processes in order to plan and make changes that support the concept of the team-based organization. This requires radical innovation and HR leadership. We began by pointing out that teams are the natural and historically pervasive way of organizing human work activity in service of performing complex tasks. To capitalize on our skills in team working in modern organizations, we have to adapt those organizations to support rather than inhibit team working.

Further Reading

West, M. A. (2004). *Effective teamwork. Practical lessons from organizational research* (2nd ed.). Oxford: Blackwell Publishing.
West, M. A. (2004). *The secrets of successful team management. How to lead a team to innovation, creativity and success.* London: Duncan Baird Publishers.

References

Ainsworth, Mary (1989). Attachments beyond infancy. *American Psychologist, 44*, 709–716.
Anderson, N., & Herriot, P. (Eds) (1995). *Handbook of selection and appraisal* (2nd ed.). Chichester: Wiley.
Applebaum, E., & Batt, R. (1994). *The new American workplace.* Ithaca, NY: ILR Press.
Armstrong, M. (2002). *Employe reward.* London: CIPD.
Axelrod, R., & Hamilton, W. D. (1981). The evolution of cooperation. *Science, 211*, 1390–13396.
Barash, D. P. (1977). Sociobiology and behaviour. New York: Elsevier.
Barchas, P. (1986). A sociophysiological orientation to small groups. In: E. Lawler (Ed.), *Advances in group processes* (Vol. 3, pp. 209–246). Greenwich, CT: JAI Press.
Barrick, M. R., & Mount, M. K. (1996). Effects of impression management and self-deception on the predicive validity of personality constructs. *Journal of Applied Psychology, 81*(3), 261–272.
Bowen, S., Gilliland, S., & Folger, R. (1999). HRM and service fairness: How being fair with employees spills over to customers. *Organizational Dynamics, 27*(3), 7–24.
Bowlby, J. (1969). *Attachment and loss* (Vol. I). London: Hogarth.
Buss, D. M. (1990). The evolution of anxiety and social exclusion. *Journal of Social and Clinical Psychology, 9*, 196–210.
Buss, D. M. (1991). Evolutionary personality psychology. *Annual Review of Psychology, 42*, 459–491.
Campion, M. A., Medsker, G. J., & Higgs, A. C. (1993). Relations between work group characteristics and effectiveness: Implications for designing effective work groups. *Personnel Psychology, 46*, 823–850.
Clutterbuck, D. (2004). *Everyone needs a mentor. Fostering talent in your organization.* London: CIPD.
Cotton, J. L. (1993). *Employee involvement.* Newbury Park, CA: Sage.
Dawson, J. F., West, M. A., Scully, J. W., Beinart, S., Carpenter, M., & Smith, D. (2004). *Healthcare commission report of national findings NHS staff survey 2003.* London: Commission for Healthcare Audit and Inspection.
Edmondson, A. C. (1996). Learning from mistakes is easier said than done: Group and organizational influences on the detection and correction of human error. *Journal of Applied Behavioral Science, 32*(1), 5–28.
Guzzo, R. A., & Shea, G. P. (1992). Group Performance and Intergroup Relations in Organizations. In: M. D. Dunnette & L. M. Hough (Eds), *Handbook of industrial and organizational psychology* (Vol. 3, pp. 269–313). Palo Alto, California: Consulting Psychologists Press.
Hackman, J. R. (1990). *Groups that work (and those that don't).* San Francisco: Jossey-Bass.
Hewstone, M., Rubin, M., & Willis, H. (2002). Intergroup bias. *Annual Reviews of Psychology, 53*, 575–604.
Hogan, R., Jones, W. H., & Cheek, J. M. (1985). Socioanalytic theory: An alternative to armadillo psychology. In: B. R. Schlenker (Ed.), *The self and social life* (pp. 175–198). New York: McGraw Hill.
Kolodny, M., & Kiggundu, M. N. (1980). Towards the development of a sociotechnical systems model in woodlands mechanical harvesting. *Human Relations, 33*, 623–645.

Leonard, D., & Swap, W. (1999). *When sparks fly. Igniting creativity in groups.* Boston: Harvard Business School Press.

Macy, B. A., & Izumi, H. (1993). Organizational change, design and work innovation: A meta-analysis of 131 North American field studies — 1961–1991. *Research in organizational change and design* (Vol. 7). Greenwich, CT: JAI Press.

Mohrman, S., Cohen, S., & Mohrman, L. (1995). *Designing team based organizations.* London: Jossey Bass.

Moreland, R. L. (1987). The formation of small groups. In: C. Hendrick (Ed.), *Group processes: Review of personality and social psychology* (Vol. 8, pp. 80–100). Newbury Park, CA: Sage.

Onstenk, J. (1997). *Innovation, work teams and learning on-the-job.* Paper for EU Seminar on Knowledge and Work, Amsterdam.

Orr, J. E. (1990). Sharing knowledge, celebrating identify: Community memory in a service culture. In: D. S. Middleton & D. Edwards (Eds), *Collective remembering* (pp. 169–189). Newbury Park, SA: Sage.

Parker, G., McAdams, J., & Zielinski, D. (2000). *Rewarding teams: Lessons from the trenches.* San Francisco, CA: Jossey Bass.

Pearce, J. A., & Ravlin, E. C. (1987). The design and activation of self-regulating work groups. *Human Relations, 40,* 751–782.

Richter, A., Van Dick, R., & West, M. A. (2004). The relationship between group and organizational identification and effective intergroup relations. *Academy of Management Proceedings.*

Richter, A., West, M. A., & van Dick, R. (in press). Managing group identification for effective intergroup relations, *Academy of Management Journal.*

Rutte, C. G. (2003). Social Loaving in Teams. In: West, M. A., Tjosvold, D., & Smith, K. G. (Eds), *International handbook of organizational teamwork and cooperative working* (Ch. 17). Chichester: Wiley.

Stern, E., & Sommerlad, E. (1999). *Workplace learning, culture and performance. Issues in people management.* London: CIPD.

Shipton, H., Fay, D., West, M. A., Patterson, M., Birdi, K. (2005). Managing people to promote innovation. *Creativity & Innovation Management, 14*(2), 118–128.

Sundstrom, E., De Meuse, K. P., & Futrell, D. (1990). Work teams: Applications and effectiveness. *American Psychologist, 45,* 120–133.

West, M. A. (2000). Managing creativity and innovation in organizations. In: P. Forrester & D. Bennett (Eds), *Responsive production and the agile enterprise* (pp. 10–18). Bradford, Yorkshire: MCB University Press.

West, M. A. (2002). Sparkling fountains or stagnant ponds: An integrative model of creativity and innovation implementation in work groups. *Applied Psychology: An International Review, 51*(3), 355–387.

West, M. A., & Borrill, C. S. (2005). The influence of team working. In: J. Cox, J. King, A. Hutchinson & P. McAvoy (Eds), *Understanding doctor" performance.* Oxford: Radcliffe Publishing.

West, M. A., Borrill, C. S., Carter, M., Dawson, J. F., & Scully, J. W. (2005). Employee involvement in health service organisations: Effects on individual and trust performance. *Report to Department of Health.* Birmingham: Aston Business School.

West, M. A., Borrill, C., Dawson, J., Scully, J., Carter, M., Anelay, S., Patterson, M., & Waring, J. (2002). The link between the management of employees and patient mortality in acute hospitals. *The International Journal of Human Resource Management, 13*(8), 1299–1310.

West, M. A., & Markiewicz, L. (2004). *Building team-based working: A practical guide to organizational transformation.* Oxford: Blackwell Publishing Inc.

CHAPTER 11

Human Resource Management Practices in the Knowledge Economy: Developing Human and Social Capital

Brenda E. Ghitulescu and Carrie R. Leana

Introduction

Over the past two decades, the relationships between organizations and employees have changed dramatically. These changes have been fueled by many factors, including an increased need for flexibility in rapidly changing markets, innovations in information technology, and changes in the nature of work and the bases of firm's competitive advantage. In the past, jobs were structured to emphasize and reinforce stability in the relationship between employers and employees. More recently, employment practices that emphasize short-term relationships (often called "free agent" employment models) are prominent in the United States and elsewhere. Through such practices as downsizing, outsourcing, and the use of contingent workers, managers are able to readily shift both the size and the composition of the workforce to meet the changing business needs.

Although such practices can also provide individuals with some level of flexibility, they carry with them significant human costs that have been the subject of public discourse and have attracted the attention of individuals, employers, and public policy makers (Cohany, Hipple, Nardone, Polivka, & Stewart, 1998; Leana & Feldman, 1992; The New York Times, 1996). Further, it is not clear that such practices actually contribute to a sustained organizational effectiveness. The extant empirical evidence on this issue is mixed (Leana & Van Buren, 2000). Cascio, Young, and Morris (1997), for example, found that in the absence of asset restructuring, downsizing was not linked to increased profitability. In another study, Flanagan and O'Shaughnessy (2005) found that downsizing has a negative impact on firm reputation, particularly for newer firms. Other researchers have reported mixed results from outsourcing (Bryce & Useem, 1998; Gilley & Rasheed, 2000) and the use of contingent workers (Lautsch, 2002) as well. Moreover, labor costs often constitute a small portion of a firm's total costs (Pfeffer, 1998b), yet they may represent assets producing the most lasting value for the firm (Bartlett & Ghoshal, 2002).

When organizations adopt "free agent" employment practices, it places them at a risk of incurring significant organizational costs by losing not only the firm specific, contextual knowledge of the workers displaced, but also the basis for the collective action that is critical for any organization to function effectively (Leana, 1996). Recent research has explored the value of relations among employees and between employer and employees for organizational performance (see Nahapiet & Ghoshal, 1998; Leana & Van Buren, 1999; Adler & Kwon, 2002). In particular, researchers have used the term "social capital" to broadly capture the assets that inhere in social relations and networks. Leana and Van Buren (1999) introduced the term "organizational social capital" as a way of articulating the competitive advantage that can be realized through social relations within an organization. They define organizational social capital as a resource reflecting the character of social relations within the firm, which facilitates a successful collective action. The argument behind social capital is that the collective knowledge, skills, and abilities that individuals bring to the workplace and, more importantly, how such knowledge is combined, produce a unique asset for the organization that supports long-term competitive advantage. And while human capital is susceptible to poaching by competitors, and technology is often easy for competitors to imitate, social capital is a unique resource that cannot be easily transferred from one setting to another.

The importance of social capital to competitive advantage is reinforced by technological innovations. Recent structural changes in organizations, due to the deployment of information technology infrastructure and intense investments by firms in digital technologies, have increased many organizations' reliance on information sharing, problem solving, innovation, and knowledge transfer among different employees or organizational units. In such a context, human resource management (HRM) practices that foster the development of not only human capital, but also social capital, can become an important source of competitive advantage.

Here we argue that the purposeful adoption of HRM and work practices that encourage the development of employee skills and foster social connections across employees can raise productivity and improve organizational performance. In this chapter we: (1) outline the organizational social capital model and its outcomes; (2) summarize recent research on the relationship between HRM, human and social capital, and organizational performance; (3) discuss the effects of current employment practices on human and social capital; and (4) describe ways in which HRM practices can build and maintain human and social capital to improve organizational effectiveness. Throughout, we discuss the implications of human and social capital using examples from research in both for-profit and not-for-profit organizations.

Human and Social Capital

The combined knowledge, natural abilities, and skills of employees — typically acquired through formal education and job experience — constitute the level of an organization's human capital. The traditional human capital view suggests that when individuals invest in their human capital by sharpening their skills and training, these investments translate into better wages and job security for workers, higher productivity for firms, and greater economic growth for the society (Becker, 1964). Indeed, research suggests that learning on the job accounted for over half of the increase in America's economic growth from the 1920s to the 1980s (Carnevale & Gainer, 1988). Investments in human capital can be general in nature, having applicability across multiple firms; or they can be firm specific, in which case they are of limited use outside of a particular organization.

Traditionally, HRM researchers have focused on creating competitive advantage through practices that enhance employees' human capital (Snell, Youndt, & Wright, 1996; Lepak & Snell, 1999). This line of research has produced an impressive body of evidence linking particular bundles of human resource practices that emphasize employee training, development, and skill enhancement with superior organizational performance. For several reasons, this perspective has been broadened over the past few years to emphasize social capital as well as human capital development (Appelbaum, Batt, & Leana, 2003). First, it has become increasingly evident that organizations achieving competitive advantage are those that are better able to create new knowledge which leads to the generation of novel organizational outcomes, such as new products or services (Nahapiet & Ghoshal, 1998; Hargadon & Fanelli, 2002). Often this new knowledge is created by the exchange of information within a scientific community, or through social interaction in workgroups or organizations. For example, in the biotechnology industry, new and fine-grained knowledge primarily occurs through collaboration and teamwork (Zucker, Darby, Brewer, & Peng, 1996). Thus, the emerging perspective argues that organizations have some particular capabilities for creating and sharing knowledge that gives them their distinctive advantage. This requires not just substantial levels of human capital among individual employees, but also consideration of the collective knowledge and knowing capability of the social community that constitutes the organization. Indeed, researchers have suggested that organizations are best understood as social communities that specialize in the speed and efficiency with which they create and transfer knowledge (Kogut & Zander, 1996).

While few doubt the importance of employees' education and training, some have questioned whether the human capital framework is sufficient for understanding the impact that employees as individuals have on organizational performance. In particular, in the current context when organizations use downsizing, outsourcing, or contract workers, employees are encouraged to think of themselves as mobile free agents pursuing personal employability, rather than as stable, long-term employees (Pil & Leana, 2000). Therefore, they are less likely to make investments in firm-specific knowledge (including norms, routines, and habits of practice) that are a critical source of sustained competitive advantage for organizations. Those employees who are most highly sought in the external labor market are continuously scanning the job market for other employment opportunities. Therefore, the use of HRM practices such as downsizing and outsourcing assumes — perhaps falsely — that the organization will be able to assemble the human capital they need on a contingent basis.

However, there are important reasons to believe that this approach is not sufficient to ensure organizational effectiveness in the long term. First, the competitive advantage that a firm's employees provide resides not only in the aggregation of the individuals' human capital; more importantly, it resides in the norms and shared understandings among workers, and in the synergies that arise from their cooperation and sharing of knowledge. Second, the employment strategies that emphasize buying labor on an as-needed basis are not likely to be sources of competitive advantage. In contrast, firms that use effective HRM practices (described by several observers as innovative, high commitment, high perform-ance, high involvement, and so forth) can produce substantially enhanced economic per-formance, as evidenced by numerous studies across many different industries (Appelbaum, Bailey, Berg, & Kalleberg, 2000; Ichniowski, Kochan, Levine, Olson, & Strauss, 1996; Pfeffer, 1998a). And these successful practices foster the development of both human and social capital by providing workers with the opportunity to intervene in the work processes and make decisions, motivating workers to contribute effort toward organizational goals, and ensuring the employees have the skills and ability to do their work (Ichniowski et al., 1996; Appelbaum et al., 2000). Finally, Coleman (1988) and others have argued that social capital is essential to the development of human capital. Indeed, as noted by Nahapiet and Ghoshal (1998), knowledge creation is a socially complex phenomenon that involves structural, relational, and cognitive processes.

A broader perspective on the traditional human capital approach to competitive advan-tage suggests that organizations need the trust and reciprocity norms that make collective action possible to fully realize the value of the human capital that resides with employees (Coleman, 1988; Nahapiet & Ghoshal, 1998; Leana & Van Buren, 1999). This perspective emphasizes the role of organizational social capital for firm effectiveness. Organizations with rich stocks of social capital are able to deploy human capital in ways that ensure indi-viduals are not working at cross-purposes, or worse, working on developing skills and per-sonal networks that benefit the individual first and the organization only secondarily, if at all (Leana & Van Buren, 1999).

Social Capital — The Hidden Value in Relationships

Social capital has become a popular topic among academics and practitioners, and has received increased attention in recent years from scholars who are interested in the eco-nomic value of social relations in general and in the workplace in particular. The notion of social capital reflects how people interact to produce additional economic value beyond that attributable to human skills and abilities and investments in equipment and technol-ogy. There is a growing body of research accumulating on the topic of social capital, which suggests that for most work settings, more of this intangible asset is generally better than less.

Despite the growing literature on social capital, the term remains difficult to define (Leana & Van Buren, 1999; Adler & Kwon, 2002). In part, this is because the term social capital has been described at different levels of analysis — used variously to explain the advantage that accrues from social relations to individuals, firms, communities, and nations or geographic regions. For example, social capital has been described as the advan-tage that individuals possess based on their location within a social structure, particularly on the basis of numerous and strategically based ties with others. Research shows, for instance, that job opportunities and income growth often depend more on whom individu-als know than on what they know (Granovetter, 1973; Burt, 2000). Others have described social capital as a societal or regional phenomenon that captures the norms, expectations, trust, and civic engagement that facilitate the formation of voluntary enterprises of mutual benefit (Putnam, 1993; Fukuyama, 1995).

According to Leana and Van Buren's (1999) model of organizational social capital, social capital resides at the organizational level and is jointly owned by the collective and each of its members. Organizational social capital is the glue that binds employers and employees together as well as employees to one another. It is a resource that resides in the character of social relations in the organization, and can be contrasted with other sources of capital such as financial resources (financial capital), plant and equipment (physical capital), and the skills and experience of workers (human capital).

Organizational social capital has two primary facets — associability and shared trust (Leana & Van Buren, 1999). Associability describes how willing and how able organizational members are to subordinate their individual goals and associated actions to the goals and actions of the collective. Associability combines elements of sociability (the ability to interact socially with others) and a willingness to prioritize group objectives over individual desires. Associability has both an affective component (for example, collectivist feelings) and a skill-based component (for example, the ability to coordinate activities). In organizations, some level of associability is necessary if individuals are to agree upon and effectively coordinate their various tasks.

The other important facet of organizational social capital is trust. Researchers generally agree that trust requires a willingness to be vulnerable (Rousseau, Sitkin, Burt, & Camerer, 1998). Trust refers to the positive expectations that employees and organizations have of each other's intentions and behavior. Trust is important to organizations because it decreases the need for monitoring and increases the employees' willingness to work for the collective organizational goals. Without trust, the costs of monitoring individuals would outweigh the benefits of a collective action in organizations. Thus, in the absence of trust, associability is unlikely to exist. Further, people are more likely to work together when they have had a successful interaction in the past. Work groups that have had a history of successful collaboration are more likely to experience higher levels of trust than those without such a history, and therefore are more likely to collaborate successfully in the future.

Trust is important in an era when organizations need to restructure work in the face of changing performance demands and competitive pressures. When employees trust management, these restructuring initiatives are more likely to be successful, because people will not fear that they will lose their jobs as a result of increases in productivity. Many of the innovative work practices adopted by organizations in recent years rely on team work and cross-functional cooperation rather than on formal control mechanisms. Thus, trust becomes central to the successful adoption of these practices because people will be more likely to cooperate when they believe their contribution to collective efforts will be rewarded. It should also be noted that trust takes different forms depending on the nature of the employment relationship, with different consequences for cooperation and collective performance. For example, firms that emphasize long-term relationships with employees are more likely to achieve sustainable performance due to the development of "resilient trust" — a form of trust where each partner is expected to exhibit a high degree of mutual concern and shared interests (Ring, 1996). In contrast, firms that emphasize short-term relationships with employees (such as in the case of using contingent workers) develop "fragile trust" — a form of trust where each partner is willing to rely on the other only to a limited extent, based on an evaluation of each party's short-term self-interest.

According to Nahapiet and Ghoshal (1998), social capital at the organizational level operates through three distinct yet intertwined mechanisms: (1) the structure of the collective network linking employees in the organization; (2) the shared norms, trust, and obligations that are leveraged through relationships among employees; and (3) the shared knowledge, language, and narratives that provide collective interpretations and systems of meanings to workers and facilitate their coordination at work. How do these three components of social capital explain why social capital creates value for organizations? There are several arguments that have been theoretically developed and empirically tested that pertain to this discussion and are outlined below.

First, the structure of the networks linking employees in the organization refers to who the employees share information with and with what frequency. Such information flowing among different employees create a competitive advantage for the organization by enhancing the organization's ability to absorb and assimilate new knowledge. For example, empirical evidence indicates that sharing knowledge among employees is a key factor in the speed with which manufacturing innovations are transferred internally or imitated from others (Zander & Kogut, 1995). Information sharing can also increase competitive advantage by facilitating individual learning in the context of work, where it has more meaning than in more formal settings using abstract approaches. For example, workers may learn how knowledge in practice may be different from formal documented practice through collaborative discussions, reflective dialogue, and storytelling (Orr, 1996), which allows them to improve their work practices continuously. More generally, information sharing among coworkers can enhance agreement on expectations among workers and mutual accountability (Sparrowe, Liden, Wayne, & Kraimer, 2001).

Second, research across several different industries has shown that trusting relations facilitate collaborative behaviors and collective action in the absence of other explicit mechanisms to foster and reinforce these behaviors (Coleman, 1990). Relationships characterized by trust among employees allow the transmission of more information as well as richer, more complex, and potentially more valuable information across individuals and organizational units. Such findings have been reported across diverse settings ranging from product development teams (Hansen, 1999) to public schools (Leana & Pil, 2006). Employees who trust one another are more likely to exchange more sensitive information that is not available to others outside the circle of trust, and are less likely to fear opportunistic behavior on the part of their colleagues, enabling a work environment characterized by collaboration and exchange that can benefit both the organizations and the individuals who work within them.

Third, when employees develop networks of social relations among them and interact as part of a collective, they develop a shared conception of work, their common goals in the organization, and a shared language to talk about their work and respective roles. This shared vision and language, and the underlying values that employees collectively hold, will help promote employee integration and a sense of shared responsibility and collective action (Coleman, 1990; Leana & Van Buren, 1999). When employees in an organization collectively hold a set of goals, there is a lower incidence of what economists call "free rider" problems. Social capital may be a substitute for the formal contracts, incentives, and monitoring systems that economists devise to control employees and ensure that they act in the interests of the organization rather than just their self interest.

Empirical evidence in several contexts suggests that social capital creates value for organizations beyond the effects of human capital. For example, Tsai and Ghoshal (1998) studied several business units of a multinational electronics company. They found evidence that social capital — manifested through the network of social interaction among units, the trust that different units had in one another, and the shared vision about work that the units had — contributed significantly to product innovation in the organization. Other researchers found evidence that social capital in product development teams facilitated an enhanced search and transfer of complex and tacit knowledge (Hansen, 1999). Recent work on coordination in uncertain, interdependent, and time-constrained environments has shown that communication and relationships characterized by shared goals and knowledge, mutual respect, and helping among employees, played an important role in achieving better patient care results in hospitals (Gittell et al., 2000), and improved quality, productivity, and fewer customer complaints in airlines (Gittell, 2000).

There is empirical evidence that both internal social ties within teams and the external relationships that cut across different employee groups are important for organizational performance. Reagans and Zuckerman (2001) studied corporate R&D teams in several corporations from seven different industries (automotive, chemicals, electronics, aerospace, pharmaceuticals, biotechnology, and oil) that focused on both basic research and applied projects (product and process development and improvement). They found that those teams that developed both types of social ties had the highest productivity levels. Another study of knowledge workers and top management teams in technology firms showed that employees' human capital and social networks predicted the organization members' ability to combine and exchange knowledge, which in turn was a significant predictor of the rate of new product and new service introduction (Smith, Collins, & Clark, 2005). And in a not-for-profit setting, Leana and Pil (2006) found evidence that the collective social capital among teachers in urban public schools, as well as the external social relations of principals with stakeholders such as parents and community groups, had a positive and sustained effect on several dimensions of school performance, most notably student achievement in literacy and mathematics. These positive effects of social capital were significant beyond the effects of teachers' human capital, suggesting that organizational social capital contributes uniquely to school performance, independent of human capital effects.

How Organizations Create and Maintain Human and Social Capital

Given the accumulating empirical evidence on the positive effects of social capital, how can organizations develop this resource? An important concern here is employee motivation: Employees will not invest in actions that build and maintain organizational social capital unless they see a benefit from doing so, even if the benefit is indirect and realized over the long run. Leana and Van Buren (1999) argue that organizational social capital is largely managed through the firm's employment practices. The most obvious way in which firms can build and maintain both their human capital and organizational social capital is by adopting HRM practices that promote stability among employees, thus fostering employees' stake in the long-term achievement of organizational goals — even if this entails subordinating their immediate individual goals. Typically this is done by making investments in training, job security, and team building, and minimizing the use of practices such as downsizing and contingent work. Organizational social capital can also operate through norms that base employee selection in part on the employees' ability and appreciation for working cooperatively. Socialization systems can also be used to promote reciprocity norms, as can the organization's reward system in the form of promotions and compensation. Employment practices that encourage a stable job tenure and reinforce trust and the willingness to work cooperatively enhance a firm's stock of organizational social capital, with a parallel benefit to the organization's ability to organize collective action.

Is there a Place for Social Capital in the Link between HRM and Performance?

Pfeffer (1998a) provides extensive anecdotal evidence that effective organizations use seven common HRM practices — employment security, selective hiring of new employees, decentralized decision making and self-managed teams, high compensation contingent on organizational performance, extensive training, reduced status distinctions and barriers, and extensive sharing of financial and performance information throughout the organization. For example, Southwest Airlines bases its successful performance in part on never having a layoff or furlough in an industry where such events are very common, and recognizes people as strategic assets rather than costs. Southwest Airlines also builds employee partnership through job security and a stimulating work environment, by putting long-term interests before short-term profitability, and keeping a smaller, but stable and more productive labor force than their competitors. In a more detailed empirical study, Gittell (2000) showed how Southwest Airlines achieved superior performance compared to its competitors by using HRM practices that emphasize selection for cross-functional teamwork — rather than selection for functional skills, and proactive cross-functional conflict resolution — rather than minimal cross-functional conflict resolution. Gittell argued that these practices led to better performance through their effects on what is commonly termed social capital — or the communication and relationships among employees, characterized by helping behavior, shared goals, shared knowledge, and mutual respect among workers.

Substantive empirical evidence has accumulated in recent years documenting the payoff for organizations adopting HRM practices that invest in the human capital of the workforce (Becker & Gerhart, 1996; Huselid, 1995; Ichniowski et al., 1996). Researchers have opened up the "black box" of management practices and documented the implementation of high involvement work systems with substantial gains in operational performance in several industries ranging from automobile assembly (MacDuffie, 1995; Pil & MacDuffie, 1996; Kochan, Lansbury, & MacDuffie, 1997), apparel and medical electronics (Appelbaum et al., 2000), semi-conductors (Bailey, 1998; Appleyard & Brown, 2001), steel mini mills, rolling mills, and finishing lines (Ichniowski et al., 1997; Appelbaum et al., 2000), telecommunication services (Batt, 1999) and financial services (Hunter, Bernhardt, Hughes, & Skuratowicz, 2001). These high involvement practices generally include coherent sets of HRM practices that enhance employee skills, participation in decision making, and motivation at work. Similar to what Pfeffer (1998a) described as successful practices, these HRM practices usually include the use of problem-solving teams, incentive pay plans, careful recruiting and selection, extensive labor-management communication, flexible job assignments, and employment security.

These HRM practices are successful in part because they foster the development of employee skills. Productivity is likely to be higher when firms invest in the skills and training of the workforce, design work so that employees may use their skills more effectively, and provide incentives to motivate workers. Some explanations explicitly focus on how such HRM practices develop firm-specific human capital as a source of competitive advantage (Batt, 2002). Such HRM practices emphasize not only the selective hiring of employees with high general skills (or formal education), but also the investment in on-the-job training (that builds firm-specific human capital). However, most research has paid far less attention to the informal networks through which employees cooperate and coordinate their work, and the patterns of peer relationships in organizations, even though such informal networks are growing in importance relative to the formal hierarchical structures in organizations (Powell, 1990).

According to Appelbaum et al. (2000) and others who study high involvement work, employers adopting high involvement HRM practices strive for workers who are accountable, adaptable, and reliable. They want employees who have a shared sense of obligation and are willing to invest the time and energy to learn the norms, systems, and structures that make the organization effective. Through the use of these practices, employers hope to develop a stable workforce that is capable of operating effectively and proactively in unstable, unpredictable global and local environments. These characteristics describe organizations rich in social capital in which employees share critical knowledge and coordinate their activities both formally and informally. The most recent research on HRM practices has begun to examine the social capital that develops among employees in organizations using these practices, as a mechanism that may account for their positive performance effects.

High involvement HRM practices can foster the development of all three dimensions of organizational social capital — structural, relational, and cognitive. With regard to the structural and cognitive dimensions, high involvement HRM practices provide opportunities for employees to interact and engage in ongoing learning through collaboration with other employees, in both "on-line" problem-solving groups (such as self-directed teams in which groups rather than individuals are responsible for many decisions) and "off-line" groups (in which employees and supervisors meet periodically). For example, sales representatives in self-directed teams in call centers had higher sales productivity than sales representatives in traditionally supervised groups, because they benefited from better learning and problem solving on how to handle customers and new technology (Batt, 1999).

Further, the incentives associated with the use of high-involvement HRM practices — such as ongoing investment in training, employment security, high relative pay, and performance management systems — support the building of trust between employees and employers. The training that organizations provide rewards the employees with additional skills and opportunities for higher-paying jobs. Ensuring employment security allows workers to suggest productivity and quality improvements without fear of losing their jobs. In these ways, organizations are more likely to achieve superior performance in part because they have a better connected workforce (structural dimension of social capital); in part because they have employees who are more attached to the organization (relational dimension); and in part because employees share knowledge and develop collective work strategies (cognitive dimension).

From the preceding summary of the research conducted across many different settings and industries, it appears that both human capital and social capital are primary means by which high-involvement HRM practices affect organizational performance. A human capital model does not satisfactorily explain the mechanisms linking HRM practices and outcomes, because it does not consider the synergies — learning, problem solving, and knowledge sharing — that occur among employees through networks of communication. At the same time, a social capital approach by itself is insufficient because it does not consider the quality of employees and the knowledge they have to offer one another (Adler & Kwon, 2002).

Only a handful of researchers have begun to grapple simultaneously with these issues in empirical settings. For example, there is evidence that the introduction of high involvement work practices led to an array of structural changes in the frequency and content of interactions among employees, between managers and workers, and between management and union representatives (Rubinstein, Eaton, & Colucci, 2002). Further, high-involvement HRM practices introduced in steel finishing lines led to a much more extensive communication network among employees, especially among production and maintenance workers (Gant, Ichniowski, & Shaw, 2002). In several acute-care hospital units, high involvement HRM practices shaped the quality of information available on hospital patients, which in turn predicted the rate of medical errors (Preuss, 2003). Finally, in high technology companies, network-building HRM practices focused on training, performance assessment, and rewards designed to help and encourage top managers to build relationships with internal organizational members and external others, led to superior financial performance through the top management teams' internal and external social networks (Collins & Clark, 2003).

These recent studies point to the importance not only of individual human capital, but also of networks of human capital, or organizational social capital. Therefore, the challenge for managers is to provide incentives and create an environment in which employees are encouraged to invest in and create networks at work, both within their workgroups and across different groups and organizational units, and external peer networks that build organizational capacities and enable the firm to meet its strategic goals. This requirement is unlikely to be met by relying solely on employees' informal networks of personal loyalty and contacts. Instead, organizations will also need to design collaborative mechanisms to build and sustain social capital.

Building Organizational Social Capital through HRM Practices

Given the trend in employment practices outlined in the beginning of this chapter, the theory and research findings we describe here may be surprising, even curious. Theory and empirical findings make clear the connections between organizational social capital and the effectiveness of HRM practices. High-involvement HRM practices rely on collective identity and trust, rather than formal monitoring and control mechanisms associated with more traditional (so-called transactional, see Rousseau, 1995) ways of managing people and organizing work. Therefore, HRM practices that emphasize transactional arrangements and human capital at the expense of social capital may retard rather than enhance flexibility. To the extent that flexibility requires informal norms for workgroup coordination and high levels of trust, it is necessary to develop HRM practices that support the development of organizational social capital.

In reality, organizations place much more emphasis on procuring human capital than on building organizational social capital (Leana & Van Buren, 2000). Many employment markets are characterized by a "winner-take-all" mentality (Frank & Cook, 1995) in which disproportionate rewards accrue to individuals with talents deemed to be scarce. For example, organizations focus on attracting and remunerating a chief executive officer with the talents and abilities that are thought to be the missing element needed to make the organization successful, without such regard for attracting and rewarding other employees. Such practices emphasize the contributions that individuals — specifically those at the top of the organizational hierarchy — make to organizational success but downplay the contributions of the collective. However, compensation schemes that are based solely on individual contributions are generally inappropriate in contexts where teamwork occurs (Pfeffer, 1998b). Because organizational social capital is intangible and thus difficult to quantify, it is often devalued by organizations in ways that other forms of capital (human, financial, or physical) are not. Thus, the likely tendency in organizations is to pay much more attention to human capital than to social capital when they devise HRM practices and systems. As we have argued here, such a narrow focus may be ineffective as it does not consider an organization's stock of social capital, which can either unleash or retard the positive effects of human capital on organizational performance.

We have several practical recommendations regarding how organizations can build and maintain social capital. As noted earlier, firms can have the greatest impact on organizational social capital through their HRM practices. Practices that build trust, stability in employment, and associability can foster organizational social capital. In contrast, practices such as downsizing, outsourcing, and the use of contingent workers destroy trust and undermine stability, thus eroding organizational social capital. Several HRM practices can promote organizational social capital and human capital. First, organizations that use job security provisions or at least provide an understanding that practices like downsizing are a last resort rather than a first measure of cost cutting, are more likely to build high stocks of organizational social capital. Second, organizations should use socialization practices that encourage collective goal setting and attainment rather than only individually focused goals. Third, equally important is the use of organization- or workgroup-based compensation systems rather than incentives based solely on individual performance. Fourth, organizations should use compensation and promotion practices that reward social capital building or enhancing behaviors, particularly among their managers. Fifth, to maintain social capital, compensation practices cannot be designed to overreward a few individuals strong in human capital at the expense of the collective capital of the workforce as a whole. Sixth, selective hiring practices should ensure that individuals who join the organization have the skills for, and appreciation of, behaviors that encourage organizational social capital. Finally, organizations should establish long-term partnerships with external stakeholders such as customers and labor unions to further enhance social capital.

Conclusions

Although cost-effectiveness is certainly important for organizations, the primary rationale for selecting a system of HRM practices should be its effects on an organization's ability to accomplish its mission. The concept of social capital centers the debate about which HRM practices enhance an organization's ability to engage in collective action, achieve organizational goals, and create what Leana and Rousseau (2000) call "relational wealth".

In this chapter, we discuss recent research on organizational social capital — a resource reflecting the character of social relations within a firm — and relate it to the current research on HRM practices and human capital. We note that organizational social capital tends to be particularly undervalued in most firms in the current environment. This is surprising in light of the accumulating empirical evidence regarding both the positive effects of organizational social capital on firm performance and the advantages of designing HRM practices that support the development of human and social capital alike. We offer an analysis of the relationship between HRM practices, human capital, and social capital, and argue that HRM practices can make a difference in an organization's stocks of both forms of capital. Finally, we provide some practical implications for firms to enhance and maintain their stocks of human and social capital.

Why should managers value organizational social capital? All other forms of capital — physical, financial, and human — can be procured from external sources. But organizational social capital is a resource that must be made, not bought, and it cannot be imitated by competitors. It is the result of shared trust among employees and among employers and employees, and of successful collective action that creates competitive advantage. Organizations try to trade off organizational social capital for increased short-term profitability through workforce reductions, curtailed expenditures on employee training, or outsourcing core business functions. These practices may save money in the short-term but harm organizational social capital and long-term organizational success.

Acknowledgment

The authors are grateful to the National Science Foundation (Award No. 0228343) for the support of Brenda E. Ghitulescu during the writing of this manuscript.

References

Adler, P. S., & Kwon, S. W. (2002). Social capital: Prospects for a new concept. *Academy of Management Review, 27*, 17–40.
Appelbaum, E., Bailey, T., Berg, P., & Kalleberg, A. L. (2000). *Manufacturing advantage. Why high-performance work systems pay off.* Ithaca, NY: Cornell University Press.
Appelbaum, E., Batt, R., & Leana, C. R. (2003). Social capital at work. *Perspectives on work.* (vol. 7.1, pp. 7–9). Champaign, IL: University of Illinois Press.
Appleyard, M. M., & Brown, C. (2001). Employment practices and semiconductor manufacturing performance. *Industrial Relations, 40*, 436–474.

Bailey, D. E. (1998). Comparison of manufacturing performance of three team structures in semi-conductor plants. *IEEE Transactions on Engineering Management, 45*, 1–13.

Bartlett, C. & Ghoshal, S. (2002). Building competitive advantage through people. *Sloan Management Review, 43*(2), 34–41.

Batt, R. (1999). Work organization, technology, and performance in customer service and sales. *Industrial and Labor Relations Review, 52*, 539–564.

Batt, R. (2002). Managing customer services: Human resource practices, turnover, and sales growth. *Academy of Management Journal, 45*, 587–597.

Becker, G. S. (1964). *Human capital*. Chicago, IL: University of Chicago Press.

Becker, B., & Gerhart, B. (1996). The impact of human resource management on organizational performance: Progress and prospects. *Academy of management Journal, 39*, 779–801.

Bryce, D. J., & Useem, M. (1998). The impact of corporate outsourcing on company value. *European Management Journal, 16*, 635–643.

Burt, R. (2000). The network structure of social capital. *Research in Organizational Behavior, 13*, 55–110.

Carnevale, P., & Gainer, L. (1988). *The learning enterprise*. Washington, DC: U.S. Department of Labor.

Cascio, W. F., Young, C. E., & Morris, J. R. (1997). Financial consequences of employment change decisions in major U.S. corporations. *Academy of Management Journal, 40*, 1175–1189.

Cohany, S. R., Hipple, S. F., Nardone, T. J., Polivka, A. E., & Stewart, J. C. (1998). Counting the workers: Results of a first survey. In: K. Barker & K. Christensen (Eds), *Contingent work: American employment relations in transition*. Ithaca, NY: ILR Press.

Coleman, J. (1988). Social capital in the creation of human capital. *American Journal of Sociology, 94*, s95–s120.

Coleman, J. (1990). *Foundations of social theory*. Cambridge, MA: Harvard University Press.

Collins, C. J., & Clark, K. D. (2003). Strategic human resource practices, top management team social networks, and firm performance: The role of human resource practices in creating organizational competitive advantage. *Academy of Management Journal, 46*, 740–751.

Flanagan, D., & O'Shaughnessy, K. (2005). The effects of layoffs on firm reputation. *Journal of Management, 31*, 445–463.

Frank, R., & Cook, P. (1995). *The winner-take-all society*. New York: Free Press.

Fukuyama, F. (1995). *Trust: The social virtues and the creation of prosperity*. New York: Free Press.

Gant, J., Ichniowski, C., & Shaw, K. (2002). Social capital and organizational change in high involvement and traditional work organizations. *Journal of Economics & Management Strategy, 11*, 289–328.

Gilley, K. M., & Rasheed, A. (2000). Making more by doing less: An analysis of outsourcing and its effects on firm performance. *Journal of Management, 26*, 763–790.

Gittell, J. H. (2000). Organizing work to support relational coordination. *International Journal of Human Resource Management, 11*, 517–539.

Gittell, J. H., Fairfield, K. M., Bierbaum, B., Head, W., Jackson, R., Kelly, M., Laskin, R., Lipson, S., Siliski, J., Thornhills, T., & Zuckerman, J. (2000). Impact of relational coordination on quality of care, postoperative pain and functioning, and length of stay. Medical Care, 38, 807–819.

Granovetter, M. (1973). The strength of weak ties. *American Journal of Sociology, 78*, 1360–1380.

Hansen, M. (1999). The search-transfer problem: The role of weak ties in sharing knowledge across organizational subunits. *Administrative Science Quarterly, 44*, 82–111.

Hargadon, A., & Fanelli, A. (2002). Action and possibility: Reconciling dual perspectives of knowledge in organizations. *Organization Science, 13*, 290–302.

Hunter, L. W., Bernhardt, A., Hughes, K. L., & Skuratowicz, E. (2001). It's not just the ATMs: Technology, firm strategies, jobs, and earnings in retail banking. *Industrial and Labor Relations Review, 54*, 402–424.

Huselid, M. A. (1995). The impact of human resource management practices on turnover, productivity, and corporate financial performance. *Academy of Management Journal, 38,* 635–672.

Ichniowski, C., Kochan, T., Levine, D., Olson, C., & Strauss, G. (1996). What works at work: Overview and assessment. *Industrial Relations, 35,* 299–333.

Ichniowski, C., Shaw, K., & Prennushi, G. (1997). The effects of human resource management practices on productivity: A study of steel finishing lines. *The American Economic Review, 87,* 291–313.

Kochan, T., Lansbury, R. D., & MacDuffie, J. P. (1997). *After lean production: Evolving employment practices in the world auto industry.* Ithaca, NY: Cornell University Press.

Kogut, B., & Zander, U. (1996). What do firms do? Coordination, identity, and learning. *Organization Science, 7,* 502–518.

Lautsch, B. (2002). Uncovering and explaining variance in the features and outcomes of contingent work. *Industrial and Labor Relations Review, 56,* 23–43.

Leana, C. R. (1996). Why downsizing won't work. *Chicago Tribune Sunday Magazine,* pp. 14–16, 18.

Leana, C. R., & Feldman, D. (1992). *Coping with job loss: How individuals, organizations, and communities cope with layoffs.* Lexington, MA: Lexington Press.

Leana, C. R., & Pil, F. K. (2006). Social capital and organizational performance: Evidence from urban public schools. *Organization Science* (forthcoming).

Leana, C. R., & Rousseau, D. M. (2000). *Relational wealth: The advantages of stability in a changing economy.* New York: Oxford University Press.

Leana, C. R., & Van Buren, H. J. (1999). Organizational social capital and employment practices. *Academy of Management Review, 24,* 538–555.

Leana, C. R., & Van Buren, H. J. (2000). Eroding organizational social capital among U.S. firms: The price of job instability. In: R. J. Burke & C. L. Cooper (Eds), *The organization in crisis. Downsizing, restructuring, and privatization* (pp. 220–232). Oxford, UK: Blackwell Publishers.

Lepak, D. P., & Snell, S. A. (1999). The human resource architecture: Toward a theory of human capital allocation and development. *Academy of Management Review, 24,* 31–48.

MacDuffie, J. P. (1995). Human resource bundles and manufacturing performance: Organizational logic and flexible production systems in the world auto industry. *Industrial and Labor Relations Review, 48,* 197–221.

Nahapiet, J., & Ghoshal, S. (1998). Social capital, intellectual capital, and the organizational advantage. *Academy of Management Review, 23,* 242–266.

Orr, J. E. (1996). *Talking about machines. An ethnography of a modern job.* Ithaca, NY: ILR Press, Cornell.

Pfeffer, J. (1998a). *The human equation: Building profits by putting people first.* Boston, MA: Harvard Business School Press.

Pfeffer, J. (1998b). Six dangerous myths about pay. *Harvard Business Review, 76*(3), 109–119.

Pil, F. K., & Leana, C. R. (2000). Free-agency versus high-involvement approaches to skill development. Enhancing relational wealth. In: C. R. Leana & D. M. Rousseau (Eds), *Relational wealth. The advantages of stability in a changing economy* (pp. 116–129). New York: Oxford University Press.

Pil, F. K., & MacDuffie, J. P. (1996). The adoption of high-involvement work practices. *Industrial Relations, 35,* 423–455.

Powell, W. (1990). Neither market nor hierarchy: Network forms of organization. In: L. Cummings & B. Straw (Eds), *Research in organizational behavior* (Vol. 12, pp. 295–336). Greenwich, CT: JAI Press.

Preuss, G. A. (2003). High performance work systems and organizational outcomes: The mediating role of information quality. *Industrial and Labor Relations Review, 56,* 590–605.

Putnam, R. D. (1993). *Making democracy work: Civic traditions in modern Italy.* Princeton, NY: Princeton University Press.

Reagans, R., & Zuckerman, E. W. (2001). Networks, diversity, and productivity: The social capital of corporate R&D teams. *Organization Science, 12*, 502–517.

Ring, P. (1996). Fragile and resilient trust and their roles in economic exchange. *Business & Society, 35*, 148–175.

Rousseau, D. M. (1995). *Psychological contracts in organizations*. Thousand Oaks, CA: Sage.

Rousseau, D. M., Sitkin, S., Burt, R., & Camerer, C. (1998). Not so different after all: A cross-discipline view of trust. *Academy of Management Review, 23*, 393–404.

Rubinstein, S., Eaton, A., & Colucci, W. (2002). *The effects of high involvement work systems on employee and union-management communication*. Working Paper, Rutgers University.

Smith, K. G., Collins, C. J., & Clark, K. D. (2005). Existing knowledge, knowledge creation capability, and the rate of new product introduction in high-technology firms. *Academy of Management Journal, 48*, 346–357.

Snell, S. A., Youndt, M. A., & Wright, P. (1996). Establishing a framework for research in strategic human resource management. *Human Resource Management, 14*, 61–90.

Sparrowe, R. T., Liden, R. C., Wayne, S. J., & Kraimer, M. L. (2001). Social networks and the performance of individuals and groups. *Academy of Management Journal, 44*, 316–325.

The New York Times Special Report. (1996). *The downsizing of America*. New York: Times Book.

Tsai, W., & Ghoshal, S. (1998). Social capital and value creation: The role of intrafirm networks. *Academy of Management Journal, 41*, 464–477.

Zander, U., & Kogut, B. (1995). Knowledge and the speed of the transfer and imitation of organizational capabilities: An empirical test. *Organization Science, 6*, 76–92.

Zucker, L. G., Darby, M. R., Brewer, M. B., & Peng, Y. (1996). Collaboration structures and information dilemmas in biotechnology: Organization boundaries as trust production. In: R. M. Kramer & T. R. Tyler (Eds), *Trust in organizations: Frontiers of theory and research* (pp. 90–113). Thousand Oaks, CA: Sage.

CHAPTER 12

Engagement with Work: Issues for Measurement and Intervention

Michael P. Leiter

Building engagement with work is a challenge. The complexity of the task arises in part from engagement's quality as a relationship: engagement with work is not an independent quality of a person but of a person's contact with a work environment. The employees' part of this relationship is a state of mind reflecting the energy, involvement, and self-efficacy they invest in their work. The work environment's part of this relationship reflects policies and practices that influence employees' options for structuring their day-to-day worklife and their long-term career aspirations. Relationships with work reflect an investment from both parties — individual employees and their organizational environments. They often settle into a consistent pattern over time: highly engaged relationships with work persist, as do relationships characterized by burnout. A significant challenge for research and management practice is identifying, developing, implementing, and assessing interventions to move relationships with work away from burnout and toward engagement. To be effective and sustained, interventions to build engagement with work encompass the perspectives of both organizations and individuals, acknowledging the benefits and risks an intervention holds for either party.

Burnout and Engagement With Work: Definitions and Measures

Burnout is a construct at the negative end of three inter-related qualities: energy, involvement, and efficacy. In terms of energy, burnout is characterized by exhaustion. In terms of involvement, burnout is characterized by cynicism and distance. In terms of efficacy, burnout reflects a poor sense of self-efficacy regarding work (Maslach & Leiter, 1997).

The most widely used measure of burnout, the Maslach Burnout Inventory, MBI (Maslach, Jackson, & Leiter, 1996), includes a distinct subscale on each of these three dimensions. The measure, using a frequency rating scale, assesses how often respondents experience the defining qualities of burnout. Most surveys of burnout indicate a broad, single modal distribution of scores on each of these three qualities. In large data sets, the striking feature is the smooth continuum of scores on these three dimensions. The distribution of scores on the three dimensions suggests that burnout is an extreme version of something that most people encounter some of the time.

Engagement with work is the opposite of burnout. In contrast with exhaustion, engagement is energetic. In contrast with cynicism, engagement is involved with people, with ideas, and with values. In contrast with inefficacy, engagement is confident of getting things done and doing them well. Engagement means more than the absence of burnout; it is an active state implying an intense, fulfilling, and productive participation in work.

In research exploring interventions that prevent and alleviate burnout, it became increasingly important to define a positive alternative. Many interventions considered to address burnout had the potential to do more than alleviate negative qualities of worklife; they could build constructive, fulfilling relationships with work. Including engagement shifted the perspective from two potential relationships with work — burnout or neutral — to three: burnout, neutral, or engaged. This shift raised conceptual challenges in defining that territory above the neutral line. It opened opportunities to put burnout models in the context of other organizational constructs, such as organizational commitment, and job satisfaction. The broadening of the focus on burnout can help to address challenges to the syndrome as lacking a credible theoretical base.

On a practical level, the engagement construct opens more opportunities for research collaboration. Field research on burnout requires active partnerships with organizations that deliver value to balance the organization's contribution to the research. Helping to assess or to alleviate burnout provides one element of that rationale. Engagement with work brings an additional and more positive focus for the project.

Measuring Engagement With Work

There are distinct approaches to defining engagement. Each has implications for defining and for measuring the construct. A separate contrast approach contrasts engagement with work with burnout, but does not define engagement strictly as the opposite of burnout. It develops a new measure to capture the distinct qualities of engagement. The single construct approach defines engagement as the opposite of burnout. It accepts the Maslach Burnout Inventory as providing a sufficient and adequate measure of burnout. Each approach has implications for intervention.

Separate Construct

The separate construct approach, taken by Schaufeli and colleagues (Demerouti, Bakker, de Jonge, Janssen, & Schaufeli, 2001; Schaufeli & Bakker, 2004), defines engagement as vigor, dedication, and absorption. This group has developed a scale (the Utrecht Work Engagement Scale, UWES) to measure these three elements of engagement. This approach reflects an assumption that engagement is not simply the opposite of burnout as measured by the MBI, but a related construct, contrasting with burnout, but including qualities other than those represented on the three MBI continua of energy, involvement, and efficacy.

With this approach, burnout and engagement lead to distinct outcomes: burnout predicts health problems but engagement does not. The approach proposes that these three qualities of engagement predict certain organizational outcomes better than the three dimensions of burnout. It argues that building engagement with work requires different strategies and initiatives than does alleviating burnout.

Adding elements may enrich the concept of engagement with work, but there is a risk of muddling the boundaries among existing concepts, such as organizational commitment, professional commitment, and job involvement. One challenge is to differentiate and distinguish this definition of engagement in contrast with other constructs. Another challenge is that measuring both burnout and engagement with work requires two distinct questionnaires. As research fatigue has become a challenge of growing importance for researchers, increasing the length of a questionnaire package is a serious decision. A second challenge is defining the relationship of engagement to burnout. Adding dimensions other than energy, involvement, and efficacy results in a construct that is not precisely the opposite of burnout. This may be a valuable contribution, especially if one views current definitions of burnout to be incomplete in important ways. But the definition requires researchers to test and contrast the implications of the definition.

Single Construct

The single construct approach accepts the three continua assessed in the MBI as a complete description of engagement with work. The combination of infrequent exhaustion and cynicism coupled with an ongoing sense of professional efficacy constitutes the essential qualities of engagement with work.

An implication for measurement is that the MBI-GS (General Scale) provides an adequate measure of engagement with work. Burnout is defined by relatively high scores on exhaustion and cynicism combined with low scores on professional efficacy. Engagement is defined by relatively low scores on exhaustion and cynicism combined with high scores on professional efficacy. This approach offers simplicity: it stays with energy, involvement, and efficacy, adding no other dimensions to the construct. It simplifies measurement, by staying with an instrument that has an extensive track record in the research literature. The 16 items of the MBI-GS remain a sufficient measure for both burnout and engagement. One limitation of this approach is that the validity and reliability record of the MBI has been as a measure of burnout. Additional psychometric analyses are necessary to establish it as a measure of engagement as well.

A variation on this approach is to accept energy, involvement, and efficacy as the defining dimensions of both burnout and engagement, but to view the existing MBI-GS scales as having insufficient range to accommodate engagement adequately. For example, on the energy dimension, the MBI includes only items that describe a state of exhaustion. The most positive score possible on the energy dimension of the MBI is to never experience exhaustion. Never feeling exhaustion is not necessarily the same thing as feeling energetic. Extending the energy scale of the MBI in the positive direction would permit the scale to provide a richer description of the energy dimension associated with engagement with work. Although this approach makes intuitive sense, it appears that being energetic is not experienced as the opposite pole from being exhausted. The original MBI-HSS (Human Service Scale) included an item — I feel very energetic — which functioned as part of the personal accomplishment scale, not as a reverse scored item on the emotional exhaustion scale. Schaufeli and colleagues (Schaufeli, Salanova, González-romá, & Bakker, 2004) found as well that the vigor dimension of the UWES was more closely associated with the professional efficacy dimension of the MBI-GS than with the exhaustion dimension. Feeling energetic appears to be a quality of professional efficacy as much if not more than it is the opposite of exhaustion.

The difficulty in defining an extended dimension of energy may be seen as support for the separate construct model. From this perspective, experiencing low energy — from mild, occasional fatigue through chronic, profound exhaustion — has a dynamic that is distinct from experiencing high levels of energy. It follows then that defining and measuring engagement with work requires a qualitative shift in focus. Vigor is not simply the opposite of exhaustion, but a distinct quality requiring a separate approach to measurement and responsive to different types of interventions.

Another interpretation, consistent with encompassing engagement with work within the existing range of the MBI-GS, is to accept a rating of 'never' on the exhaustion subscale as the most positive rating of energy. This rating may function as the most accurate assessment available of a sense of being comfortably in the moment, having sufficient energy to address any physical, social, emotional, or cognitive demand. The state described by very low scores on the exhaustion subscale may reflect a sense of centered wellbeing that contrasts subjectively with chronic exhaustion. In contrast, actively endorsing statements that one feels energetic constitutes a distinct condition. Saying 'I feel very energetic,' may further elaborate on one's sense of professional efficacy than contradict feelings of exhaustion.

Implications for Intervention

Both depictions of engagement with work lead to the conclusion that a strong positive construction of energy ('I feel very energetic') is not exactly the opposite of a negative score on the exhaustion subscale of the MBI. Feeling energetic is not intuitively the opposite of feeling exhausted and burned out every day at work. A separate construct approach views vigor as a defining quality of engagement with work. The fact that feeling energetic at work is not simply the opposite of feeling exhausted requires supplementing the MBI. The resulting construct requires a distinct measure with new dimensions.

A single construct approach acknowledges that feeling energetic is not the opposite of feeling exhausted, but takes a different resolution. It concludes that the opposite of exhaustion is not feeling energetic, but feeling centered and relaxed or some other quality inconsistent with fatigue. From this perspective, feeling energetic is a quality of efficacy, captured adequately by the professional efficacy subscale of the MBI-GS, despite the absence of specific items referring to feeling energetic as was the case in the original MBI-HSS. It follows from this perspective that engagement defined as vigor, dedication, and absorption is potentially an interesting and important construct to be studied in conjunction with burnout, it is not exactly the opposite of burnout. The opposite pole from burnout on the MBI-GS indicates infrequent experiences of exhaustion and cynicism along with frequent experiences of professional efficacy. This is a convenient construct, but it may fall short of capturing an active state of engagement with work.

In summary, this brief consideration of definition and measurement issues suggests that complex issues underlie initiatives to enhance engagement with work. Additional research, especially studies that assess the impact of interventions on the core qualities of energy, involvement, and efficacy, as well as associated constructs, such as organizational commitment, is needed. At this point, engagement with work remains somewhat tentative in its definition.

Interventions

This chapter proposes a conceptual framework for interventions to build engagement with work. The framework encompasses the targets of interventions, strategies for interventions, and potential consequences. Finally, the section considers implications for research and application.

Intervention cannot wait for questions raised above regarding the engagement construct to be settled. The only way to settle some of the questions, especially those regarding the relative utility of the distinct definitions of engagement is by intervening in workplaces to change engagement.

Targets of Interventions

Either perspective on engagement with work leads to interventions that build energy, involvement, and efficacy at work. The objective is to move any or all of these three dimensions away from the burnout end of the scale and toward engagement with work. Each dimension of engagement presents distinct challenges.

Energy   People experience energy in distinct modalities. The following is a typology that proposes distinct kinds of energy, any one of which may contribute to engagement with work. The absence of any of these forms of energy may contribute to experiencing exhaustion.

- *Physical energy* is the body's sense of vigor and capacity. It conveys the ability to move, to exert strength, or to execute complex, precise movements. Physical energy rests ultimately on biochemical processes of metabolism, but the subjective sense of available physical energy may be influenced by emotional or cognitive qualities.
- *Cognitive energy* is the capacity to concentrate mentally, to focus on demanding problems, and to comprehend complex concepts. It conveys the capacity to perform mathematical calculations, to edit text, or to analyze logic. It encompasses the capacity to focus perceptual modalities — sight, hearing, taste, smell, touch, proprioception — onto subtle qualities of sensation.
- *Emotional energy* is the capacity to respond to people or situations with appropriate feelings. It rests upon the capacity to attend to the present situation with sensitivity to other people and to the impact of events. Emotional energy was the primary focus of the original MBI-HSS, which presented emotional exhaustion as the defining quality of burnout.
- *Creative energy* is the capacity to generate new ideas, produce original work, and to perform an original interpretation of an artistic work. Creative energy is a second-order form of energy, resting upon the other forms: a combination of physical, cognitive, and emotional energy supports the capacity to create. But creativity has a distinct quality that goes beyond the sum of the other energy forms.

The extent to which these energy modalities are independent of one another is unclear. To some extent, one modality depends on another. To some extent, all forms of energy rest upon physical energy resulting from biochemical processes of metabolism. But a quality of independence is evident. For example, people may enjoy vigorous physical activity after a prolonged period of concentrated mental effort. It is less obvious that concentrated mental activity is enjoyable when one is physically exhausted. These experiences suggest that exhaustion may be limited to a specific modality, but overlapping with other modalities.

For healthy people, all of these forms of energy are available and renewable. Extended and intense activity depletes the available energy, requiring replenishment. Circumstances may facilitate or interfere with the capacity to access, sustain, or replenish any type of energy. People act, observe, think, feel, and create. They get tired. They rest and recover.

These four types of fatigue have distinct modes of recovery. Physical fatigue calls for periods of physical inactivity. Lying quietly or sleeping is the most effective means of recovery. Sleep has a distinct restorative effect on mental exhaustion (Horne, 1988). Replenishing emotional energy requires at the least a respite from immediate emotional demands. Strategies that are more complex are necessary to prevent and alleviate emotional exhaustion or creative exhaustion. Receiving emotional support from colleagues, recognition from supervisors, and enjoyable experiences in one's personal life may be more effective routes to revitalize emotional energy. Reviving creative energy requires a break from a project, rest, and perhaps uplifting experiences as well. Creative energy seems to be fickle, leaving people with writer's block despite repeated attempts to revitalize oneself.

Physical activity can alleviate mental fatigue, especially activities requiring low levels of mental concentration. Although a change of activity can alleviate mental fatigue to some extent, before too long sleep is required to support a full recovery. After rigorous evaluation, sleep research has concluded that sleep does have a specific function in alleviating mental fatigue. While lying restfully and awake may be effective in restoring physical energy, restoring mental energy requires a few hours of sleep (Horne, 1988). Research on sleep deprivation has generally found that in the short term, many cognitive functions operate well despite inadequate sleep. However, there are noticeable deficits in decision making in uncertain or managing unanticipated situations, developing innovative solutions, revising complex plans, ignoring distraction, and communicating effectively on project coordination. These are complex cognitive functions requiring the integration of information from the present situation and from memory. They require the capacity to concentrate on many dimensions of a problem, to generate new ideas, and articulate intricate plans. All of these functions require mental energy.

A defining quality of burnout, emotional exhaustion includes fatigue from addressing the emotionally charged demands of service recipients. Emotional exhaustion is a state of flat, inappropriate, or distressing affect. It indicates depletion of the capacity to engage in the usual emotional connection with people, especially those looking for a caring, confirming, and friendly relationship. In service relationships, such as health care, social services, or customer service, emotional exhaustion means an inability to do the emotional labor integral to the job. Social relationships are not the only source of emotional exhaustion. Interactions with objects, ideas, and values may be emotionally charged. And not every social interaction has a noticeable emotional quality. Interacting with people for prolonged periods in a way requiring no emotional labor will result in a specific quality of fatigue: just being tired of being with people.

Together, these four types of energy describe qualities of experience with distinct patterns of depletion and recovery in the course of worklife. Engagement with work includes some quality of all four types.

Involvement   Involvement is the capacity of people to become drawn into an aspect of their work. Regarding engagement with work, the fundamental issue with involvement is the capacity to be cognitively and emotionally absorbed by something. The specific focus of involvement is less important than the capacity to be involved. In an information/service economy that is prevalent throughout the post-industrialized world, involvement is an essential quality. The capacity of employees to attend closely to clients and to convey a sincere dedication to meeting their needs is valuable in the service industry. The capacity to become immersed in a complex idea is a valuable characteristic in an information sector that thrives on the implementation of innovation. Productivity in either of these spheres of activity requires involvement.

The original focus of the MBI-HSS was emotional involvement with service recipients, emphasizing helping relationships that were central to the original conceptualization of burnout (Maslach, 1982). The demands of providing services to others could overwhelm the service provider, especially when confronting the excessive demands with inadequate resources, which has been a persistent quality of public human service work. They withdrew emotionally from the social relationships with service recipients, imposing a flat affect that required less energy to maintain and that reduced the potential for emotionally draining interactions. The resulting depersonalization of service relationships continues to be a defining condition of burnout among human service providers. The concept captures the insidious erosion of the service relationships as it loses elements of meaningful contact.

The broader definition of burnout represented in the MBI General Scale (Leiter & Schaufeli, 1996; Maslach, Jackson, & Leiter, 1996) labels an absence of involvement as cynicism. This concept captures both the workers' tendency to distance themselves from the work and to de-emphasize its emotional and creative qualities. An optimal state of involvement has qualities of flow (Csikszentmihalyi, 1991) in which workers not only have the capacity to become absorbed in activities, thoughts, or people, but doing so is a highly enjoyable part of their work day. From the employees' perspective, the issue is finding a way of becoming pleasantly involved in something. From an employers' perspective, the additional challenge is focusing involvement on something that contributes to the organization's productivity.

Involvement is partially dependent on energy: research has consistently confirmed a path from energy to efficacy (Lee & Ashforth, 1993; Leiter, 1993; Maslach, Schaufeli, & Leiter, 2001). It follows that interventions that enhance energy could also benefit involvement. In addition, involvement may be a direct target of specific interventions.

The single construct approach to measurement operationally defines involvement as a low score on cynicism: to be involved is to never feel cynical. The separate construct approach includes items that define involvement positively: to be involved is to endorse the experience of flow and absorption in one's work. The lack of strong negative correlations with cynicism suggest that the separate construct approach is not exactly the opposite of cynicism, but a positive state that is somewhat incompatible with that state. The challenge remains for the single construct approach to establish that endorsing a position of never experiencing cynicism is synonymous with being absorbed in the flow of one's work.

Efficacy   Employees' sense of efficacy in their work includes subjective evaluations of their successes and their confidence for future performance. It also encompasses how they assess their impact. That impact may be focused on an individual service recipient, the sum total of their contribution at work, or the extent to which they contribute to making the world a better place. A challenge for organizations is aligning employees' definitions of success with its definition of productivity.

The focus of the original MBI was personal accomplishment through benefiting the lives of service recipients. The broader definition of the syndrome considers the full range of accomplishments at work. Broadening the scope shifts the focus from the service relationship to the employees' fulfillment and confidence arising from experience of success. On the other side are feelings of discouragement, frustration, and self-doubt associated with failure.

The alignment of personal and organizational values and objectives is crucial for a mutually constructive working relationship. A sense of efficacy, supported by personally relevant success at work, is a definitive quality of engagement with work. It follows that a critical component for organizations to support engagement with work is providing opportunities for employees to experience success. That support make a lot more sense — and therefore is more sustainable — if those successes also constitute a contribution to the productivity of the organization.

The separate construct approach appears to assess a construct that is the opposite of low efficacy (Schaufeli et al., 2004). This construct is more detailed and elaborated than the MBI-GS efficacy measure, giving more thorough consideration to vigor, dedication, and absorption. The greater success in contrasting with the inefficacy dimension of burnout is somewhat muted by efficacy's somewhat uneven relationship with the other two qualities of burnout. It has been argued that efficacy is not an integrated part of the burnout syndrome (Shirom, 2003). This quality suggests that the contrast between engagement and burnout is more complex than a simple opposition.

Intervention Strategies

The qualities of energy, involvement, and efficacy that constitute engagement with work benefit both employees and the organization. Strong levels of energy are instrumental in maintaining a level of activity, attentiveness, and emotional stability required for providing high-quality services. Strong mental and creative energy are necessary for initiating, developing, and implementing innovative ideas that are the fundamental unit of value in an information economy. The capacity to realize one's potential is integral to finding personal fulfillment in work and to opening opportunities in a competitive workplace. The capacity to facilitate employees' realization of their potential is a quality of an effective and attractive workplace. The issue is not deciding that engagement with work is better than burnout; the issue lies in understanding how to develop and sustain engagement with work.

Recommendations for building engagement with work are largely untested. Research on building engagement with work shares a key shortcoming pointed out for research in stress (Cooper, Dewe, & O'Driscoll, 2001): a very thin record of longitudinal studies with interventions designed for a systematic impact. Although considerable work has occurred that has mapped the correlates of burnout and engagement within organizational environments, few studies have evolved into full tests of how interventions affect these qualities over time.

The dearth of such research does not reflect a lack of interest on the part of researchers or insufficient calls to action from those reviewing research outcomes. The research is challenging conceptually. It requires significant working relationships of researchers with organizational decision makers. As is apparent through the section on organizational interventions below, actions that have an impact on energy, involvement, and efficacy constitute major changes to the management culture of an organization. Executives prefer to manage such interventions themselves. There is only a limited amount of this authority that they are willing to share with researchers.

Two Levels of Intervention

When considering interventions to build engagement with work, a potentially relevant construct is parallel to Herzberg's (1966) two-factor model of motivation. Does building engagement beyond an average level of energy, involvement, and efficacy require qualitatively different interventions from those required to alleviate burnout?

From a broad perspective, any intervention that enhances energy, involvement, and efficacy constitutes progress away from burnout and toward efficacy. It seems reasonable that having more energy puts individuals in a better position to develop a more constructive and productive relationship with work. The question raised from a two-process perspective is whether interventions that are effective for alleviating severe exhaustion, cynicism, and inefficacy are distinct from interventions that are effective for achieving exceptionally strong levels of engagement with work.

Individual Interventions

These qualities respond to a variety of initiatives on the individual, workgroup, or organizational level. Selecting an approach and adapting it to a specific situation requires thorough assessment, an inclusive process, careful implementation, and detailed monitoring. The following section identifies points to consider in developing and implementing interventions to build engagement with work.

Organizational Interventions

The diverse range of workplace qualities, structures, procedures, processes, values, and practices that have been correlated with burnout suggest the potential for a wide range of organizational interventions. This section considers interventions focused on six areas of worklife: workload, control, reward, community, fairness, and values (Leiter & Maslach, 2004; Maslach & Leiter, 1997). The driving concept in this model is that chronic mismatches between individuals and their workplaces aggravate pressures toward burnout by depleting their energy, blocking their capacity to become absorbed in their work, and undermining their sense of efficacy.

Developing engagement with work encompasses a variety of interventions that facilitate congruence between employees' aspirations and the workplace. These interventions may address issues in any of the six areas of worklife. Workplaces are not uniformly problematic or uniformly enlightened. In a given setting, employees may give markedly different ratings to the various areas of worklife (Leiter & Maslach, 2004). In a given situation, focusing on one or two areas of worklife may be sufficient to address its major mismatches. Regardless of the specific area of worklife, there are a few underlying themes pertaining to any initiatives to enhance engagement with work (Maslach & Goldberg, 1998).

Flexibility   People differ in their aspirations for work: the centrality of work in their lives, their ambition, and their personal values among other qualities. Further, these qualities evolve in the course of an individual's worklife: what if fulfilling at one career stage is inappropriate at another. A one-size-fits-all solution to build engagement with work is inconsistent with the concept of congruence. A solution may work very well for some people at least some of the time, but be inappropriate for many others. Interventions that increase the flexibility in the workplace open more possibility for successful resolutions. These interventions may have an immediate impact on organizational policies, work schedules, meeting formats, or design of workspace. They increase the range of options for employees to shape their work to be more congruent with their preferences, inclinations, skills, potentials, and aspirations, increasing their potential for engagement with work.

Participation in the process   In building engagement with work, there is a limited amount that one can do for someone else. The process of participating in planning, developing, and implementing initiatives enhances its impact. It may even be essential for an initiative to have a constructive impact. Major changes in a workplace that do not have full participation of intended beneficiaries encounter problems.

Full participation of employees in an initiative brings their thorough knowledge of the situation to the challenge of shaping the worksetting. They know their jobs — their constraints and their possibilities — better than anyone else. It is more likely that an initiative will fulfill its objectives if it includes the people it is supposed to help. They can ensure that the plan encompasses the important issues, the initiative accommodates the nuances of the work situation, and changes are feasible within the day-to-day flow of the workplace.

Areas of Worklife

Six areas of worklife provide a focus for interventions to enhance engagement with work as well as to alleviate burnout (Maslach & Leiter, 1997). Interventions that change any of these six areas — workload, control, reward, community, fairness, and values — reduce disparities of the organizational environment with the aspirations and inclinations of employees (Leiter & Maslach, 2004).

Workload

Workload encompasses the amount of work, its complexity, and its pacing. Any one of these dimensions can be the basis of a serious mismatch of employees with a worksetting. Indicators of problematic workload are evident in work assignments and deadlines that have a negative emotional impact on employees (Greenglass, Burke, & Moore, 2003).

Workload interventions to address engagement with work start with designing work as a better fit of the organization's mission with employees' aspirations. Engagement with work has a quality of relaxed intensity that is sustained over time. It is a clear contrast with both the frantic pressure and deadening drudgery associated with burnout.

Focusing on high priority tasks Pressures to increase productivity are intrinsic to today's global economy. A strategy of doing more with less often overwhelms the capacity of individuals, groups, and organizations. The result is often doing less with less. Thinning the staff often results in thinning service quality. This impact creates tension between an organization's stated commitment to quality and its actual commitment evidenced in its resource commitment.

An alternative to *doing* more with less is *focusing* more with less. By reducing its scope of activity, an organization or work team can add depth to a narrower range of products or services. This strategy requires thorough planning, as members of a team are unlikely to intuitively agree upon the elements to be enhanced and the elements to deemphasize. It is a transition point requiring leadership to establish a meaningful dialogue regarding priorities. Employees with a sincere commitment to a level of quality are likely to overextend themselves when required to do more with less. It is a risky management approach to allow employees to redesign the work without clear direction.

Effective leadership can use a transition point to build engagement with work. Individuals may retain a strong commitment to activities that have shifted from high to low priority over a transition. Clear direction is necessary to help employees to shift their commitment to new activities. Leadership at this juncture avoids wasting energy on low-priority activities and reduces the conflict individuals experience regarding the shift in organizational priorities.

Innovation Innovation builds engagement by tapping into employees' creative problem solving. Developing a new approach to a complex issue calls for focused attention and involvement in the issue. While innovation makes demands on energy, drawing time away from other priorities, it breaks from the drudgery that can develop in established work patterns. Innovation builds employees' confidence and their ongoing value to the organization, as a demonstrated capacity to innovate is valued on the individual and the corporate level of operation. Active participation in innovation is energizing, it encourages focused involvement in work, and supports a sense of efficacy. These are the fundamental qualities of engagement with work.

Control

An active participation in important decisions at work is a fundamental element of engagement with work. The capacity to influence decisions about workload has direct consequences for whether expectations will be manageable or exhausting. The prerogative for employees to determine their approach to work is empowering, building a sense of efficacy while encouraging a focused involvement in work.

Build front line decision making   A primary target for management interventions to enhance front-line decision making are group decision-making skills. Groups vary widely in their capacity to implement the basic steps of a decision-making process: defining a problem, generating alternatives, evaluating alternatives, selecting a course of action, implementing an action plan, and evaluating impact. A weakness at any one of these steps can undermine an initiative. Without a clearly defined leader for an initiative, groups are vulnerable to losing their focus on an initiative while juggling the myriad demands of their day-to-day responsibilities.

Interventions to enhance front-line decision making include team building interventions that enhance a group's capacity to work together with mutual respect and enthusiasm. They may include establishing procedures for tracking project implementation, including project management software to facilitate the capacity of group members to track progress, to cue individuals to complete their contributions, and to establish metrics for evaluating the impact of a complex project. Enhancing the technical capacity of a workgroup to solve problems and implement decisions assures management that groups will use delegated authority effectively.

Salience of organizational values and objectives   In addition to technical proficiency in decision making, management seeks assurance that groups will use distributed decision-making authority in a manner consistent with organizational values and objectives. Policies that centralize decision making may reflect a view that adherence to organizational values and objectives is central management's role.

Interventions that enhance the salience of organizational values and objectives throughout the organization provide assurance to management that distributed decisions will reflect their priorities. They build engagement by promoting a deeper commitment to these values and objectives in the employees who participate in their implementation. Opportunities to play an active role in implementing something of personal as well as organizational importance involve an employees' full attention. They also affirm policies that distribute consequential decision-making authority to workgroups throughout the organization.

Reward

Meaningful rewards build engagement. They confirm that the organization recognizes and values employees' contributions. Rewards can have an immediate energizing impact on employees. They may also sustain energy in the longer term through their confirmation that employees' activities are well directed. They confirm the accuracy of employees' priorities for their activities at work. Rewards build efficacy by providing public recognition of employees' performance. Some employees are so inner-directed that external recognition is of little personal consequence, but many are gratified and confirmed by acknowledgment from others.

Increasing the relevance of recognition events   Recognition events are vulnerable to basic flaws. The first critical issue is credibility. Employees are often skeptical of the process for selecting individuals for public recognition. Front line employees have a perspective on an organization's work that is distinct from management's perspective on the same activities. Performance that looks impressive from one perspective may appear flawed, limited, or superficial from another perspective. A process that considers a variety of perspectives — from management, supervisors, and front line employees — has a greater potential for identifying performance that is widely appreciated. Broad participation also makes the selection process more transparent to employees, increasing its credibility as well.

   In addition to credibility, the visibility of a reward influences its potential impact. The timing of an award event, the way the event unfolds, and its communication plan affects its impact.

Management and supervisor training   A fully considered plan for employee development includes enhancing the capacity of managers and supervisors to recognize effective performance, to respond encouragingly, and to support further growth and development. Managers and supervisor do not necessarily enter their positions with these abilities. A conscientious ongoing program for training and supporting managers in this role is a critical element in building engagement with work.

   The day-to-day interactions of managers with employees are the points at which they convey support to employees' efforts and at which they communicate the organizational values that are intrinsic to the organizations' work. Research has indicated consistency between the burnout levels of managers and employees within their workgroups (Leiter & Harvie, 1997). Managers play a significant role in building engagement by both modeling behaviors and attitudes consistent with engagement as well as providing instrumental support to employees. Nursing research has identified the active role of supervisors in empowering employees. The informal influence that a nurse can exercise through their interactions with supervisors increases their capacity to make use of formal power structures in the complex social world of a large hospital (Ellefsen & Hamilton, 2000; Laschinger, Sabiston, & Kutszcher, 1998). The capacity to provide mentoring and informal support are essential for maximizing the impact of an organization's formal initiatives to empower employees.

Community

In addition to the attention and support of people in positions of authority in an organization, the quality of social relationships with colleagues is an essential component of building a work environment that is conducive to engagement with work. Collegial cooperation plays a role in managing workload by coordinating tasks in ways that reduce the burden upon individuals in the team (Greenglass, Fiksenbaum, & Burke, 1994). In contrast, unresolved conflict, resentment, and bitterness among members of a work team add considerably to the demands on individuals at work, draining energy through negatively charged interactions at work. They also interfere with employees' capacity to replenish their energy outside of work, as unresolved conflict tends to resonate long after the specific event, encouraging anxiety and interrupting sleep cycles.

The social environment plays an important role in building involvement. The emotional tone of a commitment shared with supportive colleagues in a cohesive workgroup increases employees' focus at work. Interactions with colleagues reaffirm the importance of an activity and provide feedback that facilitates involvement in that activity.

The collegial environment makes a direct contribution to efficacy. The positive regard of colleagues derives power from their familiarity with the demands and challenges of the work. A supervisor's commendation references an employees' ability, but may be shaped as well by perspectives that may have more to do with the political or administrative structures of the organization. In contrast, colleagues are more reliable evaluators of one another's abilities. They know the details and are unlikely to be distracted by tangential concerns.

Teamwork   Workgroups vary widely on their capacity to be credible supports for engagement with work. Some teams are actively destructive to their members. Other teams greatly under-perform as potential sources of confirmation. Active team building can have a direct impact on a team's level of functioning and an indirect impact on the members' capacity to develop a constructive engagement work.

Teamwork builds engagement by providing social support to the group as a whole, by teaching skills for group functioning, by improving the emotional tone of interactions in the group, and by confirming the team as a fundamental element of how the organization functions. A major intervention that focuses on teams makes a statement that the organization looks to teams as being a fundamental unit of activity and that it acknowledges their potential to support effective performance.

Mediation processes   Unresolved conflict seriously inhibits progress toward engagement with work. By sapping energy at the moment and interfering with recovery later, the emotional impact of negative interactions at work influence employees toward chronic exhaustion rather than toward maintaining energy and well-being.

Workgroups can lose their capacity to function as effective supports. They may become embedded in chronic conflict, treating one another with cold indifference, or bullying colleagues through intimidating behavior. After such a tone is established within a group, it may be very difficult to change. Members of the group lack the mutual trust required to improve matters on their own. A thoroughly negative workgroup can defy the good intensions of successive managers in their attempts to improve the quality of community.

A mediation intervention introduces a leader with specific expertise in moving groups beyond enduring conflict. The mediator may be a member of the organization or an outside resource with specific expertise on mediation. The process provides opportunities for participants to articulate their concerns and listen to the perspectives of others. Most importantly, it is a format that brings strong momentum toward resolution. The process gains some of its power from a requirement to rationally discuss issues. It also communicates management's concern for the group's capacity to function effectively. By requiring employees to present rational positions for discussion, the process has a potential to move past unresolved conflict and resentment that interferes with the capacity of individuals to benefit from the dynamics of a teamwork environment.

Fairness

Mutual respect is a core quality of constructive working relationships. It is equally relevant as a quality of personal interactions of employees with one another, with management, and with clientele. Respect is conveyed through interactions of the individual with the organization as a whole. Organizational policies, especially those pertaining to personnel decisions, convey implicit values and perspectives. Employees are sensitive to the implications of these values for their place in the organization as individuals and as a part of the employee group.

Fairness is the realization of respect in decisions that affect the well-being of individuals. On one level, organizations support fairness through stating general values of respect, diversity, and justice. On another level, organizations realize these values by developing policies and procedures that monitor the quality of decisions, providing appeal mechanisms, and taking action when unfair actions are identified. The mutual trust engendered through transparent and fair procedures contributes to overall organizational effectives while supporting engagement with work (Firth-Cozens, 2004).

Equity   Interventions that support equitable treatment of employees encompass educational programs, procedures for hiring or promotion, and appeal procedures. Educational interventions state the organization's values regarding diversity of the community and respect in personal interactions. Educational programs give direction to employees in realizing these values in their work and convey the importance of these considerations in the life of the organization. Policies regarding affirmative action or equal opportunity hiring procedures specify mechanisms through which equity values shape important decisions regarding recruitment and career advancement. Appeal procedures provide a route through which individuals can address problems. The most thorough procedural structure relies on people to put the policies into action in a manner that reflects the underlying values. When the reality falls short of the ideal, appeal procedures permit individuals to address the problem. Lacking clear procedures, individuals have no way of resolving experiences of disrespect or exclusion from the organizational community.

Transparent procedures   Procedural justice — employees' perception that decisions are made fairly — has a more pervasive impact than distributive justice — employees' satisfaction with outcomes. Large organizations have been able to address widespread suspicions of cronyism and nepotism by increasing the information flow about their procedures for internal promotions and access to professional development opportunities. When these actions are taken in response to concerns expressed in employee surveys, subsequent assessments indicate improved perceptions of fairness in the organization (Leiter & Maslach, 2005).

Values

A theme through all five areas of worklife reviewed above is congruence of individual and organizational values. The indirect objective of interventions that address worklife, control, reward, community, and fairness is to develop a greater congruence of organizational and individual values.

Reviewing core values   Increasing the salience of core values throughout the work of the organization supports engagement with work. Although the primary issue is congruence of individual and organizational values, a secondary issue is the congruence of an organization's stated values and its values in action. Individual employees may not object to the values articulated in the organization's mission statement, but take exception with an inconsistent application of these values in the organization's day-to-day actions (Argyris, 1990; Bloch & Borges, 2002). The gap between espoused and enacted values creates a tension for employees, undermining their allegience to the organization. Faced with two contrasting sets of values — espoused and enacted — employees' personal values become more salient. A clearly articulated set of personal values will conflict with either the espoused or the enacted organizational values if not both.

Value conflicts are especially likely during major organizational transitions. A new structure may imply a significant shift in values and priorities. Actively addressing that shift with employees increases the possibility for maintaining engagement with work through a major transition. Failures to anticipate and establish procedures for addressing value conflicts are conducive to burnout (Burke, 2001, 2003).

An organization's most effective approach to value congruence is to enhance the congruence of its own espoused and enacted values. Emphasizing core values throughout their policies, communications, structures, and practices, organizations move values from serving as general ideals to shaping their core functions. Moving values from occasional statements by the CEO or the public affairs department to specific organizational policies embeds them in the life of the organization. They become difficult to ignore. Managers perceive these values as qualities that will shape their future within the organization. Employees perceive a single, integrated set of values that function as guiding principles for the organization.

New employee orientation   Entry is a critical point in value congruence. Employees choose to join an organization for many reasons. Value congruence may play a major role in the decision to accept a job offer, but the decision may be guided by expediency or convenience. Even when new employees perceive value congruence, they may not fully appreciate the complexity of the organization's values or their specific relevance to the employees' work. When new employees have not attended to the organization's values, they may not be prepared to accommodate their impact on the jobs. A clearly articulated description of the organization's core values and their implications for job performance, evaluation, and career advancement avoids potentially disruptive surprises (Bussing & Glaser, 1999; Mestre, Stainer, & Stainer, 1997).

Conclusion

Engagement with work is an intriguing concept that eludes precise definition. The general qualities of the concept present an opportunity to broaden the impact of interventions that address burnout in organizations. By providing a positive target for an intervention program, engagement with work serves as a deliberate focus for interventions that strive to enhance the quality of worklife to an exceptionally positive level. An assessment package that includes the MBI for measuring burnout and the Utrecht Engagement Scale would encompass a broad range of relationships with work from the most burned out to the most positively engaged. Considerable work remains to assess the impact of interventions on these qualities. There appears at this point to be a variety of approaches that would affect employees' energy, involvement, and efficacy.

References

Argyirs, C. (1990). *Overcoming organizational defenses: Facilitating organizatinol learning.* Boston: Allyn & Bacon.

Bloch, D., & Borges, N. (2002). Organisational learning in NGOs: An example of an intervention based on the work of Chris Argyris. *Development in Practice, 12*, 461–472.

Burke, R. J. (2001). Surviving hospital restructuring. Next steps. *Journal of Nursing Administration, 31*, 169–172.

Burke, R. J. (2003). Survivors and victims of hospital restructuring and downsizing: Who are the real victims? *International Journal of Nursing Studies, 40*, 903–909.

Bussing, A., & Glaser, J. (1999). Work stressors in nursing in the course of redesign: Implications for burnout and interactional stress. *European Journal of Work and Organizational Psychology, 8*, 401–426.

Cooper, C. L., Dewe, P. J., & O'Driscoll, M. P. (2001). *Organizational stress: A review and critique of theory, research and applications.* London: Sage.

Csikszentmihalyi, M. (1991). *Flow: The psychology of optimal experience.* New York: Perennial.

Demerouti, E., Bakker, A. B., de Jonge, J., Janssen, P. P., & Schaufeli, W. B. (2001). Burnout and engagement at work as a function of demands and control. *Scandinavian Journal of Work and Environmental Health, 27*, 279–286.

Ellefsen, B., & Hamilton, G. (2000). Empowered nurses? Nurses in Norway and the USA compared. *International Nursing Review, 47*, 106.

Firth-Cozens, J. (2004). Organisational trust: The keystone to patient safety. *Quality Safety in Health Care, 13*, 56–61.

Greenglass E. R., Burke R. J., & Moore K. A. (2003). Reactions to increased workload: Effects on professional efficacy of nurses. *Applied Psychology: An International Review, 52*, 580–597.

Greenglass, E. R., Fiksenbaum, L., & Burke, R. J. (1994). The relationship between social support and burnout over time in teachers. *Journal of Social Behavior and Personality, 9*, 219–230.

Herzberg, F. (1966). *Work and the nature of man.* Cleveland: World Publishing.

Horne, J. (1988). *Why we sleep: The functions of sleep in humans and other mammals.* Oxford: Oxford University Press.

Laschinger, H. K. S., Sabiston, J. A., & Kutszcher, L. (1998). Empowerment and staff nurse decision involvement in nursing work environments: Testing Kanter's theory of structural power in organizations. *Research in Nursing & Health, 20*, 341–352.

Lee, R. T., & Ashforth, B. E. (1993). A longitudinal study of burnout among supervisors and managers: Comparisons between the Leiter and Maslach (1988) and Golembiewski et al. (1986) models. *Organizational Behavior and Human Decision Processes, 54*, 369–398.

Leiter, M.P. (1993). Burnout as a developmental process: Consideration of models. In:W. Schaufeli, C. Maslach & T. Marek (Eds), *Professional burnout: Recent developments in theory and research* (pp. 237–250). Washington: Taylor & Francis.

Leiter, M. P., & Harvie, P. (1997). The correspondence of supervisor and subordinate perspectives on major organizational change. *Journal of Occupational Health Psychology, 2,* 343–352.

Leiter, M. P., & Maslach, C. (2004). Areas of worklife: A structured approach to organizational predictors of job burnout. In: P. Perrewé & D.C. Ganster (Eds), *Research in occupational stress and well being: Vol. 3. Emotional and physiological processes and positive intervention strategies* (pp. 91–134). Oxford, UK: JAI Press/Elsevier.

Leiter, M. P., & Maslach, C. (2004). Areas of worklife: A structured approach to organizational predictors of job burnout. In: C. Cooper (Ed.), *Handbook of stress medicine and health* (2nd ed., pp. 173—192). London: CRC Press.

Leiter, M. P., & Maslach, C. (2005). *Banishing burnout: Six strategies for improving your relationship with work.* San Francisco, CA: Jossey-Bass.

Leiter, M. P., & Schaufeli, W. B. (1996). Consistency of the burnout construct across occupations. *Anxiety, Stress, & Coping, 9,* 229–243.

Maslach, C. (1982). *Burnout: The cost of caring.* Englewood Cliffs, NJ: Prentice-Hall.

Maslach, C., & Goldberg, J. (1998). Prevention of burnout: New perspectives. *Applied and Preventative Psychology, 7,* 63–74.

Maslach, C., Jackson, S. E., & Leiter, M. P. (1996). *Maslach Burnout Inventory Manual* (3rd ed.). Palo Alto, CA: Consulting Psychologists Press.

Maslach, C., & Leiter, M. P. (1997). *The truth about burnout.* San Francisco, CA: Jossey Bass.

Maslach, D., Schaufeli, W. B., & Leiter, M. P. (2001). Job burnout. *Annual Review of Psychology, 52,* 397–422.

Mestre, M., Stainer, A., & Stainer, L. (1997). Employee orientation — the Japanese approach. *Employee Relations, 19,* 443–456.

Schaufeli, W. B. & Bakker, A. B. (2004). Job demands, job resources, and their relationship with burnout and engagement: A multi-sample study. *Journal of Organizational Behavior, 25,* 293–315.

Schaufeli, W. B., Salanova, M., González-romá, V., & Bakker, A. B. (2004). The measurement of engagement and burnout: A two sample confirmatory factor analytic approach. *Journal of Happiness Studies, 3,* 71–92.

Shirom, A. (2003). Job-related burnout: A review. In: J.C. Quick & L. E. Tetrick (Eds), Handbook of Occupational Health Psychology. Washington, DC: APA.

CHAPTER 13

Becoming a Talent Leader — Individual and Organizational Perspectives

Mary Beth Mongillo

Organizations must meet the demands of shareholders for profitable growth and market share, customers for innovative, cost-effective products and services and employees for growth, development and an environment in which they can do their best work. Developing a deep understanding of business strategy, key differentiators and brand identify to create profitable growth is a critical first step to achieving organizational objectives (Hamel & Pralahad, 2005; Porter, 1996). However, no matter what strategy companies pursue to meet the increasingly complex demands of the global marketplace, customers and employees, organizations that invest in developing high-quality leadership are more effective at executing their business strategies and achieving business results.

Organizational Talent Leadership — The Bottom Line

Hewitt and Associates found, a direct correlation between a company's financial performance and its approach to building leaders, based on the financial analysis of the 2005 Top Companies for Leaders (Hewitt & Associates, 2005). Hewitt reports that senior management is formally held accountable for the success or failure of leadership development program in 78% of companies that perform at the 75th percentile or higher in industry adjusted return on equity, but only 55% of companies that perform below the 25th percentile.

A review of the one-year stock growth of three of the best companies for leaders compared to their major competitors further illustrates that organizations with focused development efforts for their leaders achieve superior results. These data show that companies that have: (1) commitment to leadership development from the board of directors and senior executives, (2) clearly differentiated development paths for high potential employees and (3) hold leaders accountable for their own development as well as for the development of the broader organization show greater stock growth than companies who do not.

Integrated Approach to Talent Leadership

Strength of leadership has significant impact on a company's financial results. So why do not all companies build talent-management systems to grow great leaders? There are at least two reasons organizations struggle to ensure their companies have the leadership they need to drive business success: (1) organization leaders do not believe that the strategic management of talent will translate to bottom-line business results or (2) human resources professionals have not designed and implemented strategic, integrated talent-management processes that impact the bottom line.

Most organizations have some process in place to support the growth of individuals in significant leadership positions in their companies. Examples include redesigning performance-management systems, employee-engagement surveys or a corporate university that generates large quantities of training for leaders throughout the organization. However, the problem of growing talent is bigger than any one process or program can address. An integrated talent management strategy is required.

How do you know whether or not the talent management strategy at your company is integrated? If any of the following statements are true, there are disconnected processes, not an integrated strategy:

(i) Changes in strategic direction are taken without consideration of the talent available to execute the strategy.
(ii) All new positions are filled externally.
(iii) All new positions are filled from within.
(iv) Sudden request for talent are frequent, there is no time to develop from within.
(v) Much time goes into the development of succession plans but they wind up sitting in a binder on the shelf.
(vi) 75% of the time and resources are dedicated to the identification of high-potential employees and less than 25% on actually developing them for future roles.
(vii) As soon as times get tough, the first thing to get cut is the investment in growing the talent in the organization.

The Roadmap for an Integrated Talent Management Strategy

Figure 1 provides one approach to strategic talent management. Business analysts are inclined to use strengths, weaknesses, opportunities, threats (SWOT) analysis to determine the effect of global, socioeconomic, industry and market challenges on a company's business strategy. The astute business planner will also assess the mission, vision and values that have been constants within the company. These factors can sometimes have a stronger impact on business strategy than external forces.

The most visible example of the impact of company values on business strategy comes from the application of the 60-year-old Johnson & Johnson credo during the TYLENOL® crises of 1982 and 1986 when product was adulterated with cyanide and killed several people. With Johnson & Johnson's good name and reputation at stake, company managers and employees made countless decisions that were inspired by the philosophy embodied in the credo. The product was voluntarily recalled and Johnson & Johnson took a $100 million

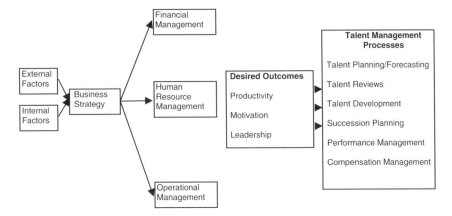

Figure 1: Strategic talent management.

charge against earnings. The company's reputation was preserved and the TYLENOL® business was regained.

The three primary areas through which business strategy gets executed are the financial, human resources and operational management systems of a company. GE is one company that has effectively integrated these three key components of company operations. In January of each year, a global leadership meeting is conducted during which the strategic direction for the year is reviewed and discussed. March brings their annual employee-engagement survey in which the clarity of priorities is validated, depth of operational commitment is assessed and emerging issues are uncovered. Financial reviews are held on a quarterly basis beginning in March and Session C — the GE talent review process in which each business reviews the human resource strengths, opportunities and development plans with senior leadership is conducted in the April/May timeframe. Strategy sessions are conducted in June and July with Session C follow-up soon thereafter. And operating plan reviews take place in the fall in preparation for the yearly cycle to kick off again in January. The outcome of an integrated governance structure like GE's is a more informed workforce focused on the strategic priorities of the business. A workforce that is motivated to contribute to the company's success because they are able to share in it. Finally, an integrated system provides the foundation for effective leaders to have significant impact in the business.

Processes to Enable Effective Talent Leadership

After aligning talent strategies with business and human capital strategies, the next step to becoming a talent leader is to develop and implement state-of-the-art talent programs or processes. The primary set of programs to develop is highlighted in Figure 1. The objective of these programs is to: (1) identify talent needs based upon business strategy, (2) determine the best method for fulfilling these talent needs, (3) understanding the level of skill that currently exists in the organization, (4) actively developing talent for current and future needs, (5) ensuring top talent is appropriately rewarded and (6) providing a working environment that results in employee retention.

Linking Business Planning with People Planning

Put very simply, integrated talent management is the effective attraction, development and retention of the right people to be available in the right place at the right time. Leaders who operate with an integrated talent management strategy, true talent leaders, are those leaders who understand the talent implications of the business strategy and constantly evaluate the people and organization capabilities required to advance their company's strategic business objectives in both the short and the long term. Neither business strategy nor talent can be viewed statically. It's not only about having the "right people on the bus" (Collins, 2001) but understanding enough about the bus' direction so people can grow their skills and capabilities to guide the bus to destinations not previously imagined. Further, it's constantly keeping an eye out for great folks to get on the bus who can help along the journey (see Figure 2).

The identification of organizational capability requirements is a critical first step in understanding the talent needs of a company. It requires depth of understanding of the internal and external factors from which both company values and business strategy derive. There are a few key elements of an integrated talent management strategy. The components required for effective talent management include: talent planning and forecasting, talent acquisition, talent assessment and review and talent development. Most organizations have implemented some or all of these talent management components or processes. However, few have been able to effectively integrate these pieces into a meaningful whole.

Talent Planning and Forecasting

Often forecasting talent needs begins as a financial exercise. Understanding the revenue generation objectives of an organization or business unit can give an initial understanding of the numbers of people needed to drive to these financial objectives. But talent forecasting is

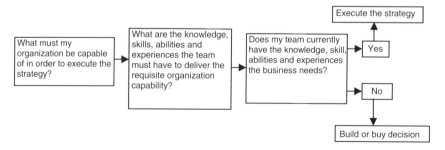

Figure 2: Integrating business planning with talent development and acquisition.

more than just a numbers game. It is first, understanding and systematically addressing the current and future business strategy and growth objectives of an organization and second, determining the knowledge, skills and abilities required to support these goals.

Let us apply this model to a specific organizational example. Dell, Inc. provides its global customers with a diversified portfolio of Information Technology products and services. Its global growth strategy relies on manufacturing and sales facilities throughout North and South America, Europe and Asia and direct relationships with customers. To support a diversified, global organization, Dell must build organization capability in rapid, global growth scenarios. Leadership skills and experience in change management, globalization, strategic analysis and talent development are needed to meet this capability requirement. Dell has a multi-pronged approach to addressing both organizational needs and individual skill requirements. First and foremost is the continuous evaluation and development of internal talent to prepare individuals for positions that will become available in the future. Our secondary strategy for building organizational capability is through talent acquisition. A simple model for translating business strategy to measurable business results is provided in Figure 3.

Talent Development Processes — Talent Review

The talent review process at Dell has three primary elements. First, each business or functional organization must present a business review that highlights the current and future

Figure 3: Talent forecasting processes.

challenges it anticipates. In many cases this dialogue begins deep in the organization at the first-line supervisor level and rolls up over the course of several months to determine the prioritized set of business challenges to be addressed in a given year. The result of this bottoms-up approach culminates in a meeting of each business leader with the CEO, Senior Vice President of Human Resources and the Vice President of Global Talent Management.

The talent implications of the business strategy are discussed next. For example, if the business strategy includes global growth, the talent discussion must include the talent needs, talent development and acquisition challenges and an action plan to address these challenges. In the talent review sessions, the dialogue may include some of the following questions:

(i) Do you have the right level of talent in your organization?
(ii) Where are your biggest gaps?
(iii) Will the talent you have today get you to where you need to be next year? Three years out?
(iv) If you have gaps, what are your plans to fill them?
(v) What are your plans to develop the high potential talent in your organization?
(vi) Who are the potential blockers in your organization? What is your plan to move them?

Next, a thoughtful and thorough review of current talent within the organization follows. This review includes an in-depth look at the current level of contribution and expected future contribution for leaders within each organization. Other information discussed in these sessions includes the strengths and development opportunities of each organizational leader as well as actions planned to leverage these strengths and address development opportunities. Finally, a discussion of the individual career goals and expectations of each leader takes place with a plan for the next position along the path to the leader's ultimate destination job.

Once an in-depth understanding of the current talent in the organization has occurred, a succession planning discussion takes place. The succession plan reflects those individuals who leadership believes could be ready to assume senior level roles within various timeframes (e.g. ready now, ready in 1–2 years, ready in 3–5 years). The individuals listed on the succession plan represent a culmination of those individuals who have demonstrated both high current performance and future potential in the organization. A robust development action plan is required for all high potential employees especially those individuals who are expected to fill critical positions in the near term.

Talent Development Processes

The development strategy at Dell is predicated on the premise that most development occurs on the job through experiences provided by the daily activities required for effective performance. Developing relationships with critical individuals throughout the organization to get perspectives on their business is also a key development activity. Finally, formal learning programs are the third approach used at Dell to ensure that individuals in the company have sufficient information and skills to be able to effectively accomplish their jobs while continuously learning and growing as professionals.

Talent Development — Learning through Experience

As highlighted by the many works of Morgan McCall and his colleagues (McCall, 1998; McCall & Hollenbeck, 2002) the most effective methods of developing employees is through the experiences they encounter on the job. However, learning through experience though is not as simple as it sounds. There are some critical conditions under which optimal learning occurs. First, the development objectives of a particular assignment must be as clearly outlined as the performance objectives are. For example, presume a high-potential leader is sent to complete an assignment outside of his or her home country — an expatriate assignment. It is likely that the company will spend a great deal of time discussing the business objectives the leader is expected to achieve as well as the metrics upon which success will be judged. However, in addition to achieving margin, revenue and unit sales targets the leader must also build capability in dealing with ambiguity and understanding and appreciating different cultural perspectives.

The second key to ensure that critical job experiences result in the learning and development desired is to ensure that the high potential leader take time on a weekly basis to reflect upon the learning that has occurred over the last week and plan for the learning opportunities that will present themselves in the coming week. Taking the time to assess one's progress toward development objectives is critical to the successful attainment of those objectives. Finally, accountability for development objectives is crucial to the ongoing prioritization and achievement of those objectives. This accountability can be accomplished when development objectives are incorporated into periodic reviews with a manager, mentor or coach who can ensure that development objectives are top of mind and progress is being made.

At Dell, experiential learning is the cornerstone of its talent development strategy. The most effective and efficient talent development process used at Dell is the movement of high-potential employees into positions of increasing scope and complexity. This allows leaders to hone previously acquired skills and acquire new knowledge, skills and establish new relationships. Job movement is strategic at Dell in that each job move is governed by two critical decision points, (1) can this leader effectively perform in the new role? and (2) will the new role provide this leader with experiences that will enhance development areas he or she possesses? If these two critical questions are answered in the affirmative job moves can take place very quickly.

Talent Development — Learning through Others

In addition to job movement, learning through others both within and outside of the organization is a critical development strategy used at Dell. Relationships are established with those through which work must be accomplished as well as those individuals with depth of experience in the industry or organization. These relationships can not only assist in the completion of job responsibilities but also provide guidance in navigating the organization, recommendations of future potential roles with the company and a testing ground for new ideas or innovations before they are ready for prime time.

Mentoring is one method for learning employed extensively at Dell. The mentoring process relies on direct relationships between mentors and mentees that are used to facilitate, guide and encourage continuous innovation and learning and to prepare the individual for the future. Most mentoring relationships are informal and grow naturally out of a mutual feeling of respect and trust. Mentors are encouraged to provide support and constructive, honest feedback from someone who is interested in the mentee's success. This will allow the mentee to gain insights, organizational know-how and lessons learned that are not typically provided through formal development programs.

Executive coaching is another method that can be used effectively to provide insight and external perspectives to assist an organizational leader in the development of his or her leadership capability. Dell's executive coaching program is intended to enhance the leadership capability of the Dell executive population globally. Coaching is utilized to enhance individual insight into the impact of behavior, style or personality on the work and team around the leader. In addition, coaching is used to assist the leader in leveraging key development strengths or enhancing development opportunities to improve overall leadership effectiveness. The critical success factor in Dell's coaching program is the interaction between the coach, the manager, the employee and the HR representative. Dell's coaching program is built on the premise that it takes a team to develop a leader and the more people surrounding the employee with feedback to enhance performance, the better.

Talent Development — Formal Learning Programs

Formal learning programs are different at Dell. All high-potential programs and the vast majority of management development programs are led by Dell leaders. This provides Dell with a unique opportunity to cascade messages throughout the organization in a systematic and sustainable way. The secret to the success of Dell's formal learning programs is the expectations that leaders will teach, providing them with the best opportunity to learn themselves. Not only does leader-led learning ensure that all leaders throughout the organization absorb the lessons provided in each of our programs, it also provides a built-in sustaining mechanism for reinforcing the learning objectives through one-on-one meeting when employees return to the job. This simple approach to learning provides an added benefit: studies show that employees prefer and are more willing to act upon information that is provided by their immediate leader.

Talent Acquisition

There are times when an internal talent-development strategy will fall short of the objective of ensuring the right people, with the right skills will be available in the right place at the right time. In the War for Talent Study conducted by McKinsey & Co. (Michaels, Handfield-Jones, & Axelrod, 2001) only 60% of corporate officers at the companies they studied said that they were able to pursue most of their growth opportunities. They have good market opportunities and the cash to invest; they simply did not have the talent to be able to take advantage of these market opportunities. A simple but useful framework is

Table 1: Key considerations talent development vs. talent acquisition.

Develop	Acquire
• The knowledge, skills, abilities and experiences can be efficiently developed in your current workforce	• The knowledge, skills, abilities and experiences cannot be efficiently developed in your current workforce
• The knowledge, skills, abilities and experiences are diffcult to find in the relevant talent marketplace	• The knowledge, skills, abilities and experiences are readily available in the relevant talent marketplace
• Your company has failed to invest in talent development of the current work-force and attrition is steadily increasing	• Your company has a history of promoting from within and seldom revitalizes through injection of new talent with fresh ideas

provided in Table 1 to determine when it may be appropriate to hire talent from outside your organization versus developing talent from within.

When acquiring talent some key lessons learned include: (1) Make a compelling case for why potential employees should choose your company. A 2005 study by Executive Development Associates (EDA, 2005) reports that companies with fewer talent shortages had a distinctive employer brand — a brand recognized in the market and clearly demonstrated in the organization. "Winning" is a core value at Dell and is a powerful recruiting tool since most people want to work for the industry's best. (2) Assure recruits that high performance leads to high rewards. Another core value at Dell is being a meritocracy. Simply put those who perform most effectively receive the highest rewards. (3) Provide challenging work that affords great learning opportunities. Most people want jobs in which they are continually learning and growing. At Dell there are limitless opportunities to add value to the business through stretch assignments in which learning is accelerated.

Driving Ownership and Accountability

In many organizations, employees are chartered with driving their own career and personal development. However, an individual owning his or her own development can sometimes translate to managerial abdication for any responsibility and engagement in that employee's development. Organizations that successfully manage talent provide employees with the tools and resources for effective development and leaders who place emphasis and importance for continuously developing oneself.

Dell's growth demands that all employees continue to grow and develop to meet the ever-increasing demands of the business. This is accomplished in a number of ways. First, the company introduced a Talent Development tool called *Talent Direct*, which houses development information on each employee throughout the organization. Some of the information available through this tool includes individual skills and experiences, global mobility preferences, leadership competency self-assessments, leadership competency manager assessment, individual development action plan and potential next jobs. This tool allows employees to pinpoint the development activities that would be most beneficial to getting ready for their next job and most critical to enhancing the development opportunities identified.

Managers are required to have development discussions with their direct reports, and each employee is expected to have a development plan and make continuous progress against it. Metrics are established through an employee-engagement survey that measures whether or not managers are living up to their employee development commitments. In addition, individuals who are effective managers of talent are frequently those who are rewarded with progressive job movement and are recognized in public forums. Further, leaders are held accountable through the performance management process for developing direct reports.

Becoming a Talent Leader

Driving the ownership and accountability for global talent management is an increasingly important responsibility of senior leaders. A talent leader must take personal ownership for attacking the talent challenge on every front — from acquisition, to development, reward and retention. Do you wait for your talent acquisition team to send you resumes for open positions in your organization or are you actively recruiting at professional societies and community events throughout the year? Are you meeting with the high-potential employees in your organization and assessing their knowledge and skill? Have you considered what job moves you will make for your high-potential employees to get them the right set of experiences to prepare them for critical roles in the future? Have you "re-recruited" your top talent — letting your best employees know through word and deed that they are critical to the success of your department and the organization at large?

Another sign of becoming a true talent leader is the adoption of a talent mindset — this means you will not have a discussion about business strategy or direction without also discussing the talent implications of such a move (i.e., no business plan without a talent plan). Take a look at your business plan and determine the knowledge, skills and experience your team will need to execute that plan. Assess your current team and determine the top three talent gaps. Assess your ability to grow those skills or experiences in the current leaders you have given the immediacy of your needs. Finally, roll out your talent development and acquisition strategy to accomplish your strategic objectives.

The final key to becoming a talent leader is to develop a "critical eye" for talent. Are you hiring for scale and building a diverse team in which new hires have the potential for promotion at least two levels? Are you inspiring your team to increasingly higher levels of performance? Are you accelerating the development of high potential employees in your organization by ensuring they have the right set of experiential learning opportunities?

There is a new "War for Talent" (Michaels et al., 2001) on the horizon and organizations that understand this challenge and are actively managing it will create a competitive advantage for themselves. Keys to becoming an organization that is a true talent leader include: (1) CEO level support for talent acquisition, development and retention activities throughout the organization, (2) developing a winning employment brand, a clear efficient recruiting process, the proper use of technology to identify the right people externally, (3) understanding who your high-potential employees are and investing in them through clear career paths and job rotations, special assignments, coaching mentoring and formal learning activities and (4) ensure that business leaders understand that best performing organizations do a better job of attracting, developing, engaging and retaining their talent.

References

Collins, J. (2001). *Good to great: Why some companies make the leap … and others don't.* New York: Harper Collins.

Executive Development Associates (EDA). (2005). *The leadership benchstrength challenge: Building integrated talent management systems.* New York: EDA.

Hamel, G., & Prahalad, C. K. (2005). Strategic intent. *Harvard Business Review*, July–August 2005, 148–161.

Hewitt & Associates. (2005). *Research highlights: How the top 20 companies grow great leaders.* New York: Hewitt & Associates

McCall, M. W. Jr. (1998). *High flyers: Developing the next generation of leaders.* Cambridge, MA: Harvard Business School Press.

McCall, M. W. Jr., & Hollenbeck, G. P. (2002). *The lessons of international experience: Developing global executives.* Cambridge, MA: Harvard Business School Press.

Michaels, E., Handfield-Jones, H., & Axelrod, B. (2001). *The war for talent.* Cambridge, MA: Harvard Business School Press.

Porter, M. E. (1996). What is strategy. *Harvard Business Review*, Nov–Dec , pp. 61–78.

Ulrich, D. (1998). A new mandate for human resources. *Harvard Business Review*, Jan–Feb, pp. 124–134.

CHAPTER 14

The Strategic Employee Survey

Jack W. Wiley

Employee surveys have been used in organizations for decades to help leaders understand how individual employees perceive their working conditions, job satisfaction, advancement opportunities, and other qualitative aspects of the workplace. While employee surveys can be used for multiple purposes, leaders are increasingly using surveys as a strategic tool to maximize productivity and meet financial and other business objectives. The traditional employee survey measuring solely employee satisfaction or happiness is declining in popularity. A recent market research study by Gilliand (2002) finds that employee surveys are more commonly being used to ask employees to assess the work environment and the support provided to help achieve business goals. Businesses are progressively beginning to use the results from surveys of employee teams and business units as *predictive* tools for customer satisfaction and business performance. Results are used to make appropriate adjustments in leadership practices, training initiatives, and business processes.

Whether used defensively or offensively — that is, to forestall anticipated threats or to drive high performance — an effective employee survey *starts* with strategy. The survey instrument should be designed with the appropriate business objectives in mind, whether this is enhancing employee retention efforts, evaluating the ethical mindset of the culture, or improving business unit performance. Employee surveys can be carefully structured to capture data that will be of maximum effectiveness in helping management take action to align its operations with its values and goals.

Higgs and Ashworth (1996) note that over the past 70 years, the goals and methods of employee surveys have substantially evolved. Surveys in the 1930s and 1940s were often conducted in order to identify worker groups with low morale that were susceptible to union organizing campaigns. Over the next several decades, employee surveys were more commonly used to measure employee satisfaction more broadly, often as a tool to improve productivity. More recently, in the past 20 years, surveys have emphasized quality of life issues, benefits, and other "employer of choice" topics, particularly as employers have become sensitive to the costs and challenges of recruitment and retention. Finally, the most current trend in surveys has been a focus on employee observations of business performance, in order to measure the effectiveness of key company strategies (Higgs & Ashworth, 1996).

Table 1: United States survey participation rates.

Survey participation by industry		
Low (34 – 48%)	**Moderate (50 – 58%)**	**High (59 – 72%)**
• Construction & Engineering	• Transportation	• Business Services
• Light Manufacturing	• Education	• Financial Services
• Heavy Manufacturing	• Government	• Hi-tech Manufacturing
• Retail		• Health Care Products
		• Communication/Utilities Services
		• Banking
		• Health Care Services

Today, between half and three-quarters of large U.S. companies regularly conduct employee surveys or otherwise track employee attitudes (Kraut, 2004). Our own research in the U.S. shows that the frequency of employee surveys varies widely by industry and company size. Fewer than 30% of companies with 100 employees or less conduct employee surveys; by contrast, nearly three-quarters of companies with more than 10,000 employees do so. This may reflect the reality that, in general, larger companies have more complex operating structures, and that management cannot "take the temperature" of a large, often distributed employee population through informal means.

When studying different industry segments, employee surveys are conducted more often in sectors where institutional knowledge and employee retention are highly valued, and where employees are often essential to the company's brand, such as financial services, technology, health care, communications, and other business services. We find a lower emphasis on employee surveys in industries such as construction, manufacturing, and retail that are often characterized by high turnover and a higher percentage of unionized workforce. Falling in the middle are highly regulated and systematized industries such as transportation, education, and government (see Table 1).

In our 30 years of conducting employee surveys for U.S. and multinational companies, we have found that the common thread among businesses that value employee survey data is that they are *strategy-driven*. In general, large companies and those that are in knowledge-based industries tend to rely on more sophisticated strategies, and in turn rely on employee data to measure the effectiveness of their strategy (often down to the unit level) and modify their business plans accordingly. But the utility of employee surveys is by no means limited according to company size or industry. For example, while retail businesses typically have a lower usage of employee surveys, we have conducted numerous surveys for retailers focused on unionization issues, store level effectiveness, and other strategic measures.

Our research has shown that organizations generally conduct employee surveys for four, sometimes overlapping, reasons:

1. to identify "warning signs" of trouble within the organization;
2. to evaluate the effectiveness of specific programs, policies, and initiatives;
3. to gauge the organization's status as an "employer of choice" among its workforce; and
4. to predict and drive organizational outcomes, including customer satisfaction and financial performance.

As shown in Figure 1, these objectives range along a continuum from defensive strategies (anticipating and defusing potential threats) to offensive strategies (driving high performance and using employee data as leading indicators of business results). Achieving the specific purpose obviously requires survey content that is tailored to the organizational objectives. For example, questions that predict an organization's vulnerability to union organizing activity are likely to be very different from those that predict external customer satisfaction.

In the remainder of this chapter, we will discuss each of the four primary purposes of conducting employee surveys. In doing so, we will outline not only how the survey content differs by purpose, but also how organizations use and follow up each type of survey instrument. We will illustrate the different purposes with case studies and/or normative data.

Employee Surveys as Warning Indicators

An employee survey can be an important source of "red flags" that highlight *potential problems* within the organization or its workforce. Such surveys can either arise as a result of specific management concerns (i.e., complaints, accidents, or other evidence that suggests a problem) or as a result of management taking initiative to *prevent* problems from occurring. Such warning signs cover a wide range of organizational issues, such as workplace safety, ethics and values, and union vulnerability.

Figure 1: Strategic survey model.

Concerns about safety may range from physical harm to employees as a result of unsafe working conditions or practices, to workplace violence or substance abuse, to security of company and personal property. Often the survey is used to identify gaps between the company's policies, procedures, and objectives with regard to safety and the reality of those safety issues as they are perceived by employees. Specifically, typical objectives of safety surveys involve:

- Using employees as observers of specific safety practices
- Measuring the level of importance employees place on safety
- Evaluating the need to make employees more conscious of safety
- Determining whether employees are willing to report safety violations
- Determining whether employees receive a satisfactory response when they report on behaviors of their co-workers or other safety issues

A safety-related survey may include employee perceptions of items such as the following:

- Management sets example for safety
- Safety valued over budget/schedule
- Response to safety issues
- Understand safety procedures
- Protected from health/safety hazards
- Sufficient medical facilities
- Company is the leader re: safety

Safety survey results are used to evaluate an organization's climate for safety and determine whether additional training for employees or management is needed. One of the most important functions of employee surveys in an area such as safety is often to disabuse management of the belief that, because they have a *policy* on a particular issue, they have successfully addressed that issue throughout the organization. Surveys tend to reveal the reality of how and whether policies and procedures are actually implemented at the workforce level.

This is also true in an area that has attracted considerable attention in recent years, namely, the issue of corporate ethics. Few organizations, of course, are likely to suffer the devastating leadership-driven ethical lapses that undermined companies such as Enron and WorldCom. But maintaining an ethical work environment and values-driven culture is a challenge that most or all organizations face and that has substantial bottom-line ramifications. A series of studies by Kotter and Heskett (1992) found that organizations with cultures focused on balancing the interests of multiple stakeholders (customers, employees, and investors) and ensuring proper management skills at all leadership levels outperformed those with a disproportionate focus on short-term financial gains. Those with balanced focus increased revenues by an average of 682%, while those more narrowly focused on short-term financial gains increased revenues by only 166% over an 11-year period. Other business results, including net income, stock prices, and workforce levels, also increased at significantly higher margins in organizations with more balanced cultures.

Organizations often rely on employee survey data to determine whether the values structure and ethical standards established by senior management are in fact being disseminated and propagated throughout the culture. Companies going through major transitions such as acquisitions or management succession may need to assess the values that are dominant within the existing culture and, subsequently, evaluate their success in establishing a new standard. The results of surveys related to ethics and values can help company leadership develop a plan of action, including targeted education and training programs for managers and employees, improved corporate communications, compliance audits, advancement and recognition programs, changes in hiring standards and performance reviews, and other specific tools.

Another common "warning sign" identified through employee surveys is vulnerability to union organizing campaigns. As Higgs and Ashworth (1996) note, this use of surveys dates all the way back to "non-unionization" efforts in the 1930s. Most businesses in North America continue to resist unionizing programs for financial and strategic reasons. In their view, unions can serve as an impediment to workforce communications by inserting a third party between leadership and workers. This can reduce the effectiveness of an organization's implementation and alignment of corporate strategy.

In many geographic regions, union drives are typically based on worker dissatisfaction over issues such as pay and benefits, respect, and physical working conditions. Employee surveys are important tools in identifying locations, worker groups, specific management practices, and "hot button" items that stoke a desire for third-party representation. From these data, management can take corrective steps to defuse the underlying worker concerns that often give an opening to unions.

For example, we conducted a survey for a large retailer in Canada that had recently acquired a new chain of stores in which employee activities related to unionization had been observed. Union avoidance was an important factor in this organization's business strategy. We measured a variety of topics in this survey, including a nine-item Union Vulnerability Index (UVI) designed specifically to identify units with the highest susceptibility to organizing campaigns. Employing a methodology designed and tested in our prior survey projects, we then ranked the retailer's 90 stores using this UVI and categorized three stores at "high risk", and 18 stores at "moderate risk" of union vulnerability. Following the study, the client informed us that known union activity had occurred in all three high risk stores identified by the vulnerability index, as well as one of the stores identified among the higher scoring locations with "moderate risk". Based on the UVI results, leadership sent a corporate employee relations team to each of the "high risk" locations and to several of the higher scoring "moderate risk" locations to investigate the sources of employee concerns and take corrective actions. All of the stores remain union-free to this day, supporting the validity of the UVI as a predictor of union vulnerability.

Employee Surveys as Program Evaluation

Employee surveys are also commonly used to evaluate the effectiveness of major corporate initiatives or influence the design of such initiatives through employee input. This includes workforce programs such as employee benefit packages, where organizations will often survey employees to evaluate the attractiveness of alternative benefit programs and elements, and then develop or modify the final package on the basis of employee feedback. In such circumstances, organizations may devote the entire survey to a single topic.

Among the most common corporate programs in which organizations rely heavily on employee survey data are initiatives related to diversity. Economic trends such as shortage of talent, global competition, and the pursuit of new international markets have put a priority on the ability of organizations to do a better job recruiting and retaining women and members of minority groups. This is an area where proper gathering and segmentation of employee data can help organizations identify key workplace factors that influence retention among specific subsets of the employee population.

Table 2 shows the results of a recent survey conducted at a major U.S. banking organization. These results demonstrate that reliance on *overall* employee statistics from employee surveys is entirely misleading and that important differences generally exist in the responses among employees of different racial and ethnic origins. For example, in 2004, while scores for the diversity theme *overall* show 63% favorable responses, a segmentation by race reveals that only 42% of African Americans responded favorably.

This particular banking organization has conducted three employee surveys since 1996 addressing diversity issues. As a result of this analysis, leadership at the organization has been able to target actions to improve these ratings and hold managers accountable for results. Between 2000 and 2004, the bank's initiatives to support diversity were highly visible and focused on training of employees and management, publicizing the status of goals, and placing diverse staff in high level positions. In 2004, expectations were high, but the survey diversity scores were lower than expected (see Table 3). Leadership concluded from

Table 2: Banking case study diversity results.

	Percent favorable by ethnic origin				
	Overall	Asian	African American	Hispanic	White
Diversity theme overall	**63**	**61**	**42**	**62**	**69**
Item: Easy to fit in	70	65	52	69	75
Item: Opinions valued regardless of age, gender, etc.	64	65	41	65	71
Item: Managers hire/retain diverse workforce	59	56	39	58	65
Item: Developed/advanced regardless of age, gender, etc.	58	56	35	56	63
% of respondents	*100%*	*6%*	*14%*	*9%*	*65%*

Table 3: Historical banking case study diversity results.

	Percent favorable for diversity theme over time				
Year	Overall	Asian	African American	Hispanic	White
1996	52	57	32	49	61
2000	66	59	47	60	73
2004	63	61	42	62	69

the results that not enough was being done to hire and promote minorities and more emphasis was necessary on achieving diversity at senior levels. Recently, the bank has increased the number of high level placements involving diverse staff.

Employee Surveys as Measures of "Employer of Choice"

Many organizations are also using employee survey tools to measure the climate within their workforce. These tools measure the attractiveness of the organization as an "employer of choice" for recruiting and retaining key employees, and the "engagement" of the workforce in terms of the willingness of workers to provide discretionary independent effort to deliver better results.

The desire to be known as an "employer of choice" derives in large part from a concern with a looming shortage of talent driven by demographics and, as a result, intense competition to recruit and retain employees, particularly knowledge workers, in the global economy. Frank, Finnegan, and Taylor (2004) note that "a growing awareness of unavoidable demographics is creating a greater urgency for HR professionals everywhere to focus more attention and energy on retaining talented employees and keeping them actively engaged in their work." They cite surveys from large accounting firms that show retention of key workers is the top priority among the HR community.

The focus on retention is not solely driven by a growing shortage of experienced workers to fill technical, professional, and managerial jobs. Most organizations are also aware of the significant costs of turnover, in terms of training, lost productivity, and lost opportunities when competent workers take their knowledge and skills elsewhere. Estimates of turnover costs range anywhere from 25% to 200% of an employee's salary and benefits (Talentkeepers, 2005). A study by Hillmer, Hillmer, and McRoberts (2004) on turnover in call centers found that the cost of turnover was roughly equal to the salary for each position vacated. Another review of turnover at a large healthcare institution found the overall cost of turnover to be 3.4–5.8% of the annual operating budget (Waldman, Kelly, Arora, & Smith, 2004).

Despite the occasional downturns caused by recession, emphasis on talent retention and employer of choice cultures has shifted the balance of power in favor of the employee. As a result, employers are recognizing that employees increasingly have choices about where and for whom they work, and that the reputation and values of the organization play a substantial role in the growing war for talent. To the extent that recruits and employees alike perceive a compelling employment opportunity and work experience at a given company, they are more likely to join and stay. As a result, organizations are closely measuring their reputation as employers and actively marketing their workforce culture, particularly their mission, vision, and values, in the recruitment process.

Employee surveys can be an important tool in measuring the effectiveness of the employer's brand as an "employer of choice". Such tools can also identify pockets of dissatisfaction down to the business unit level, as well as key drivers among the company's policies, values, and leadership practices that contribute to higher levels of turnover.

There are two main forces that impact an employee's decision to leave an organization; the "push" and the "pull". The "pull" comes from external sources, including opportunities for new jobs, advancement, more pay, etc. The "push" comes from dissatisfaction in the current employer that makes the employee more inclined to seek alternatives and more susceptible to outside recruitment efforts. Interfering with the push and pull forces is the natural friction that tends to keep people from making changes: cost, fear, uncertainty, existing relationships, family situations, etc. There is little that employers can do about the "pull" from other sources, but employers can identify and, to some extent, control the "push" of dissatisfaction through proper implementation and analysis of employee survey tools.

A statistical analysis of survey results can help the employer understand the elements of the employment relationship that most influence the employee's decision to stay or go. For example, it is common to include an item in employee surveys such as: "I am seriously considering leaving my organization within the next 12 months." Such an item can then be treated as a dependent variable in a multiple regression analysis. The other items in the survey can be treated as independent variables and regressed against the measure of turnover intention. The resultant regression equation will identify items in the survey that carry the most weight in decisions about staying or leaving the current employer.

For more than 20 years, Gantz Wiley Research has regularly conducted surveys of the U.S. workforce known as WorkTrends™. The data from this survey allows us to benchmark the results of individual company surveys against the U.S. workforce as a whole, specific industry sectors, and best practices companies. By conducting the kind of regression analysis described above using the WorkTrends survey data, we can identify the overall key drivers of employee retention. While the importance of individual drivers will vary by age, job level, and industry, we have found that these factors largely apply across the employee population (see Figure 2).

Figure 2 shows that the key drivers of retention, according to the WorkTrends survey, are:

- Career development opportunity
- Sense of accomplishment
- Job security
- Confidence in future
- Pay

The disparity in turnover intention based on these factors is dramatic, as shown in Figure 3. Where employees report a favorable opinion of their employer with regard to these factors, their intention to leave within the next year ranges from 11% to 16%. By contrast, where

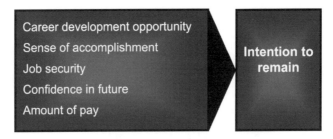

Drivers reflect *Promising Future*

Figure 2: Key drivers of retention.

employees report an unfavorable opinion on these factors, their intention to leave spikes, ranging from 35% to 53%.

The WorkTrends data also shows that these factors have remained relatively constant over the past decade. As Figure 4 shows, the importance of career development opportunities has remained unchanged throughout this period as a factor in driving turnover. Interestingly, pay has actually declined as a factor influencing turnover, while "sense of accomplishment" has gone through a parallel rise in importance. In looking at the data below in Figure 3, fewer employees who are dissatisfied with pay express their intention to leave in the coming year, compared with much higher percentages of employees dissatisfied

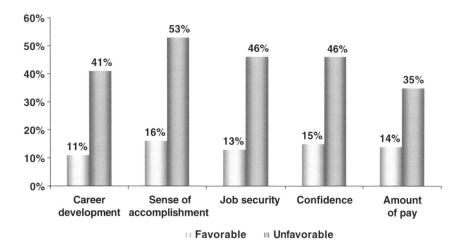

Figure 3: Impact of employer of choice practices on retention.

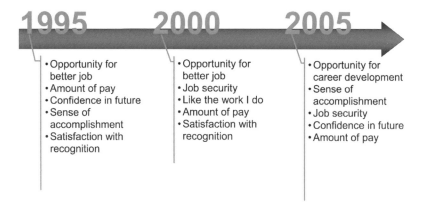

Figure 4: Historical drivers of retention.

with other key drivers of the employment relationship. These results reinforce the importance of the "employer of choice" reputation in retaining key employees.

While we can generalize about key drivers by analyzing results of national surveys of the worker population, we can also derive specific information about an individual organization by analyzing its survey results (and, in some instances, comparing their results to normative or "best practices" data). Such information can help the organization apply different tactics to different business units and job types or levels, depending on the specific importance of individual retention drivers. Not surprisingly, executive managers, scientific or technical employees, and individual contributors may all assign different weights to the various retention factors. Individual employees may be most concerned with job security, for example, whereas technical employees may be focused on their sense of accomplishment, and managers or leaders may be most influenced by career development opportunities. Understanding these different drivers will help the organization tailor its HR policies accordingly to maximize the retention influences for specific jobs.

In Table 4, we describe the results of a key driver analysis conducted at a large European consumer health products company with worldwide operations. These results demonstrate the different factors that influence retention between individual contributors and managers. While confidence in the future is the first retention driver for both groups, the importance and priority of other factors differ between the two groups. From a strategic perspective, actions designed to encourage participation in decision-making would increase retention among individual contributors. By contrast, the organization would need to address personal and career development interests and goals to increase retention among executive managers.

We have found that surveys aimed at measuring "employer of choice" attributes should include content measuring: fair compensation, recognition and feedback, job security and confidence in the future, job and company satisfaction, communication, teamwork, and career development opportunities (Wiley, Brooks, & Hause, 2003; Hause & Wiley, 1996). These topics are the most consistent predictors of employee retention and overall job satisfaction. To the extent that a specific survey reveals weakness in these items, either on an absolute basis or in comparison to "best practices" results, the organization can establish, prioritize, and implement a set of actions intended to improve employee perceptions in these areas.

Table 4: Consumer health company retention drivers.

Overall	Individual contributors	Managers
1) Confidence in future	1) Confidence in future	1) Confidence in future
2) Like the work I do	2) Encouraged to participate in decisions	2) Manager supports development
3) Manager supports development	3) Like the work I do	3) Clear understanding of my role, expectations
4) Problems in group corrected quickly	4) Problems in group corrected quickly	4) Like the work I do

In collaboration with Roy Morgan Research, we conduct a survey process similar to WorkTrends in several other countries, including Australia, the United Kingdom, and New Zealand. In Table 5, normative data for these four countries are provided for the Employer of Choice index. Australian and U.S. workers show very similar levels of satisfaction with pay and career development opportunities. While Australians indicate greater job satisfaction and are more satisfied with recognition than U.S. employees, they are also more concerned about job security within their organization.

While similarities exist in the "employer of choice" norms, there are also significant differences in how employees in these countries feel about their employers. For example, employees in the United Kingdom indicate a significantly lower rate of satisfaction with job security and pay than the other three countries. However, New Zealand employees indicate they are more satisfied than the other three countries in all five of the Employer of Choice index items.

It is important to note that surveys measuring the organization's reputation as an "employer of choice" are increasingly also focused on employee "engagement". While this includes an individual's job satisfaction, the concept of engagement is much broader. Frank, et al., (2004) define engagement as the willingness of the workforce to provide discretionary effort — i.e., to be good citizens and go above and beyond the call of duty in delivering customer service. While Frank, et al., believe that engagement is "joined at the hip with employee retention," the focus on engagement also reflects a growing use of surveys to predict organizational outcomes (see discussion below).

As outlined by Colquitt and Macey (2005), engaged employees are more adaptable to change, more proactive, more loyal, more positive, and more aligned with the culture and values of the organization. As a result, organizations that foster engagement deliver better performance, both in terms of customer satisfaction and financial results, because their employees will be more committed to the goals of the organization.

But what creates engagement? HR professionals often lean toward "employer of choice" models on the belief that happy employees — that is, those with the highest job

Table 5: Employer of choice norms by selected countries.

Employer of choice index	US*	Australia**	New Zealand**	UK**
Index score	**54%**	**56%**	**62%**	**49%**
Rate job satisfaction	70%	74%	79%	70%
Rate satisfaction with recognition	49%	56%	60%	51%
Rate job security	62%	57%	57%	47%
Rate amount of pay	52%	52%	54%	41%
Satisfied with opportunity for better job	38%	43%	49%	36%

*Sourced by Gantz Wiley Research WorkTrends USA
**Sourced by Roy Morgan Research and Gantz Wiley Asia Pacific

satisfaction — will in turn be engaged or committed employees. But our research has shown that the relationships among job satisfaction, employee engagement, customer satisfaction, and financial results are much more complex.

A study by Lundby and Fenlason (2004) suggests the possibility of a "chicken and egg" problem with employee satisfaction. In comparing the effectiveness of employee satisfaction with an organization's "climate for service" as predictors of organizational outcomes, they found that employee satisfaction had little or no predictive power beyond climate for service. A review of the research suggests that, in some cases, satisfaction may be an *outcome* of effective leadership and organizational success — in effect, that employees are more satisfied when they are part of a winning team.

Indeed, the missing link in this equation is *leadership*. Colquitt and Macey (2005) cite a study by Deci, Connell, and Ryan (1989) that suggests *managerial behaviors*, which focus on employee autonomy, positive feedback, and attention to employee opinions, are more likely to create the self-directed employee behaviors considered as engagement here.

There is limited research on the construct of engagement. The majority of operational definitions of engagement in the current literature are similar, if not the same, as traditional measures of overall job satisfaction. For example, in a recent meta-analysis by Harter, Schmidt, and Hayes (2002), significant relationships were found between employee satisfaction/engagement and business outcomes such as customer satisfaction, productivity, and employee turnover. However, they indicate that engagement, as they define it, is not clearly different than traditional definitions of job satisfaction.

Employee Surveys as Leading Indicators

A growing body of research has begun to use employee surveys as the linchpin in linking an organization's leadership practices, its employee perspectives, its customer loyalty, and its long-term financial performance. This represents the most proactive or "offensive" strategic use of the employee survey — as a tool to predict customer and business outcomes. The concept was first explored by Schneider, Parkington, and Buxton (1980), and Wiley (1996) coined the term "linkage research" to describe the body of research in this area: "Linkage research involves integrating and correlating data collected from employees with data in other key organizational databases. The purpose of linkage research is to identify those elements of the work environment — as described by employees — that correlate, or link, to critically important organizational outcomes such as customer satisfaction and business performance."

Wiley presented a comprehensive summary of the research literature that resulted in the development of the Linkage Research Model, later renamed as the High Performance Model. Further research (Wiley & Brooks, 2000) produced a taxonomy of the high performance organizational climate. Other studies (Heskett, Jones, Loveman, Sasser, & Schlesinger, 1994; Rucci, Kirn, & Quinn, 1998) have similarly demonstrated how employee surveys can be used as a tool to identify leading indicators of organizational results.

The High Performance Model, shown in Figure 5, describes how certain leadership practices (customer orientation, quality emphasis, employee training, and involvement)

Figure 5: High performance model.

create positive employee results. To the extent that employees perceive these practices emphasized in their organizations, they are more likely to report higher job satisfaction, more knowledge of and alignment with the company's vision and values, and improved teamwork and cooperation. They are also less likely to voluntarily resign. These employees are better positioned to deliver value to customers and thus drive improved customer satisfaction and customer loyalty. Over time, greater customer loyalty generates improved business outcomes, including sales growth, market share, and profitability.

Linkage research is a natural complement to other holistic models of organizational performance that emphasize leadership, such as the Service-Profit Chain (Heskett et al., 1994) and the Balanced Scorecard (Kaplan & Norton, 1996). The Balanced Scorecard, for example, is a vehicle for translating management strategy into action, by connecting the leadership practices and values of a company with its core interrelated organizational processes. The scorecard, made up of leading and lagging indicators of performance, reflects the integrated systems that impact an organization's success or failure.

In a similar way, the High Performance Model pinpoints the leadership practices that drive employee results. An employee survey focused on High Performance Model themes can help an organization diagnose its strengths and weaknesses in the cycle of performance. Rather than emphasize employee-focused items related to job satisfaction, this approach positions the employee as an observer and reporter of the organization's leadership practices and climate for service. These leadership practices (customer orientation, quality emphasis, employee training, and involvement) have shown the greatest predictive potency as leading indicators of customer satisfaction and business performance.

For example, traditional measures of employee satisfaction focus on the employee's personal experience and emphasize items such as the following:

- Job uses skills and abilities
- Job performance evaluated fairly
- Manager is good at "people management"
- Rate physical work environment
- Rate total benefits program

By contrast, our linkage research studies have demonstrated that the leadership practices outlined in the High Performance Model serve as much better predictors of business outcomes. These practices are measured using items such as the following:

- Use customer feedback to improve
- Policies and procedures are customer-friendly
- Clear standards for product/service quality
- Encouraged to participate in decisions
- Get training to keep up with customers

Additional examples of items measuring the themes referenced in the leadership practices and employee results components of the High Performance Model are shown in Table 6.

This approach to the employee survey casts the employee as an ally in assessing the organization's value proposition. Based on employee feedback, the organization can predict customer and financial performance down to the business unit level and develop an action plan that aligns unit performance with the company's strategy, including areas where leadership, training, staffing, technology, and other tools need to be evaluated and improved.

Proper analysis of surveys developed according to the High Performance Model also enables organizations to target their resources and action plans to those areas that are most likely to drive performance. The more common HR model is to focus the organization's efforts on those results that score "lowest" in the employee survey. However, we have

Table 6: High performance model sample items.

Theme	Item
Customer orientation	Customer problems are corrected quickly
Quality emphasis	Continually improving quality
Training	New employees get necessary training
Involvement	Authority needed to serve customers
Communication	Enough information about meeting group goals
Teamwork	Co-workers cooperate to get work done
Engagement	Proud to work for my company
Retention	Not seriously considering leaving

found that organizations can achieve a greater return on investment by focusing on areas that are most predictive of business outcomes (such as customer orientation, quality emphasis, training, and involvement), even if those areas rank *higher* than other items measured in the survey.

A recent case study demonstrates the power of the "leading indicators" approach to employee surveys in shaping organizational action plans. We worked with the new CEO of a global organization that had recently been formed from six business units of a consumer health products company. The CEO concluded that the keys to success for the new company would be customer service, consumer focus (reflecting the organization's wholesale and retail customers), and dynamic leadership. In order to develop an action plan to achieve these goals, the CEO and top HR executive wanted a baseline assessment of the organization's culture among its managerial and professional staff.

We worked with the company's top HR professionals to implement a survey based on the themes of the High Performance Model, in a structure we call the "InsideTrack" survey, utilizing many of the items described in Table 6. This survey was implemented with the top 2000 people in the organization with a participation rate of 79%, and the results were analyzed in comparison to industry norms and best practices established through the WorkTrends survey data. The results of the survey are shown in Figure 6, which also displays the range of results among the six business units.

The CEO led an intense, off-site review of the survey findings as part of a multi-day leadership team-building retreat. During that session, the team identified several priorities for follow-up action, reflecting the High Performance Model themes where there was the greatest gap between business unit performance and WorkTrends best practices. At the unit level, the company has implemented follow-up actions and instituted a schedule of future assessments to monitor progress.

This approach reflects the highest and best use of the employee survey: the survey content was designed and driven by the organization's top-level goals; the analysis reflected

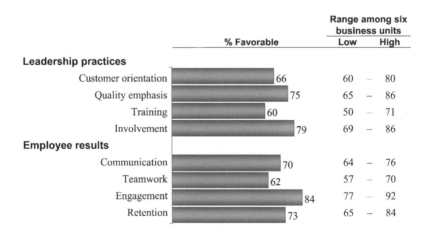

Figure 6: Global consumer health company inside track results.

those areas most predictive of future performance; and the action plan and follow-up were developed in order to align operations with the overall strategy.

Conclusion

The employee survey is an important tool for helping organizations manage their work-force and enhance their overall performance. Properly designed survey instruments can serve a number of purposes: identifying "warning signs" within the organization in areas such as ethics and union susceptibility; aiding in the design and implementation of high-priority organizational programs such as employee benefits and diversity initiatives; evaluating the organization's standing as an "employer of choice" to assist in recruitment and retention; and predicting organizational performance and measuring the effectiveness of key leadership practices.

What these purposes have in common is a focus on organizational strategy. The most effective employee surveys are developed based on a clear set of goals that are aligned with the direction established by the organization's leadership. In this way, the survey content can measure information that will provide practical, powerful results and a roadmap for specific action plans. Fundamentally, we believe that an employee survey is only of value to the extent it is *used* by management as a guide to implement strategy, improve performance, and achieve business objectives.

References

Colquitt, A. I., & Macey, W. H. (2005). *Surveys throughout the employment lifecycle: What matters, when.* Workshop given at the 20th annual conference for the Society for Industrial and Organizational Psychology (SIOP), Los Angeles, CA, April.

Deci, E. L., Connell, J. P., & Ryan, R. M. (1989). Self-determiniation in a work organization. *Journal of Applied Psychology, 74,* 580–590.

Frank, F. D., Finnegan, R. P., & Taylor, C. R. (2004). The race for talent: Retaining and engaging workers in the 21st century. *Human Resource Planning, 27,* 12–25.

Gilliand, R. (2002). *Employee survey and 360 markets: Today and tomorrow.* Unpublished data.

Harter, J. K., Schmidt, F. L., & Hayes, T. L. (2002). Business-unit level relationship between employee satisfaction, employee engagement, and business outcomes: A meta-analysis. *Journal of Applied Psychology, 87,* 268–279.

Hause, E. L., & Wiley, J. W. (1996). What do employees want most from their organizations? In: J. W. Wiley (Chair), *The attitudes of working America: A nationwide, longitudinal analysis.* Symposium conducted at the eleventh annual conference of the Society for Industrial and Organizational Psychology, San Diego, CA, April.

Heskett, J. L., Jones, T. O., Loveman, G. W., Sasser, W. E., & Schlesinger, L. A. (1994). Putting the service-profit chain to work. *Harvard Business Review, 72*(2), 164–174.

Higgs, A. C., & Ashworth, S. D. (1996). Organizational surveys: Tools for assessment and research. In: A. I. Kraut (Ed.), *Organizational surveys* (pp. 19–40). San Francisco, CA: Jossey-Bass.

Hillmer, S., Hillmer, B., & McRoberts, G. (2004). The real costs of turnover: Lessons from a call center. *Human Resource Planning, 27*(3), 34–41.

Kaplan, R. S., & Norton, D. P. (1996). Using the balanced scorecard as a strategic management system. *Harvard Business Review*, *76*, 75–85.

Kotter, J. O., & Heskett, J. L. (1992). *Corporate culture and performance.* New York: Free Press.

Kraut, A. I. (2004). How organizational surveys can be made more useful: A look at current and future survey practices. Presentation given at the second IT Survey Group Symposium, St. Leon Rot, Germany, June.

Lundby, K. M., & Fenlason, K. (2004). Service climate and employee satisfaction in linkage research. In: A. F. Bruno (Ed.), *Creative consulting: Innovative perspectives on management consulting* (pp. 125–141). Greenwich, CT: Information Age Publishing.

Rucci, A. J., Kirn, S. P., & Quinn, R. T. (1998). The employee–customer-profit chain at Sears. *Harvard Business Review*, *76*(1), 82–97.

Schneider, B., Parkington, J. J., & Buxton, V. M. (1980). Employee and customer perceptions of service in banks. *Administrative Science Quarterly*, *25*, 252–267.

TalentKeepers Webpage – Turnover cost calculator. http://www.talentkeepers-services.com/talentkeepers/costcalc.asp. 2005, June.

Waldman, J. D., Kelly, F., Arora, S., & Smith, H. J. (2004). The shocking cost of turnover in health care. *Health Care Management Review*, *29*(1), 2–7.

Wiley, J. W. (1996). Linking survey results to customer satisfaction and business performance. In: A. I. Kraut (Ed.), *Organizational surveys: Tools for assessment and change* (pp. 330–359). San Francisco, CA: Jossey-Bass.

Wiley, J. W., & Brooks, S. M. (2000). The high-performance organizational climate: How workers describe top performing units. In: N. S. Ashkanasy, C. Wilderom & M. F. Peterson (Eds), *The handbook of organizational culture & climate* (pp. 177–191). San Francisco, CA: Sage Publications.

Wiley, J. W., Brooks, S. M., & Hause, E. L. (2003). The impact of corporate downsizing on employee fulfillment and organizational capability. In: K. P. De Meuse & M. L. Marks (Eds), *Resizing the organization: Managing layoffs, divestitures, and closings-maximizing gain while minimizing pain* (pp. 108–130). Thousand Oaks, CA: Jossey-Bass.

CHAPTER 15

Developing Leaders: A Multilevel Perspective

Tjai M. Nielsen and Terry R. Halfhill

Developing Leaders: A Multilevel Perspective

What distinguishes great leaders? What contributes to leadership excellence? Many leadership scholars and practitioners would agree that leaders are not born, do not possess a specific personality profile, and do not approach leadership the same way (Bass, Avolio, Jung, & Berson, 2003; McCall, 1998; Yukl, 1994). John Kotter (2001) expresses this sentiment well in *What Leaders Really Do*, "Leadership isn't mystical and mysterious. It has nothing to do with having 'charisma' or other exotic personality traits. It is not the province of a chosen few" (p. 3). Similarly, Rooke and Torbert (2005) state, "…what differentiates leaders is not so much their philosophy of leadership, their personality, or their style of management" (p. 67). How does an organization ensure that it has enough leadership talent to succeed? One method involves executive coaching as a key component (Wasylyshyn, 2003). To be effective, however, executive coaches must learn to approach leadership development at multiple levels; individual, team, and organization. It is not enough to help an executive smooth out the rough edges by tempering an authoritative leadership style through one-on-one dialogue (individual level), facilitate a senior manager's ability to coach and motivate her team (team level), or institute a singular leadership development approach across an organization (organization level). Leadership development must be addressed at each of these levels to be successful.

In this chapter, we present a comprehensive, multilevel approach to leadership development (please see Figure 1). First, we define what is meant by leadership development, review the approach used by some organizations, and discuss specific leadership development methods. Next, we briefly review the executive coaching literature, define the primary components of executive coaching, and discuss ways in which current approaches are problematic. Finally, we explain the importance of a multilevel approach to specific phases of the executive coaching process, its benefits, and offer practical suggestions for implementation.

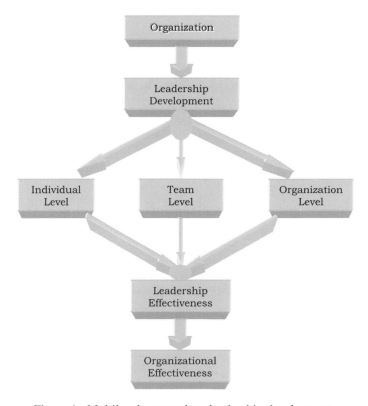

Figure 1: Multilevel approach to leadership development.

Leadership Development

We believe effective leaders: (1) actively manage change and help others manage change; (2) unify individuals and teams around a compelling vision aligned with organizational strategy; (3) motivate individuals and teams to achieve a common set of objectives aligned with organizational strategy; (4) consistently demonstrate the behavior they expect of others; and (5) place significant emphasis on identifying and developing those who may replace them. While this list is not comprehensive, it does cover important facets of leadership that contribute to effectiveness. It also highlights the complexity and challenge of being an effective leader in today's global, complex, and volatile business environment. An organization's ability to develop effective leaders is undoubtedly a key competitive advantage (Charan, 2000; Charan, Drotter, & Noel, 2001; Conger & Fulmer, 2003) and contributes substantially to organizational performance (McCall, 1998). But how do organizations approach the process of leadership development?

Organizations have taken a variety of approaches in their efforts to develop effective leaders. One of the best known examples of a company actively engaged in developing internal talent is General Electric (GE). GE spends a significant amount of time and money on leadership development and expects a significant return-on-investment (ROI). GE uses a pipeline model that focuses on preparing leaders for specific leadership transitions. Some examples of these transitional positions include, "new manager", "functional manager", "general manager", and "officer/group business leader". GE believes that effective leadership involves mastering specific skills and values at each level (Charan et al., 2001). This conceptual approach is supported by developmental activities such as training courses, seminars led by current GE leaders and business school faculty, individual readiness evaluations, and a strong focus on executive coaching. Many of these activities take place at GE's famed John F. Welch Leadership Center at Crotonville in Ossining, New York.

Another large, US-based company, Best Buy, spends significant time and resources on leadership development.

Customer centricity, Best Buy's major corporate initiative that calls for each store to focus on one or two customer segments (e.g. a soccer mom; small business owners), is being directly supported by a simultaneous focus on leadership development (McGregor, 2005). Best Buy embraces strength-based leadership (Buckingham & Clifton, 2001), which espouses the benefits of assessing and capitalizing on individual employees' strengths. Best Buy's conceptual approach is supported by leadership training, executive coaching, and a variety of other leadership-focused activities. Goldman Sachs is another organization that appreciates how crucial it is to develop internal leadership talent.

Goldman Sachs recently hired Steve Kerr, former Chief Learning Officer and Vice President at GE, to lead all of its employee development efforts. Goldman Sachs, like GE and Best Buy, is strongly committed to gaining a competitive advantage by developing effective leaders. A principle element of Goldman Sachs' approach is centered on experiential, action-based learning (Whitney, 2004). For example, vice presidents and managing directors are placed in 12- and 9-month stretch assignments at the supervisor, division, and firm-wide level that are designed to be significantly challenging and push participants out of their comfort zones. In addition to these developmental strategies, Goldman Sachs invests significantly in executive coaching.

GE, Best Buy, and Goldman Sachs are leading companies in their respective sectors, each embraces the importance of leadership development, and all three rely on executive coaching at varying levels. These organizations are representative of many others who believe in the importance of developing internal leadership talent and are taking part in the growing trend of hiring executive coaches.

Approaches to Leadership Development

Leadership development can be approached in various ways depending upon multiple forces such as organization strategy, competitive landscape, organization culture, and those in the organization responsible for driving the development process. However, there are two conceptual distinctions we would like to review before discussing specific leadership development methods.

Effective Leaders: Are They Born or Developed or Both?

Beliefs about the origins of leadership effectiveness are directly related to core assumptions regarding how leaders are developed. Morgan McCall (1998) details this idea and others in his book, *High Flyers: Developing the Next Generation of Leaders*. One camp has long held that leaders are born and that someone cannot learn to be a great leader. Tom Wolfe (1980), in his book *The Right Stuff*, suggests that great leaders are born with the "right stuff". While some in the corporate world might see this as lacking validity, it still serves as the basis for leadership development efforts at many organizations. These companies often approach leadership development by assuming that those with the "right stuff" simply need additional seasoning so they can exercise the innate talent that lies within (McCall, 1998). This logic falls short for several reasons. First, there is no reliable and valid method for assessing whether someone has the "right stuff". This prevents organizations from selecting those who would gain the most from being developed. In addition, if an organization makes a mistake and someone assigned to a high profile rotational assignment or company-wide project fails, the probability that this person will develop the necessary skills is slim. Second, since many assume someone has the "right stuff" because they perform well, there is no effective mechanism to learn from failure. In other words, since the "right stuff" is determined by success there is no mechanism for dealing with failure other than the assumption that the person who failed must not have had the "right stuff" in the first place. Fundamentally, the belief that leaders are born undermines the very notion of leadership development. Another perspective conceptualizes effective leadership as something that can be learned and developed (Law, Wong, & Song, 2004; McCall, 1998).

While effective leadership may be partially explained by innate abilities such as intelligence (Schmidt & Hunter, 2004), there are a host of other key factors that contribute to success. This concept is discussed frankly by Chuck Yeager as he writes about the reasons for his success (Yeager & Janos, 1985), "I am the sum-total of the life I have lived .... There is no such thing as a natural-born pilot. Whatever my aptitudes or talents, becoming a proficient pilot was hard work, really a lifetime's learning experience .... The best pilots fly more than the others; that's why they are the best" (p. 318). Like great pilots, effective leaders result from experience, hard work, intelligence, and a host of other factors. We unequivocally endorse this concept of leadership effectiveness and believe strongly that no leader is able to maximize his or her effectiveness without a strong commitment to their development.

The importance of leadership development has never been higher for organizations (Hernez-Broome & Hughes, 2004). One empirical example was a survey concluding that 91% of senior managers believed leadership was critical to their firms continued growth, yet only 8% considered the leadership at their firm to be "excellent" (Csoka, 1997). The importance of leadership development is clear, but the most effective methods for achieving developmental progress remain elusive.

Leadership Development Methods

In the following section, we review various methods used for leadership development. We review the most common approaches and do not attempt to be comprehensive. However, we do classify each method as being at the individual, team, or organization level to begin laying the foundation for our contention that a multilevel approach to leadership development by executive coaches is essential for achieving success.

Classroom Training

Classroom training is probably the most traditional form of leadership development and for many years, the most common. Training consists of leaders meeting in a classroom environment to be presented with material covering a wide range of topics. Training sessions include such topics as raising awareness of emotional intelligence, learning to think strategically, learning how personality impacts behavior, improving communication skill, and many others. While helpful, classroom training is often the least impactful form of development when it is not accompanied by other methods such as action learning. Training is often conducted in a group format, but is targeted toward individuals. Thus, we consider training to be at the individual level.

Executive Education

This method is often executed in a classroom format within a university setting. However, there are executive education programs implemented by university faculty within organizations. Topics offered under the rubric of executive education are numerous, including service firm leadership, leading change, marketing strategy, operating not-for-profit organizations, and finance for senior executives to name just a few. While many executive education programs offer the benefit of exposure to current theory and research, participants often note the interaction with other leaders from other companies as most beneficial. Executive education is typically targeted toward individuals, while occasionally assuming alternative formats. This leads us to categorize executive education as an individual level method.

Action Learning

Action learning involves leaders solving actual organizational issues as a way to develop. Measurable results, being able to communicate important learning, and developing leadership skills are three key objectives typically sought (Palus & Horth, 2004). Action learning is popular because it provides leaders challenging opportunities while contributing directly to the organization. However, the effectiveness of action learning often depends on the context within which it is conducted. That is, action learning activities are most effective when the issues being tackled are aligned with organization strategy and the development needs of participating leaders. Action learning is typically targeted toward individuals, but can also be used with work teams. For these reasons, we conceptualize action learning at both the individual and team levels. A method used for development containing elements of action learning is job rotation.

Job Rotation

Many organizations rotate high-potential leaders through a variety of challenging jobs in an effort to improve their leadership ability. However, the depth and commitment with which organizations approach job rotation varies greatly. Some organizations simply encourage leaders to take on challenging assignments, while others create developmental assignment matrices including their high potential leaders. When implemented effectively, the benefits of this form of development can be significant because leaders: (1) are challenged; (2) learn about another part of the organization; (3) develop relationships across the organization; (4) gain exposure to different senior leaders; and (5) further their understanding of how the entire organization operates. This method of leadership development is at the organization level.

360-Degree Feedback

The use of 360-degree feedback, an individual-level method for development, is one of the most common. This process involves leaders soliciting and receiving feedback from those with whom they work most closely including supervisors, direct reports, peers, customers, and others. It has garnered a significant amount of attention in the popular (e.g. Huet-Cox, Nielsen, & Sundstrom, 1999a) and academic press (e.g. Gillespie, 2005; Smither, London, Flautt, Vargas, & Kucine, 2003). Often used with other development methods such as coaching (Huet-Cox, Nielsen, & Sundstrom, 1999b), 360-degree feedback can be an invaluable tool for leaders who want to know more about how they are perceived by others. In addition, 360-degree feedback is one of the most common tools used by executive coaches.

Mentoring

As seen in companies like GE, Best Buy, and Goldman Sachs, a focus on developmental relationships such as coaching and mentoring is an important developmental method. Mentoring is defined as a committed, long-term relationship between two organizational members. Typically, a senior member of the organization will mentor a more junior member, but some organizations support peer mentoring programs (Bryant, 2005). Mentoring programs have become very popular in many organizations and while their effectiveness has been supported empirically in specific examples (e.g. Payne & Huffman, 2005), many mentoring efforts fall short of their promise. One key feature of successful mentoring programs is training for the mentors. Some organizations proceed with the assumption that their senior managers know how to mentor effectively which is not always accurate.

Coaching

Coaching, at its most basic level, involves practical, goal-focused forms of one-on-one learning and behavior change (Huet-Cox et al., 1999b). Coaching might be done by a peer, boss, member of human resources, or consultant. It can last a month or 20 years depending upon objectives, relationships, and organizational constraints. Executive coaching, one form of coaching at the center of this article, lasts for varying lengths of time and is carried out by a professional consultant or psychologist (Hall, Otazo, & Hollenbeck, 1999). Coaching is often conceptualized at the individual level. However, team-level coaching is receiving more attention as the use of teams becomes common (Hackman & Wageman, 2005; Kets de Vries, 2005). We view coaching as both an individual and team-level intervention across organizations.

There are multiple methods for approaching leadership development. It seems reasonable to assume no one method is most effective. GE, Best Buy, and Goldman Sachs approach leadership development differently, likely driven by their specific organization strategy, organization culture, and the person or persons responsible for driving their development efforts. However, each of these organizations share a common reliance on executive coaching to bolster their development efforts. Executive coaches (ECs) may use each of the leadership development methods reviewed previously. Coaching is central to what ECs do, but they also employ the use of training, action learning, mentoring, job rotation, elements of executive coaching, and 360-degree feedback depending on the client and context. We suggest, however, that ECs employing development methods at only one level (individual, team, or organization) will be limited in their effectiveness.

Executive Coaching

The history of executive coaching is unclear. There are many opinions about when it began (Judge & Cowell, 1997; Kilburg, 1996; Tobias, 1996) due to semantics and varying definitions. However, it is generally agreed upon that the use of executive coaches has increased dramatically in the last 10 years (Kampa-Kokesch & Anderson, 2001; Winum, 2005). This increase has occurred in unison with an increase in the literature on executive coaching.

The term executive coaching is often used with the assumption that everyone relies on a similar definition. We make no such assumption and employ the following definition of executive coaching offered by Kilburg (1996):

> a helping relationship formed between a client who has managerial authority and responsibility in an organization and a consultant who uses a wide variety of behavioral techniques and methods to help the client achieve a mutually identified set of goals to improve his or her professional performance and personal satisfaction and, consequently, to improve the effectiveness of the client's organization within the formally defined coaching agreement (p. 67)

Different definitions have been offered, but this one captures what we believe is the essence of executive coaching — a professional relationship between an executive and a coach that is formed in an effort to improve the performance of the executive and that of her organization. A key part of this definition is the inclusion of performance beyond the individual level. Many definitions and approaches to executive coaching focus exclusively on individual performance. Not only does this focus diminish the potential impact of executive coaching, it also fails to consider the needs of the organization. Executive coaching should ideally result in performance improvement at multiple levels. The relative absence of multilevel models of performance in the executive coaching literature can be partially explained by its lack of empirical focus on performance.

There is a paucity of empirical research on the effectiveness of executive coaching (Kampa-Kokesch & Anderson, 2001; Lowman, 2005). In a recent review on the executive coaching literature, Kampa-Kokesch and Anderson identified only seven (11%) studies that examined the efficacy of executive coaching empirically. Of these, only two (3%) were published journal articles examining the actual effectiveness of executive coaching (Hall et al., 1999; Olivero, Bane, & Kopelman, 1997). The vast majority of studies focused on different case studies, models, techniques, and methodologies. Since 2000 (when the review by Kampa-Kokesch & Anderson was completed), it seems that little has changed (Lowman, 2005). A 10-article, two-part special issue of the *Consulting Psychology Journal* (Kilburg, 2005) on executive coaching contained no attempts at empiricism. In a review of this special issue on executive coaching, Lowman (2005) discusses the need for more empirical work in the following statement:

> In the absence of rigorous debate, vigorous empirical tests, and the revision of theory and practice based on those findings, intervention methodologies run the risk of either falling from their own bloatedness deriving from a lack of intellectual exercise or of becoming internally consistent belief systems, preaching faithfully to the choir if unconvincingly to those who prefer to sing from other music....If executive coaching puts itself in a position in which it considers case methodology to be an adequate and sufficient substitute for empirical evaluation, relying exclusively on a "constructivist narrative" approach, its days, at least as a field that potentially belongs in the house of psychology, may be as numbered as few as were those of the dodo bird" (p. 92)

It seems that executive coaching is in need of models and theories that can be tested empirically in an effort to identify approaches to executive coaching that result in performance improvement at the individual, team, and organization level. A number of excellent efforts have been made in the development of executive coaching models (e.g. Cocivera & Cronshaw, 2004; Diedrich, 1996), but none have approached interventions and criteria from multiple levels. Current executive coaching models highlight a multitude of key elements from comprehensive planning (Diedrich) to diversity and inclusion (Katz & Miller, 1996) to a business-linked focus (Saporito, 1996). Our aim in this chapter is not to suggest a new model of executive coaching, it is to demonstrate, regardless of your conceptual model, the necessity for ECs to intervene at multiple levels in order to maximize their effectiveness. In order to understand their impact, we also suggest that ECs go beyond criteria like client satisfaction as a measure of effectiveness and assess their performance at multiple levels using objective and subjective indices (Winum, Nielsen, & Bradford, 2002).

While there have been a number of different executive coaching models suggested in the literature, many of them overlap and can be broken down into five similar steps (please see Figure 2).

The five overlapping components include: (1) context assessment and relationship building; (2) assessment; (3) feedback; (4) intervention; and (5) evaluation. While not found in many other models, we have included a sixth component, *adjustment*, because we feel that it is a critical component in *ongoing* coaching engagements. *Adjustment* would not be as relevant in short-term coaching engagements where there is little time to coach, much less evaluate the quality and effectiveness of that coaching. The five other components illustrated in Figure 2 are found in most executive coaching models.

Context assessment and relationship building are two initial steps in the coaching process that facilitate understanding of the organization within which the executive operates

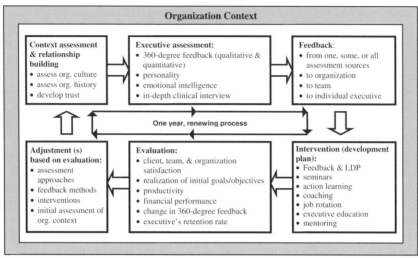

Organization Context

Context assessment & relationship building	Executive assessment:	Feedback:
• assess org. culture • assess org. history • develop trust	• 360-degree feedback (qualitative & quantitative) • personality • emotional intelligence • in-depth clinical interview	• from one, some, or all assessment sources • to organization • to team • to individual executive

⇧ ⇩ One year, renewing process ⇩

Adjustment (s) based on evaluation:	Evaluation:	Intervention (development plan):
• assessment approaches • feedback methods • interventions • initial assessment of org. context	• client, team, & organization satisfaction • realization of initial goals/objectives • productivity • financial performance • change in 360-degree feedback • executive's retention rate	• Feedback & LDP • seminars • action learning • coaching • job rotation • executive education • mentoring

Note. LDP = Leadership Development Plan

Figure 2: Model of executive coaching process. Note: LDP = Leadership development plan.

and starts laying the foundation for a trusting relationship. An organization's culture, climate, and history are all important elements that shape executive behavior and provide vital information to an executive coach regarding the context of his or her client's behavior. This phase also helps the executive coach better understand the business imperatives of the organization, which should naturally be integrated with the coaching process.

The assessment phase is common in different approaches to executive coaching. ECs must understand: (1) how their clients behave while at work; (2) how they impact colleagues; (3) what drives their behaviors; (4) their level of problem solving ability and emotional intelligence; and (5) what key events contributed to their current situation. A number of techniques are used to gather this information in the assessment phase of executive coaching, but the most common is 360-degree feedback. The 360-degree feedback process can be qualitative (information gathered through a series of interviews conducted by the EC) or quantitative (a survey designed to assess specific competencies and/or behaviors). A variety of other assessment methodologies such as personality measures, emotional intelligence inventories, and extensive one-on-one interviews are employed by ECs to gather this critical data. The information gathered in the assessment phase serves as the basis for feedback given to the executive and is critical for creating a specific, actionable, measurable, and business-related leadership development plan (LDP).

Typically, clients are given feedback in the form of an assessment profile, feedback report, or some other method of integrating data from different sources. We believe it is essential that feedback be given face-to-face by the EC. Receiving this type of feedback is a unique and often overwhelming event for most executives. It is essential that executives understand their feedback report, put the results in perspective, and begin thinking developmentally, not defensively. The absence of the executive coach during the feedback phase can permanently and negatively impact future progress. Once feedback has been provided, most coaching processes move into the intervention phase.

As we reviewed earlier, there are a variety of leadership development methods or interventions that can be employed. Each has its own merits depending on the key goals and objectives created by the EC and the client. The first step in this phase is typically the creation of an LDP. Often, this effort is led by the executive and only supported by the coach. LDPs created primarily by ECs garner less commitment, maintain lower levels of adherence, and are less effective. Other possible interventions include action learning, seminars, executive education, mentoring, and job rotation. Using multiple methods typically yields better results (McCall, 2001). To maximize effectiveness, development methods at the individual level (seminars), team level (team-based action learning), and organization level (job rotation) should be used. Using a single intervention or multiple interventions at only one level (e.g. individual) will fail to maximize development. Interventions may be short (seminar) or long-term (job rotation) lasting from 1 day to several years. Assessing the impact of the interventions used and the overall coaching process is done in the evaluation phase.

To remain competitive and be able to demonstrate value, ECs must evaluate their coaching effectiveness and demonstrate its impact (Winum et al., 2002). This phase is often the most overlooked and undervalued. Most ECs depend on their clients to let them know how things are going. Moreover, they base the assessment of their own performance and impact on the general satisfaction of the hiring manager and executive client. Too often, the difficulty of delivering negative feedback prevents hiring managers and executive clients from offering candid assessments of an EC's performance. In addition, these stakeholders frequently base their evaluations on the degree to which they like or dislike the EC. Ironically, this often happens in organizations that measure hundreds of performance indicators across a myriad of functions and types of operations. Ultimately, it is up to the EC to thoroughly evaluate his or her own performance. The key indicators of performance will vary depending on the specific coaching engagement, but at a minimum an EC should assess: (1) the degree to which initial goals were achieved; (2) change in 360-degree feedback over time (Smither et al., 2003); and (3) the change in perception of the executive's boss and colleagues. However, just as ECs should intervene at multiple levels, they should evaluate their performance at multiple levels. In long-term, ongoing executive coaching engagements, data gathered from the evaluation phase should be used to make process adjustments.

While *adjustment* was not a common element of the executive coaching models we reviewed, it is essential for long-term coaching engagements. No EC does everything perfectly the first time around. Moreover, after the initial process of coaching is concluded, the executive being coached is likely thinking, behaving, and operating differently. This, in addition to changes in organizational context and competitive landscape justify making adjustments to the coaching process.

Current models and applications of executive coaching fall short because they typically function at the individual, team, or organizational level, but not all three. We argue that executive coaching approached at one level is limited in its ability to achieve sustained success. Specifically, two key steps in the executive coaching process, the *intervention phase* and the *evaluation phase*, require a multilevel approach to maximize effectiveness.

Key Points

Maximizing the effectiveness of executive coaching requires a multilevel approach.

• Beliefs about the origins of leadership effectiveness are directly related to core assumptions regarding how leaders are developed.
• While effective leadership may be partially explained by innate abilities such as intelligence, there are a host of other key factors that contribute to success.
• A multilevel approach to leader development is a key success factor in achieving individual, team, and organizational outcomes.
• Two key steps in the executive coaching process, the *intervention phase* and the *evaluation phase*, require a multilevel approach to maximize effectiveness.
• There is a distinct absence of rigorous empiricism concerning executive coaching and objective outcomes - an issue that must be addressed in the future.

Intervening at Multiple Levels

There are three key reasons for the importance of executive coaches implementing leadership development methods at multiple levels. First, leaders work and must perform effectively at all three levels. Second, skills developed at one level do not necessarily carry over to other levels. Finally, the sustainability of learning increases at higher levels due to increased accountability and broader impact.

The majority of leaders in Fortune 500 companies and small businesses must function at the individual, team, and organization levels to be effective. Leaders perform a variety of tasks individually such as the performance appraisal of direct reports and dealing with key stakeholders such as customers or suppliers. Leaders must acquire the interpersonal, performance management, and emotional skills necessary to perform effectively at the individual level. If they do not already, most leaders will work within a team context at some point in their careers (Nielsen, Sundstrom, & Halfhill, 2005). Team leadership and performing at the team level is fundamentally different than the individual level and requires specific skills and knowledge (Hackman & Wageman, 2005; Nielsen & Halfhill, in press). Finally, leaders must perform at the organization level to be effective. Leaders who understand how components of their organizations are interdependent and operationally integrated are better able to employ a broad perspective when making decisions, prioritizing demands, and utilizing resources.

Skills developed at one level do not necessarily carry over to other levels. For example, a seminar (individual-level development method) on performance management that teaches participants how to more effectively manage direct reports and motivate them with rewards will not help an executive tasked with leading a team. Many of the knowledge, skills, and abilities necessary to be an effective leader at the team level (Campion, Medsker, & Higgs, 1993) differ from those at the individual level. Another example would include a very common leadership development intervention, teaching executives to be more emotionally intelligent (Hernez-Broome & Hughes, 2004). While greater levels of emotional intelligence (i.e., understanding emotion; perception of emotion in self and others; managing emotion in self and others; assimilating emotion to enhance thought) have been found to be related to increased performance at the individual level in a number of studies (Daus & Ashkanasy, 2005; Law et al., 2004), far fewer have found a similar relationship between emotional intelligence and performance within a team context. That is, leader emotional competence at the individual level requires different skills because team members: (1) operate interdependently; (2) are frequently subject to team-based rewards; (3) perform different tasks; and (4) perform under a myriad of circumstances depending on their type of team.

The sustainability of learning increases at higher levels due to increased accountability and broader impact. Individual-level development can be very effective, but the degree to which executives adhere to individual-level methods is limited. For example, ECs are often asked to help executives smooth out rough edges by tempering an authoritative leadership style through one-on-one dialogue (individual level). ECs frequently recommend several behavior modification techniques to assist the executive with this change. How often and consistently these techniques are used is primarily up to the executive with intermittent support from the EC. This lack of accountability decreases the likelihood that the behavioral modification techniques learned will be maintained. Team-level development methods are more likely to be sustained.

A common EC intervention at the team level involves the facilitation of open dialogue between the team leader and team members. This type of intervention is typically designed to increase the leader's understanding of relevant issues, her ability to communicate with team members, and overall team trust. The behavior changes that come out of this intervention are more likely to be sustained because it is not just the individual leader who participated in her development. The leader is now accountable to herself, everyone on the team, and the EC. In addition, since team members were a part of the process, they are more likely to help their leader adhere to new parameters of behavior. To maximize the likelihood of adherence and sustainability, ECs must also employ development methods at the organization level.

An organization-level development method like job rotation must be executed and supported at the organization level. Specifically, an organization actively engaged in job rotation to develop its leadership talent must consider a variety of issues such as: (1) How will we make up for the performance of the *executive* who left? (2) Who will take *her* place? (3) What position should the *executive* be placed in? (4) Will someone else be moved out? (5) How will we make up for the performance deficit as the *executive* assumes a new role where they lack expertise and experience? and (6) Is tracking, managing, and maintaining all this movement beneficial to individual participants and the organization? Organizations that sponsor job rotation must be fully committed (i.e., time, resources, effort) to do it effectively. When organizations commit time, money, and effort to something, they want a return on their investment. This pushes organizations to increase the support and expectations of participating executives. Increased support and expectations motivates executives to adhere to lessons learned and more actively work to sustain behavior change.

Executive coaches who seek to maximize the impact of their services must implement development methods at the individual, team, and organization levels. The importance of approaching the *intervention phase* at multiple levels necessitates the implementation of the *evaluation phase* at multiple levels.

Evaluating at Multiple Levels

To remain competitive and demonstrate value, ECs must evaluate their coaching effectiveness and demonstrate its impact (Winum et al., 2002). This phase is often the most overlooked and undervalued. There are three critical reasons for evaluating performance at the individual, team, and organization levels. First, intervening at multiple levels requires effectiveness to be assessed at multiple levels. Second, demonstrating effectiveness at multiple levels is a professional necessity. Third, the opportunity to empirically examine the efficacy of executive coaching is significantly improved.

ECs will greatly improve their effectiveness by implementing leadership development methods at the individual, team, and organization levels. Operating at multiple levels requires that ECs assess their effectiveness at each of those levels. For example, ECs are often asked to help executives smooth out rough edges by tempering an authoritative leadership style through one-on-one dialogue (individual level). Several behavior modification techniques are often recommended to assist the executive with this change. The degree to which the client achieves the target behavior change is an obvious individual-level evaluation of effectiveness. A less obvious approach would involve a second administration of a 360-degree, emotional intelligence, or personality survey that measures behaviors associated with authoritative leadership. Improvement on the associated scores would indicate improvement. A similar technique would not suffice for evaluating the effectiveness of a team-level intervention. A common EC intervention at the team level involves the facilitation of open dialogue between the team leader and team members. This type of intervention is typically designed to increase the leader's understanding of relevant issues, her ability to communicate with team members, and overall team trust. Evaluating the impact of this intervention requires assessment at the team level. In other words, it is not enough to survey individual team members regarding the relevant objectives because their perspective may not be representative of the entire team. One possible evaluation technique would involve examining aggregated team ratings of communication and trust from the second 360-degree feedback administration. This would represent team perceptions, which were an inherent part of the intervention. A similar principle holds true for organization-level interventions. A multilevel *evaluation phase* is also necessary for ECs to remain competitive.

ECs who are not willing and able to make compelling connections between their services and desired organizational outcomes will be marginalized. Almost every executive coaching engagement involves individual, team, and organizational outcomes. Demonstrating effectiveness via comprehensive evaluation at each level of work is imperative. Unlike some professional service providers like accountants and lawyers, ECs do not provide services that organizations are required to have by law. There is no captive market in executive coaching. Moreover, the majority of organizations must consider budget constraints. ECs who want to thrive must show how their services contribute value to the organization's ability to execute its mission. Thus, the ability to evaluate the impact of executive coaching and demonstrate that value is a professional necessity in order to remain economically viable. ECs who limit their demonstrations of effectiveness to one level will be quickly surpassed by those who provide evidence of impact on individuals, teams, *and* organizations. While more important for academics, evaluating effectiveness at all three levels will contribute to empirically establishing the efficacy of executive coaching.

There is a paucity of empirical research on the effectiveness of executive coaching (Kampa-Kokesch & Anderson, 2001; Lowman, 2005). While the importance of empiricism is higher for ECs from academic environments, it will have a long-term impact on non-academic ECs as well. The lack of empirical evidence showing that executive coaching works, will eventually diminish the field's credibility. Examining the efficacy of executive coaching at multiple levels offers a variety of possibilities for empirically demonstrating the impact of executive coaching and will contribute to multilevel theory building. It is beyond the scope of this chapter to offer a detailed review of multilevel research methods, but for more information we recommend reading Klein and Kozlowski (2000) and Klein, Tosi, and Cannella (1999).

Conclusion

Leadership development is a vitally important component contributing to sustained organizational success. Without it, organizations are forced to find, select, and integrate external talent, thus spending more time and money. Many organizations rely on executive coaches to aid their leadership development efforts and many executive coaches rely on individual, team, *or* organization level interventions. However, that is not enough, leadership development must be addressed at each of these levels to be successful. By not approaching leadership development at multiple levels, executive coaches necessarily limit their effectiveness and that of their clients.

Acknowledgments

We extend our sincere thanks to Sarah Nielsen for her comments on earlier drafts of this chapter.

Key Discussion Questions

1. Is leadership innate or learned?
2. Why is a multilevel perspective important for leadership development?
3. Provide examples of leadership development methods at the individual, group, and organizational levels of analysis.
4. What are some common leadership development methods and what level of analysis is each associated with?
5. What are the five common components to most models of executive coaching?
6. Why is it important for the EC to objectively evaluate his/her effectiveness?

References

Bass, B. M., Avolio, B. J., Jung, D. I., & Berson, Y. (2003). Predicting unit performance by assessing transformational and transactional leadership. *Journal of Applied Psychology, 88*(2), 207–218.

Bryant, S. E. (2005). The impact of peer mentoring on organizational knowledge creation and sharing. *Group and Organization Management, 30*(3), 319–338.

Buckingham, M., & Clifton, D. O. (2001). *Now, discover your strengths.* New York: Free Press.

Campion, M. A., Medsker, G. J., & Higgs, A. C. (1993). Relations between work group characteristics and effectiveness: Implications for designing effective work groups. *Personnel Psychology, 46,* 823–850.

Charan, R. (2000). Stand by your CEO (sometimes). *Fortune, 142*(4), 296–297.

Charan, R., Drotter, S., & Noel, J. (2001). *The leadership pipeline: How to build the leadership-powered company.* San Francisco: Jossey-Bass.

Cocivera, T., & Cronshaw, S. (2004). Action frame theory as a practical framework for the executive coaching process. *Consulting Psychology Journal, 56,* 234–245.

Conger, J. A., & Fulmer, R. M. (2003). Developing your leadership pipeline. *Harvard Business Review,* December, pp. 1–8.

Csoka, L. (1997). *Bridging the leadership gap.* Report No. 1190-97-ES. The Conference Board, New York.

Daus, C. S., & Ashkanasy, N. M. (2005). The case for the ability-based model of emotional intelligence in organizational behavior. *Journal of Organizational Behavior, 26,* 453–466.

Diedrich, R. C. (1996). An iterative approach to executive coaching. *Consulting Psychology Journal, 48,* 61–66.

Gillespie, T. L. (2005). Internationalizing 360-degree feedback: Are subordinate ratings comparable? *Journal of Business and Psychology, 19*(3), 361–383.

Hackman, J. R., & Wageman, R. (2005). A theory of team coaching. *Academy of Management Review, 30*(2), 269–287.

Hall, D. T., Otazo, K. L., & Hollenbeck, G. P. (1999). Behind closed doors: What really happens in executive coaching. *Organizational Dynamics, 27*(3), 39–53.

Hernez-Broome, G., & Hughes, R. L. (2004). Leadership development: Past, present, and future. *Human Resource Planning, 27*(1), 24–32.

Huet-Cox, G. D., Nielsen, T. M., & Sundstrom, E. (1999a). Get the most from 360-degree feedback: Put it on the Internet. *HR Magazine, 44*(5), 92–103.

Huet-Cox, G. D., Nielsen, T. M., & Sundstrom, E. (1999b). Getting results from Internet-based 360-degree feedback through coaching. *Human Resource Professional, 12*(6), 23–28.

Judge, W. Q., & Cowell, J. (1997). The brave new world of executive coaching. *Business Horizons, 40*(4), 71–77.

Kampa-Kokesch, S., & Anderson, M. Z. (2001). Executive coaching: A comprehensive review of the literature. *Consulting Psychology Journal, 53*(4), 205–228.

Katz, J. H., & Miller, F. A. (1996). Coaching leaders through culture change. *Consulting Psychology Journal, 48,* 104–114.

Kets de Vries, M. F. R. (2005). Leadership group coaching in action: The Zen of creating high performance teams. *Academy of Management Executive, 19*(1), 61–76.

Kilburg, R. R. (1996). Toward a conceptual understanding and definition of executive coaching. *Consulting Psychology Journal, 48,* 134–144.

Kilburg, R. R. (Ed.). (2005). Trudging toward Dodoville-part II: Case studies in executive coaching *Consulting Psychology Journal, 57*(1&2), (Special issue).

Klein, K. J., & Kozlowski, S. W. J. (2000). Multilevel theory, research, and methods in organizations: Foundations, extensions, and new directions. *Society for industrial and organizational psychology frontier series.* San Francisco: Jossey-Bass.

Klein, K. J., Tosi, H., & Cannella, A. A. (1999). Multilevel theory building: Benefits, barriers, and new developments. *Academy of Management Journal, 24*(2), 243–248.

Kotter, J. P. (2001). What leaders really do. *Harvard Business Review,* December, pp. 3–12.

Law, S. L., Wong, C. S., & Song, L. J. (2004). The construct and criterion validity of emotional intelligence and its potential utility for management studies. *Journal of Applied Psychology, 89*(3), 483–496.

Lowman, R. L. (2005). Executive coaching: The road to Dodoville needs paving with more than good assumptions. *Consulting Psychology Journal, 57*(1), 90–96.

McCall, M. W. (1998). *High flyers: Developing the next generation of leaders.* Boston: Harvard Business School Press.

McGregor, J. (2005). *Competing on culture* [Online]. Available (March): www.fastcompany.com/magazine/92/clear-leader-extra.html.

Nielsen, T. M., & Halfhill, T. (in press). A strategic contingency model of team leadership. In: R. Burke & C. Cooper (Eds), *Inspiring leaders.* London, England: Taylor & Francis.

Nielsen, T. M., Sundstrom, E., & Halfhill, T. (2005). Group dynamics and effectiveness: Five years of applied research. In: S. A. Wheelan (Ed.), *Handbook of group research and practice.* Thousand Oaks, CA: Sage.

Olivero, G., Bane, K. D., & Kopelman, R. E. (1997). Executive coaching as a transfer of training tool: Effects on productivity in a public agency. *Public Personnel Management, 26*(4), 461–469.

Palus, C. J., & Horth, D. M. (2004). Exploration for development. In: C. McCauley & E. Van Velsor (Eds), *The center for creative leadership handbook of leadership development* (2nd ed., pp. 438–464). San Francisco: Jossey-Bass.

Payne, S. C., & Huffman, A. H. (2005). A longitudinal examination of the influence of mentoring on organizational commitment and turnover. *Academy of Management Journal, 48*(1), 158–168.

Rooke, D., & Torbert, W. R. (2005). 7 transformations of leadership. *Harvard Business Review*, April, p. 67–76.

Saporito, T. J. (1996). Business-linked executive development: Coaching senior executives. *Consulting Psychology Journal, 48*, 96–103.

Schmidt, F. L., & Hunter, J. (2004). General mental ability in the world of work: Occupational attainment and job performance. *Journal of Personality and Social Psychology, 86*(1), 162–173.

Smither, J. W., London, M., Flautt, R., Vargas, Y., & Kucine, I. (2003). Can working with an executive coach improve multisource feedback ratings over time? A quasi-experimental field study. *Personnel Psychology, 56*, 23–44.

Tobias, L. L. (1996). Coaching executives. *Consulting Psychology Journal, 48*, 87–95.

Wasylyshyn, K. M. (2003). Executive coaching: An outcome study. *Consulting Psychology Journal, 55*(2), 94–106.

Whitney, K. (2004). *Steve Kerr: Managing the business of learning* [Online]. Available (August): www.clomedia.com/content/templates/clo_cloprofile.asp? articleid=582&zoneid=4.

Winum, P. C. (2005). Effectiveness of a high potential African American executive: The anatomy of a coaching engagement. *Consulting Psychology Journal, 57*(1), 71–89.

Winum, P. C., Nielsen, T. M., & Bradford, R. E. (2002). Assessing the impact of organizational consulting. In: R. Lowman (Ed.), *Handbook of organizational consulting psychology* (pp. 645–667). San Francisco, CA: Jossey-Bass.

Wolfe, T. (1980). *The right stuff.* New York: Bantam.

Yeager, C., & Janos, L. (1985). *Yeager: An autobiography.* New York: Bantam.

Yukl, G. (1994). *Leadership in organizations* (3rd ed.). Englewood Cliffs, NJ: Prentice-Hall.

CHAPTER 16

Developing the Adaptive and Global Leader: HRM Strategies within a Career-Long Perspective

Stephen J. Zaccaro, Gabrielle M. Wood and Jeffrey Herman

Effective leadership provides competitive advantage to organizations. Or, as Hambrick and Mason (1984, p. 194) asserted, "Top executives matter." Many studies have affirmed the real contributions that effective leadership practices and personal qualities of executives add to organizational productivity. Strategic leadership processes such as effective environmental scanning and boundary spanning have been associated with retained earnings, sales, and organizational profitability (Dollinger, 1984; Thomas, Clark, & Gioia, 1993). Miller and Cardinal (1994) found consistent evidence linking another strategic leadership process, planning, to higher organizational growth and profitability. Hart and Quinn (1993) reported that the ability of executives to exhibit behavioral complexity positively influenced organizational cash flow, profitability, sales growth, product development, and market share. The quality of top management team dynamics has been associated with income growth (Peterson, Smith, Martorana, & Owens, 2003) and return on assets (Iaquinto & Frederickson, 1997). Other studies have explicitly linked personal qualities of the CEO to organizational sales and net income growth (Miller & Toulouse, 1986), product innovation (Howell & Avolio, 1993; Howell & Higgins, 1990), and acquisition decisions (Hitt & Tyler, 1991). Peterson et al. (2003) found that CEO personality influenced organizational growth by affecting the dynamics of top management teams. Other studies have reported that CEO succession accounted for between 32% and 44% of the variance in post-succession profit margins and 47% of the variance in stock prices (Day & Lord, 1988; Weiner & Mahoney, 1981). Barrick, Day, Lord, and Alexander (1991) provided a direct calculation of possible financial impact from effective organizational leadership in 132 companies over a 15-year period. They used a decision-theoretic utility procedure to determine that organizations accrued more than $25 million after taxes from an average executive's tenure.

These and other studies (see Zaccaro, 2001 for a review) point to the powerful importance of effective leadership for organizational performance. They also suggest that the development of effective leaders should be a high priority in organizational human resource management efforts. While executive selection strategies have an important role in HRM practices, developmental strategies are more likely to produce the executives that can successfully navigate organizational change (McCall, 1998). Selection models often reflect end-state competencies that are based on prior executive performance and become increasingly obsolete when organizational environments change, along with corresponding executive performance requirements (Spreitzer, McCall, & Mahoney, 1997). Developmental strategies that foster a leader's ability to adapt and manage change will serve organizations better in such dynamic environments.

Despite widespread agreement about the importance of leader development for organizational effectiveness (Rynes, Colbert, & Brown, 2002), and the investment of large sums to leader training and development (McCall, 1998; Conference Board, 1999), such efforts are often unsystematic, *ad hoc*, and not precisely calibrated to target emerging requisite skills. Different developmental strategies employed at alternate stages of a leader's career are rarely integrated and are typically somewhat dissociated from changing performance requirements across organizational levels (Yukl, 2006; Zaccaro & Banks, 2004). Mumford, Marks, Connelly, Zaccaro, and Reiter-Palmon (2000) argued that different leader performance requirements and corresponding skill sets emerge as leaders transverse organizational levels in their career. Accordingly, leader development programs need to respond systematically to these changes. Zaccaro and Banks (2004) noted that different modes of development (i.e. formal training, operational assignments, self-learning) are rarely integrated, with systematic development reserved for relatively short term, off-site courses, and seminars. In summarizing this literature, Yukl (2006, p. 412) noted:

> In most organizations there is little integration of leadership training and development activities with each other or with related human resources practices such as performance appraisal, career counseling and succession planning. Decisions about what types of training and development to provide are often influenced by current fads and vender hype rather than a systematic analysis of essential competencies that need to be enhanced.

Today's business environment requires executives to be increasingly adaptive and global in the operations of their leadership responsibilities (Hitt, Keats, & DeMarie, 1998; Ireland & Hitt, 1999; London, 2002; Suutari, 2002). Adaptive leadership requires skills and competencies that are different from standard leadership practices (Albano, 2000; Heifetz & Laurie, 1997). Typical strategic leadership entails problem definition, organizational defense, role clarification, and maintaining internal order and structure (Heifetz & Laurie, 1997; Zaccaro, 2001). However, Heifetz and Laurie argued that leaders need to identify adaptive challenges, allow environmental change to challenge the organization, and in turn challenge existing norms and roles. Likewise, global leadership requires knowledge sets and skills not readily present in many organizational executives (Conner, 2000; Gregersen, Morrison, & Black, 1998; Suutari, 2002). Gergerson et al. reported in a survey of U.S. Fortune 500 firms that 85% of respondents indicated a deficiency in their numbers of required global leaders. These respondents also indicated that competent global leaders represented their most important organizational need, ahead of adequate financial resources, international communication technology and higher quality local work force.

Yet despite these needs, current leader development strategies lag in their ability to grow skills fostering adaptive and global leadership (Mendenhall, Dunbar, & Oddou, 1987; Zaccaro & Banks, 2004). Growing adaptive leaders require developmental strategies that differ from traditional approaches (Smith, Ford, & Kozlowski, 1997; Zaccaro & Banks, 2004). Traditional training strategies have focused either on expanding a manager's generic behavioral repertoire (e.g. giving feedback, managing time effectively) or developing skills that are applicable within specific contexts (e.g. team building or conflict management skills). The designs of these programs typically emphasize repeated practice and "overlearning" of targeted skills. The goal of such approaches is to produce highly developed, well organized, and extensive knowledge structures that can lead to automatized performance, what Holyoak (1991) called "routine expertise" (Kozlowski, 1998; Smith et al., 1997). Routine expertise results in high levels of performance when performance situations are familiar. However, such expertise does not help, and can actually hinder performance when problems become nonroutine, novel, and ill-defined (Kozlowski, 1998).

Adaptive performance reflects neither a set of trainable behavioral routines, nor a set of contextually prescribed skills. Instead, effective adaptability rests on skills in environmental pattern recognition, and pattern change recognition, skills in critical thinking and sense making, skills in formulating adaptive responses, and skills in regulating one's own behavior and that of followers (Bader, Zaccaro, & Kemp, 2004). Leader development strategies that are intended to grow adaptability skills need to use discovery learning strategies that prompt leaders to explore new ideas, challenges, and frames of reference (Smith et al., 1997; Zaccaro & Banks, 2004). Organizations typically do not provide the space for their budding executives to take such risks, preferring a form of "corporate Darwinism" (McCall, 1998), where executive "growth" comes through passing tests and clearing hurdles.

Growth of effective global leadership skills also requires different learning and development strategies. Yet companies still struggle to identify and implement best practices for such development (Suutari, 2002). Black and Gregersen (2000) argued that "the primary objective of global leadership training is stretching someone's mind past narrow domestic borders and creating a mental map of the entire world" (p. 175). Accordingly, the development of global executives would require developmental episodes targeted at different points in an organizational leader's career, to expand cultural awareness and requisite cross-cultural leadership skills. These episodes are likely to rest heavily on developmental assignments coupled with mental map reframing learning strategies (Black & Gregersen, 2000; Suutari, 2002).

The present chapter aims to summarize a framework of human resource management strategies of leader development that integrates developmental assessment and different modes and strategies of development with leader performance requirements at different career stages. Systemic and effective executive development should begin early in the leader's career, and change in concert with the job demands likely to be faced by the leader at higher organizational levels. As we describe this framework, we will use it to offer prescriptions for the development of adaptive and global executives.

Strategies of Leader Development

While a large cross section of developmental strategies exist (Day, 2001; McCauley & Van Velsor, 2004), we will focus primarily on (1) assessment and feedback, and (2) integrations of formal instruction, developmental assignments, and self-learning strategies (Zaccaro & Banks, 2004).

Leader Assessment and Feedback

Assessment has four functions in a systematic leader development program. The first function is to screen and select leaders for participation in the program. Such screening assessment should focus on (a) whether the leader has the potential to become a successful executive (McCall, 1998), and (b) whether the leader possesses a "readiness" for training and development (Noe, 2002). The assessment of executive potential rests on identifying "end-state competencies", or the attributes of successful executives, and then measuring their anticipated presence in rising leaders (Spreitzer et al., 1997). We have already noted one caveat with this approach — whether the executive competencies identified in the present will be comparably critical in a future state of the organization (Spreitzer et al., 1997). In today's rapidly changing business environment the likelihood is high that executive performance requirements will change over relatively short periods of time, along with corresponding competency models. Another concern is a lack of understanding regarding how end-state competencies exist or form in rising executives. One improbable perspective is that such leaders possess them in a less formed or "miniature" state (cf. McCall, 1998). More likely such competencies arise from targeted and tailored leadership experiences, if leaders have an ability to learn from those experiences (McCall, 1998; Spreitzer et al., 1997).

The assessment of readiness concerns the identification of attributes that predict the leader's ability and motivation to engage in developmental experiences. These attributes can include cognitive ability, functional and leadership experience, an orientation toward learning goals (i.e. increasing personal mastery, viewing errors as part of the learning process) versus toward performance (i.e. receiving positive evaluations in training, viewing errors as failure) (Ford, Smith, Weissbein, Gully, & Salas, 1998), an ability to learn from experience (McCall, 1994; Spreitzer et al., 1997), and an expectancy that developmental experiences will yield personal benefits (Baldwin & Ford, 1988) along with an efficacious belief that the leader can transfer these experiences into effective practices (Gist, 1989). The rising leaders that likely possess the strongest potential for executive leadership, and therefore are prime candidates for investment in leader development, will be those that have (a) the attributes associated with anticipated end-state competencies that are tied to future strategic goals and (b) the ability to learn and flourish in developmental contexts. Screening assessment batteries need to capture both of these components of executive potential.

The second function of development-based assessment is to evaluate the strengths and weaknesses of leaders at the onset of training. While such assessment might mirror the screening assessment, the purpose of these measures is to define more precisely critical developmental needs, and to establish a baseline for learning. Early assessment may also foster more self-awareness, which can enhance the developmental process (London, 2002).

This learning baseline is related to the third function of development-based assessment — to monitor and regulate one's progress through a developmental program. An effective program has intermediate goals that represent learning steps in development. These goals can be used in self-regulation processes to help a leader gauge the amount of personal growth that he or she is experiencing in the program, and make alterations if that growth is insufficient (London, 2002). Such processes are especially crucial in primarily self-directed and continuous learning programs. London (2002, p. 235) noted, for example that "continuous learning is self-regulated and managed. Leaders decide what they need, when they need it, and how to get it. They initiate and maintain their own learning processes." Assessment, whether formal or informal, represents a vital part of continuous and self-directed learning because it allows leaders to determine precisely what their learning needs are, and, more importantly, if their efforts are succeeding in satisfying these needs.

The fourth function of development-based assessment is to determine whether leader development programs have significant short- and long-term payoff for both the leader and the organization. Kirkpatrick (1994) referred to this form of assessment as reflecting two types of training evaluation criteria: behavior and results. Behavioral criteria represent the transfer of skills learned in training to the work setting and to on-the-job performance. Results criteria represent the utility of training and development for organizational strategy and goals. Such analyses can examine the utility of leader development against short-term costs and benefits, where fairly immediate gains are expected in leader performance and leader contributions to organizational productivity (Cascio, 1989). Mathieu and Leonard (1987) illustrated this approach in an analysis of supervisory skills training in 13 bank managers. They reported a one-year gain of $13,000, but a three-year gain of more than $100,000. This approach is not useful, however, for evaluating the utility of executive development programs in which gains are expected to emerge over a longer time frame in concert with far-reaching strategic goals. In such instances, while assessment of costs may be fairly explicit, the assessment of gains may be more tenuous and abstract.

Guthrie and King (2004) illustrated several of these assessments functions as they occur in the executive development programs at the Center for Creative Leadership. Prior to beginning these programs, leaders complete a large battery of personality and leadership skills measures, 360-degree or multirater instruments, open-ended essays and business cases, and interviews with their supervisors. The purposes of these assessments are to prepare the leader for participation in the program, establish a clear picture of personal strengths and weaknesses, and promote self-awareness and the beginning of self-insight. During the program, participants received other forms of more informal assessment including reflection exercises, peer and staff observations, videotapes and audiotapes of performance during exercises. These assessments are linked with pre-program assessments to intensify and consolidate the learning process. Post-program measures include follow-up 360-degree ratings, goal progress assessments, and informal assessment with feedback coaches. Guthrie and King portray the functions of developmental needs assessment, developmental progress assessment, and developmental results assessment. The program as described by Guthrie and King does not, however, include screening assessment or utility assessment for the leader's organization — those assessments are presumably left to the host organizations. Nonetheless, this effort combines multiple uses of assessment in an executive education program that has been ranked as one of the best in the world by *Business Week* and *The Financial Times* (http://www.ccl.org/leadership/news/2005/ft2005.aspx?pageId=735).

MultiSource Assessment and Feedback

Multisource assessment and feedback has become one of the most popular forms of leader assessment in management (Atwater & Waldman, 1998; Day, 2001; London & Smither, 1995). A number of studies have demonstrated the utility of this approach for subsequent leader development and productivity (e.g. Reilly, Smither, & Vasilopoulos, 1996; Walker & Smither, 1999). This method entails gathering assessments from different sources about a leader's attributes and performance. These sources can include self, subordinates, peers, supervisors, internal clients, and external stakeholders, customers, and suppliers (Chappelow, 2004; Day, 2001). "360-degree" feedback refers to assessments in which self-ratings are combined with ratings from direct reports, peers, *and* supervisors, with feedback provided separately for each group. The particular premise of such assessments is that leadership performance requirements differ across these sources and accordingly each one provides an alternate perspective of leader attributes, behavior, and performance.

Multisource assessments can serve as powerful tools in leader development programs. They are particularly effective in promoting self-awareness, because they can dramatize differences in how leaders perceive themselves relative to how other important stakeholders perceive them, particularly when there is consensus among ratings by others. As Chappelow (2004) noted, "managers receiving 360-degree feedback can be jarred to attention about their shortcomings by agreement among their raters" (p. 63). The existence of large perceptual differences often provides the clear spark for self-analysis and insight, especially when feedback of such differences occurs within a supportive developmental environment. Likewise the use of multiple raters can provide a more valid and comprehensive assessment of a leader's strengths and weaknesses; because perceptions of raters can differ substantially by source, measuring only a subset of leadership stakeholders will provide an incomplete summary of a leader's profile (Day, 2001).

The developmental utility of multirater assessment can vary according to the administration of feedback and the planning of follow-up exercises. Feedback from self-ratings as well as those by peers, superiors, and direct reports should be presented separately, but in a manner that facilitates easy comparisons (London & Smither, 1995). If possible, ratings should be accompanied with behavioral examples of effective and ineffective leadership (Kaplan, 1993). Such behavioral feedback is facilitated by the use of situation-based items in the assessment battery itself (Moses, Hollenbeck, & Sorcher, 1993). Developmental gains happen more readily when leaders discuss their ratings and feedback with their raters, particularly direct reports (Walker & Smither, 1999). For example, Walker and Smither reported that the highest performance increases from a 360-degree assessment occurred when rated managers met with their direct reports to gain greater insight and understanding about the ratings.

To be effective, the provision of feedback from multirater assessments needs to occur within a developmental climate, with the support of feedback coaches and the leader's organization. Also, coaches should help the leader use the ratings feedback to construct a development plan that includes learning goals as well as strategies for regulating and assessing learning gains (Chappelow, 2004). Seifert et al. (2003) contrasted conditions of giving feedback reports with or without facilitators and found that gains accrued to those individuals who received facilitated support. Chappelow (2004, p. 66) summarized the following seven excellent strategies for supporting multirater assessment and feedback:

- Establishing a systematic and safe learning environment by maintaining the confidential nature of the feedback data.
- Giving participants access to trained feedback facilitators for clarification about the data and for guidance in putting together a development plan.
- Involving superiors to gain buy-in for the participant's development plan.
- Allowing the participant and immediate boss to meet beforehand to discuss their goals for the process.
- Offering organizational support for the kinds of assignments that are known to contribute to effective development of leaders.
- Strategizing with the participant about how to receive ongoing feedback after the formal 360-degree feedback process is over.
- Structuring an organizational norm for following up periodically on the development plan.

Chappelow provides considerable details about these strategies and we refer the reader to that source. These strategies emphasize the important role multirater assessment can have in a leader development program.

Assessment and the Development of Adaptive and Global Leaders

How do the four functions of developmental assessment contribute to the growth of adaptive and global leaders? Screening assessment for executive adaptability potential should focus on the degree to which rising leaders have shown a disposition and skill to be adaptive in prior lower level leadership positions, and on the likelihood that they will be able to extend such skill to the more complex operating environment they are likely to face as executives. A disposition toward adaptability reflects such personal characteristics as openness, tolerance for uncertainty or ambiguity, resilience, optimism, and emotional stability (Bader, Zaccaro, & Kemp, 2004; LePine, Colquitt, & Erez, 2000; Kemp, Zaccaro, Jordan, & Flippo, 2004; Ployhart & Bliese, in press; Pulakos et al., 2002). These constructs are likely to predict executive outcomes. Indeed, Ritchie (1994) reported behavioral flexibility and tolerance of uncertainty as being among the strongest correlates of subsequently attained organizational level in a sample of rising managers.

Adaptive performance in current and prior positions can be assessed in several ways. Pulakos et al. (2002) developed measures that tapped one's frequency of prior experiences in situations requiring adaptability, and one's interest in working in such situations. They also developed behaviorally anchored rating scales used to measure effectiveness in situations having one or more of the following adaptive performance requirements (the definitions provided by Pulakos et al. (2002, p. 301) are indicated after each requirement):

- *Handling emergencies or crisis situations.* "Reacts appropriately and decisively to life-threatening or dangerous situations".
- *Handling work stress.* "Remains calm under pressure, handles frustration, and acts as a calming influence".

- *Solving problems creatively.* "Solves atypical, ill-defined, and complex problems".
- *Dealing with uncertain and unpredictable work situations.* "Adjusts and deals with unpredictable situations, shifts focus, and takes reasonable action".
- *Learning work tasks, technologies, and procedures.* "Anticipates, prepares for, and learns skills needed for future job requirements".
- *Demonstrating interpersonal adaptability.* "Adjusts interpersonal style to achieve goals working with new teams, coworkers, or customers".
- *Demonstrating cultural adaptability.* "Performs effectively in different cultures learning new languages, values, traditions, and politics".
- *Demonstrating physically oriented adaptability.* "Adjusts to various physical factors such as heat, noise, uncomfortable climates, and difficult environments".

Pulakos et al. administered performance scales assessing these items to supervisors of the managers being rated. Prior experience, interest in adaptive performance situations, and cognitive and personality variables predicted scores on these measures. While these assessments were not used in a developmental context, they represent good candidates for screening rising managers on their potential as adaptive executives.

The instrument developed by Pulakos et al. (2002) was not a multisource instrument, although we suspect it can be easily converted into one. A multisource instrument can provide a different assessment approach, based on its unique structure, to measuring adaptability. The premise of such assessments is that different constituencies of the leader require different sets of leadership responses, and often the leader may be less effective with one group than another. However, leader adaptability includes an ability to respond effectively to different social groups (Zaccaro, Gilbert, Thor, & Mumford, 1991; Pulakos, Arad, Donovan, & Plamondon, 2000). Accordingly, adaptability skills can be assessed not only by the aforementioned battery of measures, but also by the presence of high-effectiveness ratings across multiple rating sources. Consistency in perceptions of high performance across rating sources suggests that the rated leader is effective in adapting to the demands and requirements of different stakeholders, an adaptive performance requirement that grows in importance at levels of executive leadership (Zaccaro, 2001).

The strategies of screening high adaptability potential can apply as well to the screening of high potential global executives. Indeed, Pulakos et al. (2002) defined cultural adaptability as one of their key adaptive performance requirements. Other researchers have noted that some of the same dispositional qualities that portend high adaptability skills also apply to global leadership potential, including openness, emotional stability, and tolerance for ambiguity (Gregersen et al., 1998; Mendenhall et al., 1987; Suutari, 2002). Gregersen et al. (1998) add inquisitiveness or curiosity to this list. Connor (2000) described a global executive screening potential protocol that integrated a combination of dispositional ability and motivational attributes. She articulated the following four criteria to screen high potential for global executive leadership (p. 151):

> First, the individual was viewed as having potential to be promoted to a general manager or senior functional role within five years. Second, s/he was willing to accept either a two to three year rotational assignment outside his/her geographic division, or preferably, a permanent international career outside the home country. Third, the individual achieved exceptional

results during the last two to five years. Finally, s/he demonstrated the ability to learn and develop the skills and capabilities necessary to excel in a senior global leadership position.

Multisource assessment of these and related global leadership skills requires careful consideration of appropriate raters. Asking supervisors, peers, and subordinates from one's own national or cultural context may provide insufficient information regarding the ability to work effectively in multicultural environments. Such assessment, particularly if it is to be used to identify developmental goals and needs, must reflect a rater pool that includes an international mix of subordinates and peers, as well as supervisors that have international experience and can understand the competencies for effectiveness in global leadership domains (e.g. Gregersen et al., 1998).

The approaches that we have described to screen executive adaptability and global leadership potential can also be used for the second developmental function of assessment, that of highlighting strengths and weaknesses to define developmental needs more precisely. Once learning baselines and goals have been established, assessment tools that measure growth in adaptability skills and global leadership competencies can then be used to ascertain progress in training and development, the third function of developmental assessment (e.g. Caligiuri & Di Santo, 2001). Situation judgment tests and other forms of scenario-based assessment (Motowidlo, Dunnette, & Carter, 1990; Motowidlo & Tippins, 1993) can be used to gauge learning gains during training and development in understanding multicultural leadership issues, and in skills used to derive solutions to problems centering on such issues.

Many companies experience a significant shortage of available leaders who have the experience and skills to operate in a global environment (Black & Gregersen, 2000; Conner, 2000; Gregersen et al., 1998; Suutuari, 2002). Recall that the survey of Fortune 500 companies completed by Gregersen et al. reported that 85% of these companies "do not think they have an adequate number of global leaders" (p. 22). Accordingly, significant increases in the numbers of qualified and experienced leaders and managers who can be sent on international assignments can serve as one effective assessment of organizational gains from investments in global leadership development. Other forms of utility assessment can use more traditional dollar cost and benefits metrics of organizational training performance (Cascio, 1989), as applied in international business domains.

The assessment of organizational gains from programs targeted in the development of executive *adaptability* may be more difficult to achieve, however, because such gains may not be reflected in "routine" executive work. Instead, they may emerge more clearly in periods of organizational "revolution" (Griener, 1972) and significant change. However, while such periods provide strong opportunities for executives to demonstrate their adaptability skills, the turmoil that typically characterizes large-scale change may produce measurement "noise" that can obscure the assessment of organizational gain, especially over short-time frames. We urge that more HR research be focused on the assessment of organizational utility for developmental interventions that target executive adaptability.

Modes of Development

Leader development can occur through three modes or pathways — formal instruction, operational assignments, and self-learning programs (Day, 2001, Day & Zaccaro, 2004;

London, 2002; McCall, 1998; McCauley & Van Veslor, 2004; U.S. Army, 1999; Zaccaro & Banks, 2004). Formal instruction programs typically entail classroom-based course work, or relatively short-term workshops and seminars that provide presentations of general concepts, along with simulations and exercises. They include feedback intensive programs that involve increased self-awareness, identification of developmental needs, and construction of developmental goals and learning plans (Guthrie & King, 2004). They can also involve elaborated field exercises and large-scale simulations, such as the ones conducted by the U.S. Army at its National Training Center (Maggert, 2004).

These kinds of formal instruction programs comprise the large bulk of leader development efforts in most companies (Burke & Day, 1986; Day, 2001). However, such programs represent one part of a systematic approach to growing leadership skills. Work experiences in several forms represent another critical mode of leader development, but one that is rarely structured in most organizations. McCall (1998) noted that in companies,

> Their managers are learning from experiences, from the mistakes they make and what happens to them afterward, and from the challenges they face on the job. In this respect it is impossible not to develop people....development happens whether planned or not. The real issue is not that companies don't develop talent but rather that they aren't aware of how these unmanaged processes are working, of what their talented people are learning, or of what they could be doing to influence the kinds of leaders being produced (pp. 1–2)

Experience-based learning encompasses the leader's acquisition of skills and knowledge from encountering new job demands, tasks, roles, responsibilities, and relationships (Day, 2004; Ohlott, 2004). While leaders invariably 'learn by doing', there often exists little structure or few support mechanisms to enhance and augment lessons learned from experience. The development of effective adaptive and global leaders will require a more systematic structuring of work assignments and developmental experiences.

Researchers have specified several types of job assignments that constitute learning experiences. Zaccaro and Banks (2004) identified one set of developmental assignments as "stamping-in" experiences, where leaders complete work tasks that reflect recently acquired (presumably through formal instruction) skills and knowledge. These tasks represent the *typical* kind of job demands that the leader is likely to encounter in a particular role. To enhance development, these demands need to range from the simplest tasks that define job performance to the most complex. The intention is to develop "routine expertise" (Holyoak, 1991). Such expertise entails highly proceduralized skills that follow from well-developed, well-organized, and extensive knowledge structures about the job and its context (Holyoak, 1991; Kozlowski, 1998; Smith et al., 1997). In essence, the leader moves from a relatively novice level of skill performance to an expert level, where most job demands that comprise a particular job role are easily accomplished.

Action learning represents a slightly different form of experience-based development. In action learning programs, leaders work on real-time organizational problems (Day, 2001; Palus & Horth, 2004). These are not quite stamping-in experiences because the problems selected may pose unique challenges not previously encountered as part of existing job requirements. Leaders are expected to analyze the key elements of a problem, derive and evaluate potential solutions, and propose an action plan to senior management (Day, 2001), In some instances, action learning also entails the implementation of solutions. Palus and Horth (2004) define three objectives of such programs (p. 461):

> Delivering measurable results in service of the organization's work, learning and communication lessons specific to a particular context, and developing individual and collective capabilities for learning and leadership more generally.

Day (2001) described action learning as occurring in a "microworld," or a temporary work system that is "designed to be realistic yet safe (p. 603)." Leaders typically work as part of teams in which decisions need to be made not only about the problem itself, but also how the team will organize confront the encountered problem. Accordingly, such learning rests on the development of trust and a climate of psychological safety (Day, 2001; Edmondson, 1999).

A third kind of experienced-based learning makes use of "stretch" assignments (McCauley, Eastman, & Ohlott, 1995). Such assignments are similar to action learning projects because they also pose unique challenges to the job incumbent. However, while "stamping-in" assignments and action learning projects are designed to expand and deepen nascent expertise, stretch assignments are designed to challenge developed expertise and demonstrate to leaders the limitations of their current skill sets and knowledge structures. The purpose is to prompt them to recognize that they need to develop richer and more complex understandings of the operating environment they will encounter as they rise to higher levels of the organization. Accordingly these assignments need to reflect considerable challenge, where early failure is expected. Ohlott (2004) argued that a developmental assignment

> must be something that stretches the people, pushes them out of their comfort zone, and requires them to think differently. It may involve roles that are not well-defined, and it usually contains some elements that are new to the person. These assignments place people in challenging situations full of problems to solve, dilemmas to resolve, obstacles to overcome, and choices to make under conditions of risk and uncertainty (p. 154).

Ohlott (2004, see also McCauley et al., 1995) defined several general categories of developmental assignments that stretch the budding leader and prompt the development of new and more complex frames of reference. These include working in unfamiliar roles, being responsible for structural and policy changes in the organization, dealing with inherited problems, encountering tasks that have greater visibility and scope within the organization, working with different external stakeholders, and working in more culturally diverse groups and populations.

A third mode of leader development, self-learning, has received considerably less attention in both the applied and research-oriented literature. Self-development is a process in which the learner has responsibility for establishing the conditions, content, context, and pace of learning (Boyce, 2002; Manz & Manz, 1991; Noe, 2002; Piskurich, 1993).

Effective self-development follows from the application of several learning processes. Cortina, Zaccaro, & Chiara (2004) noted that an effective self developer (p. 6):

- Conducts a self-needs assessment,
- Defines the attributes to be targeted in self-development,
- Establishes the learning goals and objectives,
- Identifies learning resources,
- Develops learning strategies and exercises,
- Defines the pace and time frame of learning,
- Establishes the criteria for evaluating growth, and
- Evaluates gains, and making adjustments.

This form of leader development is perhaps the most difficult because it rests almost entirely on self-initiative. Managers rarely feel they have the time for such activities. When they do engage in self-learning exercises, they are likely to practice existing skills so as to make them stronger (or bring them back to higher levels of expertise) than to pursue developmental needs. However, self-learning strategies are becoming a more crucial avenue of leader development. As the pace of change increases, and leaders and managers encounter a broader range of new ideas, technologies and concepts, organizations cannot constantly revise their formal instructional programs to keep up. They will need to rely increasingly on the self-initiative and self-learning skills of their rising leaders to augment formal instruction and developmental assignments (London, 2002).

Modes of Development for Adaptive and Global Leaders

Zaccaro and Banks (2004) argued for a framework of leader development that integrates formal instruction with stamping-in and stretching developmental experiences. They also applied their framework to the development of a leader's ability to manage change, a central component of adaptive leadership.

Formal instruction in development programs targeting adaptive leadership skills needs to avoid learning strategies that emphasize over-learning and behavioral routinization. Instead, growing adaptability skills requires a focus on developing "adaptive expertise." Kozlowski, 1998, p. 119) argues that:

> Adaptive expertise entails a deep comprehension of the conceptual structure of the problem domain. Knowledge must be organized, but the structure must be flexible. The process goes beyond procedural knowledge of an automatic sort. Adaptive experts understand when and why particular procedures are appropriate as well as when they are not. Comprehension entails active processing, allowing recognition of shifts in the situation that necessitate adaptability. Adaptive experts are able to recognize changes in task priorities and the need to modify strategies and actions.

Thus, according to Kozlwoski (1998), adaptive experts have a deeper understanding of performance domains that allows them to know that certain procedures are more appropriate for certain situations, and also to know when those procedures must change. Also, these deeper and more flexible knowledge representations facilitate the formulation of novel performance strategies under conditions of environmental change and unfamiliarity (Smith et al., 1997).

Adaptability training should emphasize the development of skills in adaptive problem-solving processes, self- and team-regulation, and metacognitive thinking (Bell & Kozlowski, 2002; Kozlowski, 1998; Kozlowski et al., 2001; Smith et al., 1997; Zaccaro & Banks, 2004). Adaptive problem-solving processes include situational awareness and understanding, particularly of changing contingencies in the leader's operating environment, the specification and implementation of solutions to problems arising from organizational change, and motivation of followers to change established routines. Self- and team-regulation skills entail the specification of personal and team goals and the pathways of reaching those goals. These skills also include monitoring progress along these pathways, and adjusting behaviors when performance levels are incongruent with expected goal progress. Such skills are particularly important when environmental change introduces obstacles that block original organizational goals. In these instances adaptive leaders will need to modify these goal, modify existing goals paths, or try and remove the impeding obstacles.

Metacognitive skills refer to competencies in reflecting upon and understanding how one's own cognitive processes are operating in particular problem domains (Smith et al., 1997). Metacognitive problem-solving skills reflect an expertise in knowing what cognitive abilities are applicable in particular problem domains and in evaluating the products of their application. Individuals use such skills to recognize change and, more importantly, when existing performance strategies no longer suit changing environmental conditions (Smith et al., 1997). They also use metacognition to facilitate the application of self- and team-regulation skills in problem solving (Bell & Kozlowksi, 2002; Smith et al., 1997).

Adaptability training programs that use formal instruction should effectively integrate adaptive problem-solving skills, self-regulation, and metacognitive thinking. They should utilize discovery learning strategies, where participants actively explore and experiment with new ideas and concepts (Kozlowski, 1998; Smith et al., 1997). Instructors can lead or prompt this process, but participants are left to discover the targeted principles.

Stretch assignments represent a key means of developing adaptable leaders (Zaccaro & Banks, 2004). Such assignments are explicitly designed to challenge the leader's existing frame and encourage him or her to adopt new ways of thinking and new behavior patterns. Accordingly, they encourage use of the kinds of skills that reside at the heart of adaptive leadership. Repeated experiences with such assignments should also establish deeper levels of adaptive expertise where leaders are able to examine and understand the processes of change at a broader and more comprehensive level. The development of such expertise from developmental assignments should also lead to greater realization of how processes of change apply to and influence strategic decision-making.

Global leadership requires adaptability, as leaders need to respond to diverse cultural demands and influences (Pulakos et al., 2002). Accordingly, the training and development of global leadership skills includes several of the aforementioned recommendations for developing adaptive leadership. However, training for effective global leadership entails some unique features as well. Formal instructional programs need to focus on such knowledge and skills as cultural awareness and sensitivity, cross-cultural communication, multicultural team leadership, perspective switching (from global to local and vice versa), international business knowledge, international strategy formulation and visioning, international organizational design; conflict management and negotiation, and building global alliances (Alldredge & Nilan, 2000; Black & Gregersen, 2000; Brake, 1997; Dalton & Ernst, 2004; Gregersen et al., 1998; Maznevski & DiStefano, 2000; Morrison, 2000).

Most formal instructional programs for global leadership emphasize information about relevant countries and/or cultures the leader may operate within, along with some limited cultural sensitivity and language training (Mendenhall et al., 1987; Mendenhall & Stahl, 2000). This training typically occurs just prior to an international assignment, or in a post-arrival class containing all of the expatriates working in-country (Mendenhall & Stahl, 2000). The concerns with these forms of training pertain to their specificity regarding the locus of the international assignment. Pre-assignment training conveys information primarily about the assignment-based culture, without emphasizing broader multicultural leadership skills. In-country training also emphasizes such knowledge, but does not typically cover the range of unique cross-cultural challenges that different expatriates need to confront (Mendenhall & Stahl, 2000).

Salas, Burke, Wilson-Donnelly, and Fowlkes (2004) suggested the use of event-based scenarios in multicultural leadership training. Such training uses scenarios that represent critical catalysts of skill-based behavior. These scenarios can be constructed to target a range of multicultural leadership competencies. Specifically, Salas et al. argued for three types of event-based scenarios that can be used for leadership development in cross-cultural contexts. These are (p. 317):

> (a) scenarios that serve to illustrate the cultural biases inherent in the leader's own culture (own cultural awareness), (b) scenarios that serve to promote cultural awareness of broad cultural dimensions and how they are manifested with regard to key leadership functions and teamwork, and (c) scenarios that develop the knowledge, skills, and attitudes that leaders need within these domains (essentially giving them strategies and opportunities to practice in a simulated context).

Note that this approach emphasizes a broader perspective to multicultural training than the typical information-based programs. Trainees are provided with skills that can generalize across most cultural domains, not just the culture they happen to be headed to on assignment. As such, this approach represents a useful platform for formal instructional programs.

Another approach taken by companies represents an integration of formal instruction with some developmental assignment, typically an action-learning project (Black & Gregerson, 2000; Mendenhall & Stahl, 2000). These programs have the advantage of facilitating skill transfer from artificial training domains to real-time, real-place work situations. Many researchers and practitioners agree that overseas work assignments represent one of the most effective means of growing effective global leaders (Gregersen et al., 1998; Kohonen, 2005; Oddou, Mendenhall, & Ritchie, 2000; Stroh, Black, Mendenhall, & Gregersen, 2005; Suutari, 2002; Yan, Zhu, & Hall, 2002). Gregersen et al. (1998) reported in their survey of company executives that 80% of them "identified living and working in a foreign country as the single most influential experience in their lives" (p. 30). These are prototypical stretch assignments because they are intended to break leader mono-cultural perspectives and help them develop broader and deeper frames of reference. These more complex frames are likely to encompass different cultural perspectives as well as an integrated mental model of global business dynamics.

Career Perspectives of Adaptive and Global Leadership Development

We have outlined some leader development strategies and applied them to the training of global and adaptive leaders. However, most leader development models fail to take an integrated career-long perspective that accounts for shifting leader performance requirements as leaders rise through organizational ranks. In this final section, we examine one career perspective model of leader development and apply it to the development of adaptive and global leaders.

A Career Model of Leader Development

Mumford et al. (2000) specified a systematic *prescriptive* model of leader career growth that identifies the kinds of developmental issues that generally occur at different career points, and links these issues to alternate kinds of instructional and operational experiences, that ought to occur at each different career points. We present only a brief summary of their model in this chapter and refer the reader to that source for more details. Figure 1 illustrates the first part of their model covering the early part of a leader's career. This part of the model would prescribe the developmental path for managers and leaders from junior levels to middle management. Figure 2 presents the rest of Mumford et al.'s model as it applies to rising executive leaders.

According to Mumford et al. (2000), the developmental issues that are likely to be pertinent early in a leader's career involve the learning of organizational norms, rules, and basic processes involved in implementing policies and procedures. As novices begin to gain experience, the developmental issues change to the development of coherent knowledge structures that integrate real-world experience with basic declarative concepts (i.e. the emergence of elaborated tacit knowledge). Other developmental issues for early leaders include the development of basic problem-solving skills, evaluation standards, and a more affective commitment (cf. Meyer, Allen, & Smith, 1993) to organizational goals.

The training and assignment experiences of entry-level leaders begin with initial technical training and socialization, typically through formal course instruction, followed by very structured work experiences under close supervision. Most performance requirements for these leaders are technical in nature with some limited responsibilities for leading small teams. As they gain routine expertise, such leaders can be given more autonomy, some low-level stretch assignments, and greater responsibility for developing others. In terms of early career development, the major dynamics center on an orientation toward enculturation and a growing organizational identity.

As leaders gain organizational and career tenure, along with basic experiences in small group leadership roles, they typically receive more advanced technical training, and then may be tasked with problems having multiple components, decisions involving more autonomy and discretion, and projects with greater supervisory responsibilities. Note that these experiences correspond to both the stamping-in and stretch experiences (in order of complexity)

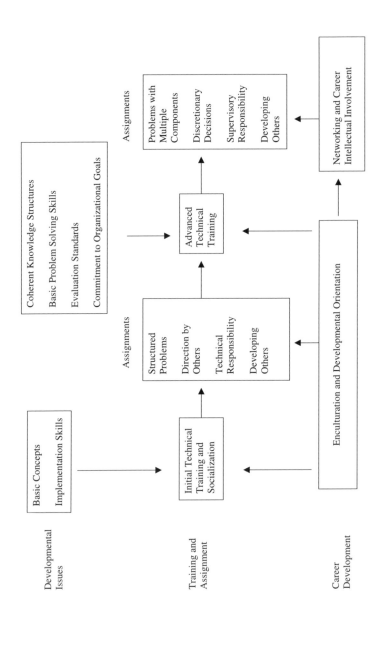

Figure 1: Conceptual Model of Leader Development – Early Career Stages (adapted from *The Leadership Quarterly*, 11, Mumford, Marks, Connelly, Zaccaro, & Reiter-Palmon, *Development of Leadership Skills: Development and Timing*, p. 91, copyright (2000), with permission from Elsevier).

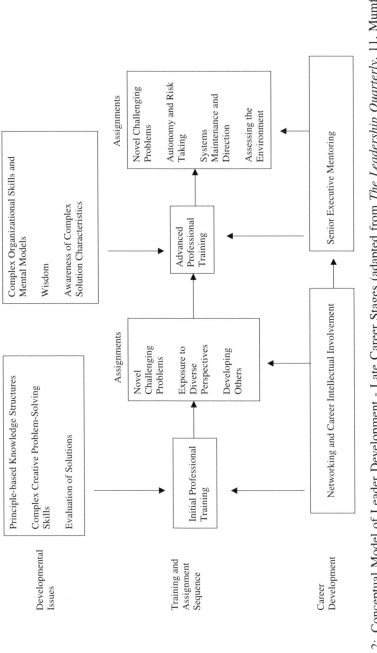

Figure 2: Conceptual Model of Leader Development - Late Career Stages (adapted from *The Leadership Quarterly*, 11, Mumford, Marks, Connelly, Zaccaro, & Reiter-Palmon, *Development of Leadership Skills: Development and Timing*, p. 91, copyright (2000), with permission from Elsevier). Note : The contents of the first "Assignments" box and the second "Professional Training box" in this figure have been modified from the original source to more accurately reflect the text from Mumford et at. (2000). p. 90.

described earlier. At this stage, the career developmental dynamics begin to change to more network building, and a greater intellectual involvement in one's work and career.

As leaders move into higher organizational ranks (into levels of middle management), developmental issues turn to the acquisition of more elaborated principle-based knowledge structures, along with complex problem-solving skills, and greater ability to evaluate novel and long-term solutions. The central concern at this leadership level is growth in the ability of these rising leaders to develop more comprehensive and complex mental models that encode their correspondingly more complex operating environment. Training and formal instruction begins to reflect professional skills and issues, as well as organization-wide dynamics. Middle and upper middle-level leaders can receive developmental assignments that involve solving novel and more challenging problems and working with multiple individuals and groups, especially those having very diverse perspectives. The career development dynamic at this point remains primarily the building of networks, acquisition of broader social capital, and greater career involvement.

As organizational leaders begin to approach executive levels, the developmental issues become the acquisition of complex organizational and system-wide problem-solving skills, the development of broader social perspective and understanding (i.e. wisdom), and a growing awareness of complex system-level solution characteristics. That is, these organizational leaders need to acquire skills in solving organization-wide problems that can have long-term systematic implications. Developmental assignments include continuing experience with novel and challenging problems, except from a more system-wide scope and longer time frame than previous problems, greater autonomy and risk-taking in decision making, more responsibility for organizational system maintenance, and for scanning and interpreting the organization's external environment. The career dynamics shift at this point to senior executive mentoring.

Mumford et al.'s (2000) model provides a useful, prescriptive approach to a leader's career progression. It specifies the kinds of experiences that will likely be more beneficial at different career points. It also associates developmental work experiences with key developmental goals and dynamics, and arranges these in a progression from early to late career development. The model can cover many years of a leader's career. Mumford et al. noted (p. 90)

> It may take up to 20 years before leaders acquire all of the skills needed to solve novel, ill-defined organizational problems. Moreover, development in this sense is progressive, moving from simple knowledge structures and straightforward technical and social skills, to complex integrated knowledge structures that support the effective application of creative problem solving and systems skills. Finally, it should be recognized that the kinds of experiences [that] promote skill development at one point in a leader's career are different from those that may be beneficial later.

Developing Adaptive and Global Leaders

Mumford et al.'s (2000) model suggests that adaptive and global leadership requirements will vary across the career span of the company leader. Developmental interventions need to change accordingly. For entry level and junior leaders, work demands are fairly structured and more predictable than at higher organizational levels (Katz & Kahn, 1978; Jacobs & Jaques, 1987). Such leaders are primarily responsible for establishing short-term goals for themselves and for small organizational units within the context of objectives established by managers at higher levels. Adaptive performance requirements (cf. Pulakos et al., 2002) at this level are likely to consist of learning new roles, tasks, and responsibilities, dealing with unexpected blocks to established goals, dealing with stress in high work load situations, and interacting with subordinates from diverse backgrounds. Junior leaders in global organizations may be required to coordinate their work activities with peers and supervisors from other nations and cultures.

A significant component of junior-level leadership involves goal setting and unit task completion. Accordingly, formal instruction in adaptability at this level should focus on self-regulation and metacognitive skill development (Smith, et al., 1997). These skills will facilitate goal progress and help leaders recognize when they need to adjust their tasks and activities as their environment changes. Because some adaptive performance requirements at this level involve social demands, formal instructional programs should also target social competencies, especially those that help leaders adjust their leadership style to the diversity among their subordinates (Caruso & Wolfe, 2004; Zaccaro, 2002).

Global leadership performance requirements at entry and junior levels of organizational leadership typically involve interactions in small group settings with culturally diverse subordinates and peers. Accordingly, the social competencies that would be targeted in adaptability training can also apply to multicultural leadership. Formal instructional programs for multicultural leadership development at lower levels should also foster greater cultural awareness and cross-cultural communications skills.

At the entry level of leadership, work roles are sufficiently unfamiliar to the leader that they provide ongoing developmental experiences. However, these experiences are more likely to be stamping-in assignments with the goal of producing routine expertise. As these leaders gain such expertise and greater trust from their supervisors, they can be given stretch experiences, such as temporary assignments to other functional domains, responsibility for handling difficult subordinates, and new jobs having slightly higher scope and visibility. Such assignments begin to challenge the leader to think in different ways and sow the seeds for more effective adaptation.

Developmental work experiences that foster multicultural leadership development at junior levels include travel to international conferences, short-term international assignments, and membership on culturally diverse project teams (Dalton & Ernst, 2004). As junior leaders gain expertise and experience, they can be given longer international assignments, asked to lead culturally diverse teams, and even transferred to international job positions having comparable or slightly expanded scope and scale (Suutari, 2002; Oddou et al., 2000; Gregersen et al., 1998). Each of these assignments has the capacity to broader the leader's cultural perspective and frame of reference in correspondence with his or her level of work complexity. These assignments, coupled with formal instruction targeting the aforementioned skills, can provide a sound foundation for international leadership at the next organizational level.

Performance requirements at middle management levels entail managing multiple small business units, each often having competing demands and needs (Zaccaro, 2001).

Middle managers are also tasked with translating the strategic goals and decisions established by company executives into more concrete goals and tasks for lower level units (Katz & Kahn, 1978). Their decisions to allocate resources among different units need to reflect these executive priorities. Adaptive performance requirements at middle management levels include not only those that characterize lower level leaders, but also handling unit-level diversity and dealing with greater uncertainty and unpredictability as their work becomes less structured. International leadership requirements may include responsibilities for managing groups that are functionally linked but geographically dispersed across cultural boundaries. Also, the translation by middle level leaders of strategic organizational policy to more short-term plans and goals may require greater accommodation and assimilation of international economics and policy dynamics.

Because middle level leaders work with and supervise sometimes competing units, formal instruction for adaptive leadership should focus on conflict management and negotiation (Zaccaro, 2001). Such instruction should also include large-scale change management skills (Zaccaro & Banks, 2004). Formal instruction for international middle managers should center on skills in leading different multicultural units, and switching perspectives from global to local domains. Such instruction should also include knowledge of international business dynamics (Gregersen et al., 1998), and awareness of how different cultural dimensions can influence such dynamics (Salas et al., 2004).

Developmental assignments that prompt growth of adaptability skills in middle managers should entail greater involvement in strategic thinking and decision-making processes. Examples of such assignments include working on strategic-level project teams, reorganizing a division or major unit within the company, or confronting and managing a large-scale business crisis or large-scale organizational change effort (Ohlott, 2004). The management of several culturally diverse teams or multiple culturally homogeneous teams, with each team coming from a different culture, constitutes developmental assignments for international middle managers (Maznevski & DiStefano, 2000). Also, extended expatriation and action learning on strategic-level international projects will provide opportunities to challenge and stretch existing cultural perspectives of middle level managers (e.g., Oddou et al., 2000). These and similar assignments involve exposure to novel responsibilities that are somewhat strategic in nature. They also require consideration and management of complex issues from multiple business units. The resolution of these assignments should enhance middle managers' abilities to manage change and adapt to dynamic organizational-level circumstances, including those that extend across national boundaries.

Executive level performance requirements include analysis and interpretation of the organization's external business environment and making strategic decisions in reaction to environmental shifts (Zaccaro, 2001). Executive leaders need to develop a frame of reference that makes sense of the complex organizational environment and can be used by lower level managers for their own sense making and planning (Jacobs & Jaques, 1987). They are responsible for long-term visioning, the introduction of structural changes and the formulation of corporate-wide policies (Katz & Kahn, 1978).

Executive leadership entails near constant adaptive performance requirements because of the high levels of informational and social complexity that comprise executive job demands (Hambrick, Finkelstein, & Mooney, 2005; Zaccaro, 2001). Informational complexity reflects the amount and pace of information that the executive must assimilate and the complexity and diversity of that information (Zaccaro, 2001). Social complexity arises from the complex array of internal and external stakeholders that the executive must consider, as well as the need to balance the demands and requirements of these different stakeholder groups when implementing social change in organizations (Zaccaro, 2001). These forms of complexity create constant demands on executives for adaptability. Because most companies today are increasingly international in scope, executive informational and social complexities extend beyond national and cultural boundaries.

Formal instruction that targets adaptive and global executive-level leadership should focus on principles of strategic decision making, analysis of national and international business trends, and the formation of global alliances (Alldredge & Nilan, 2000; Gregersen et al., 1998). However, effective development of executive leaders is more likely to proceed from repeated developmental experiences in dynamic, novel, global, and increasingly strategic problem domains. Such experiences can include integrating strategic decision making for national and foreign subsidiaries of a global corporation, starting or heading a new foreign-based division of the corporation, participating in corporate-level strategic meetings, and representing the organization to high-level stakeholder groups (cf. Suutari, 2002). These developmental experiences provide opportunities for rising executives to develop mental models and frames of reference that correspond to the high levels of social and informational complexity characterizing their operational environment. They also facilitate the use of these highly complex mental models in strategy formation and implementation. Accordingly, the successful completion of these assignments should produce the highly adaptive executive who can operate comfortably in an international environment.

Conclusion

The intent of this chapter was to elucidate HRM strategies that contribute to the development of adaptive and global leaders. We described the contributions of assessment and feedback to such development. We also described how different modes of leader development, particularly formal instruction and developmental assignments, can be integrated to provide a systematic approach to the training of leadership skills for effectiveness in dynamic and international environments. Perhaps, the most important conclusion of this chapter is that such an integration of leader development strategies needs to evolve across the leader's career as he or she rises through different levels of organizational leadership.

This point requires that organizations build integrated and systematic development programs that reflect leadership performance requirements at different levels. Organizations that construct such programs can gain considerable competitive advantage because their leaders will have access to learning opportunities and assignments that correspond to their developmental needs. Many researchers and practitioners cited in this chapter have noted the inadequacy of current leader development programs in growing significant numbers of effective global and adaptive leaders, and the need for better and more comprehensive approaches to such development. The strategies and principles articulated here should begin to address this need.

References

Albano, C. (2000). *What is adaptive leadership?* Online paper from http://www.selfgrowth.com/articles/calbano.html.

Alldredge, M. E., & Nilan, K. J. (2000). 3M's leadership competency model: An internally developed solution. *Human Resource Management, 39*, 133–145.

Atwater, L., & Waldman, D. (1998). 360-degree feedback and leader development. *Leadership Quarterly, 9*, 423–426.

Bader, P. K., Zaccaro, S. J., & Kemp, C. F. (2004). Predicting leader adaptability with leader trait patterns. Paper presented at the *19th annual conference of the Society for Industrial and Organizational Psychology*, Chicago, IL, April 2–4.

Baldwin, T. P., & Ford, J. K. (1988). Transfer of training: A review and directions for future research. *Personnel Psychology, 41*, 63–105.

Barrick, M. R., Day, D. V., Lord, R. G., & Alexander, R. A. (1991). Assessing the utility of executive leadership. *Leadership Quarterly, 2*, 9–22.

Bell, B. S., & Kozlowski, S. W. J. (2002). Adaptive guidance: Enhancing self-regulation, knowledge, and performance in technology-based training. *Personnel Psychology, 55*, 267–306.

Black, J. S., & Gregersen, H. B. (2000). High impact training: Forging leaders for the global frontier. *Human Resource Management, 39*, 173–184

Boyce, L. (2004). *Propensity for leadership self-development: Understanding, predicting, and supporting leadership self-development performance.* (Doctoral dissertation, George Mason University, 2004). *Dissertation Abstracts International, 65*(01), 468.

Brake, T. (1997). *The global leader: Critical factors for creating the world class organization.* Chicago: Irwin Professional Publishing.

Burke, M. J., & Day, R. R. (1986). A cumulative study of the effectiveness of managerial training. *Journal of Applied Psychology, 71*, 242–245.

Caligiuri, P., & Di Santo, V. (2001). Global competence: What is it and can it be developed through international assignment? *Human Resource Planning, 24*(3), 27–36.

Caruso, D. R., & Wolfe, C. J. (2004). Emotional intelligence and leadership development. In: D.V. Day, S. J. Zaccaro & S. M. Halpin (Eds), *Leader development for transforming organization* (pp. 237–266). Mahwah, NJ: Lawrence Erlbaum Associates.

Cascio, W. F. (1989). Using utility analysis to assess training outcomes. In: I. L. Goldstein (Ed.), *Training and development in organizations* (pp. 63–88). San Francisco: Jossey-Bass.

Center for Creative Leadership. (2005). *Financial Times* survey ranks Center for Creative Leadership among top 10 worldwide in executive education. Retrieved December 23, 2005 from http://www.ccl.org/leadership/news/2005/ft2005.aspx?pageId=735.

Chappelow, C. T. (2004). 360-degree feedback. In: C. D. McCauley & E. Van Velsor (Eds), *The Center for Creative Leadership handbook of leadership development* (pp. 58–84). San Francisco, CA: Wiley.

Conference Board. (1999). Developing leaders. *HR Executive Review, 7*, 1–19

Conner, J. (2000). Developing the global leaders of tomorrow. *Human Resource Management, 39*(2, 3), 147.

Cortina, J., Zaccaro, S. J., & Chiara, J. (2004). *Promoting realistic self-assessment as a basis for effective leader self development.* Alexandria, VA: Mirum Corporation.

Dalton, M. A., & Ernst, C. T. (2004). Developing leaders for global roles. In: C. D. McCauley & E. Van Velsor (Eds), *The Center for Creative Leadership handbook of leadership development* (pp. 361–382). San Francisco, CA: Wiley.

Day, D. V. (2001). Leadership development: A review in context. *Leadership Quarterly, 11*, 581–613.

Day, D. V., & Lord, R. G. (1988). Executive leadership and organizational performance: Suggestions for a new theory and methodology. *Journal of Management, 14*, 453–464.

Day, D. V., & Zaccaro, S. J. (2004). Toward a science of leader development. In: D. V. Day, S. J. Zaccaro & S. M. Halpin (Eds), *Leader development for transforming organization* (pp. 383–399). Mahwah, NJ: Lawrence Erlbaum Associates.

Day, D. V. (2004). Leadership processes and follower self-identity. *Personnel Psychology, 57*(2), 517–520.

Dollinger, M. J. (1984). Environmental boundary spanning and information processing effects on organizational performance. *Academy of Management Journal, 27*, 351–368.

Edmondson, A. (1999). Psychological safety and learning behavior in work teams. *Administrative Science Quarterly, 44*, 350–383.

Ford, J. K., Smith, E. M., Weissbein, D. A., Gully, S. M., & Salas, E. (1998). The influence of goal orientation, metacognitive activity, and practice strategies on learning outcome and transfer. *Journal of Applied Psychology, 83*(2), 218–233.

Gist, M. E. (1989). The influence of training method on self-efficacy and idea generation among managers. *Personnel Psychology, 42*(4), 787–805.

Gregersen, H. B., Morrison, A., & Black, J. S. (1998). Developing leaders for the global frontier. *Sloan Management Review, 40*(1), 21–33.

Greiner, L. E. (1972). Evolution and revolution as organizations grow. *Harvard Business Review, 50,* (July–August).

Guthrie, V. A., & King, S. N. (2004). Feedback-intensive programs. In: C. D. McCauley & E. Van Velsor (Eds), *The Center for Creative Leadership handbook of leadership evelopment* (pp. 25–57). San Francisco, CA: Wiley.

Hambrick, D. C., & Mason, P. A. (1984). Upper echelons: The organization as a reflection of its top managers. *Academy of Management Review, 9*, 195–206.

Hambrick, D. C., Finkelstein, S., & Mooney, A. C. (2005). Executive job demands: New insights for explaining strategic decisions and leader behaviors. *Academy of Management Review, 30*, 472–491.

Hart, S. L., & Quinn, R. E. (1993). Roles executives play: CEOs, behavioral complexity, and firm performance. *Human Relations, 46*, 543–574.

Heifetz, R. A., & Laurie, D. L. (1997). The work of leadership. *Harvard Business Review, 75*, 124–134.

Hitt, M. A., Keats, B. W., & DeMarie, S. M. (1998). Navigating in the new competitive landscape: Building strategic flexibility and competitive advantage in the 21st century. *Academy of Management Executive, 12*, 22–42.

Hitt, M. A., & Tyler, B. B. (1991). Strategic decision models: Integrating different perspectives. *Strategic Management Journal, 12*, 327–351.

Holyoak, K. J. (1991). Symbolic connectionism: Toward third-generation theories of expertise. In: K. A., Ericasson & J. Smith (Eds), *Toward a general theory of expertise* (pp. 301–336). Cambridge, England: Cambridge University Press.

Howell, J. M., & Avolio, B. J. (1993). Transformational leadership, transactional leadership, locus of control, and support for innovation: Key predictors of consolidated-business-unit performance. *Journal of Applied Psychology, 78*, 891–902.

Howell, J. M., & Higgins, C. A. (1990). Champions of technological innovation. *Administrative Science Quarterly, 35*, 317–341.

Iaquinto, A. L., & Frederickson, J. W. (1997). Top management team agreement about the strategic decision process: A test of some of its determinants and consequences. *Strategic Management Journal, 18*, 63–75.

Ireland, R. D., & Hitt, M. A. (1999). Achieving and maintaining strategic competitiveness in the 21st Century: The role of strategic leadership. *Academy of Management Executive, 13,* 43–57.

Jacobs, T. O., & Jaques, E. (1987). Leadership in complex systems. In: J. Zeidner (Ed.), *Human productivity enhancement.* New York: Praeger.

Kaplan, R. E. (1993). 360-degree feedback PLUS: Boosting the power of co-worker ratings for executives. *Human Resource Management, 32*(2&3), 299–314.

Katz, D., & Kahn, R. L. (1978). *The social psychology of organizations* (2nd ed.). New York: Wiley.

Kemp, C. F., Zaccaro, S. J., Jordan, M., & Flippo, S. (2004). Cognitive, social, and dispositional influences on leader adaptability. Paper presented at the *19th annual conference of the Society for Industrial and Organizational Psychology*, Chicago, IL, April 2–4.

Kirkpatrick, D. (1994). *Evaluating training programs: The four levels.* San Francisco, CA: Berrett-Koehler.

Kohonen, E. (2005). Developing global leaders through international assignments: An identity construction perspective. *Personnel Review, 34*(1), 22.

Kozlowski, S. W. J. (1998). Training and developing adaptive teams: Theory, principles, and research. In: J. A. Cannon-Bowers & E. Salas (Eds), *Decision making under stress: Implications for training and simulation* (pp. 115–153). Washington, DC: American Psychological Association.

Kozlowski, S. W. J., Toney, R. J., Mullens, M. E., Weissbein, D. A., Brown, K. G., & Bell, B. S. (2001). Developing adaptability: A theory for the design of integrated-embedded training systems. In: E. Salas (Ed.), *Advances in human performance and cognitive engineering research* (Vol. 1, pp. 59–123). Amsterdam: JAI/Elsevier Press

LePine, J. A., Colquitt, J. A., & Erez, A. (2000). Adaptability to changing task contexts: Effects of general cognitive ability, conscientiousness, and openness to experience. *Personnel Psychology, 53,* 563–593.

London, M. (2002). *Leadership development: Paths to self-insight and professional growth.* Mahwah, NJ: Lawrence Erlbaum Associates.

London, M., & Smither, J.W. (1995). Can multi-source feedback change self-evaluation, skill development, and performance? *Personnel Psychology, 48,* 375–390.

Maggert, L. E. (2004) Leadership challenges for the future. In: D.V. Day, S. J. Zaccaro & S. M. Halpin (Eds), *Leader development for transforming organization* (pp. 32–40). Mahwah, NJ: Lawrence Erlbaum Associates.

Manz, C. C., & Manz, K. P. (1991). Strategies for facilitating self-directed learning: A process for enhancing human resource development. *Human Resource Development Quarterly, 2,* 3–12.

Mathieu, J. E., & Leonard, R. L. (1987). Applying utility concepts to a training program in supervisory skills: A time-based approach. *Academy of Management Journal, 30,* 316–335.

Maznevski, M. L., & DiStefano, J. J. (2000). Global leaders are team players: Developing global leaders through membership on global teams. *Human Resource Management, 39*(2,3), 195.

McCall, M. W. (1998). *High flyers: Developing the next generation of leaders.* Boston: Harvard Business School Press.

McCauley, C. D., Eastman, L. J., & Ohlott, P. J. (1995). Linking management selection and development through stretch assignments. *Human Resource Management, 34,* 93–115.

McCauley, C. D., & E. Van Velsor (Eds). (2004). *Handbook of leadership development* (2nd ed.). San Francisco, CA: Jossey-Bass.

Mendenhall, M. E., Dunbar, E., & Oddou, G. R. (1987). Expatriate selection, training and career-pathing: A review and critique. *Human Resource Management (1986-1998), 26*(3), 331.

Mendenhall, M. E., & Stahl, G. K. (2000). Expatriate training and development: Where do we go from here? *Human Resource Management, 39,* 251–265.

Meyer, J. P., Allen, N. J., & Smith, C. A. (1993). Commitment to organizations and occupations: Extension and test of a three component conceptualization. *Journal of Applied Psychology, 78,* 538–551.

Miller, C. C., & Cardinal, L. B. (1994). Strategic planning and firm performance: A synthesis of more than two decades of research. *Academy of Management, 37,* 1649–1665.

Miller, D., & Toulouse, J. M. (1986). Chief executive personality and corporate strategy and structure in small firms. *Management Science, 32,* 1389–1409.

Morrison, A. J. (2000). Developing a global leadership model. *Human Resource Management, 39*(2,3), 117.

Moses, J., Hollenbeck, G.P., & Sorcher, M. (1993). Other people's expectations. *Human Resource Management, 32*(2), 283–297.

Motowidlo, S. J., Dunnette, M. D., & Carter, G. W. (1990). An alternative selection procedure: The low-fidelity simulation. *Journal of Applied Psychology, 6,* 640–647.

Motowidlo, S. J., & Tippins, N. (1993). Further studies of the low-fidelity simulation in the form of a situational inventory. *Journal of Occupational and Organizational Psychology, 66,* 337–344.

Mumford, M. D., Marks, M. A., Connelly, M. S., Zaccaro, S. J., & Reiter-Palmon, R. (2000). Development of leadership skills: Experience, and timing. *Leadership Quarterly, 11,* 87–114.

Noe, R. A. (2002). *Employee training and development* (2nd ed.). Boston, MA: McGraw-Hill Irwin.

Oddou, G., Mendenhall, M., & Ritchie, J. B. (2000). Leveraging travel as a tool for global leadership development. *Human Resource Management, 39*(2,3), 159–172.

Ohlott, P. (2004). Job assignments. In: C. D. McCauley & E. Van Velsor (Eds), *The Center for Creative Leadership handbook of leadership development* (pp. 151–182). San Francisco, CA: Wiley.

Palus, C. J., & Horth, D. M (2004). Exploration for development. In: C. D. McCauley & E. Van Velsor (Eds), *The Center for Creative Leadership handbook of leadership development* (pp. 438–464). San Francisco, CA: Wiley.

Peterson, R. S, Smith, D. B., Martorana, P. V., & Owens, P. D. (2003). The impact of chief executive officer personality on top management team dynamics: One mechanism by which leadership affects organizational performance. *Journal of Applied Psychology, 88,* 795–808.

Piskurich, G. M. (1993). *Self-directed learning: A practical guide to design, development and implementation.* San Francisco: Jossey-Bass Publishers.

Ployhart, R. E., & Bliese, P. D. (in press). Individual ADAPTability (I-ADAPT) theory: Conceptualizing the antecedents, consequences, and measurement of individual differences in adaptability. In: S. Burke, L. Pierce & E. Salas (Eds), *Understanding adaptability: A prerequisite for effective performance within complex environments.* Amsterdam: Elsevier.

Pulakos, E. D., Arad, S., Donovan, M. A., & Plamondon, K. E. (2000). Adaptability in the workplace: Development of a taxonomy of adaptive performance. *Journal of Applied Psychology, 85,* 612–624.

Pulakos, E. D., Schmitt, N., Dorsey, D. W., Arad, S., Hedge, J. W., & Borman, W. C. (2002). Predicting adaptive performance: Further tests of a model of adaptability. *Human Performance, 15,* 299–323.

Reilly, R.R., Smither, J.W., & Vasilopoulos, N.L. (1996). A longitudinal study of upward feedback. *Personnel Psychology, 49*(3), 599–612.

Ritchie, R. J. (1994). Using the assessment center method to predict senior management potential. *Consulting Psychology Journal: Practice and Research, 46,* 16–23.

Rynes, S. L., Colbert, A. E., & Brown, K. G. (2002). HR. professionals beliefs about effective human resource practices: Correspondence between research and practice. *Human Resource Management, 41,* 149.

Salas, E., Burke, C. S., Wilson-Donnelly, K. A., & Fowlkes, J. E. (2004). Promoting effective leadership within multicultural teams: An event-based approach. In: D.V. Day, S. J. Zaccaro & S. M. Halpin (Eds), *Leader development for transforming organization* (pp. 293–324). Mahwah, NJ: Lawrence Erlbaum Associates.

Seifert, C. F., Yukl, G., & McDonald, R. A. (2003). Effects of multisource feedback and a feedback facilitator on the influence behavior of managers toward subordinates. *Journal of Applied Psychology, 88*(3), 561–569.

Smith, E., Ford, J. K., & Kozlowski, S. W. J. (1997). Building adaptive expertise: Implications for training design. In: M. A. Quinones & A. Ehrenstein (Eds), *Training for a rapidly changing workplace: Applications of psychological research* (pp. 89–118). Washington, DC: American Psychological Association.

Spreitzer, McCall, M. W., & Mahoney, J. D. (1997). Early identification of international executive potential. *Journal of Applied Psychology, 82*, 6–29.

Stroh, L. K., Black, J. S., Mendenhall, M., & Gregersen, H. B. (2005). *International Assignments.* Mahwah, NJ: Lawrence Erlbaum Associates.

Suutari, V. (2002). Global leader development: An emerging research agenda. *Career Development International, 7*, 218–233.

Thomas, J. B., Clark, S. B., & Gioia, D. A. (1993). Strategic sensemaking and organizational performance: Linkages among scanning, interpretation, action and outcomes. *Academy of Management Journal, 36*, 239–270.

U. S. Army (1999). *FM22-100: Army leadership.* Washington, DC: U. S. Army.

Walker, A.G., & Smither, J.W. (1999). A five-year study of upward feedback: What managers do with their results matters. *Personnel Psychology, 52*, 393–423.

Weiner, N., & Mahoney, T. A. (1981). A model of corporate performance as a function of environmental, organizational, and leadership influences. *Academy of Management Journal, 24*, 453–470.

Yan, A., Zhu, G., & Hall, D. T. (2002). International assignments for career building: A model of agency relationships and psychological contracts. *Academy of Management. The Academy of Management Review, 27*(3), 373–391.

Yukl, G. (2006). *Leadership in organizations* (6th ed.). Englewood Cliffs, NJ: Prentice-Hall.

Zaccaro, S. J. (2001). *The nature of executive leadership: A conceptual and empirical analysis of success.* Washington, DC: APA Books.

Zaccaro, S. J., & Banks, D. (2004). Leader visioning and adaptability: Bridging the gap between research and practice on developing the ability to manage change. *Human Resource Management Journal, 43*, 367–380

Zaccaro, S. J., Gilbert, J. A., Thor, K. K., & Mumford, M. D. (1991). Leadership and social intelligence: Linking social perceptiveness to behavioral flexibility. *Leadership Quarterly, 2*, 317–347.

Zaccaro, S. J. (2002). Organizational leadership and social intelligence. In: R. E. Riggio, & S. E. Murphy, (Eds), *Multiple intelligences and leadership* (pp. 29–54). Mahwah, NJ: Lawrence Erlbaum Associates.

Subject Index

Note: Page numbers with f and t denote that entries are taken from figures and tables, respectively.